W9-BXN-209

The United States and the Americas

Lester D. Langley, General Editor

This series is dedicated to a broader understanding of the political, economic, and especially cultural forces and issues that have shaped the Western hemispheric experience—its governments and its peoples. Individual volumes assess relations between the United States and its neighbors to the south and north: Mexico, Central America, Cuba, the Dominican Republic, Haiti, Panama, Colombia, Venezuela, the Andean Republics (Peru, Ecuador, and Bolivia), Brazil, Uruguay and Paraguay, Argentina, Chile, and Canada.

The United States and the Americas

Canada and the United States

John Herd Thompson
and Stephen J. Randall

Canada and the United States: Ambivalent Allies, Second Edition

The University of Georgia Press
Athens and London

Set in 10 on 14 Palatino

The paper in this book meets the guidelines
for permanence and durability of the Committee on
Production Guidelines for Book Longevity of the
Council on Library Resources.

Printed in the United States of America

01 00 99 98 97 P 5 4 3 2 1

Library of Congress Cataloging in Publication Data

Thompson, John Herd, 1946–
Canada and the United States : ambivalent allies / John Herd Thompson and Stephen J. Randall. — 2nd. ed.
p. cm. — (The United States and the Americas)
Includes bibliographical references (p.) and index.
ISBN 0-8203-1929-5 (pbk. : alk. paper)
1. United States—Relations—Canada. 2. Canada—Relations—United States. I. Randall, Stephen J., 1944– . II. Title.
III. Series.
E183.8.C2T46 1994
303.48′273071—dc20 93-29652
CIP

British Library Cataloging in Publication Data available

Published simultaneously in Canada
by McGill-Queen's University Press

to Isa and Ema—JHT

to my family—SJR

Contents

Maps

Acknowledgments to the Second Edition

We thank purchasers of the first edition and the University of Georgia Press for giving us the opportunity to do a second edition. The theses and premises of *Ambivalent Allies*, we feel, have stood the test of critical assessment, but we have corrected errors that reviewers were kind enough to point out to us. We have substantially rewritten chapter 10 and the epilogue, adding a new section on NAFTA and trilateralism and an extended discussion of recent U.S. congressional impact on the bilateral relationship. The revised bibliography incorporates scholarship that has appeared since completion of the first edition.

JHT SJR

Acknowledgments

Nations have no friends, only interests. Historians are much luckier. Many others in addition to the two men credited on the title page labored on this book: the staff of Duke's Lilly Library, and Colleen Seguin, Danny Calhoun, and Sarah Wells Caldwell, my research assistants. Hilda Pärtelpoeg never expected her scrapbooks of Royal Tours of Canada to provide me with invaluable insight into the role of the British connection in shaping Canada's bilateral relationship with the United States. *Ambivalent Allies* would have been much poorer without the comments of my Duke colleagues Calvin Davis, Patrice Leclerc, and Alex Keyssar; it would have been impossible without those of my best North Carolinian friend Tim Tyson. With many Canadians, Tim shares an ambivalence about "Yankees" that helped to put my own less critical views into perspective. Finally (why do families always come last?) I thank Katrin, Anne, and Mark Thompson. Katrin has quietly sustained my scholarship for twenty years, and Anne has miraculously grown old enough to copy and collate. And Mark lets me read him *Horton Hatches the Egg;* there could be no more inspiring example for a historian.

JHT

This volume is the work of two historians, friends and former colleagues for almost two decades at McGill University. Differences between us in style and interpretation have been few, and it is my hope that any differences that remain will be invisible to the reader. My first thanks thus go to my co-author John Thompson. At the University of Calgary, the University Research Grants Committee provided funds to conduct research on the United States dimensions of the project and to enlist the research assistance for Canadian materials of Paul Dougherty, who not only located obscure documents and quotations but also added his own intellectual insights. Various colleagues and friends offered insights and guidance directly and indirectly, among them: Kenneth McNaught, Robert Bothwell, David Bercuson, Kim Richard Nossal, Jack Granatstein, Edgar Dosman, Leonard Waverman, Harold Klepak, Shel Silverman, David Marshall, Don Barry, Reginald Stuart, Thomas Paterson, and Michael Hogan. A special thanks is due my friend and cartographer Bill Mills. My own dedication of the volume is to my family, extended and nuclear. No dedication could be more appropriate, since they have all sustained me in different ways. Sadly perhaps, for my children *Horton Hatches the Egg* is a fading memory; collating holds little appeal for those with busy lives of their own; they are all more likely to make informed and critical assessment of their father's (and spouse's) academic work.

SJR

Lester Langley conceived this series and decided that Canada was sufficiently of the Americas to merit a place in it. Karen Orchard committed the University of Georgia Press to bringing Lester's vision into print. Both of them were patient, gentle, and when necessary, firm with the authors. Hundreds of Canadian and several dozen American scholars contributed to *Ambivalent Allies* through their books, articles, and theses. Bob Babcock of the University of Maine provided a close reading of the manuscript and sixteen single-spaced pages of suggestions. We accepted fifteen pages of them, and apologize for those we declined. George Rawlyk of Queen's University corrected errors in chapter 1. Mistakes of fact and interpretation no doubt persist despite all the help we've received. None of them, of course, is our fault.

JHT SJR

Canada and the United States

Introduction

The inclusion of a volume on Canada in a series on *The United States and the Americas* is an ironic reflection of changing international realities. For most of its history, Canada has not been discussed as an "American" nation; rather it has been considered British and European in its roots, its politics, its foreign policy, its cultural orientation. This traditional view has given way in recent years to a greater appreciation of Canada's strong ties to the Western Hemisphere. These were emphasized during debates over the 1987 Free Trade Agreement between Canada and the United States, in the decision of the Conservative government of Brian Mulroney in 1989 to join the century-old Organization of American States, and in the 1993 North American Free Trade Agreement encompassing Canada, the United States, and Mexico.

For more than two hundred years, the relationship between the United States and what emerged from the second British Empire as an independent Canada has been intense. Over those two centuries there have been substantial and minor conflicts, bilateral and multilateral institution building, tranquility and turbulence. Some authors emphasize the "undefended" border that has allegedly existed since the conclusion of the War of 1812 and argue that a "special friendship," or "special relationship," links Washington and Ottawa. Such studies assert that the U.S.-Canada relationship is unlike any other international interaction, and that the fundamental maxim of international relations — that nations have no friends, only interests — has been suspended in the interest of amity and harmony.

Such platitudes belie the dissonance of the nineteenth century and exaggerate the harmony of the twentieth. They are more useful for saccharine speeches at binational gatherings than for understanding the binational relationship. What is important for historians is the shifting nature of the international context in which the Canadian-American relationship evolved over two hundred years. Despite the differences in economic and military power between Canada and Latin America, the central fact of the U.S.-Canada relations has been similar to the United States position in Latin America: its essential one-sidedness. One may speak of a relationship in which influence flows in both directions, as indeed it sometimes has; but the essential reality has been the imbalance in power. Canada in the nineteenth century was little more than an appendage of the British Empire and would not have survived as a political entity distinct from the United States without that imperial connection. In the twentieth century, as the United States emerged first as a major power and then as a superpower, Canada was at best a "middle" power, although that term exaggerates the political, economic, and especially the military power of Canada in the world arena. Under what criteria could Canada be considered a "middle" power in the post-1945 era, for instance, in comparison to the economic and military capabilities of such nonsuperpowers as Israel, South Africa, India, and even Iran and Iraq in more recent years? Hence, it was logical that there should be an ambivalence in the way in which the two countries have related to one another.

The asymmetry in the bilateral relationship is reflected in a number of ways, among them the imbalance between the relative attention Canadian and American scholars give to the relationship. An observer of the professional literature in history or political science would be struck by the prodigious industry of Canadian scholars who specialize in the study of what they call "Canadian-American relations," and by the prevailing neglect on the American side. Scores of Canadian professors have built careers in the field, but only a handful of American senior scholars (Robin Winks and Seymour Martin Lipset the most notable) have reached the front ranks of the academy by writing about Canada. The leading historians of U.S. foreign policy in the twentieth century, from Samuel Flagg Bemis and Thomas Bailey to Robert Farrell, Robert Divine, and Thomas Paterson, mention Canada in their general studies of American foreign relations only when Canada intrudes dramatically: the War of 1812, the boundary settlements of the nineteenth century, the Washington Treaty of 1871, the Alaska boundary dispute of 1903, and perhaps a reference to the Hyde Park Declaration of 1941. Thereafter Canada vanishes, in spite of the facts that it was a critical member of America's cold war alliances, and that the two nations developed the largest bilateral trade in the history of the world.

Canada also has been a matter of similarly consuming disinterest to the United States public and to most of its leaders. America's image of Canada was formed by Hollywood between 1920 and 1950, as a frozen wilderness inhabited by half-breed savages, moose, red-coated mounted policemen, and a sufficient number of beautiful women to sustain the interest of Hollywood's leading men. As Gary Cooper told his co-star in *Northwest Mounted Police* (1940), "before I came to Canada I thought the women would be like the mountains—cold and distant." Presidents Richard Nixon, Gerald Ford, and Ronald Reagan shared another common misunderstanding: each learned to his surprise that Canada, not Japan, was the United States' largest trading partner. On the eve of President George Bush's visit to Ottawa in 1989, *Toronto Globe and Mail* columnist Jeffrey Simpson summed up two centuries of Canadian resentment of their neighbor's ignorance: Americans, Simpson claimed, "know and care the square root of squat about Canada."

Simpson's bitterness reflects a deep-rooted anxiety in the Canadian psyche. Canadian, especially English-Canadian, nationalism has been shaped largely in reference to the presence of the United States to the south. Canada came to exist only in reaction to the United States. It was a political nation created from those British (former French) North American colonies that rejected the American Revolution. America's most despised traitors became Canada's mythical founding fathers; one country's Tory was the other's United Empire Loyalist. It would have been unimaginable, as political parties came into being in the course of the nineteenth century, for the United States to have spawned a "Tory" party, even if many of the "Tory" values have been adopted by the Republicans in the twentieth century.

Canadians were not a colonized people who struggled to be free and then claimed uniqueness among the community of nations; rather English Canadians chose to retain a parliamentary constitution and to remain a constitutional monarchy within the British Empire. French Canadians in 1776 chose the lesser of two threats—British imperialists seemed less dangerous than would-be American liberators. At the very least, they were farther away. In 1867, English and French Canadians chose the confederation of their colonies in part as a defense against perceived ambitions from the United States in the context of the Anglo-Canadian-American conflicts that the Civil War engendered. Canadian Conservatives explicitly designed their "National Policy" for economic development to create a transcontinental Canada in defiance of the United States. In subsequent generations fear of American domination continued to feed Canadian nationalism. Significantly, the abandonment of that National Policy with the Mulroney government's move toward free trade with the United States in the 1980s produced a significant backlash from those who held a different vision of Canada. The contemporary counterparts of those who in the 1911 Reciprocity election had called for "no truck nor trade with the Yankees," suggested in the 1980s that the strategy for Canadian salvation was to "Free Canada, trade Mulroney." Canadians took Patrick Buchanan's *Los Angeles Times* pipedream of "a republic that, by the year 2000, encompasses the Maritime and Western provinces of Canada" far more seriously than did any of Buchanan's American readers. Behind Canada's anxiety as the 1995 Quebec referendum threatened to shatter their country was Canadian fear of how vulnerable the English-speaking remnant would be to the United States—despite the fact that the United States showed not the slightest sign of malevolent intent.

To every generation of Canadians, the American presence has been an unavoidable fact of everyday life. Since there was no other external threat to Canadian autonomy and identity save the United States, it was against Americans that Canadians repeatedly pledged to "stand on guard" in the English-language lyrics of their national anthem. As historians S. F. Wise and Robert Craig Brown suggest in their account of Canadian views of the United States in the nineteenth century: "The average Canadian . . . appears to have leaped from the womb fully equipped with a lifetime's antagonism toward the United States."[1]

That the United States has always been far more important to Canada than Canada is to the United States exacerbates this antagonism. Canada takes up more space on the map, but its population, huddled within a hundred miles of the border, has been consistently one-tenth that of its southern neighbor. Except for brief periods of unusual circumstance—the aftermath of the American Revolution, the Fraser and Yukon River gold rushes, the opening of the Canadian west, and the Vietnam War resistance—the United States continues to be a not-so-distant magnet pulling Canadians south. The United States has had by far the richer geographical endowment when measured in terms of accessible arable land. Americans have been the "people of plenty"; Canadians have been a people of relative scarcity, despite their forest, ocean, and mineral resources. French mariner Jacques Cartier may have been too harsh when he described the rugged granite that covers half of Canada as "the land God gave to Cain," but he understood the inhospitable northern environment. The Canadians who extracted its natural resources became progressively more dependent on markets in the United States, so that by 1995, trade with the United States accounted for one-fifth of Canadian gross national product (GNP), about ten times the percentage of American GNP, which depended on trade with Canada.

The historical development of U.S.-Canada relations should be understood both in terms of bilateral developments and in the context of the evolution of the international system and the vast expansion of America's role within it. This volume situates the U.S.-Canada relationship in the broader framework of American foreign policy more fully than does the traditional historical literature. The American and Haitian revolutions and then the Spanish American wars for independence left Canada, with the British West Indies, Cuba, and Puerto Rico, among the few remaining outposts of European colonialism in the Western Hemisphere. Canada's British colonial connection served to isolate it from larger "American" concerns, especially with the articulation of the Monroe Doctrine in the 1820s and its subsequent modifications over the next two centuries. Britain and America were the only real powers in the Western Hemisphere in the course of the nineteenth century, although many others—from Russia and France to Germany and Italy—at times claimed a presence. Bilateral Anglo-American tension made Canada a pawn in great power rivalry.

The rise of the United States and of Germany to great power status in the late nineteenth and early twentieth centuries gradually altered the relative importance of Canada in the Anglo-American relationship. Britain faced both a shift in the balance of power in Europe as well as problems within its own empire by the 1890s, with the result that Britain needed a friendly United States on its western flank. Canadian interests could in large measure be sacrificed to those larger geopolitical goals. By the end of World War I, the financial capital of the world had shifted from London to New York, and the United States had become a military power in its own right. With Britain in evident decline and its powerful neighbor on the rise, Canada had to strive for an American policy, and in turn the United States had to give at least fleeting thought to its Canadian policy. The result was the emergence in the first thirty years of the twentieth century of a more independent, distinct, and mature Canadian foreign policy and of a more distinctly bilateral Canadian-American relationship.

Had there been any doubt after World War I of the preeminence of U.S. power, there could be none by the end of World War II. With Britain and France sapped by their struggle with the Third Reich, Germany's dismemberment left the United States and the Soviet Union as two self-consciously distinct political systems, glowering at one another over a prostrate Europe. The decline of Britain, the intensity of the cold war, the hegemony of the United States and the impossibility of nonalignment pushed Canada further into the American orbit. If it was important to the United States to ensure that insignificant nations in Central America, East Asia, and the Pacific remained in the capitalist, free world camp, it was even more imperative that there should be no significant deviation from the United States' closest and most important neighbor. Canada showed little inclination to deviate, from the North Atlantic Treaty Organization and the North American Air Defense Agreement in the 1940s and 1950s through the Korean and Vietnam wars and the Cuban and Central American crises in the 1960s, 1970s, and 1980s. The process that transformed Canada from a European to an American nation was a slow one and was arguably not complete even in the 1990s; perhaps the trilateral North American Free

Trade Agreement has finally completed the process. This shift profoundly altered Canadian-American defense, political, and economic relationships, just as the sheer weight of American cultural presence pressed constantly upon Canadians.

Ambivalence has characterized the U.S.-Canadian bilateral relationship throughout more than two centuries, but *Canada and the United States: Ambivalent Allies* emphasizes the years of "America's rise to world power" during the second century, in particular the period since 1941 when the two countries became formal allies. From 1776 to 1903, British North America/Canada was, as a British colony, essentially only an issue in the relations between the United States and Great Britain. Between 1903 and World War II, Canada moved toward the establishment of an independent foreign policy; in this period the two countries erected many of the bilateral institutions and mechanisms that governed their relationship in the twentieth century. From their wartime alliance after 1941 through the end of the 1950s, the two countries united in a World War and cold war alliance based on economic interest and shared assumptions about the nature of the world and their responsibilities within it. The years from 1960 until 1984 most merit our subtitle *Ambivalent Allies,* as this binational consensus fragmented, and the two countries moved apart in their approaches to the cold war, defense relations, trade, foreign investment, and cultural policy. Division escalated as Canada sought a global "Third Option" that could increase its independence of the United States.

In 1984, Brian Mulroney's Conservative party—the "Tory" party/"les Tories" in the political slang of both of Canada's official languages—fervently proclaimed the continental harmony of the 1950s. The ultimate irony in the relationship had occurred: the Tories, named out of the legacy of an American Revolution rejected in 1776, embraced the United States with an ardor never before experienced by the Canadian body politic. Nurtured on the milk of anti-Americanism, many segments of traditional Canadian society protested; but the Conservatives won reelection in 1988, as the issue of free trade with the United States figured more prominently than any single issue ever has in a Canadian national election. The massive rejection of the Conservative party in 1993, and its replacement with a Liberal government under Prime Minister Jean Chrétien, in part reflected the electorate's judgment against Mulroney's attempted new intimacy with the United States.

In spite of its commitment to reverse the pro-American policy of its predecessors, the Chrétien government effectively altered nothing in the bilateral relationship. Having committed themselves to redrafting the NAFTA accord, the Liberals came to embrace it. The saga of the ambivalent alliance has no ending, happy or otherwise. If the past is our guide, the U.S.-Canada relationship in the future cannot be other than intense, close, and cooperative, yet conflictual in both its details and its fundamentals.

1 A Revolution Repeatedly Rejected, 1774–1871

Between 1774 and 1783 the American Revolution fragmented the North American centerpiece of the British Empire. From the turmoil two countries emerged: with no little irony, the revolution that created the United States also created Canada. Twice in one generation, from 1776 to 1781 and again from 1812 to 1815, the American colonies and then the fledgling United States fought the world's most powerful state in two wars that determined the fate of the continent. As Canadian historian A. R. M. Lower wrote: "Of greater moment than the boundary settlement was the parting itself. Here surely was the profoundest depth of the Revolution. For the parting had been in bad blood. The race was broken." What transpired in North America during and immediately following the American Revolution, which led to the creation of the two nations that have since shared the northern half of the continent? Was the division a conscious choice, a "revolution rejected" by "Canadians" and those "Americans" who sought refuge in British North America and pledged continued loyalty to the British Crown? Did the split between what became Canada and the United States derive from fundamentally different political orientations or from the pragmatic military realities of the moment?[1]

Breaking Up the First British Empire

When the American colonists turned their muskets against British imperial authority at Lexington and Concord, Britain controlled four colonies to the north that became part of nineteenth-century British North America and eventually modern Canada: Newfoundland, Prince Edward Island (called St. John's Island until 1799), Nova Scotia, and Quebec. As among the thirteen colonies to the south, differences among these colonies were profound. Tiny Prince Edward Island, with a population of perhaps thirteen hundred farmers and fisherpeople, and Newfoundland, with a population of fifteen thousand scattered in fishing villages along its rugged coast, were remote from the ideological and military conflicts of the Revolution. Nova Scotia, which geographically included both modern Nova Scotia and New Brunswick, had an economy based on agriculture, the fishery, shipbuilding, and international trade. In language, religion, and ethnicity, Nova Scotia was more akin to Massachusetts than to Quebec. More than half of its twenty thousand people were Yankee migrants, many who had come to take up the farms of the French Acadians deported by the British in the 1750s. But Halifax, the colonial capital on the Atlantic coast, was an important harbor for the Royal Navy.

Quebec, the official name for what was usually called "Canada," had been taken from France by force during the Seven Years' War, 1756–63. Quebec was the most populous of these northern colonies, and the largest geographically after the Quebec Act of 1774 expanded the colony into the interior almost to the boundaries of preconquest New France. Montreal was the entrepôt of the fur trade of this vast western territory. The garrison town of Quebec was the colony's administrative capital, but four-fifths of Quebec's European descended population of one hundred thousand were peasants who farmed under the seigneurial system, the feudal system of landholding left untouched by their British conquerors. Except for the Montreal merchants who controlled the fur trade and the British soldiers and administrators, Quebec was French-speaking, Roman Catholic, and without the elective political institutions in place in every other colony of British America save Newfoundland. Britain had confirmed all of these peculiarities—Roman Catholicism, seigneurialism, nonelective government—in the Quebec Act of 1774. This act enraged those colonials to the south suspicious of imperial designs: its real object, wrote Alexander Hamilton, was "to encircle the Thirteen Colonies in a ring of British steel." Such fears precipitated the revolutionaries toward independence. Historians have demonstrated that their anxiety was unfounded, and that the Quebec Act should not be considered among the "Intolerable Acts"; but the authors of the Declaration of Independence, with the benefits of neither hindsight nor archival access, may be forgiven the conclusion to which they jumped.[2]

The concentration of British military power to the north of the thirteen colonies made Nova Scotia and especially Quebec of substantial strategic importance to the fledgling American government, the Continental Congress, meeting in Philadelphia. The revolutionary leadership was profoundly ambiguous about both colonies. Many Nova Scotians had blood ties to New England, and French Canadians had little reason for loyalty to Britain, so that they were regarded as potential revolutionary patriots. In 1775, Thomas Jefferson believed that "the delegates of Canada will join us in Congress and complete the American union," and Article XI of the Articles of Confederation provided that on application "Canada shall be admitted into and entitled to all the advantages of the union." Yet both colonies were thought of as threats to American security, bases for potential British blows against the Revolution. "I hope we shall secure to the United States Canada [and] Nova Scotia by our arms," wrote Samuel Adams in 1778; "we shall never be on a solid footing till Britain cedes to us what Nature designs we should have, or till we wrest it from her." This ambivalence was demonstrated in letters from the Congress that circulated in Canada and Nova Scotia, which invited the "oppressed inhabitants" to share "the Transcendent Nature of Freedom," but threatened severe reprisals if they dared support British authority. It was further demonstrated to French Canadians when two American forces under Richard Montgomery and Benedict Arnold invaded Quebec in 1775. The invasion was defensive expansionism; the St. Lawrence was a vital strategic artery, and American leaders had little choice but to attempt to deny it to the British. Montgomery captured Montreal and joined Arnold in an unsuccessful winter siege of the town of Quebec, but the siege was lifted and Montreal abandoned the following spring when British reinforcements arrived. The British counterstroke was equally ineffective: General Burgoyne's defeat in 1777 at Saratoga brought the French into the war as formal American allies. Britain had the naval capacity to contain the rebellion within the thirteen colonies but not to defeat it.[3]

Internal Canadian considerations also militated against any general pro-American uprising in support of Montgomery and Arnold, although American officers reported that the local populations were (wisely) friendly. The Quebec Act was not universally popular among the English merchants of Montreal, who received a delegation from the Boston Committee of Correspondence in 1775; one of them, James Price, traveled to Philadelphia as an unofficial representative to the Continental Congress. According to Donald Creighton, however, the minority of English merchants who supported the Revolution did so because of personal ties to the thirteen colonies; those who were involved in the fur trade were commercially connected to Britain and would have lost considerably in the event the Americans gained access to the fur trade in the Ohio and Mississippi river valleys. The Quebec Act promised political and economic stability to the French-Canadian elite of landholders, the legal profession, and the Roman Catholic Church, making them the most enthusiastic supporters of British authority. They appealed to their tenants and parishioners to oppose the Americans. Nonetheless, the local French population at Montreal would not fight in support of British Governor Guy Carleton in 1775, forcing him to flee upriver. The *habitants* may have been hostile to the Quebec Act, which restored their ecclesiastical and seigneurial economic obligations. Hostile to the Quebec Act or not, most of the local population showed no inclination to fight for either side. French-Canadian peasant grievances fit poorly with political models and ideals imported from revolutionary America, and the invading American soldiers were poor emissaries of colonial solidarity against the British. Although George Washington's circular to the people of Quebec, designed to prepare the way for invasion, assured them that the army came "not to plunder, but to protect you," one general dismissed the French-Canadian peasants as "but little removed from savages." Such attitudes, another American general admitted, led to "scandalous excesses" by the American volunteers, so that "few of the inhabitants escaped abuse" at their hands. Thus although Quebec remained loyal to the Crown, it cannot be classified in any real sense as a Loyalist or Tory area, to the extent that such areas of anti-Revolution sentiment existed in parts of New York and Georgia, where individuals made conscientious decisions to oppose the Revolution. As French-Canadian nationalist Henri Bourassa put it a century later, French Canadians had to choose between two evils—the British or their English colonists to the south—and the English in London seemed farther away and less imminently threatening. Thus, though there were loyalists and rebels scattered throughout Quebec, self-interest dictated caution and neutrality.[4]

Neutrality is also the best word to describe Nova Scotia's response to the American Revolution, although it was a neutrality dictated by different conditions. Historians debate the degree of support for the Revolution, and there was no doubt discontent against British authority. There was, however, no revolt, apart from some pro-Patriot feeling in western Nova Scotia revealed by a comic-opera Patriot invasion from northern Maine. For the Halifax merchant elite, provisioners of the Royal Navy and linked to London with ties of credit, the balance sheet decreed loyalism. Many of the transplanted Yankees around the Bay of Fundy and in the South Shore fishing villages sympathized with their brethren to the south, and several communities petitioned the governor not to require them to bear arms against their New England neighbors and relatives; but their reformist inclinations burned more brightly in the religious revival of the Great Awakening than in revolt against British imperial authority. Washington asserted that Nova Scotia was superfluous to his defensive strategy, and the Continental Congress accepted his judgment. Geography and British sea power made a serious Patriot attack unlikely to succeed if it had been undertaken. Instead the Revolution was carried to Nova Scotia by marauding privateers whose hit-and-run raids undermined whatever revolutionary sympathies their victims might have held before they were robbed at pistol point. Isolation, economic interest, British sea power, and the lack of means for Nova Scotia inhabitants to raise rebellion had they so desired determined the fate of Nova Scotia.[5]

Thus, as General Cornwallis surrendered his British army at Yorktown to combined French and American troops in 1781, the colonies that would become Canada were firmly under British control. The envoys the Continental Congress sent to France to negotiate peace—John Jay, John Adams, and Benjamin Franklin—were instructed to request Canada as reparations for war damage caused by British military operations. Despite their best diplomatic efforts, however, it remained British when the Treaty of Paris was concluded in 1783. The fate of Quebec and Nova Scotia had been determined less by ideology and political preference than by geography and the realities of the balance of military power between Great Britain and the thirteen American colonies. But for whatever reasons, the American Revolution had not spread and could not be carried into the northern colonies, and that failure gave birth to Canada and permanently shaped the subsequent U.S.-Canadian relationship.

From Revolution to the War of 1812

The Treaty of Paris in 1783 resolved the issue of independence for the thirteen colonies: Jay insisted that Britain recognize them as the United States of America before a final draft was prepared. British negotiators sought a rapprochement with the new American nation, and the treaty accordingly made concessions beyond those the military situation would have dictated. Thus for the British colonies to the north, American independence brought several consequences. The first was a substantial territorial loss: the American-Canada boundary was set at the forty-fifth parallel, cutting off the vast interior hinterland that had been reconnected to Quebec in 1774. The United States and Nova Scotia were separated along the St. Croix River, but cartographical error left disagreement about precisely which river was in fact the St. Croix; the result was several generations of border disputes. Equally serious for the Atlantic colonies was the loss of the anticipated exclusive access to the fisheries off their coasts. Samuel Adams loudly insisted that "God Almighty . . . gave the people of

America a right" to them, and threatened to "enkindle a new war" for Newfoundland and Nova Scotia to obtain them. Britain accordingly conceded the New Englanders the "liberty" of continued access, but the issue remained as a contentious legacy of the treaty.[6]

But the most momentous legacy for the northern colonies from American independence was ideological: it launched them on the divergent political path of fundamental importance in understanding the distinctions between the two modern nations. An estimated half-million residents of the thirteen colonies—20 percent of the population—remained loyal to Britain during the Revolution. Sixty to one hundred thousand of them—historians disagree—committed, in Roger Daniels's words, "the most profoundly un-American act that one can imagine": they left America. More than forty thousand of these émigré Tories—Loyalists to Canadians—went north, three-quarters of them to Nova Scotia and Prince Edward Island, and the remainder to Quebec, where they settled in the Gaspé Peninsula to the east and along the north shore of Lake Ontario. Who were these anti-Americans, and why did they come? The plethora of Loyalist studies defies easy summarization, but Neil MacKinnon's conclusion about those who came to Nova Scotia will serve as a generalization: "the motives of these immigrants . . . ranged all the way from pathetic necessity to naked opportunism [and] their origins were as mixed as their motives." The Loyalists came from every one of the thirteen colonies, although New York predominated, and were "not simply an upper-class fragment [but] cross-sections of the American social pyramid." A disproportionate number were members of religious or ethnic minorities, two thousand of them were African-American freedmen and former slaves, and one thousand Iroquois. One thing united them, a bond that they shared with the French Canadians. "Almost all the loyalists," writes W. H. Nelson, were "in one way or another, more afraid of America than they were of Britain."[7]

These Loyalists exercised a remarkable influence on British North America. Their arrival forced Britain to create two new colonies. In 1784 the western shore of the Bay of Fundy was detached from Nova Scotia to become New Brunswick, and in 1791 Britain divided the old province of Quebec into Upper and Lower Canada, which later became Canada West and Canada East, and ultimately Ontario and Quebec. With Loyalists as their founding parents, Upper Canada and New Brunswick became bastions of a British North American identity built on the precepts of Loyalism: strong support for the Crown and British institutions, and a rejection of American republicanism. For many Loyalists, America was "Satan's Kingdom," a "land of banditti" doomed to be destroyed by the "Tyrannic power of a republican Government." The Loyalist goal—at least that of the Loyalist elite—was to build a superior society in the provinces to which they had fled, a society in which, said New York–born Upper Canadian Richard Cartwright, "under the epitome of the English constitution, we enjoy the greatest practical political freedom." As an important link within a worldwide empire, British North America would be, in the words of Massachusetts-born New Brunswicker Edward Winslow, "the envy of the American states."[8]

This sense of mission and the extravagant anti-Americanisms replete in Loyalist writings were the products of an elite; several thousand ordinary Loyalists abandoned Nova Scotia to return to the United States in the 1790s. The Loyalist myth built up around them in Canada in the nineteenth century (like all national myths, America's included) is only tangentially linked to the historical reality of the eighteenth. Sociologist Seymour Martin Lipset exaggerates when he ascribes the differences between Canada and the United States to the "continental divide" of revolution and counterrevolution. But the Loyalist myth, though never uncontested, did become sufficiently hegemonic to form the base of the "extremely constricting ideology" (to use historian S. F. Wise's words) from within which British North Americans would view the United States.[9]

There was, however, an inescapable ambivalence in this evolving colonial ideology: as much as British North Americans criticized America, they were simultaneously obsessed with it. The United States became the standard against which they measured not only the moral purity of their own society but also its material progress. Until 1812 the border was wide open to commerce, and transborder travel was heavy enough that one Burlington, Vermont, tavern keeper painted George Washington's portrait on the south side of his sign and Admiral Horatio Nelson's likeness on the north. British North America imported agricultural and transportation techniques from the United States. The Canadas also imported people: between 1791 and 1812, fifteen thousand New Englanders moved north to the Eastern Townships of Lower Canada and fifty thousand New Yorkers and Pennsylvanians settled the lands of Upper Canada, granted almost free by the British Crown. George Rawlyk and Jane Errington have pointed out that even the Loyalist elite's anti-American critique was copied directly from the writings of American Federalists, who were similarly alarmed with what they saw as the democratic excesses of the Jeffersonian Republicans. British North Americans drank to George III's health on 4 June, the king's birthday, instead of to American independence a month later, but if the colonials were developing a society that was spiritually British, they were also building one that was materially American, or at least North American.[10]

Day-to-day interaction among peoples ran more smoothly than the relationship between the British and American governments; between 1783 and 1812, Anglo-American tensions made the future of British North America uncertain. For the fledgling United States, the post-revolutionary period was one of economic growth, of political experimentation, and of uncertainty and weakness in international affairs. Hemmed in on the seaboard, with Britain, Spain, and France still colonial powers in the hemisphere, a sense of vulnerability and isolation shaped U.S. foreign policy in this generation and influenced the course of the Anglo-American relations, and by default, those with British North America. American leaders were compelled to come to terms with the continued dominance of Britain to the north and on the seas. It seemed, as H. G. Nicholas has put it, that the treaty of 1783 "had bought peace largely by imprecision and omission," and left "not a clean break, but a line of ragged connections" between Britain and the United States. The border of New England and Nova Scotia remained in dispute, as did American commercial rights in the British West Indies. The French Revolution, the wars of the French Revolu-

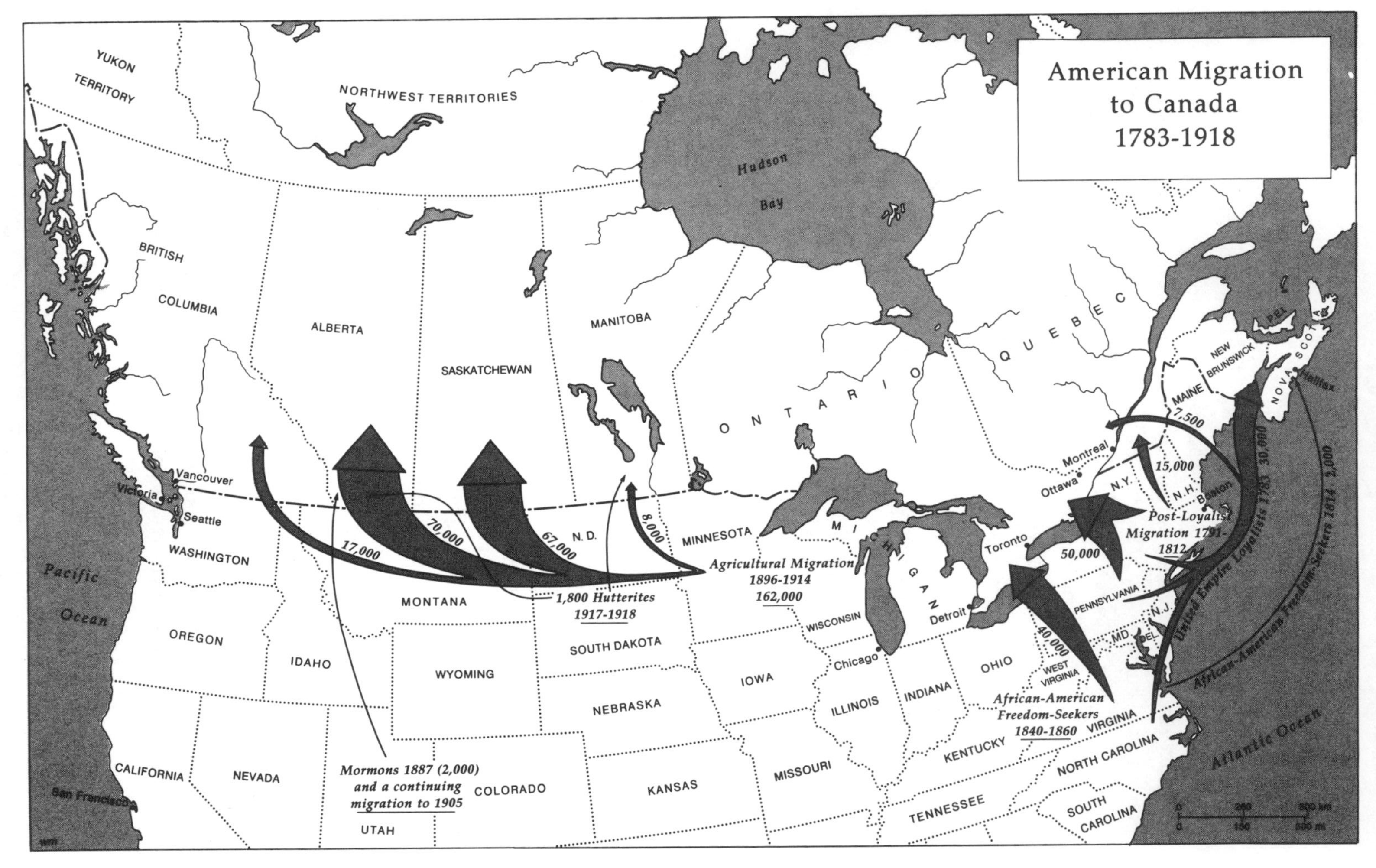
American Migration to Canada 1783-1918
YUKON TERRITORY
NORTHWEST TERRITORIES
Hudson Bay
BRITISH COLUMBIA
ALBERTA
SASKATCHEWAN
MANITOBA
ONTARIO
QUEBEC
NEW BRUNSWICK
NOVA SCOTIA
Halifax
PEI
MAINE
7,500
15,000
N.H.
Boston
N.Y.
Montreal
Ottawa
Post-Loyalist Migration 1791-1812
United Empire Loyalists 1783 30,000
African-American Freedom-Seekers 1814 2,000
50,000
Toronto
Detroit
40,000
African-American Freedom-Seekers 1840-1860
Agricultural Migration 1896-1914 162,000
8,000
67,000
70,000
17,000
1,800 Hutterites 1917-1918
Mormons 1887 (2,000) and a continuing migration to 1905
Vancouver
Victoria
Seattle
WASHINGTON
Pacific Ocean
Atlantic Ocean
OREGON
CALIFORNIA
San Francisco
NEVADA
IDAHO
UTAH
MONTANA
WYOMING
COLORADO
N.D.
SOUTH DAKOTA
NEBRASKA
KANSAS
MINNESOTA
IOWA
MISSOURI
WISCONSIN
MICHIGAN
Chicago
ILLINOIS
INDIANA
OHIO
KENTUCKY
TENNESSEE
WEST VIRGINIA
VIRGINIA
NORTH CAROLINA
SOUTH CAROLINA
PENNSYLVANIA
N.J.
MD
DEL
0 250 500 km
0 150 300 mi

tion and then the Napoleonic Wars added to these points of friction chronic disputes over the neutrality of the seas and the impressment of American merchant seamen into the British navy. A critical issue that directly affected Canada was the continued presence of British troops in forts in the Ohio Valley a decade after the Treaty of Paris had required them to withdraw. From the American perspective, this violated international law, allowed Montreal merchants to steal the profits of the fur trade, and enabled the British to incite the Indian nations in the area to attack American settlers. In 1794, the Washington administration dispatched John Jay to London to resolve this question as well as the tensions over British seizures of American ships and men on the high seas. Jay won no concessions on British maritime policy but made a breakthrough on the question of the western forts. The British abandoned their Indian allies, helping make possible General Anthony Wayne's defeat of the Indian Confederacy at the Battle of Fallen Timbers. Ratified in 1795, Jay's treaty provided for British withdrawal from the Ohio Valley and made legal the extensive intercourse already going on across the forty-fifth parallel. The claim of some historians that Jay's treaty established the tradition of "exceptionalism" in Canadian-American relations is exaggerated, but the treaty did assure, as Alexander Hamilton put it, "good neighborhood between the United States and the bordering British Territories." It created what historian Bradford Perkins refers to as "the first rapprochement" between Britain and the United States, and although it left the most irritating Anglo-American disputes unresolved, it delayed for two decades their explosion into war between Britain and the United States—a war with Canada as the scene of battle and the potential prize.[11]

The War of 1812

Historians have long debated the causes of the War of 1812. The interpretive consensus emphasizes maritime tensions between the United States and Britain as the determinant in the U.S. decision to go to war, with the invasion and possible annexation of Canada as a distant secondary consideration. The most recent interpretations stress the desire of the young republic to vindicate the American Revolution, to strengthen republican institutions, and to enhance the political fortunes of the fledgling Republican party of Jefferson, James Madison, and James Monroe. In both versions, however, taking Canada is dismissed as (in Reginald Horsman's words) "a useful side benefit of a war that had become necessary largely because of British maritime policy." There can be no doubt of the psychic and economic significance to the United States of British seizure of American ships engaged in trade with French-controlled Europe and the continued searching of American ships for deserters from the British navy, significance symbolized by the HMS *Leopard*'s attack on the USS *Chesapeake* in 1807. President Jefferson's controversial and narrowly approved embargo act of that year, and the non-intercourse act that replaced it in 1809, dramatically reduced American trade (and correspondingly increased domestic manufacturing) with serious dislocation for those American merchants who exported agricultural products to European markets. But neither act could solve the maritime problems so long as Britain feared Napoleonic France infinitely more than American enmity. To John C. Calhoun in 1812, Britain left Americans "an alternative only between the base surrender of their rights, and a manly vindication of them [by] an immediate appeal to arms." [12]

The "land hunger" explanation of the War of 1812—the thesis that maritime rights were simply "righteous pretexts" for Americans like Calhoun who coveted Canada's "rich bottom land"—has been largely dismissed by historians, if not by subsequent generations of Canadian school teachers.[13] But difficulties on the western frontier did contribute to the escalation of British-American conflict and had implications important for understanding subsequent U.S.-Canadian relations. Western Americans continued to claim, inaccurately, that only British support allowed Tecumseh and Tenskwatawa ("The Prophet"), leaders of the Algonquian confederacy, to continue to resist American traders and settlers who sought their lands. Although the Indians bought their weapons from British merchants, they were, in the words of Richard White, "independent political agents" who needed no British incitement to continue their century-long war against American expansion. But such perceptions fueled demands from such westerners as Henry Clay of Kentucky that Canada be invaded, as did the two hundred Americans killed when General William H. Harrison won a fiercely fought battle with the Indian confederacy at Tippecanoe Creek in November 1811. Hezekiah Niles's *National Intelligencer,* founded that same year, demonstrated the increase in United States interest in British North American affairs that marked the eve of war. Niles shared with many of his countrymen the belief that Upper Canada could and should be captured, but that this should be done not for territorial expansion but to expel the British, who manipulated the Indians and imposed authoritarian European values and institutions on British North America. Niles agreed with Michigan territorial governor William Hull that conquest would bring "civil, political and religious liberty" to the Canadians. As they had been forty years earlier, however, Americans were ambivalent about the colonies and the colonials to their north. John Randolph of Virginia and John Stanley of North Carolina dismissed Canadian lands as of little use, the climate as inhospitable, and its people as unenlightened. Niles's newspaper reflected this ambivalence: it would be easier to "manufacture the Devil into a christian," he editorialized, than "to make a republican of a Canadian Frenchman or an imported Scotchman."[14]

In June 1812, President Madison asked Congress for a declaration of war against Great Britain. The president emphasized maritime issues, relegating British incitement of the "savages" to an afterthought, but the congressional votes that carried the war declaration came from the West and the South, with a reluctant commercial New England—the region to which maritime issues should have been most important—pulled along in the wake of nationalist pro-war sentiment. For the "war hawks" of the West and the South, an attack on Canada seemed not only a logical way to defeat the Indian confederacies and open the way for westward expansion but also the only strategic means by which the United States could counter British naval supremacy. Canada was to be seized as a hostage rather than captured as a prize of war.[15]

The large numbers of American-born in the Canadas made American leaders confident of easy victory. Thomas Jefferson, in a prediction often quoted derisively by Canadian historians, thought that victory would be "a mere matter of marching." As from 1775 to 1776, however, most Canadians showed little interest in the unique brand of liberty offered to them by their potential conquerors. Instead, they identified the Americans with Napoleonic France, "the greatest tyranny that ever oppressed the world," as an Upper Canadian newspaper put it. U.S. forces met resistance from British regulars, from Britain's Indian allies, and eventually, from the Canadian militia. The Canadian militia's resistance toughened as the war continued because the invading American army did not behave like liberators: after their first advance into Upper Canada was repelled, General George McClure's New York militia put the Niagara peninsula village of Newark to the torch, turning residents out into a subzero December night. But although every American invasion of Canada faltered, the United States did not "lose" the War of 1812. American captains embarrassed the Royal Navy on the high seas, on the Great Lakes, and on Lake Champlain, thwarting British counterinvasions, and American troops repelled British amphibious assaults on coastal cities. In this sense, the War of 1812 was a decisive dead heat that confirmed the postrevolutionary military stalemate.[16]

As the end of the Napoleonic Wars in Europe threatened British escalation of the war in North America, President Madison welcomed negotiations to resolve the conflict. Britain's initial hard line—demands for American recognition of a distinct Indian buffer state, boundary adjustments south of the Great Lakes, and nullification of American fishing rights in British North American waters—softened with military reverses at Plattsburgh and Baltimore. The price for continued war weighed too high against the prospective gain, so that as the year drew to a close, Britain consented to the Treaty of Ghent, ending the war without territorial gain for either combatant. The War of 1812's real losers were the native peoples who had fought as Britain's allies, a cruel irony, given their importance in turning back the American invasions of Canada. Instead of a state of their own, they were left to choose between the charity of the British Crown and an American Indian policy made increasingly brutal by memories of the war.[17]

The Treaty of Ghent and the Rush-Bagot agreement of 1817 together set the terms for Anglo-American, and thus U.S.-British North American relations for the next generation. As on other occasions when Britain negotiated with the United States, British North American interests were secondary to imperial considerations. The treaty established boundary commissions to settle territorial disputes, particularly over lands occupied by British forces during the war, but it was ominously silent on the main issues Madison had identified as the causes of war: neutrality on the seas and impressment of American seamen. The subsequent Rush-Bagot agreement saved both the United States and Britain from a potentially costly arms race to protect their respective borders. The naval limitation provisions applied only to the Great Lakes and limited the number of armed vessels on Lake Champlain and Lake Ontario to one each and to two on each of the other Great Lakes. There were no limits on land fortification, on the other hand, and both Britain and the United States built extensively. True to the spirit of the Treaty of Ghent, the two parties also concluded a convention in 1818 in which they agreed to a Canadian-American boundary from Lake of the Woods to the Rocky Mountains along the forty-ninth parallel, leaving the sensitive Pacific boundary unresolved. In the interim, the Oregon Territory was considered open to the citizens of both nations. By the same agreement, American fishermen gained the "liberty" to use the fisheries off the Newfoundland and Labrador coasts, a "right" American fishermen felt they already possessed, with the result that this too would return to trouble later generations.[18]

The battles and diplomacy of this "Second American Revolution" quickly became less relevant than the new social realities it bequeathed. By neutralizing the military power of the native peoples and ending liberal British land policies for immigrants from the United States, the War of 1812 deflected American migration away from Upper Canada and westward to Ohio and Michigan. The War of 1812's most substantial legacy was its imprint on the public historical memory of the United States and Canada. It retaught the lessons of the Revolutionary War and further inculcated separate national identities into the minds of ordinary folk of each country. Nationalist mythmakers rewrote weary survival into glamorous victory. For Canadians, the War of 1812 eventually became chapter 2 in their rejection of American republicanism, a chapter with a happier ending and with gallant heroes who were winners, not losers: Sir Isaac Brock, dead defender of Queenston Heights, the Canadian militiamen, and Laura Secord, who crept through the American lines to warn of the Yankee attack at Beaver Dams. (The history primers never mentioned that British regulars and Indian allies won most of the battles, or that Laura Secord was Massachusetts-born, the daughter of a major in the Massachusetts militia!) In America, every schoolchild memorized Oliver Hazard Perry's laconic summation of his victory on Lake Erie: "We have met the enemy and they are ours." Andrew Jackson—a "Symbol for an Age," John William Ward has called him—won his national fame with his "brilliant and unparalleled victory at New Orleans [which] has closed the war with a blaze of Glory [and] placed America on the very pinnacle of fame." It is entirely appropriate that the War of 1812 provided both the setting for "The Star-Spangled Banner" and the inspiration for the interminable repetitions of "We stand on guard for thee" in the English-language chorus of "O Canada."[19]

Manifest Destiny and Imperial Rivalry

In the decades between 1820 and 1860 British North America and the United States continued to move away from their earlier common colonial heritage, but they did so at very different rhythms. For the United States, the 1820s brought the first stirring of sectionalism over the westward expansion of slavery, which Thomas Jefferson worried was a "fire bell in the night." Political power shifted from the Massachusetts-Virginia revolutionary establishment that had dominated the first half-century of the young nation to new leaders from the expanding regions of the country, men such as Andrew Jackson, symbol of the more mythical than real age of the common man. Stimu-

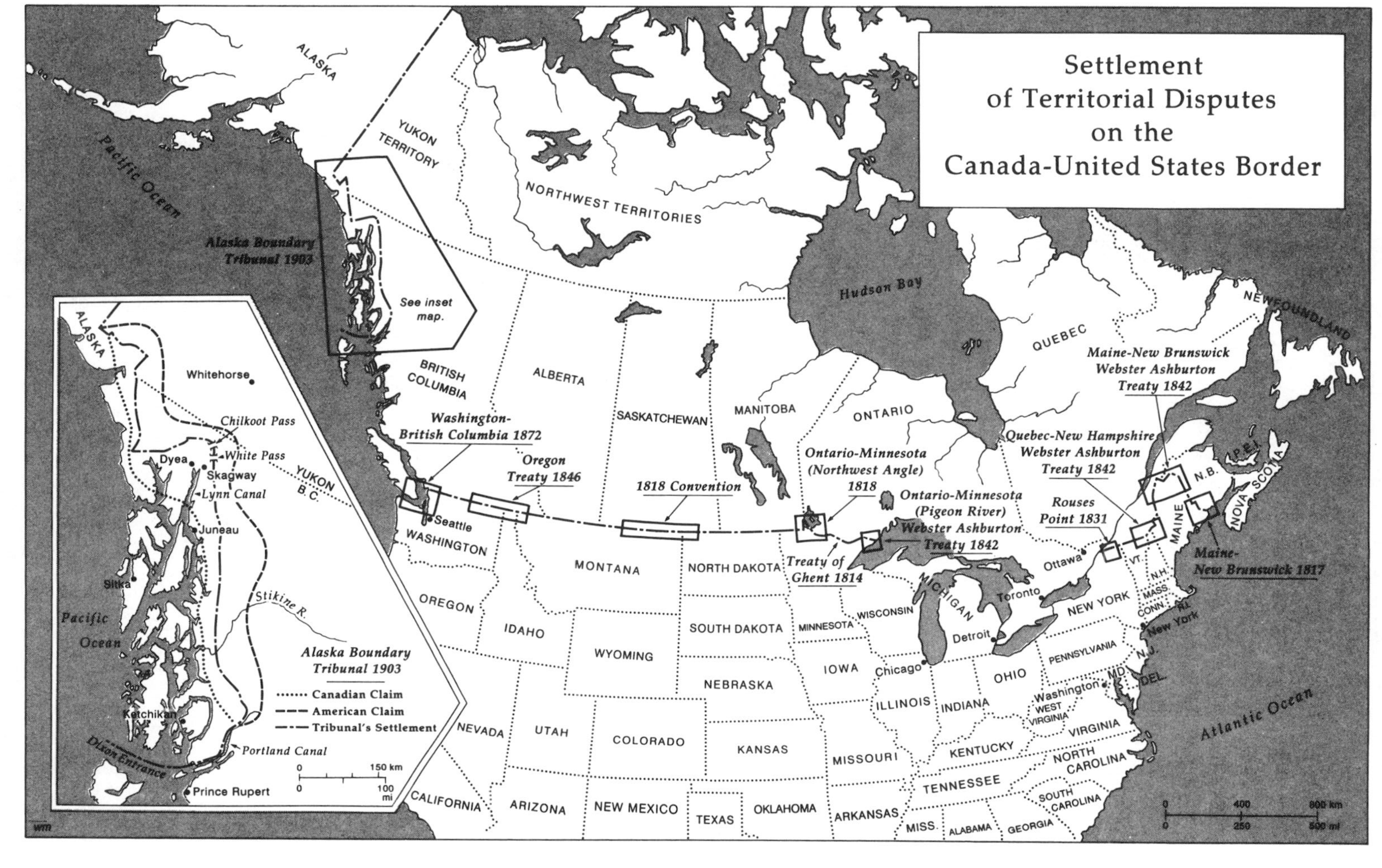
Settlement of Territorial Disputes on the Canada-United States Border
Alaska Boundary Tribunal 1903
See inset map.
Washington-British Columbia 1872
Oregon Treaty 1846
1818 Convention
Ontario-Minnesota (Northwest Angle) 1818
Ontario-Minnesota (Pigeon River) Webster Ashburton Treaty 1842
Treaty of Ghent 1814
Rouses Point 1831
Quebec-New Hampshire Webster Ashburton Treaty 1842
Maine-New Brunswick Webster Ashburton Treaty 1842
Maine-New Brunswick 1817
Pacific Ocean
Atlantic Ocean
Hudson Bay
ALASKA
YUKON TERRITORY
NORTHWEST TERRITORIES
BRITISH COLUMBIA
ALBERTA
SASKATCHEWAN
MANITOBA
ONTARIO
QUEBEC
NEWFOUNDLAND
N.B.
P.E.I.
NOVA SCOTIA
WASHINGTON
OREGON
CALIFORNIA
NEVADA
IDAHO
MONTANA
WYOMING
UTAH
ARIZONA
COLORADO
NEW MEXICO
NORTH DAKOTA
SOUTH DAKOTA
NEBRASKA
KANSAS
OKLAHOMA
TEXAS
MINNESOTA
IOWA
MISSOURI
ARKANSAS
WISCONSIN
ILLINOIS
MICHIGAN
INDIANA
OHIO
KENTUCKY
TENNESSEE
MISS.
ALABAMA
GEORGIA
SOUTH CAROLINA
NORTH CAROLINA
VIRGINIA
WEST VIRGINIA
PENNSYLVANIA
NEW YORK
MD.
DEL.
N.J.
CONN.
R.I.
MASS.
VT.
N.H.
MAINE
Seattle
Chicago
Detroit
Toronto
Ottawa
Washington
New York
0 400 800 km
0 250 500 mi
Alaska Boundary Tribunal 1903
Canadian Claim
American Claim
Tribunal's Settlement
Whitehorse
Chilkoot Pass
White Pass
Dyea
Skagway
Lynn Canal
YUKON
B.C.
Juneau
Sitka
Stikine R.
Ketchikan
Portland Canal
Dixon Entrance
Prince Rupert
0 150 km
0 100 mi
wm

lated first by Jefferson's embargo and then by protective tariffs, the first factories rose against the pastoral landscape of New England. Irish Roman Catholic and German immigrants crowded the nation's cities, providing a labor force for an American industrial revolution. Culturally, although European intellectual currents swept through the East, American intellectuals attempted to demonstrate that the United States was not English; James Fenimore Cooper's novels, for example, "struck a responsive chord in American readers." One of the best modern surveys of American history describes the period as "the Creation of the American National Character." Agitation for change on a broad range of issues confronted established traditions and institutions: religious revivalism, temperance, women's rights, abolitionism—all had their spokespersons.[20]

The United States and British North America were so close geographically and so similar ethnically (save for the French Canadians of Lower Canada and New Brunswick) that many American ideas spilled north. The stirrings of *Democracy in America* that so fascinated Alexis de Tocqueville during his stay in the United States in the 1830s seemed to be reflected in Upper and Lower Canadian rebellions in 1837. Religious revival found a Canadian analog, not surprising given kinship ties and the fact that Upper Canadian Methodists did not separate from the American Methodist Church until 1828. On both sides of the border, Protestant men and women railed against the evil of liquor; in 1836 British North American temperance societies began to affiliate with the American Temperance Union. The movement for common schools and curriculum reform in English Canada paralleled similar developments to the south. The Anti-Slavery Society of Canada cooperated actively with American abolitionists.[21]

Similarities there were; but it is critical not to confuse these affinities with fundamental agreement. The antislavery movement in Canada owed at least as much to British as to United States influence. In the area of educational reform, Upper Canadian Methodist school promoter Egerton Ryerson shared the American goal of an educated citizenry, but he denounced textbooks published in the United States as "anti-British" and pronounced the purpose of the common school to be to make "this country British in domestic feeling." British North America at midcentury was emphatically that—British. Between 1820 and 1860, the colonies welcomed almost one million immigrants from the British Isles; in the first Canadian census of 1851, the British-born made up more than 20 percent of the population and outnumbered the American-born seven to one. In Upper Canada in particular, where they were overrepresented among the colony's political leaders, there was a conscious emulation of British traditions. After Britain allowed the colonies to assume virtual autonomy in local affairs in the 1840s, French-Canadian elites came to admire their British system of government almost as fervently. "We will never forget our allegiance," vowed E.-P. Taché, "till the last cannon which is shot on this continent in defence of Great Britain is fired by the hand of a French Canadian." For those who rejected this Loyalist consensus, British North America had a safety valve: they could simply walk across the open border to the United States. Beginning in the 1840s, substantial numbers of British North Americans did exactly that—250,000 in total by 1860—but their motivation was economic rather than political discontent.[22]

British North America confronted the same agonies and pleasures in the nineteenth-century transition to industrial capitalist society, but it did so at a slower pace and within the bosom of the British Empire. Trade across the border was brisk, especially after the completion in 1825 of the Erie Canal linking Buffalo and Albany. But Canadian merchants pressed for the completion of the Welland Canal to bypass Niagara Falls between Lakes Ontario and Erie, strengthening the Great Lakes–St. Lawrence route and firming the ties between Upper and Lower Canada that Donald Creighton has labeled "The Commercial Empire of the St. Lawrence." As part of a competing world system, British North America shared its mother country's clash with the United States over economic opportunity, trade, resources, and territory. For U.S. foreign policy, the period was marked by the pretense to hemispheric domination expressed in Monroe's statement of 1823, later enshrined as the Monroe Doctrine, and by the burst of youthful nationalist chauvinism embodied in John L. O'Sullivan's concept of "Manifest Destiny." The defensive expansionism of America's first half-century gave way to what William Goetzmann aptly calls the years "when the eagle screamed," as the United States consolidated its borders to the north, west, and south against potential competing empires and began to people the continent between Mexico and British North America.[23]

In an era in which the United States took half of Mexico in a short but bloody war, and American privateers filibustered in Central America and the Caribbean, Anglo-American disputes over boundaries, over border violations after the rebellions of 1837, over fugitive slaves seeking sanctuary, and over control of western territories and resources were without exception resolved without further war. Such settlements reflected caution on the part of both parties after the costly stalemate from 1812 to 1814, growing political and international maturity in the United States, and the skill of individual diplomats. But war remained a very real possibility: the peaceful resolution of these conflicts should not mask their intensity. Nor should peaceful resolution be cited (as some historians and many politicians have subsequently cited it) as evidence that a "special relationship" has existed between Canada and the United States from 1818 to the present day. British North America was the pawn—and the hostage—in Anglo-American disputes.

The tensions surrounding the 1837 rebellions in Upper and Lower Canada, for example, were heated. The rebellions were the product of maturing societies with groups that neither shared the values nor accepted the dominance of the established order; to that extent they mirrored what took place in electoral politics in Jacksonian America. In the Upper Canadian case, radical reformers identified with William Lyon Mackenzie, who advocated political democratization along lines that they believed emulated the United States. For Mackenzie, the American influence was very direct. He had met President Jackson in 1829—subsequently describing him as the best of "these modern Romans"—and been impressed by what he saw in American politics. Yet his pro-American position evolved slowly and remained ambivalent. Like virtually all British North Americans, he was appalled by slavery, the basic contradiction between the rhetoric of liberty and the reality of American life. American politicians, he wrote in 1827, "mock the ear with the language of freedom in a capital polluted with Negro slavery." Yet he admired the representativeness of the American system of government, the use of nominating conventions to nominate candidates for office, the election of higher officials, and (he imagined incorrectly) the Senate. He attributed America's economic progress and entrepreneurial spirit to republican institutions and pressed their virtues on his countrymen. Mackenzie's ignorance about the technique of selecting U.S. senators is less significant than his ideological isolation. More representative among Upper Canadian reformers were moderates committed to the imperial connection, who sought to emulate British, not American, electoral and economic reformers.[24]

In Lower Canada ethnic divisions exacerbated the conflict, as a French-Canadian majority in the elected legislature contested an English-Canadian oligarchy based on an appointed executive grouped around the British governor. French-Canadian rebels echoed arguments heard in Virginia and Massachusetts a half-century earlier, and marched as "les fils de la liberté"—the sons of liberty. Their principal spokesman, Louis-Joseph Papineau, Speaker of the Assembly, evolved from an anti-American to an advocate of annexation to the United States, praising republican institutions rather than English radicalism as "our model and our study." Closer examination of Papineau's political program, however, reveals his profound misconceptions about what statehood would portend for French Canadians. His assumption that the French language, laws, and institutions of Lower Canada would be forever protected by the principle of states' rights is remarkably naive. Alexis de Tocqueville understood the United States better: "if the [French] Canadians united with the United States," he wrote, "their population will be soon absorbed."[25]

John L. O'Sullivan's *Democratic Review* urged support for "the cause of the Canadian rebellion," an Albany newspaper headlined "Hurra for Papineau and Freedom," and a half-dozen Vermont towns voted small sums for the Canadian patriots. But no U.S. intervention was ever contemplated, and the rebels were crushed. What involved the United States was not the exportation of American ideals but the flight of the defeated rebels—Mackenzie and Papineau among them—to the United States. Mackenzie established a provisional rebel government on American soil, and his followers, reinforced by a handful of American sympathizers, made minor incursions into Canada that provoked Anglo-Canadian retaliation. In December 1837, the Upper Canadian militia crossed the border at Navy Island in the Niagara River and burned an American ship, the *Caroline,* which was being used to provision the rebels. One American was killed in the fighting, but it might well have been one hundred, given the vociferous reaction that swept northern U.S. border cities and communities. Sir George Arthur, Lieutenant Governor of Upper Canada, feared war was imminent; President Martin Van Buren and his cabinet wanted peace, Arthur believed, "but how are they to help if the People will it?" Van Buren acted quickly: General Winfield Scott went to New York to prevent reckless military ventures against Canada that would have provoked a full-scale Anglo-American war—the rebels' goal. Mackenzie and others were taken into custody, and crisis was deferred until November 1840, when a Canadian named Alexander McLeod was arrested in Lewiston, New York, as the self-proclaimed killer of the single American casualty of the destruction of the *Caroline.* British Foreign Secretary Lord Palmerston warned the American minister in London that "McLeod's execution would produce war . . . frightful in its character," and both sides prepared for its outbreak. Fortunately for the United States, Britain, the Canadas, and especially for McLeod, the jury believed his plea that his exploit at Navy Island had been nothing more than a drunken boast. McLeod escaped the gallows, and Americans and Anglo-Canadians avoided looking at each another through gunsights yet again.[26]

Conflict between Maine and New Brunswick lumbermen over access to timber exacerbated the tensions built by the McLeod trial. The so-called Aroostook War illustrated a unique problem of Anglo-American diplomacy created by American federalism: the governor of Maine sent the state militia to the long-disputed border to rattle its sabers in support of Maine timber barons. As in New York, Winfield Scott intervened to hold the state government in check until diplomats set the machinery in motion to reach a settlement. By 1842, Secretary of State Daniel Webster and the British minister to Washington, Lord Ashburton, had come to terms on a Maine–New Brunswick boundary. Their success illustrates the sometimes determinant role of individuals in international relations. Webster was a strong Anglophile, highly regarded in England; Ashburton was connected to Baring Brothers Bank, which had loaned millions of pounds in the United States, and was married to an American. The Webster-Ashburton Treaty was a sound compromise. It drew the boundary far enough south to enable the British to construct a military road linking Quebec to New Brunswick and divided the disputed forests almost equally, much to the chagrin of Maine. The agreement also explicitly defined the boundary from Lake Superior to the Lake of the Woods, and a separate exchange of notes made verbal amends for the *Caroline* affair.[27]

No such graceful compromise characterized the resolution of the Oregon question. In the 1840s, five thousand American settlers followed the missionaries and fur traders into the area to challenge the Hudson's Bay Company, Britain's instrument of indirect rule. Whig secretary of state John C. Calhoun offered in 1844 to simply extend the forty-ninth parallel to the coast to divide the region, but Democratic presidential candidate James K. Polk vowed to take all of the territory to fifty-four degrees, forty minutes—effectively cutting British North America off from the Pacific. Given the tenuous American presence in and claim to the area, Polk's "Fifty-four, Forty or Fight" was campaign rhetoric, but once victorious, it became his campaign promise. Polk's secretary of state James Buchanan more realistically renewed the forty-ninth parallel proposal, but this time Richard Pakenham, British minister to Washington, rejected the compromise. Polk escalated the dispute into the Oregon Crisis by reiterating the Monroe Doctrine's assertion that the United States would not tolerate "any European interference on the North American continent," a claim so absurd given the British colonial presence in North America that it raised doubts about Polk's capacity for higher office. Publicly the president refused British offers to discuss the boundary, but U.S. war with Mexico loomed, and British foreign minister Lord Aberdeen was deadly serious in mobilizing a British fleet and land forces in Canada for war. The Democratic administration eventually saw the wisdom of negotiation, the Senate concurred, and in 1846 the boundary was set at the forty-ninth parallel to the Strait of Juan de Fuca, precisely where it could have been before Polk's irresponsible bellicosity.[28]

If there was interest in the United States in acquiring Britain's North American possessions peaceably, there was none at all in taking them by force, and Great Britain had demonstrated that force would be necessary. But if Britain stood firm against wholesale concessions of territory to the United States, the 1840s nonetheless brought important changes to imperial economic policies: Parliament dismantled the mercantilist tariff preferences that had created protected British markets for colonial grain and timber. Outraged merchants in Montreal sought economic salvation in the United States. In October 1849, the Annexation Manifesto called for "Friendly and peaceable separation from British connexion, and a union upon equitable terms with the great North American confederacy of sovereign States." Given that the Montreal business community had been politically Tory and traditionally inclined to see the United States as an "insatiable democracy" guilty of "dreadful crimes," some Americans misinterpreted the manifesto as sincere rejection of monarchy and an embrace of American republicanism. The *New York Tribune* rushed a special correspondent north to report on the impending annexation. But by 1850, support for annexationism had become ephemeral on both sides of the border. Some in the northern free states believed that the acquisition of Canada would shift the political balance in their favor on the issue of the extension of slavery, but as William Lloyd Garrison reminded abolitionists, Canada would never wish to be annexed to the United States "while a slave remains on our soil." Slavery was only one star in the constellation of ideological reasons for which the majority of British North Americans rejected annexation to the United States. Without strong support in New Brunswick, Nova Scotia, or Canada West, the Annexation Manifesto drew a dozen angry denunciations for every expression of support. The initiative it began died of natural causes four years before it was rendered irrelevant by the reciprocity treaty.[29]

In 1854, the U.S. Congress and the colonial legislatures of British

North America endorsed a ten-year reciprocity agreement negotiated in Washington between Canadian governor general Lord Elgin and Secretary of State William Marcy. The accord provided for free movement of products of "land, mine and sea": grain, coal, livestock, timber, and fish. American fishermen were formally allowed unrestricted access to coastal fisheries north of the thirty-sixth parallel—legal recognition of the de facto practices of the New England fleet—and shippers were granted mutual access to American-controlled Lake Michigan and the Canadian-controlled St. Lawrence canals. Although greeted with mixed feeling in the Maritime colonies because of the fishery concessions, the accord was eagerly welcomed by the Canadas as evidence that the threat of American aggression had diminished. In the United States, southern senators rationalized support for reciprocity as insurance against annexation, a guarantee that British North Americans "will not undertake to join the North to disturb the political balance," which was how one senator put it. North-south trade had always been significant, and the treaty accelerated it (although econometric historians debate the precise dimensions of its contribution). American capital and expertise moved north in what Canadian historian Arthur Lower calls a "North American assault on the Canadian forest" to cut the lumber to construct the American Middle West. The interconnections of commerce were symbolized by the engineering marvel of the age, the great international railway suspension bridge that spanned the Niagara River. For the moment, economic reciprocity reflected public will on both sides of the border and the growing Anglo-American accord in the Western Hemisphere in the 1850s. In less than a decade, however, the same sectional strains had expedited the Senate's passage of reciprocity and abruptly severed this arrangement.[30]

Division and Consolidation

The two momentous events in the history of the United States—the Revolution and the Civil War—have equal moment in the history of Canada. Born in the Revolution, modern Canada came together as a political nation as the United States moved toward seeming disintegration in the Civil War. America's forty-year sectional contest over states' rights and slavery, the contest of two very different political economies and cultures—capitalist and neofeudal, Yankee and cavalier—burst into the bloodiest war of the nineteenth century at Fort Sumter in 1861. Britain and its North American colonies were not disinterested bystanders. British and British North American sentiment had long been strongly antislavery. Britain had led the international movement against the slave trade since the beginning of the century and had formally abolished slavery within its empire in 1834, thus acquiring the self-righteous certitude of a former sinner about America's "peculiar institution." Nova Scotia, New Brunswick, and the Canadas shared this tradition. Asked by American abolitionists about settlement possibilities for former slaves in Upper Canada, Lieutenant Governor Sir John Colborne told them to "tell the Republicans on your side of the line that we do not know men by color." Black communities began to be founded in southwestern Upper Canada in the 1820s, and the province was the terminus of the "Underground Railroad." Some historians have argued that Euro-Canadians were as prejudiced against blacks as Euro-Americans were, pointing to the fact that the refugees were received with a racism only slightly less virulent than that in the United States. But forty thousand African Americans—many of them free—chose Canada. "I have enjoyed more pleasure here in one month," wrote one of them, "than in all my life in the land of bondage." Prominent abolitionists Frederick Douglass, Harriet Tubman, Levi Coffin, and John Brown visited these communities and lectured in Canadian cities; Brown's disastrous assault on the federal arsenal at Harper's Ferry was conceived near Chatham, Canada West, in 1858. One of his coconspirators, Samuel Gridley Howe, pronounced Canada a "reliable ally" and "immense moral aid" in the antislavery cause. It is impossible to determine how much of this support was deeply felt abolitionism and how much ritualistic anti-Americanism, such as that of the New Brunswick editor who used "the slave-holding Republic" as a foil to "the British flag—the *true* emblem of *true* liberty."[31]

British North American opinion on the Civil War defies easy categorization. Opposition to slavery did not lead to automatic support for the Union. *Harper's Weekly* warned against "the singular delusion" held by some Americans that "in the event of a separation between the Northern and the Southern States, Canada would leap into the arms of the former. . . . Canadians are intensely loyal to their Sovereign; and intensely hostile to Americans and American institutions." But this anti-Americanism did not translate to support for the Confederacy. Until Lincoln's emancipation proclamation in September 1862, the British North American consensus was that the war had been caused by economic differences between North and South rather than humanitarian concerns over slavery. Civil conflict thus represented the preordained failure of American republicanism, brought about by an excess of democracy, overly strong states, and a weak central government. As in Britain, there was cynical speculation about the advantages to be gained at the expense of a dis-United States. Advocates of a broad federation of the British North American colonies saw long-term opportunity: "In consequence of the fratricidal war," said Canadian co-premier John A. Macdonald, "Canada had every prospect of being the great nation of this continent." Canadian leaders also saw immediate danger. "The shot fired at Fort Sumter," wrote Thomas D'Arcy McGee, "told the people of Canada to sleep no more, except on their arms, unless in their sleep they desire to be overtaken and subjugated."[32]

The combination of British North American proximity and British international ambitions meant that "the fratricidal war" would not be contained within purely domestic bounds. Britain quickly issued a proclamation of neutrality and refused to recognize the Confederacy, but could hardly ignore the fact of southern belligerency. Three battalions of infantry and an artillery battery rushed ostentatiously across the Atlantic to reinforce the British North American garrisons. The British cabinet feared Abraham Lincoln's secretary of state, William Seward, whom British prime minister Lord Palmerston described as a "vapouring, blustering, ignorant man." They had good reason to do so, for Seward seriously contemplated a diversionary war with Britain as a tactic to reunite the North and the South. Lincoln stopped such madness but did not countermand Seward's appointment of a secret emissary to Canada in an attempt to ensure that Canadian actions and opinions were consistent with northern desires. News of this appointment soon leaked to the press, a revelation that appropriately angered British authorities, since all U.S. diplomatic representation with Canada had to be channeled through the British ministry in Washington. The incident underlined a larger problem that plagued British North American-U.S. relations throughout the war: the American determination that Canadian territory not be used as a base for Confederate operations or a source of Confederate weapons. That issue arose early, with a diplomatic note from Seward protesting the sale of the lake steamer *Peerless* to "rebel" agents for use as a privateer to attack northern shipping. The allegations were groundless—the purchasers were New Yorkers—but the heated exchange of notes illustrated how delicate the Canadian position would be throughout the Civil War.[33]

Most incendiary of the border incidents was the raid on St. Albans, Vermont, by some twenty Confederate sympathizers in October 1864. The raiders terrorized the small community, murdered one man and wounded others, and looted the banks of two hundred thousand dollars before returning to the Canadian side of the border. There they were arrested, but Canadian and British authorities refused Seward's demand that they be extradited to the United States. Canada's sincere efforts to bring the raiders to justice were confounded by a Montreal magistrate who defined them as belligerents, rather than criminals, and thus beyond his jurisdiction. The raiders went free. The Canadian legislature at once enacted an alien act that provided for deportation of aliens who engaged in hostilities against a friendly country, but American anger was not assuaged. Instead, it was compounded by Canadian refusal to return the fifteen thousand Union "skedaddlers"—deserters and draft dodgers—who fled to Canada, and by the depredations of the *Alabama*, a Confederate warship that was built in a British shipyard and preyed with deadly success on Union merchant vessels.[34] In turn, the Union naval blockade of the Confederacy revived the Anglo-American dispute over neutrality of the seas. In November

1861, the British mail ship *Trent* was stopped and searched in international waters off Cuba by the USS *San Jacinto.* Union Captain Charles Wilkes arrested two Confederate envoys en route to London, James Mason and John Slidell. An outpouring of chauvinistic anti-British nationalism awaited Wilkes in port, but President Lincoln and Charles Sumner, chairman of the Senate Foreign Relations Committee, both understood the diplomatic and military consequences of his rash decision. Britain prepared immediately for war with the United States. The North American garrisons were tripled with fourteen thousand reinforcements, and British strategists planned preemptive strikes along the border to forestall the American invasion. The strategists held out little hope of holding Canada against concerted American attack. Instead the Royal Navy would force an American retreat: one cabinet minister spoke of "the regrettable necessity of having to burn New York and Boston." Lord Palmerston assured Queen Victoria that her forces were ready "to inflict a severe blow upon and to read a lesson to the United States which will not soon be forgotten." Britain's cautiously drafted ultimatum, however, left the United States space for a face-saving de-escalation. Seward asserted the United States' right to stop and search on the high seas but disavowed Wilkes's actions and, most important, freed Mason and Slidell.[35]

The defeat of the Confederacy, symbolized by Robert E. Lee's surrender at Appomattox Court House in April 1865, did not resolve these Civil War stresses to Anglo-American relations. Some American voices, none of them significant ones, echoed the *Chicago Tribune*'s call for the Union to retaliate against Britain by devouring its North American colonies "as quickly as a hawk would gobble a quail." The contentious atmosphere led Britain, and especially British North America, to take such threats too seriously. Henry Adams wrote from London that it was "whispered about that with the . . . Union restored, and a great army is left in our hands, the next manifestation will be one of hostility to this country. The various steps to rescind old treaty obligations, especially relating to Canada, . . . are cited as proof of our intentions to attack that country at once." The "old treaty obligations" were the 1817 Rush-Bagot agreement on Great Lakes armament, which

Seward threatened to abrogate but did not, and the Reciprocity Treaty of 1854, which became the final casualty of the Civil War. John Potter, American consul in Montreal, publicly boasted that "in two years from the abrogation . . . the people of Canada themselves will apply for admission to the United States."[36]

Several thousand Irishmen living in the United States seemed disinclined to wait even that long. The Irish Republican Brotherhood—the Fenians—hoped that military action against British North America would somehow achieve their goal of an independent Ireland. Demobilization of the Union army swelled the movement with Irish-born veterans and enabled the Fenians to launch a series of forays northward between 1866 and 1871. The Fenian grand strategy was convoluted: it was never clear if these attacks were simple terrorism, serious attempts to capture hostage territories, or provocations to an Anglo-American war that might create an opening for rebellion in Ireland. Their tactics, on the other hand, were all too apparent to the British North American militiamen who were killed and wounded while repelling the raids. Although some Fenian leaders believed they had secret support from Secretary of State Seward, there was no U.S. complicity in Fenian incursions. But the reluctance of American politicians to alienate an ethnic group growing in electoral importance contributed to a lack of official enthusiasm for serious U.S. action to control the Brotherhood's activities.[37]

Thus the Civil War and its aftermath steered Britain's North American colonies toward union as the Dominion of Canada. There was a complex agenda of domestic reasons for the union, but the external threat represented by the United States—economic, military, and Fenian terrorist—provided essential momentum to the movement to confederation. The American challenge persuaded those who made the decision—the British government and the colonial elites of Nova Scotia, the Canadas, and especially New Brunswick—that in union lay the hope, if not the promise, of future strength. Defensive expansion against the United States motivated the incorporation of Manitoba in 1870 and British Columbia the following year; with the exception of island provinces of Newfoundland and Prince Edward Island, Canada had expanded to its present boundaries by 1871. W. L. Morton, a Conservative-nationalist historian of Canada, has described the *Trent* crisis as "the Canadian Lexington and Concord, the definite initiation of Canadian independence." Frank H. Underhill offered a more iconoclastic summation. "Somewhere on Parliament Hill," he suggested, "there should be erected a monument to this American ogre who has so often performed the function of saving [Canada] from drift and indecision."[38]

Lingering post–Civil War disputes and some long-standing issues were resolved in 1871 in the Treaty of Washington. The northern triumph and the emergence of unified nation states in Germany and Italy made Britain conscious of the need to keep a relatively cooperative United States on its western hemispheric flank; even more than in 1783, American goodwill was more important than a defense of seemingly narrow and less significant (at least to Britain) Canadian interests. Yet the discussions on the Treaty were a tiny first step toward Canadian-American, as opposed to Anglo-American, relations, for Prime Minister John A. Macdonald of Canada served as one of five British members of the Joint High Commission that conducted the negotiations. The British government was more eager that Macdonald participate than he was; it was, he knew, inevitable that he offend Britain, the United States, or the Canadian electorate. Macdonald's difficulties anticipated a recurring difficulty of mutual British and Canadian conduct of the relationship with the United States—British and Canadian interests were not always compatible.

In 1871, the contentious matter was the inshore fishery. The abrogation of reciprocity meant that American fishermen were excluded from the waters of the Maritime provinces. The Macdonald government's fisheries protection cruisers enforced the exclusion vigorously, seizing interlopers and fining their captains. The United States was sufficiently annoyed that President Grant complained in his 1870 message to Congress of "the colonial authority known as the Dominion of Canada," a "semi-independent but irresponsible power [which] has exercised its delegated power in an unfriendly way." Macdonald hoped to win renewed reciprocity in exchange for fishing rights, but Republican secretary of state Hamilton Fish was adamantly protectionist. Under British pressure, Macdonald capitulated. The Anglo-American Treaty of Washington granted the United States access to an ocean resource they had long coveted. In return, Canadian fishermen obtained the right to sell their catch duty-free in U.S. markets and to navigate on the mostly frozen rivers of the new United States territory of Alaska. The United States disclaimed responsibility for the Fenian raids and refused to consider compensation for them. The other provision of the treaty that directly concerned U.S.-Canadian relations was the agreement to submit the unresolved section of the Pacific coast disputed to arbitration by the emperor of Germany (how better to draw a boundary than with a German ruler, wags observed), who awarded to the United States the disputed island of San Juan south of Vancouver Island.[39]

For Canada, the treaty provided little tangible reward for a century of loyalty to the Crown; yet on another level, the Treaty of Washington was a preliminary phase in confirming American acceptance of Canadian borders and the reality of the Canadian Confederation. Legally, emotionally, and especially in American eyes, Canada remained a British colony for generations to come. Along with the remaining Spanish colonies in the Western Hemisphere, the Dominion's existence as a "semi-independent" power reminded the United States that it was neither omnipotent nor alone on the continent. By 1871, it was clear that Canada had joined the United States and Mexico as the nations of North America.

2 Canada in the Shadow of Industrial America, 1871–1903

The triumph of northern nationalism and industrialism over southern decentralization and agrarianism coincided not only with the Canadian Confederation but also with movements of national unification elsewhere in the world. Germany, Italy, Argentina, Mexico, Colombia—all emerged from mid-nineteenth-century turmoil as more unified nations and passed into periods of rapid economic growth and development. Confronted by Germany as a rival imperial power in Europe, Africa, and Asia, Britain disengaged rapidly from the Western Hemisphere. The Treaty of Washington signaled the withdrawal of the Royal Army from North America, despite Canadian protests. By 1872, the only red-coated regiments left in Canada were the garrisons at the naval bases of Halifax and Esquimalt. The United States was suddenly close to the principal objective of its Canadian policy: it need no longer actively fear British military power on its northern border. Britain remained the ultimate guarantor of Canadian security, however. "The true defence of our colonies," Colonial secretary Edward Cardwell warned the world, was "that war with them is war with England." But if Canada was any less a hostage in Anglo-American relations, Canadians felt that they had not been released so much as abandoned to their own resources in North American relations.[1]

Canada's view of "the Great Republic" was encapsulated in the Canadian editorials recognizing America's centennial in 1876. "Every well-wisher can rejoice in progress as steady as it has been remarkable," began the *Toronto Globe,* "even though he may hold by a very different political system, and may render allegiance to a very different, and in his estimation greatly preferable, political power." "Let us rejoice that so much good has been accomplished, not that so much evil is still manifest." A list of "symptoms of degeneracy among our neighbors" followed, little changed from Loyalist critiques: "the increasing unscrupulousness of public men, . . . the murders, the frauds, the failures, the falsehood, the immoralities." Comparing the speeches on Dominion Day—July First—with the "spread-eagle" rhetoric on the Fourth of July, the editor noted that Canadians "may have little talk about fighting and dying for the Dominion, but let them be put to the test and they will show satisfactorily what they are able to do." The *Globe* was among the least anti-American newspapers. The almost universal Canadian assumption was that the United States coveted its northern neighbor and plotted annexation. In Canadian political caricature, the United States was "Brother Jonathan," a skinny, avaricious version of Uncle Sam who invariably pressed his unwanted attentions on fair "Miss Canada."[2]

No corresponding caricature of Canada ever appeared in political cartoons in the United States: in fact, few Americans paid much attention to Canada at all. After a visit to Washington, a Canadian cabinet minister was shocked by "the crass ignorance of everything Canadian among leading public men." Who would want to know anything about a "bleak, arid and provincial . . . frigid colony?" asked Henry James. President Andrew Johnson had pointedly not congratulated Canada on the first Dominion Day; on the Confederation's birthdays thereafter, American editorialists continued the tradition. "The average American," writes Lester B. Shippee, "ignored the fact that a colony was disappearing and a nation was rising in its place." Active annexationism was passé, replaced by the assurance that the continental fulfillment of America's Manifest Destiny would not require recourse to arms. As Representative William Munger of Ohio told the House in 1870, now that "England's star has passed its zenith, . . . Canada will fall into our lap like a ripe apple." To help shake the tree, throughout the late nineteenth century the United States tested Canadian national sovereignty in boundary, fisheries, and sealing disputes. Important as these issues were—especially to Canada—they were matters of local rather than national interest to the United States and of indifference to Britain, until the Venezuela and Alaska boundary disputes at the end of the century. No one yet spoke of an "undefended border" between Canada and the United States, and each country planned for

———

"Coming Home from the Fair," *Canadian Illustrated News* (1876). Courtesy Metropolitan Toronto Reference Library.

"Brother Jonathan," a skinny, avaricious version of Uncle Sam, invariably proved his unwanted attentions on fair "Miss Canada."

the possibility of war with the other. But by century's end, armed conflict became increasingly improbable and there was gradual movement toward an actual bilateral U.S.-Canadian relationship.[3]

Westward the Course of Empires

This gradual movement is more apparent to historians in retrospect than it was to contemporary decision makers who lived during the period. Canadians were bent on extending their new nation to the Pacific, an expansion they justified with their own northern vision of "maintaining the honor of the British Flag" westward to the Pacific. The *Montreal Star* caught this vision: "The Dominion has an opportunity . . . of showing the world what can be achieved by a people living under free institutions, and whose constitution is based upon the principle of right and justice to all men." There was considerable concern in Ottawa and some in London that this western patrimony would be usurped by Americans unless Canada acted decisively to claim it. Prodded by the Andrew Johnson administration's purchase of Alaska from Russia, the infant Dominion had made an emulous acquisition of its own. In 1869, Canada bought the vast northwestern empire of the Hudson's Bay Company for $1.5 million and passed the Act for the Temporary Government of Rupert's Land to extend the formality of Canadian colonial authority over the region from the American border on the south and the Ontario border on the east to the Continental Divide in the west and the Arctic to the north. Effective control proved more difficult to establish. The Red River Settlement, the largest community in the region, demanded better terms for the transfer to Canada, turned back the new lieutenant governor, and established its own provisional government at Fort Garry. The focal point of the Red River Resistance was the Metis, the mixed-blood descendents of French traders and native mothers, but Metis spokesman Louis Riel had broad support in his negotiations with the Macdonald government.[4]

The resistance created an opening for Americans anxious to assist Canada's new Northwest to fulfill its "manifest destiny," among them the businessmen of St. Paul, Minnesota, and Jay Cooke, promoter of the Northern Pacific Railroad. Control of Red River, the geographic gateway to the Pacific, would strangle their northern commercial rival in its cradle. As Representative Ignatius Donnelly, one of their congressional spokespersons, explained: "If the revolutionists of the Red River are encouraged and sustained by the avowed sympathy of the American people, we may . . . see the Stars and Stripes wave from Fort Garry, from the waters of Puget Sound, and along the shores of Vancouver." About two hundred of the two thousand white residents of Red River were like-minded Americans, who formed an active annexationist group around Oscar Malmros, the saloon keeper who served as U.S. consul. Two of them infiltrated Riel's provisional government, Colonel Enos Stutsman, a U.S. treasury agent, and W. E. B. O'Donoghue, an Irish-American adventurer. They kept the State Department informed of the situation and urged support for the resistance, as did another American secret agent in Red River, James Wickes Taylor. But the annexationists faced an insurmountable obstacle: Her Majesty's subjects at Red River did not want to become Americans. Riel's provisional government flew the Union Jack over its headquarters at Fort Garry and rejected at gunpoint W. E. B. O'Donoghue's attempt to replace it with a rebel flag of his own design. However dissatisfied with the original terms of their union with Canada, no group in the settlement other than the Americans saw joining the United States as an attractive alternative.[5]

Annexation also failed because Washington refused to help Malmros and his fifth column further destabilize Red River. The American ambassador in London, J. L. Motley, warned Secretary of State Hamilton Fish that U.S. intervention would provoke a British response, and Fish and President Grant were loathe to trade a long-term U.S. objective—British withdrawal from Canada—for an uncertain prospect of territorial expansion. Lest they be tempted to do so, the Macdonald government dispatched a joint Anglo-Canadian military expedition west in 1870 to show the United States that Britain intended Canada to inherit the Northwest. Fish briefly denied the expedition's supply vessel passage through an American canal at Sault Ste. Marie, but on reflection relented. Once in Red River, the troops accomplished their purpose without firing a shot. It was the last British military action in North America—"a long way to come," remarked a lieutenant, "to have the band play *God Save the Queen.*" Riel won most of the better terms that he sought (although not a personal amnesty) and Manitoba became a Canadian province in July 1870.[6]

The incorporation of the western interior into the Confederation left British Columbia as the last piece of Canada's transcontinental puzzle. The Pacific coast colony had immense commercial and strategic value to the British world system. Beyond the potential of its coal, mineral, and forest resources, the port at Victoria linked North America to extensive British interests in the Pacific and Indian oceans. At the height of the British Columbia gold rush, from 1858 to 1862, annexation to the United States had seemed a probable future for the colony. Forty thousand of the fifty thousand miners who panned the rivers for placer gold were American "forty-niners," hardened veterans of the California rush. They poled their skiffs up the Fraser River with grunted choruses: "Soon our banner will be streaming / Soon the Eagle will be screaming / And the Lion, see, it cowers / Hurrah Boys! The river's ours!" The colony's trade ties were largely North-South, and with a transcontinental railroad in progress in the United States, closer political integration along the same economic axis carried considerable logic. The California legislature certainly thought so: it resolved that all "fair and honorable means" be used to detach British Columbia from its "Kingly Empire" and attach it to the American Union.[7]

But like the expansionists in Minnesota, the Californians lacked the support they needed in the part of British North America that they coveted. In British Columbia, the American miners ran out at the same time that the placer gold did. The American consul in the colonial capital of Victoria assured Washington that the British Columbians were "restless and dissatisfied," and thus eager for annexation, but only forty-eight signed an 1869 petition asking President Grant for annexation, and only three of those were British subjects. Even during the gold rush, the British minority had controlled the political institutions on Vancouver Island and on the mainland; in combination with the British navy this proved formidable. Lieutenant Governor Anthony Musgrave made clear that Britain's will was that British Columbia confederate, and economic self-interest confirmed the decision. Canada promised a rail link to eastern markets within ten years (a promise unkept), and businessmen in Victoria knew that as part of the United States, their city would be a satellite of San Francisco instead of the imperial entrepôt en route to Asia. There was little love for the Canadian federation, as an anonymous poet explained in verse: "True loyalty's to Motherland / and not to Ca-na-da. / The love we bear is second-hand / To any step-mama." Whatever reason tipped the balance in favor of the empire and Canada, British Columbia became Canada's Pacific province in March 1871. Now, like the United States, Canada stretched from sea to sea. The arbitration of the Strait of Juan de Fuca boundary in 1872 completed (with the significant exception of the Alaskan boundary) the diplomatic process begun ninety years before.[8]

But this western boundary existed only in a diplomatic sense; in terms of human and economic geography, national perimeters remained undefined. The Great Plains and the mountain ranges were oblivious to the political ambitions of men and women, and it was thus inevitable that problems would spill over the dividing lines that men drew in the dust and rocks of the frontier. Miners, ranchers, and farmers poured into the American West between the Mississippi and the mountains, bringing with them railroads and repeating rifles, barbed wire and boom towns. It was a process characterized by special forms of violence and lawlessness: the conflict between Indians and whites, stagecoach robbery, vigilantism, lynching, and gunfights. The simultaneous Canadian westward movement was, historians allege, very different. The occupation of western Canada, writes Paul F. Sharp, was "orderly [and] well-planned," in contrast to the "violence and hatred south of the forty-ninth parallel." The Northwest Territories, adds Stan D. Hansen, were "free from the more lurid episodes associated with the American frontier." The contrast between a "wild" and a tranquil West is an article of faith among Canadians, in Desmond Morton's words, "one of those self-congratulatory myths which bind a nation together." Like all myths, it has some foundation in reality. Canadian mining camps in British Columbia and the Klondike were relatively free of crime and disorder. The Canadian ranching frontier was not a northern extension of its competitive American counterpart, but an Anglo-Canadian cattle oligopoly. Ranchers' cartels replaced range wars, and rustlers met a magistrate rather than a rope. The starkest divergence was the temper of relations between Indians and whites. *Harper's Weekly* lamented after the Battle of the Little Bighorn that "over the Canadian line the relations between Indians and whites are so tranquil, while on our side they are summed up in perpetual treachery, waste and war." Between 1866 and 1895, the United States army fought 943 military engagements with native peoples; Canadian troops fought seven, all but one of them a battle of the 1885 North West Rebellion.[9]

Why were the two Wests so different? There are circumstantial explanations: slower settlement, fewer native people, and fewer white settlers. And all parties learned from the U.S. example. America's Indian wars taught the Plains tribes in Canada the futility of confronting white weaponry, and the Assiniboine, Cree, and Blackfoot knew that the Canadian government could call on the same weapons to destroy them. In 1885, the Gatling Machine Gun Company of Chicago provided the Canadian militia with two Gatling guns and crews to help suppress the Cree. The Gatlings were not all Canada borrowed: most of the institutional framework for western expansion was copied directly from the United States, most obviously the railway land grant policy and the free homestead system. As the *Nation* observed in 1877, even in Indian administration "the general form and professed objects of the two systems are almost identical." Both countries used similar bureaucracies, signed treaties, and confined Indians on reservations ("reserves" in Canada) with the avowed goal of assimilating them into white society. What made the difference, concludes Hana Samek, was that "the settlers who arrived in the [Canadian] territories brought with them a tradition of respect for 'Queen's Law' and a deference to authority, traits that many Americans are proud to note were absent from their frontier population." As Canada's minister of the interior,

David Mills sanctimoniously explained to his American counterpart, Carl Schurz, that America's western disorder stemmed not from its inability to control Indians, but from its unwillingness to control white men.[10] Canada had to control its settlers because the country simply could not afford a "wild" West, militarily or monetarily. Instability along the border that threatened American lives or property, such as the 1873 Cypress Hills Massacre, would have brought American expeditions into Canada as it had into Mexico. Killing Indians was also expensive: in 1869, the United States spent more on Indian wars than the entire revenue of the Canadian government! Ottawa kept tight control over the Northwest Territories, granted representative government to the white settlers reluctantly, and extended provincehood much more slowly than the United States extended statehood. Alberta and Saskatchewan became provinces only in 1905 and were denied full provincial status until 1930. Canadian Indian policy was similar in legal form to American, but the officials who administered it were more paternalistic than their American counterparts. They lacked the American zeal to force Indians to accept private land ownership, so that reserves in Canada were not broken up into individual allotments as they were in the United States.[11]

The most significant institutional divergence between the United States and Canadian wests was the North West Mounted Police (NWMP). It should be noted that the Macdonald government's decision in 1873 to establish the force was greeted with the hearty approval of Secretary of State Hamilton Fish and that the second contingent of the NWMP went west on American railroads to Fargo, Dakota Territory, before they rode north to Manitoba. The mounties, concluded an American Indian affairs expert in 1911, were Canada's "one great advantage in dealing with her Indians over the United States." In the Canadian West, they filled not only the role played in the United States by the U.S. Army but also of the locally elected sheriffs and judges who had no interest in protecting Indians from the white electorate. As Wallace Stegner melodramatically phrases it, the scarlet Norfolk jackets worn by the NWMP made "the International Boundary . . . a color line: blue below, red above, blue for treachery and unkept promises, red for protection and the straight tongue." The United States made three treaties with the Blackfeet in Montana and, because of settler's demands for Blackfeet land, respected none of them; Canada made one with the Blackfoot (as they were called in Canada) and in general lived up to its terms. Canadians, searching as ever for the Republic's feet of clay, denounced U.S. Indian policy as "white savagery." In this they were simply echoing domestic American critics such as Helen Hunt Jackson, whose *Century of Dishonor* (1884) held up Canada as an example for the United States to emulate. Even defenders of American policy admitted that "in the Dominion . . . the plighted faith . . . once made to the Indian tribes, has never been violated. The red men can trust the Crown . . . and are therefore as loyal as any other British subjects."[12]

The most written-about comparison between the United States and Canadian wests is the case of Sitting Bull and the Sioux. In the 1870s, gold miners moved into the Black Hills of the Dakota, Wyoming, and Montana territories, guaranteed to the Sioux by an 1868 agreement. The U.S. government sought revision of the agreement to remove the Sioux from the area, but Chief Sitting Bull and his people rejected all attempts to buy their hunting grounds and sacred places. In the Spring of 1876 the U.S. Army moved to force the issue. On 25 June, Colonel George Armstrong Custer and his regiment of the Seventh Cavalry stumbled onto 2,500 Sioux warriors on the Little Bighorn River. It was the greatest Indian triumph of the long Plains war. In death, Custer and his 264 troopers became America's most celebrated martyrs; in victory, Sitting Bull became a Native Napoleon, the most dangerous Indian America had ever confronted. More important for Canadian-American relations, the chief and three thousand Sioux evaded capture and fought a strategic retreat north into Canadian territory.[13]

Sitting Bull remained on Canadian soil for five years, a constant worry to Assistant Superintendent James Walsh of the NWMP and the small detachments he assigned to watch them. The Sioux situation became the subject of considerable triangular diplomatic correspondence among Canadian and American authorities. The Sioux hunted across the border and occasionally raided white settlers and Crow reservations in Montana. Secretary of State William Evarts protested "these propensities for murder and plunder" and claimed that Canadian merchants were arming the Indians. These accusations notwithstanding, the mounted police monitored Sitting Bull's movements with much better success than the Seventh Cavalry had been able to. The Indians needed some ammunition, for they had to hunt the dwindling buffalo herds to feed themselves. Although the *New York Herald* wished "the Great Mother joy of her new subjects," the Sioux were consistently denied status as "British Indians," however much loyalty Sitting Bull professed to the "Great Mother," Queen Victoria. Canadian Indian administrators were unwilling to share the meager allotment for "Canadian" Indians with refugees from the United States, and the Sioux controlled no land of their own to exchange for support. In 1881, impending starvation forced the Sioux to reluctantly retrace their path to Montana. In their five years in Canada, noted a Montana editor with admiration, "these Sioux . . . have behaved themselves well, comparatively speaking." Sitting Bull was killed a decade later during a final act of defiance against American authority.[14]

"Annexing Canadians": Patterns of Migration

Extensive transborder migration has been an ever-present fact of the U.S.-Canada relationship. Marcus Lee Hansen's term for it—"The Mingling of the Canadian and American Peoples"—is singularly inapt, however. "Mingling" implies reciprocity, a numerical equivalence that has never existed. Despite Canada's much smaller population, the southward flow of Canadians has been a torrent compared to the trickle of American residents who moved north. Further to vitiate the "mingling" concept, the Canadian and the American emigrants have been strikingly different. Sitting Bull and his people were typical of American migrants to Canada. Like the exiled Tories after the Revolution and the fugitive African-American passengers on the Underground Railroad, the Sioux saw Canada as a refuge from the United States that was nonetheless enough like America to be familiar. In

1887, a similar search for sanctuary propelled members of the Church of Jesus Christ of Latter-Day Saints—the Mormons—from the Utah Territory to the Northwest Territories of Canada. The Mormons had moved west to escape America, only to have America itself move west to engulf them. The Senate insisted that the Latter-Day Saints renounce their practice of polygamy as the price of Utah's admission as a state. Church elders decided that statehood was worth a monogamous marriage, but not all church members accepted this decree as divine revelation. Led by Charles Ora Card, Brigham Young's son-in-law, two thousand of them trekked to the District of Alberta. The Canadian government welcomed these experienced dryland farmers with more enthusiasm than it had the Sioux, overlooking their conjugal idiosyncrasies for a time in favor of economic development and increased population. This pattern of concessions to religious minorities was repeated with Mennonites, Hutterites, and Doukhobors, who considered the United States but eventually chose to settle in western Canada. Twentieth-century Canadians cite this as an example of the tolerant cultural pluralism of their "multi-cultural mosaic." In the late nineteenth century, however, the admission of dissident minorities was a confession of the inability of the Canadian West to compete for population with its American analog.[15]

In their national anthem "O Canada," English Canadians pledge to love their "home and native land" and French Canadians to honor the "terre de nos aïeux"—the land of their ancestors. Between 1870 and 1900 more than a million Canadians broke that pledge, including Calixa Lavallée, the composer of the song. American census takers counted 1,179,922 Canadian-born residents in the United States in 1900, 785,461 English-speaking, and 394,461 French-speaking. This influx was almost a quarter of Canada's 1901 population. "The Americans may say with truth," observed Goldwin Smith, "that if they do not annex Canada they are annexing the Canadians." Although diverse in origins and destinations, these emigrants shared an economic motivation for migration southward: underemployed Maritimers found work in the "Boston States," French-Canadian day laborers and their families moved to the "facteries" of industrial New

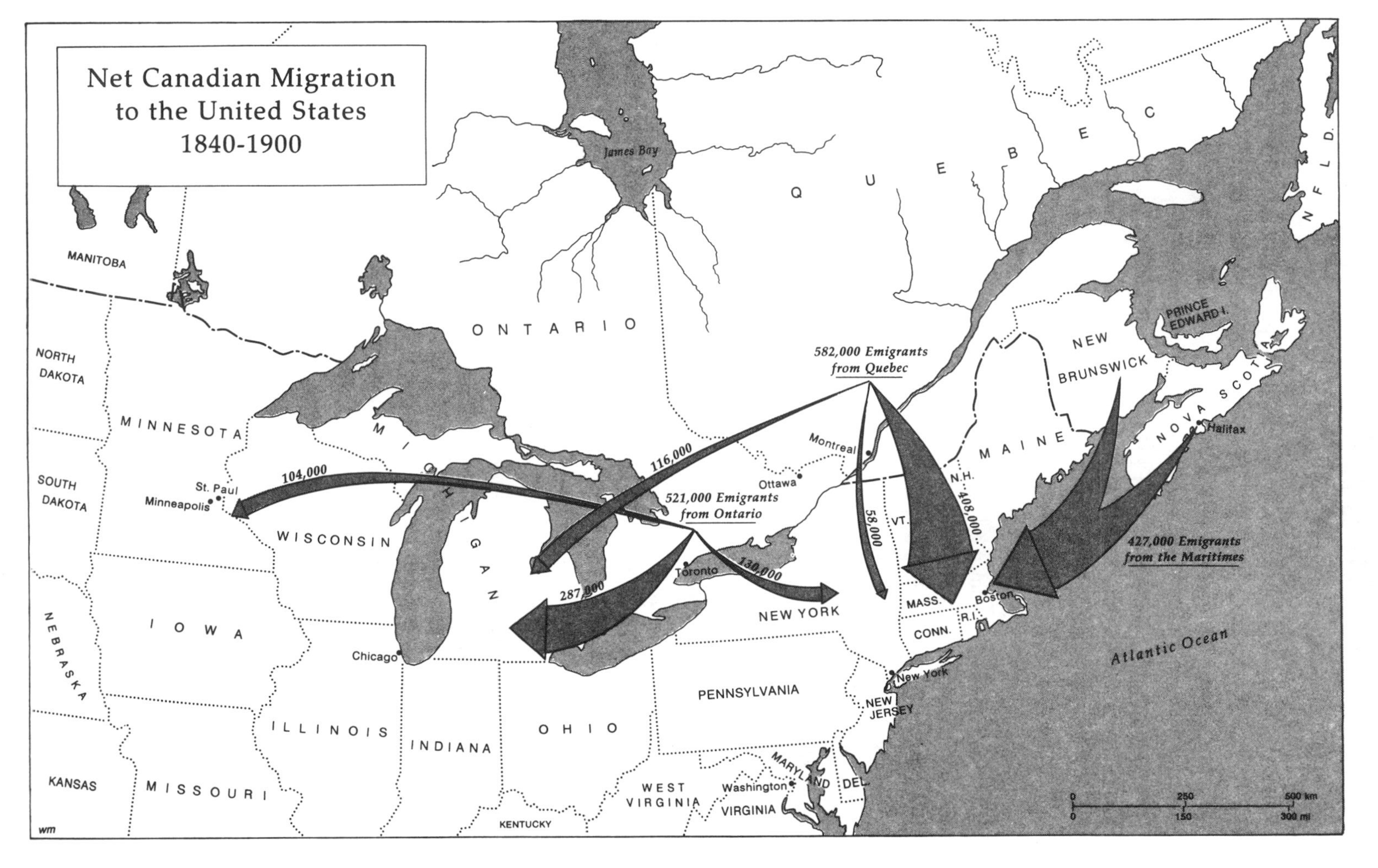
Net Canadian Migration
to the United States
1840-1900
582,000 Emigrants
from Quebec
521,000 Emigrants
from Ontario
427,000 Emigrants
from the Maritimes
116,000
104,000
287,000
130,000
58,000
408,000
James Bay
ONTARIO
QUEBEC
MANITOBA
NORTH DAKOTA
SOUTH DAKOTA
MINNESOTA
WISCONSIN
MICHIGAN
IOWA
NEBRASKA
KANSAS
MISSOURI
ILLINOIS
INDIANA
OHIO
KENTUCKY
WEST VIRGINIA
VIRGINIA
PENNSYLVANIA
NEW YORK
NEW JERSEY
MARYLAND
DEL.
CONN.
R.I.
MASS.
VT.
N.H.
MAINE
NEW BRUNSWICK
NOVA SCOTIA
PRINCE EDWARD I.
NFLD.
Atlantic Ocean
St. Paul
Minneapolis
Chicago
Toronto
Ottawa
Montreal
New York
Boston
Halifax
Washington
0 250 500 km
0 150 300 mi
wm

England, and Ontarians farmed the Middle West or clerked in Chicago. Sitting Bull had a Canadian counterpart in Big Bear, a Plains Cree chief who led his band from Saskatchewan to Montana in search of the disappearing northern herd of buffalo. Big Bear was refused a reservation by the United States just as Sitting Bull had been by Canada.[16]

Euro-Canadians were more welcome. Their migration was the continuation of a movement that had begun in the 1840s but was amplified and altered after the Civil War. Before 1870, many of the migrants had been seasonal workers such as lumbermen or fishermen, who returned after a season in the woods or on the banks. After 1870, sojourning turned to settlement, and more migrants became permanent residents. Canadians were ambivalent about their countrypeople in the Republic. Quebec orators denounced the emigrants as "deserters, cowards, loafers, and delinquents." Ontarians agreed that "we have kept the winnowed grain while the chaff has gone to them." Canadians in the United States had traded "comfort and plenty" for "privation and misery," another journalist-patriot assured his readers. "They remain only because they are too poor or too proud to return in rags to their Canadian friends." Realists worried that "Uncle Sam absorbs the bone, sinew and youth of British America," that Canada was losing the flower of its younger generation. Both optimists and pessimists took pride in the achievements of individual Canadians in "the States": railroad entrepreneur James J. Hill, or the five chaired Harvard professors born in Nova Scotia or New Brunswick, or "Tip" O'Neill, the outfielder from Woodstock, Ontario, who led major league baseball with a .435 batting average in 1887. In the late nineteenth century, however, most of the migrants were unskilled; the expression "Brain Drain" would not become part of the Canadian vocabulary until the 1920s.[17]

How did these expatriate Canadians—the second largest immigrant group in America—behave, and how did Americans react to their presence? We know much more about French- than English-Canadian immigrants because their language and religion set them further apart from the American mainstream and made the Roman Catholic Church, the Quebec government, and state governments sufficiently anxious about them to commission investigative studies. They faced the same virulent nativism as European immigrants, but nineteenth-century French-Canadian immigrants in New England fiercely resisted the "melting pot" of assimilation. "The Canadian French are the Chinese of the Eastern States," concluded a much-quoted Massachusetts report in 1881. "They are a horde of industrial invaders, not a stream of stable settlers. . . . Rarely does one of them become naturalized." This last accusation was accurate. Sustained by clerical and lay elites in Quebec who saw them as an "advance guard" of French Canada, the immigrants re-created "little Canadas," complete with schools, newspapers, and voluntary institutions, and battled with the Irish-American Catholic episcopacy for control of their own French-language parishes.[18]

English-Canadian immigrants to the United States deserve more attention from historians, who assume too easily that their language permitted them to melt easily into an American milieu. They did what other émigrés did: published newspapers, joined social clubs, and celebrated distinctive holidays. The *Canadian-American* of Chicago reported on "the many social organizations" made up of immigrants who "wished not to forget their Dominion birth," and after a boisterous Dominion Day in 1880, a Michigan newspaper complained that it seemed as if "about half the population of Canada has arrived here during the month past." Like French Canadians, English Canadians had low rates of naturalization relative to other immigrant groups or delayed becoming United States citizens until late in life. James Naismith, Canadian inventor of what George Will has called the "uniquely American" sport of basketball, left McGill University for Massachusetts at thirty but remained a subject of Their Majesties until he was sixty-five. These Canadian-Americans were, it seemed, almost as ambivalent about the United States as were the families they left behind.[19]

Tariffs, Trade, and Economic Integration

The hemorrhage of Canadians to the United States painted the backdrop against which Canadian governments played out their tariff and trade strategies. The promise of economic growth to rival America's, explicit in confederation, proved elusive—thus the exodus southward. Remembering the prosperity of the 1850s, both the Macdonald Conservative (1867–73) and the Alexander Mackenzie Liberal (1874–78) governments sought reciprocal trade agreements with the United States. Neither succeeded in persuading Washington that renewed reciprocity held any advantages for the United States. Civil War tariff increases that had stimulated manufacturing continued in force, and the victorious Republicans remained a resolutely high-tariff protectionist party; the Democrats, tied more to agriculture than industry, sought reduction of the tariff but never its abolition. The negotiations in 1874 between Republican secretary of state Hamilton Fish and Canadian finance minister George Brown revealed another stumbling block to freer U.S.-Canada trade. Fish shocked Brown with the demand that Canada maintain a higher tariff against British goods as a condition for lower tariffs within North America. The draft treaty that emerged from their discussions met a barrage of criticism in both Congress and Parliament, and died without a decision in either legislature, largely because, as historian Allan Nevins concludes, "the selfish special interests were too strong." Canadian import duties remained lower than American, so that during the recession of the mid-1870s, American manufacturers used Canada as a "slaughter market," dumping excess inventory north of the border. Canadian producers of everything from shoes to stoves appealed to Ottawa for tariffs of their own.[20]

The Macdonald Conservatives, returned to office in 1878, finally absorbed the message. Resolved upon "paying [the] U.S. in their own coin," the prime minister and his cabinet introduced the National Policy, a comprehensive system of tariffs designed to promote Canadian manufacturing in steel, textiles, coal, and petroleum products, and via a Canadian Pacific Railway, to facilitate the internal exchange of agricultural and industrial products between western and eastern Canada. "We have no manufacturers here [and] our working people have all gone off to the U.S. . . . , adding to the strength, to the power and to the wealth of a foreign nation instead of adding to ours,"

Macdonald told Parliament. Without the National Policy, Canadians were condemned to be "hewers of wood and drawers of water." Macdonald's development strategy has been hailed as the foundation of Canadian autonomy, the master stroke of nation building. In reality, Washington dictated that Canada would have high tariffs through its persistent disinterest in lower tariffs. The *Canadian Monthly and National Review* answered critics of "high tariff walls" bluntly: "Those who talk idly of a 'Chinese Wall' seem to forget that it has been already erected by our neighbors." The National Policy was not only made necessary by U.S. trade intransigence: it was the mirror image of U.S. policy, and as such was quietly protested by the British government. Its architects looked to the American experience of commercial nationalism, concluding that the protectionist American tariffs were the cause of the all-too-obvious emergence of American industrial might in the course of the nineteenth century. Finance Minister Leonard Tilley went so far as to import an assistant from the U.S. Bureau of Statistics to advise him on drawing up the new Canadian tariff schedule![21]

The further paradox of the National Policy as economic nationalism was its role in the continental integration of United States and Canadian economies. As soon as the tariff was raised in 1879, American capitalists began to invest directly in Canada to leap over the protective tariff wall. As Michael Bliss has trenchantly observed, protection sowed "the Roots of the Branch Plant" and led to the presence of large numbers of wholly owned subsidiaries of American corporations in Canada. One of the earliest of American multinationals in Canada was the Singer Manufacturing Company, which had sold its sewing machines through franchised dealers since the 1860s; now the tariff forced Singer to manufacture them in Montreal. A wide range of American companies followed: International Harvester, National Cash Register, Westinghouse, James B. Duke's American Tobacco Company; the *Monetary Times* reported sixty-five such branch plants by 1887. In 1886 the American capitalist Samuel Ritchie incorporated the Canadian Copper Company to develop the rich nickel deposits of the Sudbury region of Ontario, a metal that became in high demand for its military application in armor plating. By 1890 Sudbury, Ontario, was the world's center of production, and in 1902 the American-based giant International Nickel Company of Canada emerged from a consolidation of a smaller number of competing firms. Other U.S. companies expanded by taking over Canadian ones: Standard Oil moved into Canada with its acquisition of a controlling interest in Imperial Oil. In 1900, direct and portfolio U.S. investment in Canada was 14 percent of total foreign investment, still well behind the 85 percent represented by British capital. But investment climbed steadily, exceeding 23 percent by 1914 in comparison with Britain's declining share of 72 percent. By 1913, one-quarter of all U.S. overseas investment was in Canada, in comparison to the one-half that was in all of the Latin American countries combined. The result of this activity was that between 1897 and 1908 Canada passed Mexico as the most important single target of U.S. direct and portfolio investment.[22]

Canadian tariff policy alone cannot explain the significant movement of U.S. capital into Canada in these years. Companies such as Western Union and New York Life Insurance operated in Canada with no obvious need for tariff protection. American Bell Telephone, later AT & T, bought its one-third interest in Bell Canada in order to forestall the growth of a Canadian rival that one day might threaten its virtual monopoly. Geographic proximity was an obvious factor enticing U.S. investment north, and Canada was a relatively stable market for American goods and capital, with a commonality of language, at least with English Canada. Canada also had specific raw materials required by American industry. And as elsewhere in the Western Hemisphere (including the United States itself), as British economic influence declined that of the United States emerged to replace it. Classic Marxist explanations of American imperial expansionism stress the primacy of the search for markets and for secure investments. John A. Hobson contended in 1902 that American capitalism could not find adequate domestic markets for its goods and capital, an argument refined in Lenin's *Imperialism: The Highest Stage of Capitalism.* Such revisionist historians of U.S. foreign policy as Walter LaFeber and William A. Williams stress the critical importance of the 1890s depression in the United States as a catalyst in combining a complex range of strategic, intellectual, political, and economic forces to stimulate American expansion. Debate continues among scholars over these arguments, but there can be no doubt that both American business and government placed considerable importance on foreign markets and access to raw materials. By the turn of the century, capital expansion had become a goal in American foreign policy that influenced relations with Canada just as it did those with other countries.[23]

A Renewed Critique of the Republic

Canadians made no complaint about American economic imperialism; bringing foreign capital into the country was an explicit goal of the National Policy. But because it brought no sudden solution to Canada's economic problems, the National Policy shortly had critics. The goal of the Commercial Union movement that surfaced in the 1880s was the establishment of a common market between the United States and Canada, with a mutual protective tariff against the rest of the world. Promoted by such men as Erastus Wiman, a Canadian-born New York businessman whose Great Northwest Telegraph Company operated in both countries, the concept was popularized by Commercial Union clubs on both sides of the border. Unlike more limited Canadian proposals for freer trade, the wholesale economic merger explicit in Commercial Union attracted support in Washington—"Brother Jonathan," observed a Liberal member of Parliament to his leader Wilfrid Laurier, "wants all or nothing." Despite such misgivings within the party, the Liberals built a form of Commercial Union into their platform in 1888 that they called "Full and Unrestricted Reciprocity." The Liberals—most of them, at least—did not seek political union with the United States. Commercial Union clubs in Canada concluded their meetings with cheers for Queen Victoria. As Sir Richard Cartwright told the New York Board of Trade, "we have our history, our traditions, our aspirations, just as you have yours"; unrestricted reciprocity was a simple business deal, to be "dealt with on business principles."[24]

But if not all the supporters of unrestricted reciprocity were annexationists, all the annexationists supported unrestricted reciprocity. Most outspoken among them was Goldwin Smith, a former Oxford Regius Professor of History who taught briefly at Cornell University before marrying a wealthy Toronto widow and settling into a career as an independent commentator on virtually everything. Smith had preached annexation since 1878, launched the idea of Commercial Union in 1880, and regularly reminded Canadians that their destiny lay as part of the American Republic. His sharp wit and quick pen contributed intellectual respectability to the first strong expression of continentalism since 1849. Smith lampooned Canada's hopelessly ambivalent feelings about the United States: they enjoyed their economic relationship with America, but wanted it to be close, but not too close. Despite the high tariffs, in per capita terms Canada was America's largest trading partner: 38 percent of Canada's exports went to the United States (53 percent to Britain) and 60 percent of its imports came from America (24 percent from Britain). In 1890, fears of losing that American market intensified the debate about unrestricted reciprocity. In 1890, Congress passed the highly protectionist McKinley tariff, which threatened to devastate Canadian agricultural exports. The Republican administration of Benjamin Harrison, in particular Secretary of State James G. Blaine, had no desire to be gentle with Canada. A former senator from Maine, Blaine thought of Canada only as a competitor for fish and timber, a competitor best annexed. He rejected the overtures of the Canadian Conservative government toward the easing of tariffs on natural products. Publicly, Blaine declared himself "teetotally opposed to giving the Canadians the sentimental satisfaction of waving the British Flag . . . and enjoying the actual cash remuneration of American markets. . . . I do not mean that they shall be Canadians and Americans at the same time." Privately, he told President Harrison that by refusing any reciprocity short of Commercial Union, Canada would be forced to "ultimately, I believe, seek admission to the Union."[25]

Sir John A. Macdonald turned Blaine's rebuff to spectacular political advantage. He made the Canadian election of 1891 a national referendum on the relationship with the United States, describing the Liberal policy of unrestricted reciprocity as "veiled treason," a synonym for annexation. A Conservative majority, he told crowds, "will show to the Americans that we prize our country as much as they do, that we would fight for our existence." In industrial areas of the country the Tories warned of idle workers and idle capital if the Americans were granted unrestricted access to Canadian markets, but the appeal was more emotional than economic. Conservative editors summoned up images of a "crisis not less momentous" than the American invasions from 1775 to 1776 and from 1812 to 1814. "Is Canada to be wiped out?" screamed the *Regina Standard:* "Shall the Union Jack droop and the British lion cower while the eagle screams and the stars and stripes wave triumphantly from Alaska to the Gulf of Mexico?" In Quebec, the Roman Catholic clergy warned against the evils of encroaching American cultural values. The loyalty campaign worked: the Conservatives were returned to office and increased their share of the popular vote.[26]

The sensitive debate over closer economic links with the United States did not end with the Conservative election victory. For a century after 1891, support for the tariff became a prerequisite for national political success in Canada. The Liberals had to adopt the essence of the National Policy before the electorate would entrust them with power. The "specter of annexation" honed the blades of anti-Americanism and sharpened the Canadian critique of the Republic. The public schools, complained Goldwin Smith, were turned "into seedplots of international enmity by implanting hatred of the Americans into the breasts of our children." Their parents read in antireciprocity polemics that in the U.S. "criminals go unpunished, and life and property are insecure; . . . lawless lynchings are of almost hourly occurrence; . . . Sunday is devoted to dissipation: drinking, dancing, gambling [and] vulgar rowdyism of men and women." In 1892, business and political elites in New York and Toronto, including Goldwin Smith, Andrew Carnegie, and Theodore Roosevelt, established a Continental Union League. It was an idea whose time was yet to come. Although it anticipated the important role that binational elite organizations would eventually play in propagandizing the idea of continentalism, it lasted barely two years. In the 1890s, interest in such links within American political circles was too feeble and Canadian antagonism to the United States much too strong. In July 1892, the *New York Times* reported two incidents in which "excited Canadians" tore down (and tore up) American flags flown in Canada on Dominion Day.[27]

Resources and Boundaries

More than the anger aroused by reciprocity prompted these attacks on the Stars and Stripes. The headline of the same page of the *Times* that described the desecrations of Old Glory reported "25 'British' Sealers Seized in Alaska." The sealing vessels flew the Union Jack, but they were in fact from British Columbia, evidence that the perennial diplomatic quarrels over boundaries and resources continued to mark the trilateral British-Canadian-American relationship between 1871 and 1903. The reconciliation over fishing rights contained in the Washington Treaty of 1871 did not endure. By 1885, the United States had abrogated the section of the treaty that pertained to fishing rights, and tensions mounted between Canadian and American fishermen. In the 1890s, quarrels over access took on a new environmental dimension, as conservationists in both countries expressed alarm at the rapid decline of fish stocks in the Great Lakes brought about commercial overfishing and industrial pollution. In 1892, a joint investigative commission, established by the United States and by Britain acting on Canada's behalf, began a four-year study of the contiguous fisheries. The inquiry produced reams of evidence but no regulatory results. Each country suggested different solutions; neither country acted.[28]

Sovereignty and self-interest engendered conflict on the Pacific coast as well. The dispute over pelagic sealing (that is, sealing in the open seas) was the most emotional ocean-resource conflict of the late nineteenth century. On the surface the issues seemed clear enough. The United States controlled the Pribilof Islands in the Bering Sea, where the fur seal herds in the region concentrated; but even the Americans could not control the migratory, mating, and fishing habits of the seals, and it was the killing of seals on the high seas that posed the main problem. Within American territorial waters, policy prohibited the slaughter of females and young seals and placed limits on the seal harvest as a whole. The immutable problem was how to deal with the high seas harvest. American officials claimed that killing seals in the open sea resulted in a disproportionate kill of females and threatened the long-term viability of the hunt. In 1889, President Benjamin Harrison brought the issue officially to Canadian attention, warned of U.S. action against violators, and followed the cautionary warning with the seizure of several Canadian vessels. The British government, so often accused by Canadians of "apparent indifference to . . . the young Dominion across the sea," did not hesitate: warships moved into the sealing waters to protect Canadian sealers against American coast guard cutters. The two parties reached a temporary accommodation in 1891, halting sealing for that season, and the following year the British and Americans assented to arbitration by an international tribunal on which the American delegates were outvoted. The tribunal determined that pelagic sealing within limits should continue and also awarded more than four hundred thousand dollars in compensation to Canadians, but the resulting destruction of the herds in the next two decades led to a more determined resolve to end the problem. In 1911, the United States obtained British, Russian, and Japanese cooperation in establishing strict regulations over the industry. The 1911 agreement rejected U.S. claims to jurisdiction outside the three-mile limit and established a conservation agreement between Canada and the United States that provided for catch limits on a shared basis.[29]

In environmental terms, the United States held the better argument on the issue of pelagic sealing; the Russians also prohibited the kill except on land. But the symbolic importance of Canadian access to the seal fishery in the Bering Sea was as vital to the dispute as the economic question, with the result that the conflict assumed greater proportions than "the actual value of the seals involved." Domestic politics also played a role in shaping U.S. foreign policy positions. The Republican party was the party of commercial expansionism, and the

North American Commercial Company, which controlled the American hunt, had important Republican connections, including D. O. Mills, the father-in-law of Whitelaw Reid, editor of the *New York Tribune*, and S. B. Elkins, a financial advisor to Secretary of State James G. Blaine. As much as "humanitarian" and environmental considerations shaped U.S. policy toward pelagic sealing, so too did the desire of Republican businessmen to contain foreign competitors.[30]

The issue of American access to Canadian and to Newfoundland (not a Canadian province until 1949) fisheries paralleled the dispute over sealing. The tribunal established by the Washington Treaty offered a ruling that placed such a high price on American access to Canadian fisheries that President Chester Arthur abrogated the agreement in 1885, thus leaving the two countries in the same state of uncertainty as had prevailed since the War of 1812. Efforts by the Harrison administration in the 1890s to circumvent the Canadian government and obtain a separate agreement with Newfoundland, including reciprocity, ran aground on the shoals of Canadian leverage in London, with the result that the British government overruled the Newfoundland initiative. The fisheries issue lingered as a nagging reminder of the basic competition between the two nations until an international arbitration ruling in 1910.[31]

The fur seal controversy, with its naval threat and counterthreat, was a minor aberration in what H. G. Nicholas has called the "longest period of amicable inanition that Anglo-American relations have ever known." In this context, the dispute between Britain and the United States over the boundary between British Guiana and Venezuela erupted with astonishing suddenness. In July 1895, Secretary of State Richard Olney blustered his way into the history of American foreign policy with an aggressive defence of the Venezuelan claim and a blunt demand that Britain agree to arbitration. Olney based his command on the Monroe Doctrine: the United States would not let European powers push around small nations in the Western Hemisphere. America was "master of the situation and practically invulnerable; . . . on this continent . . . its fiat is law." At the same time, Olney noted that as long as European powers were "permanently encamped on American soil" the United States had no alternative but to be "armed to the teeth." When the British government stalled, Democratic president Grover Cleveland announced that he would personally arbitrate the boundary and enforce his decision with American arms. The threats and fears of previous war scares were immediately disinterred by military planners and the popular press. Britain would launch amphibious attacks on the American Atlantic coast; the United States would capture Canada. Canadians pretended to believe that their "resistance would be a hard nut for the invader to crack" and that "the American spread eagle . . . will find himself pretty light poultry." This, too, was bluster. Neither side wanted or was prepared for war, and British prime minister Lord Salisbury eventually accepted binding neutral arbitration (which went in Britain's favor). The Venezuela crisis, writes C. P. Stacey, "was the last occasion when active military preparations were made in Canada for defence against the United States."[32]

The crisis spurred Britain to renewed efforts to placate the United States and was thus a turning point in America's rise to world power. The crisis, concluded Captain Alfred Thayer Mahan, champion of American sea power, "indicates the awakening of our countrymen to the fact that we must come out of our isolation . . . and take our share in the turmoil of the world." The Spanish-American War demonstrated America's strength. Canada maintained a neutrality that helped the United States more than the Spanish, who would have purchased Canadian coal for their fleet. Canadians prickled at the self-satisfactions of "l'impérialism yankee," such as when American editors compared Dewey's victory at Manila Bay to Nelson's at Trafalgar. In rapid succession, the United States gained effective control over the Philippines, Cuba, Puerto Rico, Hawaii, and Panama. At century's end, the Republican McKinley administration copied Britain's Open Door policy toward China, while in Latin America, the Anglo-American Hay-Pauncefote Treaty of 1901 paved the way for an American canal across the isthmus. America was on its way to becoming a world power. Neighbors to the north could only watch with their usual combination of envy and tense expectation.[33]

Conflict on the Alaskan Frontier

The last section of what was to become the "undefended border' was the boundary between Alaska and British Columbia. Beyond simple lines on a map, much more was at stake: harbors, minerals, and not least, prestige. The conflict can only be understood in the context of the emergence of the United States as an imperial power and British concern about changes in the balance of power in Europe and the Far East with the rise of Germany and Japan. Canada was not an innocent bystander in turn-of-the-century imperialism and militarism, of course. Canadian involvement in the Boer War gave Canadians a taste of the jingoism that ran through parts of American society during the Spanish-American War. Like the United States, Canada looked to expand its economic horizons. As an example, because it was illegal before 1914 for U.S. banks to operate international branches, their Canadian competitors carved a dominant niche in the Caribbean.[34]

The discovery of gold in 1897 on Bonanza Creek in Canada's unsettled Yukon Territory meant that the Alaskan boundary question could be deferred no longer. Fifty thousand prospectors rushed for the gold. Most of the miners—and according to Canadian authorities, all of the prostitutes, gamblers, and gunmen—were American citizens. Interpreting this presence as a threat, the Canadian government promptly organized a territorial government and dispatched a "Yukon Field Force" of two hundred regular troops overland from British Columbia to assist the North West Mounted Police in maintaining order and asserting Canadian sovereignty. Their task was exacerbated by the near impossibility of reaching the gold fields by any route that passed entirely through Canadian territory. Most migrants came by sea, landed at the American port of Skagway in the Alaska Panhandle, and trekked through the White or Chilkoot Pass into Canadian territory. The riches of the region—more than a million ounces of gold in 1900—made jurisdiction over coastal access points contentious. Although a lengthy border was in question, the principal issue was which country controlled the mouth of the Lynn Canal, the strait that joined Skagway to the North Pacific. Both sides took extreme positions at the outset. Canada claimed the boundary followed a line along the mouths of the ubiquitous inlets that ran into the mountains from the Pacific, thus incorporating the Lynn Canal, including Skagway, into Canada. The United States conversely claimed a line that would have brought under American jurisdiction a significant portion of northern British Columbia and the Yukon.[35]

In May 1898, an Anglo-Canadian-American conference in Washington had established a trilateral Joint High Commission to settle all unresolved boundary questions, but the commission dissolved in dissension in less than a year, unable to agree on a formula for Alaskan arbitration. In the Hay-Pauncefote Treaty of 1901, Britain relinquished its right to participate in the Panama Canal and lost a potential bargaining chip on the Alaskan boundary. Given the British desire for American friendship, the mother country likely would not have supported the more extreme boundary demands of its North American colony, regardless of which party had the stronger legal claim. Because legal opinion favored the United States, the Canadian cause was hopeless. Nineteenth-century Russian and British maps confirmed the area in question had been Russian before 1867 and had become American with the Alaska purchase. Nor, in subsequent years, had Anglo-Canadian authorities protested the development of Skagway.

Although the United States granted Canada temporary use of the head of the Lynn Canal in 1899, and the Liberal government of Sir Wilfrid Laurier accepted, jurisdiction remained unsettled in 1901 when an assassin's bullet killed William McKinley in Buffalo and brought Vice President Theodore Roosevelt into the White House. Roosevelt added his aggressive personality to an already difficult situation in Canadian-American relations. Roosevelt's vision of American national security involved the linking of the Atlantic and the Pacific, and Alaska represented an important strategic stepping stone to the Far East. Even if national honor had not been at stake, control of the approaches to Alaska was simply too important to leave to chance, the Canadians, or third-party arbitration. Instead, he dispatched several hundred American troops as a sign of U.S. resolve to control the area against both international interlopers and the unruly local population. Roosevelt adamantly refused arbitration, arguing that the Canadian case was too weak to be taken seriously. "There are cases where a nation has no business to arbitrate," he told an English friend. "If we suddenly claimed a part of Nova Scotia you would not arbitrate." British desire not to alienate the United States contributed to an agreement early in 1903 to submit the boundary dispute to a mixed boundary commission of six "impartial" jurists, three to be appointed by each party. President Roosevelt showed his disregard for the spirit of the agreement and his understanding of the need for Senate approval of his actions by appointing strong partisans: Secretary of War Elihu Root, prominent Massachusetts Republican senator Henry Cabot Lodge, and former Republican senator from Washington, George Turner. In fairness to Roosevelt, there is no evidence that the two Canadians among the British appointees—Sir Louis Jetté, lieutenant governor of Quebec, and Allen B. Aylesworth, a Toronto lawyer—approached their assignments without prior assumptions about the merits of the case. The third British representative, Lord Alverstone, chief justice of England, was a man not to be envied. Roosevelt belligerently issued private warnings to the British through Associate Justice Oliver Wendell Holmes, Jr., that if the commission failed to sustain the U.S. position, he would use American military forces to achieve the same end.[36]

The outcome of the commission's inquiry is infamous in Canadian historical mythology. Lord Alverstone, this version runs, sold out Canada in the interest of Anglo-American accord, and the two Canadians on the panel accordingly refused to sign the decision. The commission awarded the critical control of the head of the Lynn Canal and the vital coastal strip north from fifty-six degrees forty minutes north latitude to the United States. There were minor concessions to Canada, such as the award of several islands in the Portland Channel, but these were of little consequence. Under the award, two commissioners were appointed to determine the precise delimitation of the boundary, a task that was completed in 1905. Any fair assessment of the merits of the case, however, indicates that Lord Alverstone would have been remiss to find otherwise, and that the Canadian members of the panel were in a political dilemma that made it virtually impossible for them to have acted differently in the emotional drama of the moment. The Alaskan boundary dispute was a decisive moment in Anglo-Canadian relations with the United States. Its resolution removed what Theodore Roosevelt referred to as the last serious point of friction between the United States and Great Britain. The appointment of a majority of Canadians to the boundary commission proved useless in guarding Canada's interests, but by its failure was part of the emergence of an independent Canadian tradition in foreign policy. For Canadians, the boundary dispute was a spur to Canadian nationalism, anti-Americanism, and more than a tinge of resentment against British authority, a sentiment that tended to give English and French Canadians common cause. The *Montreal Herald* editorialized that "no Canadian government will be again likely to lay itself open to such treatment as meted out to Canada, whose ministers were tricked and deluded from first to last."[37]

The boundary dispute also underlined the stark asymmetry of power between Canada and the United States. No Canadian accepted this disparity as permanent. In the thirty-five years since confederation, Canada had crossed the continent, and the original four provinces had become nine. "The Americans have 100 years the start of us. The United States cannot go on making the same progress," Dominion Day speakers assured Canadians. Canada, with its superior political inheritance from Britain, would catch up, and Canadians would build a country materially equal to America and morally superior to it. "As the nineteenth century was the century of the United States," said Prime Minister Laurier from innumerable platforms, "so shall the twentieth century belong to Canada."[38]

3 Beginning a Bilateral Relationship, 1903–1919

The first two decades of the twentieth century witnessed dramatic changes in the world context of U.S.-Canadian relations. Britain and its European rivals—France, Germany, Austria, and Russia—declined in relation to an emergent America. During the Republican presidencies of Theodore Roosevelt and William Howard Taft, the United States came to terms with its newly won status as a world power, built a battleship navy, and consolidated its political and economic influence in the Caribbean and in Central and South America, and extended it in the Pacific. The upheavals of World War I made the United States an international creditor and a military force able to compete with Britain even at sea, where the Royal Navy had ruled for a century. The temporary eclipse of Germany, the Bolshevik Revolution that reduced Russia's international influence, the rise of Japan: all these things tilted the world strategic balance to the United States' advantage. At home, a series of reform movements strained the United States body politic. Under the umbrella of the Progressive Movement a diverse range of reforms—prohibition, women's suffrage, the labor movement, civil rights, consumer protection, and social work—attempted to transform American society in response to the massive economic changes of the last quarter of the nineteenth century. Government assumed a larger role in the activities of the private sector, foreign trade, and overseas investment among others.

Because Canada was undergoing the same industrial capitalist revolution, albeit at its own pace, most of the reforms that shook the United States had their counterparts in Canada in these years. Nor was any country more affected than Canada by the global emergence of the United States and the relative decline of Great Britain. Trade relations with the United States continued to preoccupy Canadian domestic politics as well as cross-border relations, as did the growing cultural influence of the United States on Canadian society. Canadians were much less concerned about the increasing levels of American investment in Canadian resources and manufacturing. In its relations with Canada, however, the United States neither employed the heavy-handed dollar diplomacy nor played the role of international policeman that it had in the Caribbean in the early twentieth century. The many points of friction were smoothed without resort to any force more violent than political rhetoric. On the formal diplomatic front, the Canadian government quietly explored an increasing autonomy from Great Britain in the conduct of its affairs with the United States. To the extent that one can consider any historical development inevitable, the growing bilateralism in Canadian-American relations was dictated by the new realities of international economic and military power. British strategic planners viewed war with the United States as "a contingency which, however improbable, is not impossible," but they secretly conceded that a successful defense of Canada was impossible. First Sea Lord Sir John Fisher privately suggested that Britain "not spend one man or one pound in the defence of Canada." Given this military forecast, maintaining troops and a naval presence in Canada had lost even symbolic value to Britain, or at least a symbolic value that equaled the cost to the exchequer of keeping them there. In 1906, the last British garrisons withdrew from Halifax and Esquimalt, British Columbia, and were replaced by infantry from Canada's minuscule army. The establishment of a tiny Canadian Department of External Affairs in 1909 was another of the only slightly more than symbolic gestures of growing Canadian autonomy from Great Britain in the international sphere. The department was a small step toward a Canadian foreign policy, even if the real decisions were still made in London and in the British embassy in Washington. Prime Minister Sir Wilfrid Laurier did not look on the creation of the department as the launching of an independent Canadian foreign policy. The impetus came from British ambassador James Bryce in Washington, who complained that Canadian-American relations tied up three-quarters of the embassy's attention and who demanded "a sort of Foreign Office" in Ottawa through which Canadian affairs in Washington could be coordinated. Britain remained a significant political presence in the Canadian-American relationship, however, and the British Empire remained a potent emotional presence. London gently resisted independent Canadian representation in Washington, which might interfere with imperial designs, but ultimately conceded it to the Dominion in the 1920s.[1]

The Beginnings of Bilateral Relations

As in the previous century, shared boundaries, fisheries, and natural resources were the staples of Canadian-American relations. What was significant about the twentieth-century Canadian-American approach to the outstanding points of contention was the effort to institutionalize and depoliticize the mechanisms of conflict resolution, an approach that the United States also pursued, although with less success, with Mexico. This preference to avoid diplomatic disputes that might become hotly debated public issues paralleled the emergence of a more bureaucratic and "scientific" approach to conflict management during the years of progressive reform. Whether it was the creation of a Bureau of Corporations under Theodore Roosevelt, the establishment of a U.S. Tariff Commission under Woodrow Wilson, or the attempts by John D. Rockefeller, Jr., to development a new industrial relations system that would eliminate strikes, the thrust of the Progressive Era was toward organization, systematization, stability, and conflict reduction. This approach found a harmonious echo in Canada: Rockefeller's expert consultant on industrial relations was William Lyon Mackenzie King, former Canadian minister of labor and future prime minister. It was thus not surprising that the United States and Canada sought to establish bilateral bureaucratic institutions to deal with contentious common problems.[2]

The first important initiative was the establishment of the International Boundary Commission (IBC) in 1908. Stripped of their military implications in the new atmosphere of Anglo-American harmony, boundary questions became suddenly less intractable. As James Bryce commented about an obscure island on the Maine–New Brunswick boundary, "a century ago, it might conceivably have been . . . a spot on which to construct a small fort. . . . Today no use could be made of it except to erect a tiny summer cottage or perhaps an afternoon tea house." The IBC's mandate was to clarify the international boundary between Canada and the United States, with the exception of the Great Lakes and St. Lawrence boundary, which was surveyed and reported on by the International Waterways Commission under the 1908 treaty. There were several main projects: settle the boundary in the perennially difficult area of the St. Croix River and Bay of Fundy through Passamaquoddy Bay; determine the boundary from the mouth to the source of the St. Croix River; survey the boundary from the source of the St. Croix River to the St. Lawrence River; and "ascertain and re-establish accurately" the location of the international boundary from its intersection with the St. Lawrence River near the forty-fifth parallel to the mouth of the Pigeon River on the western shore of Lake Superior. From there the commissioners had the task of clarifying the boundary to the Lake of the Woods, on to the Rocky Mountains, across the mountains to the Gulf of Georgia, and finally across the boundary between Vancouver Island and the United States. They also set the boundary along the 141st meridian from the Arctic Ocean to Mount St. Elias.

The IBC's mandate has always been reasonably specific and technical in nature, a fact that kept its operation relatively free of controversy and public debate. In theory, each commissioner appointed to the IBC has been "an expert geographer or surveyor," as stipulated by Article II of the 1908 treaty, although among United States appointments there have been such exceptions as John Illinski, an insurance broker and beer distributor appointed by Harry Truman. Some of the commissioners have served sufficiently lengthy terms to provide important continuity. O. H. Tittman, appointed by Theodore Roosevelt, served from 1909 until 1915, and E. Lester Jones, appointed by Harding, served under three presidents until his death in 1929. On the

Anglo-Canadian side, W. F. King served for the first decade (1906–16), with J. J. McArthur beginning his appointment in 1917 and remaining until 1924.[3]

The IBC could not resolve everything—a separate Passamaquoddy Bay Treaty was negotiated as a "diplomatic sideshow" in 1910—but the commission cut a new and nonconfrontational pattern for U.S.-Canadian relations. The commission produced results on the Arctic–Mount St. Elias boundary by 1918. In the 1952 report, the commissioners were still looking at the boundary between Tongass Passage and Mount St. Elias; by 1925, the more controversial St. Croix–St. Lawrence River boundary report was complete. Not until 1934 did the IBC produce its fifth report, this one on the boundary from the source of the St. Croix River to the Atlantic Ocean. That boundary had been under review since at least 1794, when earlier commissioners had attempted to define the boundary. Resolution of that border with minimal controversy and technical expertise, in keeping with the entire ethos of the Progressive Era and the increasingly "professional" and technical nature of Canadian-American bilateral relations, was no small accomplishment. Anyone inclined to make political mileage from the commissioners' reports would have had first to wade through volumes of charts, "geodetic datum," and "triangulation and traverse stations"! The age of Taylorism and scientific management had come to Canadian-American relations.[4]

The second and more significant bilateral mechanism was the International Joint Commission, established 11 January 1909, when British ambassador James Bryce and Secretary of State Elihu Root signed the Boundary Waters Treaty. This permanent commission, working outside normal diplomatic channels to resolve water use problems, was a more broadly conceived successor to the International Waterways Commission. The Boundary Waters Treaty was in fact negotiated by two members of the International Waterways Commission, George Clinton for the United States and George Gibbons for Canada. The only British contribution to the discussion—other than Bryce's advice to the Canadians to settle for less than they eventually achieved—was the ambassador's signature. Composed of three United States and three Canadian appointees, the IJC was to advise both governments about water levels, pollution, power development, the impact of dams on fisheries and other downstream activities, and irrigation. Its establishment was a diplomatic victory for Canadian prime minister Sir Wilfrid Laurier, who had pressed vigorously for the establishment of a commission that would take thorny boundary water issues out of the public eye and, he hoped, beyond political logrolling. He did so against the advice of Ambassador Bryce, who preferred ad hoc solutions to problems as they arose, and over the opposition of Secretary of State Root. Because the Boundary Waters Treaty was an Anglo-American agreement, high-level support was essential to diplomatic success; Laurier received it from Governor General Earl Grey and from President Theodore Roosevelt. Grey regarded Anglo-American friendship as the primary goal of British foreign policy. Accordingly, on his appointment to Ottawa in 1904 he made the settlement of U.S.-Canadian differences his personal project. Roosevelt was recruited to the boundary waters cause through his conservationist background. The American Civic Association warned him that without an international agreement the scenic beauty of Niagara Falls would be lost to unregulated water diversion for hydroelectric development. The president's confidant on conservation matters, Gifford Pinchot, was able to bend Root away from his opposition to a bilateral commission. The less-political approach to the bilateral relationship, the major achievement of the Boundary Waters Treaty, also conformed precisely to Roosevelt's progressive perception of how reform should be managed.[5]

The importance of a bilateral commission between two countries whose border is one-third water and whose rivers flow into one another's territory should be self-evident. The pressing problems of 1909 increased as power generation, industrialization, and water pollution intensified. By 1929, the IJC had dealt with twenty-seven cases, either submitted by private citizens or referred by the Canadian or U.S. governments. Cases ranged from the 1913 approval of the construction of the St. Mary's River Dam by the Michigan Northern Power Company to the 1928 recommendations on fumes generated by the

Trail B.C. Smelter, recommendations that were rejected by the United States. The commission's decisions touched the lives of ordinary Canadians and Americans: its correspondence reveals their concerns about flooding, soil erosion, pollution, and property damage.[6]

The IJC has never deserved the fulsome praise heaped on it after World War I, when it was described as "the memorial dome to Anglo-American peace," and offered as a model for resolving the boundary between France and Germany. But the commission provided an institutional mechanism within which Canada and the United States could, in the words of international lawyer P. E. Corbett, "deal with matters . . . before they get to the stage of national bitterness." It signified, concludes Canadian scholar-diplomat John Holmes, "the triumph of the tradition of restraint . . . in quiet contradiction to the noisier thrust of Manifest Destiny." Yet leading university textbooks in Canadian history ignore the IJC, as does the leading textbook in American foreign policy. In the most recent assessment, J. L. Granatstein and Norman Hillmer contend that the impact of the IJC has been exaggerated because its actual powers have been advisory, and its ability to invoke binding arbitration restrained by Congress and the executive in the United States, and by the Senate and Cabinet in Canada. One of the major failings of the treaty, according to both contemporary and later analysts, was its application only to waters that actually straddled the border, thus excluding, for instance, rivers that flowed into boundary waters or across the borders. However short they fall of their most idealistic descriptions, the Boundary Waters Treaty and the International Joint Commission represent the development of depoliticized decision making outside the boundaries of formal diplomacy in Canadian-American relations. If the much-vaunted "special relationship" between the United States and Canada has any substance, the IJC is its essence. Whatever one decides about the "special relationship," the Boundary Waters Treaty was negotiated by Canadians and thus represented a significant step on the road to formal bilateral diplomatic relations between North American neighbors.[7]

The difference between the official text of a treaty and the reality of its implementation was further evident in violations of the spirit and letter of the Rush-Bagot Treaty of 1817, which had theoretically demilitarized the Great Lakes. The Rush-Bagot Treaty had been breached during the Civil War and was breached again in the 1890s, when the Harrison, Cleveland, and McKinley administrations began a serious naval building program, inspired by the writings of Alfred Thayer Mahan and the realities of American imperial expansion. The United States sought the convenience of naval crews on the Great Lakes, and of sending warships, with their weapons dismounted, to the Lakes via the Canadian canal system, the only one deep enough to accommodate larger vessels. The United States punctiliously requested permission for these voyages, and Canada never refused, although Laurier's acquiescence was condemned as "madness" by Canadian patriots, who feared that the Americans might launch surprise attacks en route. Several of the U.S. ships that violated the Rush-Bagot agreement were built by Great Lakes shipyards that were eager for their share of the naval construction bonanza. The State Department explained away the *Gresham,* nine hundred tons and armed with modern guns, on the technical grounds that it was a "revenue cutter" and not a warship. British support for Canada on the naval issue was limited, and Canada lacked the military clout to deter the United States and feared that an open confrontation might only make Washington more belligerent. Both London and Ottawa conceded reality, agreeing that although warships were forbidden on the lakes, two armed training vessels and six revenue cutters would not add up to a warship! Between 1900 and 1910, the American inland navy exceeded these agreed limits, a point emphasized in 1909 with the USS *Nashville,* a modern fighting ship whose four-inch guns could launch a thirty-pound shell five miles. The niceties of formal diplomacy were observed: the *Nashville*'s guns were dismounted in Canadian waters, and after complaints from the Laurier government, the Taft administration graciously promised Ambassador Bryce that in the future it would adhere to the spirit of the Rush-Bagot Treaty. One historian has referred to the diplomatic meanderings as an "invisible revision of the Rush-Bagot Agreement."[8]

Fisheries disputes remained the thorniest perennial in U.S.-

Canadian relations and in U.S.-Newfoundland relations. American access to Canadian and Newfoundland fisheries had been contentious since the American Revolution, because the 1818 agreement continued to mean different things to both parties. Only about two thousand New Englanders actually fished these waters, but the case took on greater importance because the fishermen were represented in the U.S. Senate by Henry Cabot Lodge, the most powerful member of the Foreign Relations Committee. Thus a final interpretation became part of the larger effort of the Laurier government and the Roosevelt-Taft administrations to "clean the slate." As with boundary waters, the preferred method of resolution was to remove the problem from the vagaries of the political arena. In 1908, the United States and Great Britain agreed to establish the International Fisheries Commission. Early in Taft's presidency in 1909, the Laurier and Taft administrations agreed to submit outstanding claims over the fisheries to a tribunal formed from among the members of the Permanent Court of Arbitration at the Hague. That arbitration process produced a North Atlantic Coast Fisheries Agreement that clarified the terms of the ancient accord—and clarified them in language that satisfied Canada's Maritime Provinces and Newfoundland yet allowed New Englanders to fish subject to "equitable and fair" regulation. In 1911, further trilateral discussions followed in Washington over the details of Canadian fisheries regulations. Canada agreed to amend or repeal a number of Canadian regulations that American captains contended disadvantaged them. Negotiators further agreed that any additional differences over the fisheries that could not be resolved through normal diplomatic channels would be referred to the Permanent Mixed Fishery Commission, as recommended by the Hague tribunal.[9]

Diplomacy lacks the drama of the wars and near-wars that marked the nineteenth century—one reason, no doubt, why relations with Canada almost vanish from the pages of U.S. diplomatic history after the Alaskan boundary dispute. C. P. Stacey notes, for example, that only seventeen pages of the two volumes of Philip C. Jessup's *Elihu Root* (New York, 1938) are devoted to Root's remarkable accomplishments in U.S.-Canadian relations. Between 1905 and 1911, with Britain's considerable cooperation, the two countries concluded eight treaties or agreements and "cleaned the slate" of long-standing quarrels. Peter Neary's description of these six years as a "new departure in Canadian-American relations" seems appropriate. The most significant departure was that there were now de facto direct relations between Ottawa and Washington, with only minimal British supervision. Things went more smoothly with "John Bull" on the sidelines, concluded Canadian diplomat Sir George Gibbons. With Great Britain "out of the game," he noted to Laurier, "there will be little prestige in tackling a little fellow." The United States had indeed resisted the temptation to bully its small neighbor and assert the obvious asymmetry of power between the two countries. In the shadow of the Alaska debacle, Laurier had gained substantial diplomatic ground. Who suspected that the government which had managed relations with the United States so competently was soon to be electorally crucified on the altar of Canada's anti-Americanism?[10]

The Americanization of Canada?

One reason for Laurier's bold assertion that the new century would "belong to Canada" was that the torrent of emigrants to the United States finally decelerated. Between 1896 and 1914, the number of American residents moving north came closer to equaling the number of residents of Canada heading south. The exact dimensions of these migrations remain elusive, because contemporary statistics of annual immigrant arrivals collected by the Canadian and U.S. governments disaccord dramatically with the decennial censuses. The most extravagant Canadian figures claim that 785,000 Americans came north, but census figures for the American-born are much more modest. Some migrants who came to Canada were born outside North America and are counted as Europeans; others were Canadians returning from sojourns in the United States; others, however, were Americans who came, saw, and returned south. The most convincing estimate sets the total number of Americans who came to Canada at 243,000, leaving a net outmigration of slightly fewer than 200,000 Canadians between 1896 and 1914. This was a spectacular improvement over the preceding half-century. French Canadians, albeit in smaller numbers, continued to leave Quebec for the "facteries" of New England. What broke the pattern of Canadian outmigration was not so much that Americans moved to the Canadian West, but that Canadians who left the Maritimes and Ontario chose the Canadian West as their destination rather than the United States.[11]

The inexpensive farmland beneath the short grass prairie of Saskatchewan and Alberta that attracted these eastern Canadians also persuaded Americans to join the trek to the "last, best West." The Canadian government actively recruited farm families in the midwestern states, and railroads cooperated by offering special rail rates for the emigrants, their livestock, and their equipment. Others made the journey overland by prairie schooner from states bordering Canada. Once there, the newcomers found a familiar land survey and distribution system, which Canada had adapted from the United States Homestead Act: every adult male could claim a quarter-section, 160 acres, if he and his family were hardy enough to survive on it. A few of the migrants became successful agri-businessmen, such as "Wheat King" A. J. Cotton, or Charles Noble, who employed 160 workers to till his thirty thousand acres of southern Alberta. The majority, however, were simple farm families moving up the "agricultural ladder" from tenant farming to independence on a modest homestead of their own—fulfilling their "American dream" in Canada. One critical element, however, was missing: the southern parts of the Canadian prairies received much less rain than Minnesota, Nebraska, or even the Dakotas. For a third of the American migrants, the Canadian sojourn dissolved in the blowing dust of the droughts from 1917 to 1926.[12]

Minority groups continued to prefer Canada to the United States, as had the Mormons in 1887. Canadian land regulations permitted transplanted cultural communities to settle in close proximity, Canada promised exemptions from military service, and provincial governments provided minority language public schools. Attracted by these assurances that they could preserve their distinctiveness, Jewish homesteaders abandoned North Dakota to found six agricultural colonies in Manitoba and Saskatchewan, and seventeen hundred Hutterites left South Dakota for Manitoba and Alberta. Despite Canada's eagerness for farmer-settlers, and its greater official tolerance of ethnic minorities, African Americans were unwelcome. Immigration bureaucrats did their best to deny admission to blacks secretly, by limiting recruiting in states with large African-American populations, by refusing African Americans the inducements available to Euro-Americans, and by stringently applying medical regulations. When W. E. B. DuBois complained of this discrimination in *Crisis*, the newspaper of the National Association for the Advancement of Colored People, the official response was blunt: "There is nothing in the Canadian immigration law which disbars any person on the ground of color, but since colored people are not considered as a class likely to do well in this country all other regulations respecting health, money etc., are strictly enforced, and it is quite possible that a number of your fellow countrymen may be rejected on such grounds." Had this form of restriction failed, however, Canada was ready to apply more overt racism: a federal order barring black immigrants was passed but never implemented in 1911.[13]

One group of Americans was always welcome in Canada: capitalists with money to invest. United States investment in Canada multiplied twelvefold between 1900 and 1920, from $167 million to $2.1 billion (U.S.). Most of the new investments went into resource extraction and into secondary manufacturing. Separate patterns developed in each sector. To avoid paying United States tariffs against manufactured products, the resource companies tried to do as little secondary processing in Canada as possible, and to ship their wood, ore, or asbestos back to the United States in unrefined form. After 1900, the provincial governments of Ontario and Quebec began to confound these attempts by banning or taxing the export of unprocessed logs and ore. American secondary manufacturing companies had been blackmailed since 1879 into opening branch plants by the Canadian protective tariff and by Canadian patent law, which denied patent protection to manufacturers without a domestic factory. These companies sold their products almost exclusively in the Canadian market and exported almost nothing. Canadians seemed unconcerned that a large percentage of their economy belonged to Americans. Two critical sectors of the Canadian economy, transportation and banking, were almost untouched by U.S. capital. As large as American investment in Canada was, a far larger percentage of foreign investment—three times as much in 1914—belonged to British investors; in Canada, British investment was scarcely considered "foreign" investment at all.[14]

In Canada's trade union movement, the relationship between British and American participation was the reverse: few British unions had locals in Canada, but many American unions had affiliates there. American craft unions—iron molders, coopers, railway engineers, typographers, shoemakers—first appeared in Canada in the 1850s, and for the next century, the history of the Canadian trade union movement followed many of the contours of the American. In the 1880s, the craft unions were joined by the Knights of Labor. Founded in Philadelphia in 1869 as a fraternal organization dedicated to labor reform, the Knights erupted in the 1880s into almost a national industrial union, organizing semiskilled and unskilled workers ignored by craft unions, fighting strikes when necessary, and working to create a "co-operative commonwealth" to replace American industrial capitalism. The Knights reached their apex in the massive industrial conflict of the mid-eighties, and thereafter perished in the face of employer resistance, economic depression, and conflict with the craft unions affiliated with the American Federation of Labor (AFL) established in 1886. The AFL's agenda for the American workers was defined by its president, Samuel Gompers, as "pure and simple" craft unionism aimed at improving wages and working conditions. Independent political action was anathema: American workers were to accept the world as it was rather than "dream of what might be," as the Knights would have it. Paradoxically, the Knights of Labor lived on vigorously in Canada for two decades after they became moribund in the United States. In Ontario and Quebec, local assemblies of the Knights were the vanguard of a nascent working-class movement in both its industrial and its political struggles. Knights guided the Trades and

Labor Congress (TLC), Canada's national labor federation, for the first decade after its birth in 1886.[15]

But it was craft unions affiliated with the American Federation of Labor that assumed the leadership in the prosperous years at the beginning of the new century, as union membership began to grow rapidly. Craft workers who crossed the international boundary wanted an American union card so that they could work in the United States. Canadian unions themselves sometimes sought affiliation with experienced American unions with money for organizational work. United States unions came to Canada in order to guarantee that American employers could not use it as a northern nonunion sanctuary. There was also an element of internationalist idealism in this North American focus: "There is no 49th parallel of latitude in Unionism," declared one British Columbia miner. "The Canadian and American workingmen have joined hands across the Boundary line for a common cause against a common enemy." Samuel Gompers appealed to such idealism in more restrained language: "We are more than neighbors; we are kin . . . our labor problem with all its ideals, aspirations and ambitions is alike for both of us." Lest any Canadian worker challenge the official AFL definition of those "ideals, aspirations and ambitions" (and perhaps encourage American workers to question them as well), after 1900 Gompers and his Canadian colleagues moved quickly to establish their authority within the Trades and Labor Congress of Canada. Their targets were the Knights of Labor and "dual" unions—autonomous Canadian or British unions whose membership included craftsmen (and they were virtually all crafts*men*) for whom a competing AFL union already existed. Their victory was swift: at the Trades and Labor Congress convention in Berlin, Ontario, in 1902, Gompers's candidate John Flett became TLC president. The Canadian Congress then expelled the remaining Knights of Labor delegates and all those representing "dual" unions, and granted the AFL the ultimate authority in jurisdictional disputes—to determine, in other words, which unions would be allowed to become members of Canada's most important labor federation. Samuel Gompers, said the *Montreal Herald,* was now "the Napoleon of Labor, with a continent for his kingdom." Like the branch plant industry, branch plant unions became the norm within the Canadian labor movement; the United Brotherhood of Carpenters and Joiners or the United Mine Workers of America were similar to Gillette or General Motors in this regard.[16]

What difference did this make for Canadian workers? The immediate effect of the Berlin decision of 1902 was increased fragmentation of the Canadian working-class movement by region, as most of the groups expelled were from Quebec. It was difficult for AFL unions operating in English to make up these losses, and the way was cleared for the Roman Catholic church to establish a system of Catholic unions within the province. The longer-term effect, writes Robert Babcock, was that "the international craft unions brought to Canada structural characteristics and policy predilections that were products of the America environment[:] craft union organization, short-term economic goals, apolitical unionism." Under AFL tutelage, the Canadian labor movement grew in the direction of a narrow business unionism preoccupied with the immediate interests of its members, rather than that of social movement unionism, dedicated to broader working-class objectives. Samuel Gompers's dictum to support individual "friends of labor" in the Republican and Democratic parties might have been sound advice in a congressional system, but it was structurally unsuited to a parliamentary system, in which individual Conservatives and Liberals had no legislative autonomy from their party's position.[17]

But it would be too simple to attribute all the limitations of the Canadian labor movement to the malevolent influence of what critics called the American "separation" of labor, and to use the United States as a convenient scapegoat for Canadian problems. Canadian craft workers voluntarily chose American unions to represent them, and by 1915, these unions spoke for 119,000 of them, 90 percent of the organized workers in Canada. Craft unionists in Canada practiced Labourist politics, in spite of the AFL interdiction against them. And if there is a conservative binational labor heritage, there is also a "radical heritage" of binational challenges to AFL/TLC hegemony: the Western Federation of Miners, the American Labor Union, and the Industrial

Workers of the World. Canadian employers were sufficiently alarmed by American union organizers that a bill passed the Canadian Senate in 1903 that provided two years' imprisonment for any U.S. citizen who came to Canada to support striking workers. There had been "no difficulty in settling the labour disputes in our factories" before American organizers came north, argued one Senator during the debate; Samuel Gompers should never "be allowed to come to Canada . . . to destroy our peace and harmony."[18]

Trade unionism was the worst of a series of objectionable importations from the United States that troubled Canadian elites. Immigrants to the Canadian West might bring America's wild West along with them: "Alberta," worried a member of Parliament, "might be regarded as a typical American state." College fraternities, baseball leagues, and business associations were integrating the continent on north-south lines. "Our theatres, sports, magazines, newspapers, are all more or less of the Yankee sort," lamented Rodolphe Lemieux, Canada's postmaster general. The tracts of Canadian social reformers cited American rather than British examples, beseeching Canada to "listen to a warning voice from the Republic to the South." It seemed, concluded Sir Andrew MacPhail, as if "the American spirit" was "at war for the possession of Canada's soul." In his Columbia doctoral thesis published in 1907, Samuel E. Moffett described the Americanization of Canada with an air of satisfaction inappropriate to a social scientist. "The Americans and the English Canadians have been welded into one people. Canadians . . . are already Americans without knowing it." Canada had survived the nineteenth century, Moffett concluded, only because of "a long series of American mistakes"; in the twentieth century it would soon be absorbed into the United States.[19]

Moffett proved not only a poor political scientist but a poor prognosticator. Others who studied Canadian society reached very different conclusions. French sociologist André Seigfried recognized "American ideas, habits, and tendencies" but found these superficial: "at bottom, by taste and tradition, English Canadians are very English still." Seigfried might have added Scottish, Irish, and Welsh: between 1901 and 1921, 752,000 immigrants came to Canada from the British Isles, three times as many as from the United States. A German journalist touring the Canadian West, supposedly the most "Americanized" region of Canada, remarked that "the Canadians belong to the British Empire not merely out of habit, not for practical considerations, but from a warm feeling of kinship." He found "no trace whatsoever of leaning toward the United States." English travel writer John Foster Fraser assumed that the tobacco-chewing Albertan in overalls he interviewed standing beneath a sign for "The Beer That Made Milwaukee Famous" would be an American immigrant. Appearances aside, Fraser's subject proved a passionate British Canadian, whose "dislike of the States almost equal[ed his] loyalty to the Empire." Asked about the possibility of commercial union with the United States, he told Fraser that "we're not frightened of those Yankees and their tariffs. It ain't us wants reciprocity with Uncle Sam, but Uncle Sam who'd like to get a smile from Miss Canada."[20]

Reciprocity Repulsed

Nothing better illustrates all the dimensions of Canada's ambivalent relationship with the United States than the neverending issue of reciprocal trade. The Canadian craving for a reciprocal trade agreement never really went away, however much it was dulled by the prosperity of the first decade of the new century. Even as Canadian voters rejected unrestricted reciprocity in 1891—an agreement that the United States had never formally offered—Sir John A. Macdonald had made clear that a "fair" reciprocity agreement remained a Canadian goal. On assuming the prime ministership in 1896, Wilfrid Laurier announced that there would be "no more pilgrimages" to Washington for trade agreements. The Liberals won four consecutive majority governments (1896, 1900, 1904, and 1908) with a protective tariff policy that seemed a carbon copy of that of the Macdonald Conservatives. Yet Laurier admitted that should the United States "come and knock on our door," he was ready to negotiate a free trade agreement. There were pragmatic economic reasons for this ambivalence between tariff protection against and freer trade with the United States. As intended, the high tariff attracted American branch plants to Canada, but the counterargument in favor of reciprocal tariff reductions was Canada's chronic trade deficit with the United States: 1910 figures showed an imbalance of $242 million to $97 million. During the North Atlantic fisheries negotiations, Canada had repeated its offer to exchange access to the inshore fisheries for U.S. tariff concessions on Canadian primary exports, but the offer was rebuffed as it had been previously. It was thus a surprise when Finance Minister W. S. Fielding came home from discussions in Washington in 1910 with a bigger catch than Ottawa had anticipated—a large-scale trade agreement that satisfied most of the conditions Canadians had sought since the United States abrogated the Elgin-Marcy Reciprocity Treaty in 1866. There was to be near free trade in natural products, which made up virtually all Canadian exports to the United States: the draft agreement removed all tariffs on pulpwood, most minerals, and unprocessed agricultural products, and lowered tariffs on processed farm products. To the delight of the Laurier government, there would be only limited reductions in the tariffs on manufactured goods, which made up about three-quarters of U.S. exports to Canada. Most Canadian tariffs against U.S. manufactured goods remained in place, including the "imperial preferences" that permitted British manufactures into the Canadian market at rates lower than those from the United States. "Making allowance for changed conditions," said the *Winnipeg Free Press,* the new agreement was "the treaty of 1854 all over again." There was one important difference: the agreement was to be enacted not by treaty but by concurrent legislation of Congress and Parliament, so that neither two-thirds approval in the U.S. Senate nor British diplomatic participation would be necessary.[21]

Historians debate why an agreement so favorable to Canada suddenly originated from Washington. Albert K. Weinberg, echoing the fears of Canadian critics of the accord, interpreted reciprocity in the tradition of Manifest Destiny, as "the tinder which set into flame the expansionist impulse, inactive recently but still combustible." The most generally accepted explanation is that the United States had no thought of annexation, that Taft hoped an agreement would shore up Republican electoral fortunes. After promising in the 1908 campaign that the Republican party was "unequivocally for revision of the tariff," his administration was feeling political heat generated by the 1909 Payne-Aldrich tariff, which had indeed revised tariff rates—upward. Without a reciprocity agreement with Canada, Payne-Aldrich would have required the United States to apply new maximum penalty rates to Canadian exports, the first shot in a possible trade war. President Taft was also pushed toward reciprocity, L. E. Ellis suggests, by the eagerness of the American Newspaper Publishers' Association to have untaxed access to cheaper Canadian newsprint. Richard Gwynn argues that Taft made his "offer of almost unbelievable generosity" because of his affection for Canada, a love nurtured by years of happy vacations and hearty meals at his summer home in Murray Bay, Quebec. A more comprehensive explanation of U.S. motivation for reciprocity has been offered Robert E. Hannigan and by Paul Wolman, who interpret the agreement as part of a broader attempt by a group of political and industrial "tariff revisionists" to chart new directions for American capitalism. Reciprocity was evidence, writes Hannigan, of "a new American continentalism, distinct from the annexationist variant prominent during the nation's first century," one with "very significant global implications." Its goal was to prevent Canada from developing into a "core" industrial state (the term is from Immanuel Wallerstein's *Capitalist World Economy,* discussed in chapter 2), which could compete with the United States, and "to guarantee for the American economy a cheap and continuous supply of Canadian natural products." Some of the tariff reductions in the reciprocity agreement did indeed run counter to the short-term interests of some American industries, but this was not United States benevolence to Canada. Taft and the tariff revisionists, Wolman points out, thought "not only in terms of immediate self-interest but in terms of the collective future of their nation as the world's dominant economic power." Other than among those who would specifically be hurt by its provisions, the deal had widespread support in the United States. A month after Taft announced the agreement to Congress on 26 January 1911, the *New York Times* reported that reciprocity was "backed by such a force of public sentiment as we do not recall behind any measure in our political history," and that America's business leaders were "eager for Canadian reciprocity."[22]

Initial reaction in Canada to the announcement of the agreement was incredulous enthusiasm at the Liberal government's coup of improved access to U.S. markets at little apparent cost to Canada. The Conservative opposition was shocked into silence, and its crestfallen leader Robert Borden reported "the deepest dejection in our party." But resistance to the agreement mobilized rapidly outside Parliament. Eighteen prominent Toronto businessmen, all of them Liberals, denounced reciprocity as a threat to "Canadian autonomy and Canadian nationality." It would, said their manifesto, prevent Canadian development of "her own resources in her own way and by her own people, . . . weaken the ties which bind Canada to the Empire, . . . and make it more difficult to avert political union with the United States." Buoyed—and bankrolled—by new business supporters, the Conservatives regained their composure and fought reciprocity throughout the country and in Parliament as a Trojan horse for Americanization, or worse, for annexation. "I fear the Greeks when they are bearing gifts," said Conservative spokesman George Foster; reciprocity would be "the conquest of Canada by peaceful means and large gifts." By July, exasperated by Conservative filibusters, Laurier despaired of forcing the agreement through Parliament and asked the governor general for an election.[23]

Reciprocity's American advocates unwittingly gave its Canadian opponents the tools they needed to win the election to pry the deal apart. The alacrity and the large majorities by which the reciprocity agreement sped through Congress (268 to 89 in the House of Representatives, 53 to 7 in the Senate) frightened Canadians. Could anything about which the United States was so unanimous possibly be good for Canada? American politicians had no idea of the intense scrutiny with which their every utterance on the subject would be analyzed and re-analyzed in Canadian newspapers. The congressional debates on reciprocity featured several old-fashioned spread-eagle annexationist speeches, the most quoted of which was by the Speaker of the House of Representatives. "I hope to see the day when the American flag will float over every square foot of the British North American possessions clear to the North Pole," said Missouri Democrat James Beauchamp "Champ" Clark. "I do not have any doubt whatever that the day is not far distant when Great Britain will see all her North American possessions become a part of this Republic." President Taft himself made the equally impolitic remark that Canada was at the "parting of the ways," which Canadian opponents of the agreement took to mean that Canada had to choose between America and Britain rather than between reciprocity and protection. "The talk of annexation is bosh," he told the press. "The United States has all it can attend to with the territory it now has." But the president's private assessment of the agreement, confided in a letter to Theodore Roosevelt on 10 January 1911, painted a different portrait. The agreement, Taft explained, "would produce a current of business between Canada and the United States that would make Canada only an adjunct of the United States. It would transfer all their important business to Chicago and New York, with their bank credits and everything else, and it would increase greatly the demand of Canada for our manufactures. I see this is an argument made against reciprocity in Canada, and I think it is a good one." Several historians cite this letter as a second Taft indiscretion that undermined the agreement. The letter, however, was not made public until April 1912 and therefore played no role in the defeat of reciprocity by the Canadian electorate.[24]

Taft's private analysis suggests, however, that the extravagant discourse that surrounded the reciprocity issue from 1910 to 1911 was more than simple America-bashing. The Toronto eighteen and the other Canadian capitalists and politicians who opposed reciprocity shared with Robert Borden the belief that Canada's "marvelous material resources" destined the country for "the highest position within this mighty Empire." They were determined, in other words, that within a British world system, Canada could become a "core" nation and need not be relegated to a peripheral role as America's "hewer of wood and drawer of water." The campaign—as much as any election campaign in a parliamentary democracy can revolve on a single issue—became a referendum on reciprocity. Familiar anti-American themes were revived. "Reciprocity means Annexation," warned the Montreal Woman's Anti-Reciprocity League, and annexation would mean "injury to home life and the marriage tie, [and] a lessening of national religion and morals." The newspaper *Le Devoir* pointedly asked French Canadians if they would enjoy the same religious and lingusitic guarantees if Quebec became a state of the American Union. The choice, said a Conservative candidate, was between "the Union Jack and British connection as opposed to the Stars and Stripes and Yankee domination—the domination of a flag . . . conceived in treason and born in rebellion."[25]

The election's result echoed more emphatically Canada's 1891 rejection of the United States. It was a Liberal disaster—seven cabinet ministers, including the architect of the agreement W. S. Fielding, lost their parliamentary seats—as the Conservatives won a comfortable majority of 134 to 87 in the House of Commons. Theodore Roosevelt attributed the defeat of reciprocity to "ill-judged remarks" by "three or four prize idiots, including the Speaker of the House," but the Canadian election of 1911 tells us much more than that about the relationship between the United States and Canada. Champ Clark struck the match, but the Canadian forest he set ablaze had been dried to tinder by a century and a half of anti-Americanism. "The man in the street [and only men could vote in Canada in 1911]," wrote a political science professor, voted against reciprocity "in order to show his resentment of long years of United States hostility and condescension." The *Varsity*, the student newspaper of the University of Toronto, put it more pithily: "Canada was indignant, and wiped America's eye." New prime minister Robert Borden tried to disavow the chauvinistic symphony he had conducted so skillfully during the campaign. "In rejecting reciprocity," he said in a postelection statement, "Canada has simply affirmed her adherence to a policy of national development which she has pursued for many years." That much was true. "The verdict was in no way dictated by any spirit of unfriendliness to the great neighboring republic," he continued, for "no such spirit exists." This was a convenient fiction by which Borden admitted a larger truth: that Canada had now to get on with everyday life next door to imperial America.[26]

"America Counted Her Profits; Canada Buried Her Dead"

Borden and his government matched his conciliatory words with equally conciliatory actions. Finance Minister Thomas White (one of the eighteen Toronto businessmen who had opposed reciprocity) journeyed to New York to assure Wall Street that Canada remained "a fine field for investment of their surplus funds," and the Conservatives gave final approval to the North Atlantic fisheries agreement that Laurier had hesitated for two years to confirm. To William H. Taft, this agreement summarized the new relationship he had worked to achieve among the United States, Canada, and Britain. In his last annual message in December 1912, the "lame duck" president—Taft had been defeated in November by Democrat Woodrow Wilson—noted with pride the "final conclusion" to the "century-old controversy."[27]

Intoxicated by Anglo-American amity, Prime Minister Borden expounded a new vision of the trilateral relationship in which Canada would play a unique mediating role in assuring harmony between the United States and Britain. As he explained to a New York audience, it was "the duty of Canada to become more and more of a bond of goodwill and friendship between this Great Republic and our Empire." There is no evidence that the Department of State of the British Foreign Office noted Borden's offer, which he repeated on several occasions to United States audiences, and nothing to suggest that it would have been taken seriously had it been noted. But this "linchpin" theory rapidly became a fundamental conviction of Canada's infant foreign policy, enduring even into the 1960s. An example was the remarkable rapidity with which Canadian leaders turned from manipulating the anti-Americanism of their countrypeople to memorializing the centenary of the end of the War of 1812. In August 1913, with

Secretary of State William Jennings Bryan at the head table, Thomas White reminded a New York audience that "next year we celebrate a hundred years of peace." It would, he predicted, be the first century of "a thousand more years of peace between the two great English-speaking races." A trinational British-Canadian-United States committee (chaired in Canada by Sir Edmund Walker, another of the Toronto Eighteen) set to work to plan the celebration of "the 100th Anniversary of peace between the United States and the British Empire." Their celebrations were cut short by the cannons of August 1914.[28]

As a British colony, Canada entered World War I (the "Great War," as it was universally known until the 1940s) automatically with King George V's declaration of war against Germany. Canada was "ready, aye ready" to "answer to the call of duty," promised Sir Wilfrid Laurier; few disagreed—in part because Canadians thought their empire would win a speedy victory. Instead, the war stalemated into appalling carnage between the trenches on the western front, with casualties counted in the hundreds of thousands. Borden and his government committed Canada, with a population of fewer than eight million, to maintain an army of half a million men in Europe, a commitment that meant the imposition of a military draft which split the country profoundly along French-English lines. To English Canadians, who by and large supported this commitment and the military draft, the war became more than an exercise in British Empire solidarity. Long before the United States entered the war, they came to understand it as a crusade for democracy, a struggle to rescue tiny Belgium from ruthless German oppression.[29]

Because the United States had long and loudly professed such values (and had twice invaded Canada to save it from ruthless British oppression), President Wilson's declaration of neutrality seemed to Canadians hypocrisy. Wilson asked that Americans be "impartial in thought as well as in action" and went so far as to ask audiences in movie theaters not to cheer either side during newsreels of the war. His refusal even to lend moral support to the Allies (with whom Wilson personally sympathized) was incomprehensible to Canadians, and Secretary of State William Jennings Bryan's frequent criticism of Britain outraged them. European purchases of food, raw materials, and munitions in the United States stimulated both the American economy and Canadian resentment. "America waxed richer and stronger," complained a bitter Canadian, while "Canada suffered, fought and sacrificed her prosperity and her sons." Official expressions of resentment were muted—like the British government, the Canadian government prayed for American intervention—but private expressions were scathing. "The United States made its big mistake in allowing the Belgian tragedy . . . without lifting its voice in protest," wrote a Montreal lawyer to a friend serving overseas in the Canadian army. "Our big neighbor is big no longer. . . . The true American hangs his head in shame. . . . He is not a citizen of a nation, but belongs to a conglomeration of races undigested and undigestible; how he envies us our British citizenship and curses the spirit that has made his country a by-word and reproach among men with red blood in their veins."[30]

"Conglomeration of races" referred to Irish Americans and German Americans, whose antipathy to Britain was assumed to be one of the sources of Wilson's policy of neutrality. The possibility that German agents would recruit border raiders within these ethnic communities troubled the Canadian military and the Canadian public. The German Foreign Office seriously considered several plans for such attacks, but their military attaché in Washington achieved virtually no results in implementing them. The total damage from his campaign of sabotage was one slightly damaged New Brunswick railway bridge. It was evident, Canadians conceded, that "the conspirators were well watched from Washington." The most frustrating Canadian-American wartime problems, as in the nineteenth century, stemmed from the issue of neutral rights at sea, an issue exacerbated by the development of the submarine. The Royal Navy commanded the surface of the Atlantic, so that Britain's trade with America could continue, but the Wilson administration forbade the sale of warships to belligerent nations. The British Admiralty secretly contracted with an American company to assemble "clandestine submarines" and coastal patrol vessels in Canadian shipyards, in defiance of both United States neutrality and Canadian customs and labor laws. In 1916, a German submarine freighter, the *U-Deutschland,* surfaced in Baltimore to load a cargo of nickel mined at Sudbury, Ontario. Canadians were outraged that metal mined by an American branch plant might be used against Canadian soldiers, sailors, and airmen. The submarine incident that most aroused Canadians was "the day's worth of havoc" of the *U-53* in October 1916. The first German combat submarine to cross the Atlantic, the *U-53* paid a courtesy call on the U.S. naval base at Newport, Rhode Island. American naval officers and their families toured "the long gray visitor," the *New York Times* reported, and brought gifts to the German commander and his men. The *U-53*'s crew declined the many invitations to dinners ashore in Newport; instead they returned to sea to sink five Allied merchant ships just outside the three-mile limit. One was the British-registered *Stephano,* a liner bound from New York to Halifax, sent to the bottom while two U.S. Navy destroyers waited compliantly to rescue the *Stephano*'s passengers. To have intervened would have been to "violate their duty of neutrality," Assistant Secretary of the Navy Franklin D. Roosevelt told the press; the American captains had acted in "absolute accordance with international law." But to Canadians, the American navy was an accomplice in an act of piracy; these protestations of even-handedness infuriated them all the more. "The time will come when American Democracy will need to explain," editorialized the *Toronto Globe.*[31]

Submarines ultimately brought America into the war on the side of the Allies in April 1917. Germany's announcement that its U-boats would torpedo all merchant ships trading with Britain without warning and without regard for their nationality put Wilson in Madison's position of 1812, and he made the same decision for war. America fought, he told Congress, because "the world must be made safe for democracy." Canadians welcomed their mighty neighbor to the Allied ranks. "Uncle Sam . . . definitely sets the scales of conflict in favor of democracy," wrote an Alberta editor, even if the United States was likely to be "no great force in the war." The most ironic evidence that Canada and the United States were fighting on the same side was the Canadian government's invitation to AFL president Samuel Gompers to visit Ottawa to address the Parliament, which fifteen years earlier had debated forbidding him entry the country. In April 1918, Gompers was no longer an "alien agitator" but a "sane, masterful leader"; in a series of speeches, he told Canadian trade unionists that "this War is a people's war—labour's war," and urged them to show their support by pledging not to strike for the duration of the war effort. Although they now shared a common enemy, there was little military cooperation between the United States and Canadian armed forces. In France, their armies fought under separate commands. In the North Atlantic approaches, relations between the two navies were cordial, but the U.S. Navy was too preoccupied with shepherding American merchant ships to coordinate antisubmarine defense with the Royal Canadian Navy. Nor did World War I substantially increase economic integration of the newfound Allies. In both countries, the demands of total war brought about an unprecedented degree of government intervention into economic affairs, intervention accomplished by parallel federal wartime bureaucracies. Canada's food controller W. D. Hanna visited U.S. food administrator Herbert Hoover, and the Imperial Munitions Board of Canada and the United States Ordnance Department signed an agreement to coordinate production of artillery shells. But so little real binational coordination took place before the war ended in November 1918 that the contacts had more symbolic than practical significance. Continental integration for total war lay twenty-five years in the future.[32]

The war did, however, accelerate the de facto development of independent Canadian representation in Washington. In October 1917, Borden cabled the Canadian high commissioner in the United Kingdom, stressing that it was urgent that a special Canadian representative be appointed in Washington, a position supported by Lord Northcliffe, then head of the British War Mission in Washington. Borden stressed that "the multiplicity of departments and commissions at Washington leads to disastrous delay if negotiations are conducted through the Embassy which is overwhelmed with a multitude of important matters not directly concerning Canada." The proposal was to appoint a Canadian official who would serve in the British embassy but would communicate directly with the U.S. government in matters concerning Canadian affairs. Before the end of World War I, Canada enjoyed a very distinct position as a British Dominion in its representation in Washington. The reality was that most negotiations between not only the Department of External Affairs and the State Department were conducted directly, with the consent of the British embassy, but also that this became the normal practice with other government departments as well. As British ambassador Cecil Spring Rice observed to the governor general in early 1918, "the part that the Embassy plays is merely to inform the State Department and to stand aside until the negotiation is completed." Nonetheless, such arrangements were informal and at the indulgence of the British and American governments. This suggests the importance of Borden's success in having established in February 1918 a formal Canadian War Mission in Washington, headed by businessman Lloyd Harris. Borden followed a few weeks later with an official visit to President Wilson. By the end of the war, Canada was in practice well on the road to formal, independent relations with the United States.[33]

But twenty months as comrades in arms could not reverse the resentment Canadians felt at three years of U.S. neutrality. Historian Michael Bliss concludes that Canadian and U.S. businessmen "were experiencing different wars"; given that Canada fought for three years longer and had ten times the proportional casualties, it was "a more profound experience for Canadians than it was for the Americans." Allying to fight the kaiser did not change the Canadian stereotypes of the United States ingrained by a century and a half of anti-Americanism. Canadian reporters noted that during the 1918 Fourth of July parade in New York, William Randolph Hearst, the "malignant figure" who published ten "anti-British" newspapers, had "remained seated with his hat on" as Canadian troops marched past carrying the Union Jack. When William Jennings Bryan spoke at a prohibition rally in Toronto in 1918, he was greeted by war veterans wearing gas masks and shouting "Go Home, You Pro-German" and "Shut the Sauerkraut Up." The former secretary of state protested that "My country raised an army of one and a half million," but the veterans' choruses of "God Save the King" and "The Maple Leaf Forever" forced Bryan from the platform without finishing his speech. Prime Minister Borden, just back from his visit to Washington, described the incident as "no doubt a misunderstanding" but concluded his curious apology by calculating that "to equal Canada's record [the United States] would have to place 5,500,000 men in the field." Canadian sensitivity about their country's contribution to defeating Germany was compounded after the Armistice, when the U.S. press, Hollywood, and Tin Pan Alley bragged that America had won the war. During the 1920s and 1930s, no Canadian forgot that Canada, with one-tenth the population, had more killed and wounded than the United States. In a study of U.S.-Canada relations published in 1929, H. L. Keenleyside suggested that, as a result of such memories, "Canadian dislike for the United States was definitely increased . . . and time has not yet entirely healed the wound." A few pages later, he provided an unintentional example: "America," wrote the young Canadian historian, "counted her profits while Canada buried her dead."[34]

4 The New Era, 1919–1930

World War I was a watershed for both Canada and the United States. At war's end, Canada took its tentative first steps into the international community and the United States affirmed its world power. U.S. foreign policy in the postwar decade seemed paradoxical: a trend toward political isolationism, best exemplified by the rejection of the League of Nations, at the precise moment at which America achieved global military and economic reach. Yet there was no contradiction in this policy of "independent internationalism," argues historian Joan Hoff Wilson; government and business cooperated to gain foreign markets and raw material in a way that allowed business to retain maximum freedom of action. The continued ascendancy of the United States paralleled the decline of the British Empire and the simultaneous evolution of greater Canadian autonomy in the conduct of its foreign affairs. The war also shaped the bilateral relationship in other ways beyond diplomacy: it stimulated industrial growth in both nations, encouraged a closer working relationship between business and government, and accelerated the expansion of American investment into the Canadian economy. The United States evinced little inclination toward isolationism in the area of capital expansion and in providing diplomatic protection for its investments overseas. Congress remained highly protectionist in the Republican years after World War I—protectionism expressed in the Fordney-McCumber tariff in 1922 and in Smoot-Hawley in 1930. The United States also sought expanded outlets for its industrial production and its capital, and Canada was an important target of both. As American money came north, Canadians went south. The postwar decade saw the renewal of the southward migration of the nineteenth century. Other issues from the past continued to assert their importance in the bilateral relationship, including the fisheries of both coasts and the development of the hydroelectric potential and the transportation possibilities of the St. Lawrence waterway. No longer afraid of a military threat from the United States, Canadian elites worried about a new invasion of American movies, magazines, and radio broadcasts.[1]

By the 1920s, an Anglo-American war involving Canada was universally described as "unthinkable," even though soldiers on both sides of the border still thought about it. Canada's Defence Plan No. 1 called for the use of "flying columns" to capture "key invasion bases" such as Seattle and Minneapolis in order to stall an American drive northward until the British army arrived. The U.S. Army's Strategic Plan Red hypothesized a conquest of Canada in the event of war with Britain, after which the "territory gained . . . will become states and territories of the Union [and] the Dominion government will be abolished." Not even the soldiers, however, took these plans very seriously; the U.S. War Department obtained the maps of western Canada it needed for invasion planning by writing to the Canadian government and requesting them![2]

A Formal Diplomatic Relationship

The Canadian bureaucrat who sent the maps to the War Department was flattered that the Americans had shown an interest; Canada's biggest diplomatic difficulty was to persuade the United States that the nation to the north could be simultaneously a British Dominion and an international citizen with an independent role on the international stage. The United States opposed Canadian membership in the Pan American Union of western hemispheric states on the grounds that it was still a colony—although Canada did not want to join in any event. Along with a fear of being drawn into war through the League-imposed collective security, American antagonism toward a separate Canadian seat in the League of Nations was one of the most frequent reasons for the U.S. Senate's hostility toward the Treaty of Versailles. In his defense of the League, President Woodrow Wilson urged that Canada have full membership. Canada occupied a position of "considerable importance in the industrial world," he told American Federation of Labor president Samuel Gompers, and because the "problems of the chief British Colonies and Dominions are much more like our own than like Great Britain's," Canada would be inclined toward the United States. During his 1919 tour to build public support for the League, he asked an audience in Colorado, "Is not Canada more likely to agree with the United States than with Great Britain? Canada has a speaking part." But the Senate won out; Wilson lost his League and his Democratic party lost the White House in 1920.[3]

Canadian leaders were profoundly disappointed by the United States rejection of the League of Nations and the apparent trend to isolationism under new president Warren G. Harding. Canadians were, however, equally unwilling to participate in military or economic actions to enforce collective security, as required under Article X of the League of Nations Covenant. Both countries blamed Europe as the source of the world's problems (although Canadians made a clear distinction between Britain and Europe) and moralized about how much better North Americans got along together than did European neighbors such as Germany and France. In Europe, anti-League senator William E. Borah liked to say, "there's not a square foot that hasn't been ankle-deep in blood"; Canadian delegate N. W. Rowell said the same thing in the assembly at Geneva, blaming "European statesmen, European policies and European ambitions" for having "drenched the world in blood." The United States avoided Article X and collective security by refusing to join the League; Canada became a member and bored (in both senses of the verb) from within with long-winded speeches about the lessons the world could learn from "three thousand miles of undefended frontier" between the United States and Canada. Canada's first major international achievement was amending and redefining the League Charter to disable its collective security provisions. By 1925, Canadian delegates at Geneva had reshaped the League along exactly the lines Senator Henry Cabot Lodge had proposed in the Senate Debate over the League six years earlier! To Canada's disappointment, however, this did not persuade the United States to change its mind.[4]

After the Senate repudiated President Wilson's treaty and thus the League, Canadian leaders concluded that American politicians were infantile, unaware, and afraid of their responsibilities to the postwar world. "The U.S. has simply got to get back into the international game," *Manitoba Free Press* editor John W. Dafoe wrote to his publisher Clifford Sifton in 1921. Whatever their reservations about the U.S. nonparticipation in the League of Nations, Prime Minister Robert Borden and his colleagues had built their hopes for the postwar world in part on the continued blossoming of the Anglo-American alliance. Such cooperation would insulate Canada from American hostility and allow the country to bask in a glorious Pax Anglo-Americana.[5]

The Canadian desire to strengthen the Anglo-American relationship was evident in the position Arthur Meighen's short-lived Conservative government took at the London Imperial Conference of 1921. Meighen strongly pressed Britain to abrogate the 1902 Anglo-Japanese naval alliance in the interest of Anglo-American solidarity. Like the outgoing Wilson administration, President Harding and Secretary of State Charles Evans Hughes were determined to sever the British-Japanese alliance, fearing that Japanese expansionism in the Pacific would provoke a regional war in which Japan could require British support. The Anglo-Japanese naval alliance could not serve American interests in the Pacific, since it significantly enhanced Japanese naval potential. Although there were differences between the Admiralty and the British Foreign Office, the latter carried the day against the alliance. When delegates gathered later that year in Washington for the naval disarmament conference summoned by Secretary of State Hughes, former prime minister Robert Borden represented Canada in the British delegation; Japan was cut adrift in the interest of Anglo-American solidarity. The Washington treaties doomed the Anglo-Japanese alliance, provided verbal guarantees of mutual Japanese-American respect for their respective territorial possessions in the Pacific, imposed a heavily qualified ten-year moratorium on the construction of battleships, and established an international ratio of naval power that gave the Royal Navy and the U.S. Navy parity. From the perspective of Hughes, the agreement spared the United States and the world an expensive and potentially destructive arms race. Yet there were problems with this strategy unforeseen by Borden and the Americans. Without the Anglo-Japanese alliance, Japan was more isolated and more insecure in the Pacific; it was not surprising that it came into conflict with British and American interests in the following decades. The American and British positions had also been compromised. The United States was still not capable of or committed to maintaining stability in China and the Far East; Australia and New Zealand were more vulnerable, and Canada could make no contribution at all to a balance of power in the Pacific. This was but one of the reasons, as J. L. Granatstein and Norman Hillmer note, that Canada's weakness made it essential in the 1920s that it increase its dependency on the United States.[6]

Canada's relationship with the United States had become almost as important as that with Britain, in practical if not in emotional terms. Former cabinet minister Clifford Sifton contended that Canada's "only real foreign policy must be with them [the United States] and the main business of Canada in foreign relations is to remain friendly with the United States while preserving its own self-respect." By the end of the war, Canada had set out on the road to formal independent relations with the United States, but the ad hoc wartime arrangements ended with the peace, and so the Canadian government pressed for the appointment of a Canadian minister at Washington. The British Colonial and Foreign offices dragged their feet, concerned with creating a precedent that would end with imperial disintegration, but American secretary of state Bainbridge Colby and Senator Gilbert M. Hitchcock, chairman of the Foreign Relations Committee, anticipated "good results" would follow from putting "us in direct relation with the Canadian Government." After negotiation among Ottawa, Washington, and London, the Borden government announced in 1920 that a separate Canadian minister would be appointed. In keeping with Canada's continued desire for a degree of British Empire unity, the new minister would serve in the additional capacity of second-in-command of the British embassy and "also speak as a representative of the Empire though primarily as a Canadian." The Conservative government was defeated before such a hybrid ambassador could be appointed.[7]

Canadian foreign policy underwent an important transition when Liberal prime minister William Lyon Mackenzie King took office in January 1921. King rejected a dual assignment for a Canadian representative in Washington; better, he suggested, to "let British diplomatists manage British affairs and let us manage our own affairs." Greater Canadian autonomy was a consistent theme of King's long prime ministerships (1922–30, 1935–48). Representative of the change was the appointment of Queen's University political economist O. D. Skelton as under secretary of the fledgling Department of External Affairs and the most powerful civil servant in the King government. Even more than King, Skelton sought a Canadian external policy autonomous of the British Colonial and Foreign offices. Their approach was critical to the emergence of a more independent, bilateral U.S.-Canada relationship. But because public opinion and his own cabinet were divided on the matter, King waited five years to establish separate Canadian representation in Washington.[8]

Instead, Mackenzie King's first venture in diplomacy was a personal trip to Washington in July 1922 with the ostensible purpose of revising the Rush-Bagot agreement of 1817 on Great Lakes naval armament. The *New York Times* pointed out that "there has been no suggestion formally from this [Harding] administration that modification was considered necessary," and no new agreement came about. It was the visit itself that interested King. He dropped in on Secretary of State Charles Evans Hughes, chatted with President Harding, and issued a statement to the press that Canadian-American friendship was "an object lesson to the continents of Europe and Asia of New World methods in the maintenance of international peace." The trip was an example of what would become King's favorite technique for conducting Canadian-American relations: during his twenty-three years as prime minister he was to make twenty-four such visits for "summit diplomacy" with Presidents Coolidge, Roosevelt, and Truman.[9]

The real and symbolic significance that King attached to the United States in Canada's external policy was demonstrated again in March 1923 when he chose Washington as the place to establish a historic precedent, the signing of a treaty between a dominion and a foreign state without the cosignature of a representative of the British government. The treaty concerned was yet another attempt to resolve the neverending fisheries disputes, for the U.S. Senate had rejected two bilateral treaties dealing with the protection of the Pacific salmon and halibut fisheries. King seized on the renegotiated Pacific Halibut Treaty as a step toward a broader diplomatic goal of an independent Canadian voice in Washington. Charles Evans Hughes signed for the United States; with the acquiescence of the British government, Canadian minister of marine and fisheries Ernest Lapointe ignored the objections of the British ambassador and signed the treaty alone. "This may turn out to be a very significant day in the history of relations between Canada and the United States," Hughes is alleged to have commented, but discussion in the U.S. Senate contained no hint of any recognition of Canada and instead described the treaty as a "convention between the United States and Great Britain." The only extensive news coverage the agreement received was in British Columbia and Washington State, where fishermen cared more about the halibut than the constitutional precedent.[10]

A more portentious constitutional moment came three years later, when the report of the Imperial Conference of 1926 defined Canada and the other British Dominions as "autonomous Communities within the British Empire, in no way subordinate [to Britain], . . . though united by a common allegiance to the crown." Mackenzie King waited for this declaration to announce that there would at last be formal Canadian representation in Washington. The 1920 formula in which the Canadian minister would be second-in-command of the British embassy was forgotten: the new appointee would represent only Canada. To demonstrate to Britain and the United States that Canada still valued its British connection, the terms "minister" and "legation" were used instead of "ambassador" and "embassy," and the new minister, Toronto industrialist Vincent Massey, was appointed via London through appropriate Privy Council and Royal channels. Massey was chosen in part for his Oxford training and his anglophilia—he and his wife, Alice, went to England to purchase all the furnishings for the new Canadian legation house—and he worked closely with British ambassador Sir Esme Howard, creating in practice the sort of British-Canadian cooperation in Washington that Borden had once envisaged. Massey soon voiced the Canadian lament that Americans were ignorant about their northern neighbor. When he presented his credentials in February 1927 to Calvin Coolidge—who had been born and raised in the border state of Vermont and spent his entire political career in Massachusetts—the President asked if Massey's hometown of Toronto were anywhere near Lake Ontario! Coolidge initially dismissed the idea of a U.S. legation in Ottawa, arguing that the diplomats would have nothing to do, but Massey's arrival prompted reciprocal action. In June 1927, William Phillips, a career foreign service officer and former American ambassador to Belgium, arrived as the first U.S. minister to Canada. This formal exchange of diplomatic representatives marked the culmination of two decades of gradual transition to truly Canadian-American relations, and the energy, abilities, and commitment of Massey and Phillips cemented ties of state between the two neighbors during their three years in office. The varying circumstances of their appointments, however, showed how much more important the Canadian-American relationship was to the smaller neighbor than it was to the larger one.[11]

The most contentious issues that the two legations faced were the ongoing problems created by attempts to prohibit the sale of alcohol. Prohibition was a last legacy of the vanished idealism of progressive reform, and both Canada and the United States attempted it. In Canada, like so many other things, liquor was a provincial responsibility; accordingly, the attempt was more easily abandoned. Quebec never declared itself dry, and seven of the other eight provinces returned rapidly to varying degrees of moisture during the 1920s. The United States imposed prohibition on a national scale in 1919 by the Eighteenth Amendment to the Constitution. The "noble experiment" was a disaster from the outset, for the Volstead Act that Congress passed to implement the arid millennium was virtually unenforceable. Instead the act became an economic windfall for Canada, as entrepreneurs on both sides of the international boundary immediately understood that vast profits awaited those who connected legal Canadian liquor with thirsty American throats. Prohibition-era earnings founded several Canadian fortunes, and launched Canadian distillers to North American dominance in the industry. Some of the profits were made legitimately from increased tourism, as Canadian cities attracted U.S. vacationers and convention-goers. Winnipeg, Manitoba, advertised itself in the United States Midwest as "the city of snowballs and highballs." Much greater profits were made when Canadian "rum-runners" exported liquor to American "bootleggers." Canada, reported the *Ladies' Home Journal,* was "the headwaters of the Niagara of booze"—a million gallons of spirits a year—that was drowning prohibition in the republic. But prohibitionists refused to countenance repeal; prohibition came to stand for the rearguard action rural and small-town America fought against the forces of urbanization and modernism. Organized into a powerful lobby called the Anti-Saloon League, American drys demanded that Washington enforce its own laws.[12]

Washington asked frequently for Ottawa's help. Prohibition enforcement was the largest single subject in U.S.-Canada diplomatic correspondence during the fourteen years of the Eighteenth Amendment. American officials requested that Canada (and Britain) deny shipping clearances to cargoes of alcoholic beverages which might wind up in the United States. The Canadian public was openly unsympathetic to such requests, as was an *Ottawa Journal* editorial that suggested that "U.S. enforcement, like charity, should begin at home." It was legal to distill whisky and brew beer in Canada and legal to export them. If some of the liquor Canadian customs cleared for export wound up in the United States, Canada admitted no wrongdoing. Chicago gangster Al Capone followed this example; "I don't even know what street Canada's on," he told a grand jury curious about the origins of the alcohol in his speakeasies. Canada dragged its feet on the question of clearances for liquor exports to the United States until the end of the decade. After informal bilateral discussions in Montreal in 1929—informal so that the United States could avoid looking like a bully and Canada avoid appearing to give in—Canada accepted the inevitable. In 1930, Prime Minister King himself grudgingly introduced legislation to ban liquor to countries under prohibition.[13]

Both before and after the ban, the illegal traffic in liquor resulted inevitably in high-speed automobile chases and high-seas pursuits of Canadian rumrunners by U.S. law enforcement agencies. Equally inevitably, diplomatic disputes between Canada and the United States followed. The United States won a treaty in 1924 extending the right of search on the seas from three miles to twelve, but in a number of cases, overzealous American Coast Guard captains went well beyond even the twelve-mile limit. The most acrimonious of these was the sinking in 1929 of the Canadian rumrunning schooner *I'm Alone* by the USS *Dexter*, two hundred miles from the Louisiana coast in the Gulf of Mexico. Canadian newspaper accounts emphasized that the *I'm Alone*'s captain, Jack Randell, was a Royal Navy veteran decorated for bravery during World War I, and that the United States, "the great protagonist of . . . freedom of the seas," had become "the bully of the high seas." American papers praised the Coast Guard for standing up to "foreign bootleggers." The State Department at first officially informed the British embassy in Washington before being firmly redirected to the Canadian legation. If nothing else, prohibition gently reminded the United States government that Canada was no longer simply a British colony to be dealt with through London.[14]

Economic Continentalism

The United States and Canadian economies followed parallel tracks in the aftermath of World War I. Thirty percent inflation in 1919 was followed by sudden contraction in 1920 and by the sharpest short-term economic downturn either country had yet experienced. Recovery came in 1922 in the United States and followed more slowly in Canada because the U.S. Fordney-McCumber tariff impeded Canadian exports. The recovery heralded an unprecedented economic expansion that in both countries lasted until the end of the decade, long enough for President Herbert Hoover to declare that the United States was close to "the final triumph over poverty." The way in which Canada's business cycle echoed that of its larger trading partner was a pattern that the 1920s accentuated, a pattern later commentators would describe with a medical metaphor. When the United States was in good economic health, went the analogy, so was Canada; if the American economy caught cold, they quipped, the Canadian economy developed pneumonia.[15]

Canada's share of the new economic era was created by a resource boom that was inspired by demand in the United States and carried out in part with imported American capital. Growth of Canada's newsprint paper industry, for example, was tied to the growth in circulation and size of the American newspapers, in particular the massive weekend editions: the Sunday *Chicago Tribune,* for example, required fifty thousand tons of newsprint a year from the *Tribune* corporation's Quebec mill. Canadian provincial governments refused to allow the export of unprocessed pulpwood to make newsprint in the United States, so that Americans had to buy newsprint from Canadians, or, like Colonel John McCormack, owner of the *Tribune,* come to Canada to manufacture it. By 1929, over a third of Canada's pulp and paper industry was owned and controlled by American capital. Unrestricted access for Canadian newsprint to the United States market was guaranteed by the Underwood Tariff Act, which was passed by Congress in 1913 and eliminated the import duty on newsprint. American publishers used the power of their newspapers to protect this privilege; even in the protectionist atmosphere of the 1920s, Republican Congresses never dared to reimpose the duty.[16]

As with newsprint, demand for Canadian base metals came primarily from the United States; the automobile, electrical, and radio industries were heavy users of copper, nickel, lead, and zinc. Most of the instruments mining engineers used to discover ore deposits also originated in the United States. The creation of a large-scale mining and smelting enterprise required large amounts of capital, much of which was imported from the United States. The two largest copper-gold deposits opened during the 1920s were both controlled by the

United States: Hudson Bay Mining and Smelting, in Manitoba, by the H. P. Whitney Company of New York, and Noranda Mines, in Quebec, by a syndicate that included a Rockefeller and a Du Pont. By 1930, 40 percent of mineral production in Canada was in the hands of American companies. Canadian politicians, national and provincial, welcomed foreign capitalists and assisted them with the necessary infrastructure of railways and hydroelectric power plants. The generating potential of Canada's northern rivers was one of the attractions to United States investment; hydropower inspired American multimillionaires James B. Duke and Andrew W. Mellon to bring the Aluminum Company of America to Quebec in 1924.[17]

American capital went into Canada's secondary manufacturing sector as well, in particular into the rapidly expanding auto industry. Next to the United States, Canada had the highest per capita registration of motor vehicles in the world. Canadian automobile ownership would have been even greater had there not been an ad valorem Canadian protective tariff of 35 percent on imported passenger cars. But the tariff did what it was intended to do, encouraging American auto makers to establish branch plants in Canada. The president of Studebaker bluntly explained that his company assembled cars in Canada "purely because of the tariff." Studebaker, Packard, Willys-Overland, and the small American manufacturers only assembled cars in Canada; Ford, General Motors, and Chrysler established factories that actually built automobiles. This enabled them to take advantage of the preferential duties allowed by Canada's membership in the Empire-Commonwealth to export cars to Britain, Australia, New Zealand, South Africa, and the West Indies. The auto industry was unusual among Canadian manufacturing industries in that almost one-third of its products were sold outside the domestic market.[18]

As a "miniature replica" of the American auto industry, Canadian automobile production followed the trend of the 1920s toward concentration into a small number of very large corporations. Every independent Canadian auto maker vanished. The McLaughlin Motor Car Company of Oshawa, Ontario, most successful among Canada's auto pioneers, merged with General Motors in November 1918 and renamed its product the McLaughlin-Buick. By 1930, three of every four cars made in Canada were Ford, General Motors, or Chrysler products; a new car rolled off the Ford assembly line in Walkerville, Ontario, every three minutes. Hundreds of small U.S. manufacturers also failed to survive, but "automotive amalgamation" illustrated the problems of Canada's manufacturing economy that made it particularly vulnerable to the phenomenon. As the owner of a Canadian company absorbed by General Motors explained, "in Canada . . . the problems of distribution are so severe on account of the tremendous distance over which a product must be scattered to meet the market of a small population. . . . That is why the successful companies of Canada have found it necessary to affiliate themselves with American interests, because with our small and limited outputs it is impossible to carry the tremendous burden of engineering expenses."[19]

American business had no fears about Canada as a source of supply for raw materials or as a market; it was also a place to carry out monopolistic activities that would have been illegal in the United States because of stronger American antitrust laws. By the 1918 Webb-Pomerone Act, Congress made it legal for U.S. corporations to violate those laws in their operations abroad. Canada scarcely seemed alien to American capitalists used to the vagaries investment in Latin America. As historian Mira Wilkins puts it, "governments were stable and friendly . . . people, institutions, values, and customs were similar . . . risks [were] minimal." Food processors such as Swift, Borden, Kellogg, and Kraft even found that "tastes seemed similar to those in the United States." Coca Cola discovered that "climatic . . . and racial factors"—cold weather and French Canadians—didn't hurt the sales of Coke. Canadians actually enjoyed "the pause that refreshes" more often per capita than Americans did, and Canadian sales more than doubled between 1926 and 1929, until the Montreal bottling plant became the second largest in the world.[20]

Canadian development had always been financed in part by foreign investment, and in relative terms, Canada was actually somewhat less reliant on foreign investment in the interwar period than it had been before 1914; during the 1920s, however, foreign capital was extremely important in absolute terms in the four industries that grew dramatically: pulp and paper, mining and smelting, hydroelectricity, and automobile manufacturing. What was most significant about foreign investment of the twenties was that both its source and its nature changed. Great Britain, Canada's "mother country," was displaced by the United States as Canada's principal creditor sometime in 1922, when American investment exceeded British for the first time; the American advantage continued to widen thereafter. American investment in Canada continued to differ from British in that a greater proportion of it was *direct* investment ("subsidiaries and branch plants controlled by externally based parent corporations") than *portfolio* investment ("the import of foreign capital by the sale of bonds or debentures or non-controlling equity stock"). The *Journal of the Canadian Bankers' Association* explained the difference to its readers with a concrete example: "the capital for Canadian railways has come chiefly from England, and the lenders remained at home; the capital for mining . . . has come largely from the United States, and the investors have often come with it in person to see it put into the ground." British capital had rarely been used to establish branch plants; American capital owned 466 of them in 1918 and established 641 more in the next twelve years. British portfolio investments in the form of bonds or common stock could expire or be patriated; American direct investments remained and grew larger from the profits earned in Canada. The expansion of the American-owned automobile industry, for example, was financed primarily by reinvested earnings in Canada, not by actual exports of American capital; thus American control increased even if the international flow of investment slackened. As of 1930, one-fifth of the "book value" of Canadian industry and more than two-fifths of mining, smelting, and petroleum was controlled by American firms.[21]

A half-century later, economists began to suggest that heavy reliance on U.S. direct investment had stunted the development of the Canadian economy. They argued that the American companies that came to Canada exported raw materials with little processing in Canada and frustrated Canadian attempts to expand their country's secondary manufacturing industries: U.S. capital put U.S. interests first. As Jose Igartua has put it, "resource regions of Canada were simple pawns on the continental, even global, chessboard of American corporate capitalism, . . . [and] Canadian capitalists were not very formidable knights." But during the 1920s, serious criticism of the growing American economic presence in Canada was seldom heard. Old Tory businessmen grumbled about "the absence of guts" of Canadian entrepreneurs in the face of the American challenge, and the handful of Labour members of Parliament lamented Canadians' role as "hewers of wood and drawers of water to American capitalists," but their views were not representative of Canada's business community or its AFL-affiliated labor movement. The most persistent critique of American investment came from French-Canadian nationalists, concerned about the effects of urbanization and industrialization on Quebec society. No critic offered Canadians a serious alternative path to economic development; instead, textbook descriptions of the Canadian economy assured students that the importation of capital from the United States was but a temporary phase in Canada's rise to its predestined industrial might. Annexation no longer frightened anyone. "The [American] flag," concluded the *Regina Leader,* "does not follow cash." The owners of the branch plants, far from advocating continental economic unity, became the most vociferous defenders of the protective tariff; after all, that was why they had come to Canada in the first place. Canada raised no barriers to continued U.S. investment and expressed less concern about it than any other country in which American corporations did business. In July 1923, Warren G. Harding made the first visit to Canada by a president in office. Before a crowd of forty thousand in Vancouver, he praised Canada's cooperativeness. "We think the same thoughts, live the same lives and cherish the same aspirations. . . . Since the Armistice . . . approximately $2,500,000,000 has found its way from the United States into Canada for investment. That is a huge sum of money and I have no doubt it is employed safely for us and helpfully for you."[22]

The "Mingling" of the Canadian and American Peoples

In the 1920s, what most disturbed Canadians about the United States was its seeming attraction to so many of their countrypeople, for during that decade the southward flow of population resumed at almost the levels of the 1880s. One of the justifications for actively seeking U.S. investment, as it had been a half-century earlier, was to create economic growth to give Canadians jobs at home. "Import dollars and keep our children," was how Quebec's premier Louis-Alexandre Taschereau put it; better "to import American dollars than to export Canadians to the United States." But the inflow of capital failed to check the outflow of people. The U.S. Immigration Act of 1921 imposed quotas on Europeans but exempted Canadians from restrictions, despite some congressional demands that they be included. By 1923, observers noted that "the tide is once more flowing freely," and U.S. immigration statistics record over a million arrivals from Canada between 1919 and 1930. Canadians increased from about 6 percent of total immigration into the United States to more than 25 percent. These statistics exaggerate the number of permanent migrants—more sophisticated calculations show net migration from Canada to the United States at about 385,000—but even so, this was 4.3 percent of the total Canadian population. In the 1930 U.S. census, the 1.3 million Canadian-born were the third largest group of foreign-born, after only Germans and Italians.[23]

As before, the émigrés went south for work. *Canadian Forum* speculated that "there is not a man in Canada under fifty years of age who would not pack up and move to the States tomorrow if he got a good business offer." American employers found Canadians to be "reliable" employees, which meant, wrote a sarcastic Canadian commentator, "that they are more afraid of losing their jobs than are native-born Americans." A survey for the Canadian magazine *Maclean's* reported that eight out of ten of the emigrants preferred Canada but chose the United States for "better opportunities." Before World War I, unskilled workers and farm families had made up most of the exodus from Canada; after 1920, skilled workers and the well-educated accompanied them in greater numbers, like band leader Guy Lombardo and his "Royal Canadians," university professor John Kenneth Galbraith, and bank robber Alvin Karpis—a future "Public Enemy Number One." Because American branch plants dominated the advanced sectors of the Canadian economy, industrial research was done in the home laboratories of the parent corporations; thus Canada lost a substantial percentage of the "trained brains" graduated each year from her universities. *Maclean's* discovered that between 1919 and 1926, 11 percent of University of Toronto graduates, 15 percent of Western Ontario graduates, and 36 percent of graduates from Nova Scotia's Acadia University had moved to the United States. In medicine and engineering, the figures were substantially higher. Canada was losing, commented J. B. Brebner, "if not the cream, at least the top milk of her population." The best American graduate schools attracted some of the best young Canadian scholars, many of whom took academic appointments in the United States after they completed their doctorates. In 1927, six hundred Canadians taught in U.S. universities, twice as many as twenty years earlier. Although this was often cited as an example of "intellectual internationalism," writes historian Carl Berger, "it was emphatically a one-way street": very few American students or professors came to Canada.[24]

Cultural "Imperialism" and Cultural Sovereignty

Myriad other cultural forces drew Canada closer to the United States after World War I. The middle-aged members of the Imperial Order of Daughters of the Empire (IODE) worried because "hundreds of energetic young women" were joining the "Junior League" rather than the IODE. Thousands of their husbands attended the weekly luncheon of a Canadian chapter of an American "service" club. Rotary had been the first to come north in 1920; by 1928 it had eighty-five Canadian chapters. During the twenties, Rotary was joined by the Lions, Kiwanis, and Gyro clubs, each of which expanded rapidly throughout Canada. Clubs in Canadian provinces were linked with those in adjoining American states; a Gyro pamphlet proudly proclaimed that the club "recognizes no boundary between the United States of America and the Dominion of Canada." Every summer at binational conventions, Rotarians, Gyros, Lions, and Kiwanians met in happy celebration of the "invisible border" and babbled boosterish cant about "the harmonious relationship that has always existed between the United States and Canada." More alarming to cultural nationalists than the vapid Babbittry of the service clubs was the web spun north of the border by American radio programs, spectator sports, magazines, and movies. Although American mass culture touched every nation-state on the planet to some degree, Canada's situation would remain unique. First, Canada's exposure is not mediated by language: 70 percent of its population shares a language with the United States. Second, English Canadians had no long history of national existence on which to build a national identity: like Americans, they trace their ideological roots back to seventeenth-century England. Finally, Canadian exposure to U.S. mass culture is not mitigated by distance: 80 percent of the Canadian population lives within sixty miles of the U.S. border.[25]

This explains why Canada has been in quest of "cultural sovereignty" almost as long as America has been exporting popular culture. Prodded by a nationalist intelligentsia concerned with Canadian national identity, and by Canadian cultural industries seeking the same sheltered market enjoyed by other Canadian manufacturers, successive governments have groped to cope with American mass culture. The invariable first step has been to investigate. After royal commissions or parliamentary committees have issued weighty reports, one of two types of legislation usually follows: attempts to *protect* Canadian cultural industries with regulatory or tariff barriers, and attempts to *promote* indigenous Canadian mass culture through subsidies or government-sponsored creation of cultural infrastructure. Policies have not always been clear-cut; protectionist and promotional solutions were sometimes applied alternately or even simultaneously.

Canada directed its first unambiguously protective cultural legislation against American magazines. In 1925, each of four American magazines had larger circulations than the leading Canadian journal (then as now *Maclean's*) and the *Saturday Evening Post* rubbed salt into the circulatory wounds of its Canadian competitors by accurately describing itself as "Canada's best-selling magazine." The subsequent campaign against American magazines illustrates the typical alignment of commercial and cultural forces behind campaigns for cultural sovereignty. Publishing entrepreneurs seeking an advantage against their American competitors combined with a nationalist intelligentsia who argued that American magazines were "a menace to Canadian ideals and to the moral development of the youth of this country." It was difficult to portray *Saturday Evening Post* or *Ladies' Home Journal* as immoral influences, so the target became "pulp" magazines imported from the United States, with such titles as *Black Mask, Dime Detective,* and *Spicy Adventure,* "the off-scourings of the moral sewers of human life, . . . a putrid flood of undisguised filth." Aroused Canadians demanded that something be done "to dam this trash flowing over the border." The King Liberal government evaded demands for a magazine tariff in the 1920s by offering Canadian publishers a tax incentive, a "drawback" on the import duties they paid on special grades of papers. In 1930, R. B. Bennett's new Conservative government obliged the Magazine Publisher's Association of Canada with a tariff that quickly had the desired effect: by the mid-1930s, Canadian circulation was up 65 percent and that of American magazines down an equal amount.[26]

Legislation to promote alternative mass cultural industries offered an alternative to protection. The first direct mass cultural subsidy was made in 1903, when the Canadian government provided Canadian Associated Press, a newspaper wire service, with an annual grant of sixty thousand dollars to distribute news from Britain that had been overlooked by American-based Associated Press, from whose wires all Canadian dailies received their European news. The subsidy failed to accomplish its purpose, and the experiment ended in 1910. Unlike their magazines, the newspapers Canadians read were owned and published in Canada, but after World War I, Canadian dailies became much more like their American counterparts. Wire services reinforced homogeneity, using the new teletype machine to speed stories simultaneously to a network of subscribing newspapers, which reprinted them with little editing or rewriting. Canadian newspapers, whether English or French, drew virtually all of their international news from Associated Press and United Press. Thus Canadian readers learned about British-American relations from stories written in the United States and viewed their own delegates to the League of Nations through the eyes of American correspondents in Geneva in stories that reflected America's attitude as an isolationist nonmember. Canadian front pages emulated U.S. dailies by using larger photos, bolder type, and banner headlines to report sports, crime, and the marital problems of movie stars. Editors padded the inside pages with columns on bridge, hobbies, auto repair, and personal advice distributed by United States syndicates. The most popular new feature was the American "comics," black-and-white strips on weekdays and a color section on Saturday—Canada was not yet ready for newspapers on the Christian sabbath. Circulation of the *Toronto Star Weekly* doubled when it acquired *Bringing Up Father, Barney Google, Mutt and Jeff,* and five other American strips in 1923. The audience for the comics was not restricted to children or to the semiliterate; Prime Minister Mackenzie King was said never to miss his favorite strip, *Tillie the Toiler*.[27]

American mass culture dominated the sports pages as well, as journalists hammered larger-than-life heroes out of Babe Ruth, Jack Dempsey, and Bobby Jones. Just as with the comic strips, America's sports heroes became Canada's, and America's national sport became the Canadian summer game. As S. F. Wise notes bitterly, "mesmerized by baseball's big league glamour, and spoon-fed by the American wire services, sports editors and reporters gave major coverage to baseball at the expense of lacrosse," with the result that both professional and senior amateur lacrosse became extinct in the interwar years. Every Canadian community had an amateur baseball team, and cities and larger towns had franchises in minor professional leagues. "Organized baseball had been a good thing for the towns that have participated," wrote "Knotty" Lee, manager of the Brantford, Ontario,

Red Sox of the Michigan-Ontario League. Large crowds followed the fortunes of the Montreal Royals and Toronto Maple Leafs, who played in the International League, one step below the majors. Toronto's 1926 victory over Louisville in the Little World Series occasioned an outpouring of local and national pride, pride accented because one Maple Leaf outfielder, Lionel Conacher, was actually a Canadian! Yet every Canadian ball fan reserved the deepest love for a team in the American or National League. By the midtwenties baseball's World Series had become Canada's greatest "national" sporting event, with crowds packed in front of newspaper offices to watch the games charted out on a scale-model diamond from a wire-service description.[28]

During the 1920s, American money also revolutionized Canadian hockey. In 1924, Boston millionaire Charles Adams bought the first U.S. franchise of the National Hockey League (NHL). The Bruins won only six of thirty games on the ice but were champions at the box office. Before the next season began, bootlegging baron William V. "Big Bill" Dwyer bought the Hamilton Tigers and moved them into the new Madison Square Garden as the New York Americans. Dwyer's publicity man, Paul Galico, ignored hockey's grace, speed, and finesse to emphasize its violence: played by "men with clubs in their hands and knives lashed to their feet," it was "almost a certainty that someone will . . . fleck the ice with a generous contribution of gore." New York drew two hundred thousand customers to their seventeen home games—more than the combined attendance of any four cities of the Western Canada Hockey League. It was painfully obvious that such teams as the Saskatoon Sheiks would find the new hockey era too rich for their blood. "How long will Canada be able to hold its teams?," asked a Toronto sportswriter, who predicted that "star puck chasers will gravitate to the place where they can fatten their exchequers." When the NHL awarded franchises to a Chicago financier, a New York coffee tycoon, and a Detroit syndicate that included a Ford and a Kresge among its members, hockey entrepreneurs in small Canadian cities sold such stars as Eddie Shore and Dick Irvin to the U.S.-based teams before the players could "jump" themselves. The Stanley Cup, emblem of the championship of Canadian hockey, became in

1927 the permanent possession of the "National" Hockey League, and Canada's game had been transformed into a continental commercial spectacle. Only four of the ten NHL teams were based in Canada, and the league's "Canadian" division was brought up to full strength by adding the New York Americans! In 1928, the New York Rangers became the first of the American NHL teams to win the cup and Governor General Lord Stanley's trophy to honor "the leading hockey club in Canada" began to spend time in the United States.[29]

Government intervention to protect Canadian commercial sport lay half a century in the future. What became the most characteristic Canadian promotional response to the conundrum of cultural sovereignty was the approach adopted in broadcasting: the creation of publicly financed infrastructure. Only a month after station KDKA Pittsburgh baptized the American airwaves with a broadcast of the 1920 presidential election, radio in Canada began with station CFCF Montreal, but subsequent development of the medium in the United States was much more rapid. During the next decade, the fundamental decisions that would create the American broadcasting industry were taken: radio was to be a private enterprise supported financially by the sale of advertising time, with the government's role limited to regulation by the Federal Radio Commission. Ten years after KDKA's inaugural broadcast, there were 612 stations operating in the United States, and two private networks had spread across America, the National Broadcasting Company and the Columbia Broadcasting System. In Canada, both business and governments moved more slowly, unwilling to decide whether Canada should follow the private commercial model of the United States or make radio broadcasting a public noncommercial monopoly as in Britain.[30]

By a U.S.-Canada agreement reached in 1924, Canada obtained exclusive use of six frequencies and partial use of another eleven of the ninety-five then in operation. Canadian broadcasters grumbled that "86 percent of the impulse carrying power of the atmosphere" had been handed over to extol "the superior qualities of American soap, pills and jazz"; the weak signals of their small transmitters wouldn't reach many parts of rural Canada, while in others interference from more powerful American stations drowned them out. Canadians bought 297,000 radios by 1929, but most of them were tuned to American stations. Even the mounties at northern detachments of the Royal Canadian Mounted Police got their daily bulletins over KDKA Pittsburgh. More than reception alone influenced these choices. Canadian stations offered news, lectures, or recorded music, while the American network stations featured comedy, drama, and live variety. Canadian listeners quickly made clear that they preferred such American shows as "Amos and Andy" to Canadian programs such as "Uncle Dick's Talks for Boys and Girls." Commercial stations in Canada soon decided that the best way to compete with American stations was to buy American shows to broadcast themselves. CFRB Toronto affiliated with CBS, CKGW Toronto countered by joining the NBC network, and stations in other cities hurried to follow. By the end of the twenties, an estimated 80 percent of the programs Canadians listened to were American. As one writer protested, "Canada's radio consciousness" was "throwing us all the more under United States influence."[31]

The Liberal King government's solution was to refer the broadcasting question to a royal commission, chaired by a bank president, Sir John Aird. Aird and his fellow commissioners visited Europe and the United States and held public hearings before concluding that broadcasting in Canada should be a public monopoly with strictly limited commercial content. The Canadian Radio League, which lobbied for the report's adoption, rallied extensive popular support for public broadcasting with the slogan "Britannia rules the waves—shall Columbia rule the wavelengths?" To Canadians with reservations about public enterprise, league spokespersons explained that the choice was either "the State or the United States!" The creation in 1932 of the Canadian Radio Broadcasting Commission, which became the Canadian Broadcasting Corporation (CBC) in 1936, marks the most visible difference between the cultural industries of Canada and the United States: Canada has a publicly owned and publicly financed national broadcasting system and the United States does not. Significantly, however, the CBC was not given a monopoly; private broadcasting continued and flourished. Canadian broadcasting remained a mixed public and private enterprise, borrowing from both the British and the American answers to the radio question. American programs did not disappear. Among the most popular shows on the new coast-to-coast public radio network were those the CBC bought from NBC and CBS![32]

Canada found no satisfactory dam to repel the crest of the northbound tidal wave of American mass culture, the motion picture. On weekends in the mid-1920s, over a million Canadians sat in the dark in front of the screen, and 98 percent of the movies they watched were products of the suddenly famous Los Angeles suburb of Hollywood. Canada's small-scale feature film industry succumbed rapidly to Hollywood competition after World War I. It died for economic rather than artistic reasons, for a host of talented Canadians contributed to Hollywood's golden age: director Mack Sennett, producers Louis B. Mayer and Jack Warner, and too many performers to be counted. Gladys Smith—better known as "America's Sweetheart," Mary Pickford—learned her craft in Toronto, and Canadians won the first two Academy Awards for best actress, Norma Shearer of Westmount, Quebec, and Marie Dressler of Cobourg, Ontario. Perhaps the supreme irony was that Raymond Massey, Hollywood's best Abraham Lincoln, was Vincent Massey's younger brother! But American films dominated the screens of the world, not simply those of Canada. U.S. moviemakers gained a head start on Europe between 1914 and 1917 and consolidated their position by vertically integrating production, distribution, and marketing during the 1920s. Giant predatory Hollywood studios devoured Canada's independent Canadian producers not because they were Canadian but because they were independent. Within the American industry itself, the "Big Five"—Paramount, MGM, Warner Brothers, Fox, and RKO—produced 90 percent of all feature films by 1929. These major studios regarded Canada as part of their "domestic" box office, and they extended their distribution and marketing northward through Famous Players Canadian Corporation. Famous Players monopolized the giant "movie palaces" in prime urban downtown locations and forced independent theaters to "block book" films from the major studios if they were to have films to exhibit. The Canadian federal government used its toothless antimonopoly legislation—the Combines Investigation Act of 1923—to prepare a report on Famous Players, but a 1931 Ontario prosecution based on the evidence in the report was dismissed. The judge found Famous Players's practices to be ruthless but not technically illegal.[33]

Canada quickly came to terms with American cinematic supremacy. With no Canadian film industry to add a commercial voice, Canadian cultural nationalists met the American movie menace on moral terrain. Each Canadian province censored motion pictures, watching out for films that demeaned clergymen or marriage, and for "the revolver that every he-man seems to have on one hip." Some features were retitled: "The Golden Bed" and "Flames of Desire" became "Tomorrow's Bread" and "Strathmore" in Canada. Censors also snipped "spread-eagle Americanism"—closeups of the Stars and Stripes and movies in which the U.S. Army won the world war were particularly vulnerable to the scissors. Canadian elites worried that by holding authority figures up to ridicule, American movies might do more to inspire social unrest "than all the Bolshevist agitators." They need not have been concerned; during the Depression of the 1930s, Hollywood's "dream factory" became one of the most important buttresses of the status quo in both countries. Four provinces followed Britain's lead in enacting a quota requiring that a percentage of movies shown be filmed within the British Empire, but none of these quotas was ever actually imposed. Even staunch Anglo-imperialists admitted that "the Hollywood production was on the average vastly superior to the British." Instead, Canadian governments attempted to neutralize Hollywood by making their own movies. The Canadian Government Motion Picture Bureau (CGMPB) and provincial film agencies in British Columbia and Ontario were modest operations that made scenic documentaries which were virtuous but dull. When civil service pictures were screened, Canadian audiences headed to the lobby for popcorn; like moviegoers everywhere, they wanted entertainment not education, and the cinematic experiments of Ontario and British Columbia ended in the 1930s. The CGMPB survived to make a more substantial contribution after it was restructured as the National Film Board in 1939.[34]

Americans found it difficult to take Canadian complaints about movies, magazines, and radio seriously. Historian Emily Rosenberg describes the ideology of Americans who dealt with foreign nations as "liberal-developmentalism": "the belief that other nations could and should replicate the American experience." To do this, foreigners had not only to welcome American trade and investment but also to accept "the free flow of information and culture." When Canada's Parliament first discussed restricting American magazines, for example, the *New York Times* laughed at Canadian fears of "cultural extinction" and invoked the First Amendment's promise of freedom of the press. "We have learned better, . . . the Canadians, too, may learn." If Canada did ban U.S. magazines, the *Times* suggested "an agreeable form of reciprocity. As Canada bootlegs rum to us, we could bootleg literature to Canada." The U.S. government and the industries concerned took Canadian cultural policies more seriously. Earnings from cultural exports were significant, so that the federal Department of Commerce cooperated with cultural exporters such as the Motion Picture Producers and Distributors of America (MPPDA) to keep foreign markets open, part of the process historian Michael Hogan has called government-business "associationalism." The State Department instructed American consuls in Canada (and everywhere else the United States did business) to monitor cultural nationalism closely. Canada's cultural concerns were invariably interpreted as masks for economic protectionism—which they sometimes were—but Americans were seldom able to distinguish economic protectionism from genuine concerns about culture and nationality. The State Department and the MPPDA, for example, protested provincial movie censorship as a cultural trade barrier.[35]

By and large, however, Canada's timid cultural nationalism gave the United States little to worry about compared to that of Britain, and not all of Canada's cultural sovereignty policies were perceived as equally threatening. Overt cultural protectionism usually drew an immediate response, but Canadian attempts to promote domestic mass culture (and domestic high culture, for that matter) were usually ignored because these attempts did not seriously threaten the profits of the U.S. exporters. The documentary niche chosen by the National Film Board represented no danger to Hollywood's domination of feature film production, nor did American broadcasters fear the demonstration effect of Canadian public radio. Corporate America showed a great deal more hostility to Ontario Hydro, the government-owned electrical power utility, than it did to experiments in public film production or broadcasting.[36]

Did the continentalization of popular culture prove that Canada was being turned into a cultural as well as an economic colony of the United States? Americanization, concluded the *Canadian Forum*, was "like baldness; once caught there is no escape from it." Yet in many respects Canada in the interwar period had a better sense of itself as a nation than it had ever had. To use sport as an example, Canadian football evolved under unique rules distinct from those used in the American game, even though teams hired American "imports" to help them win the national championship, the Grey Cup. Every Canadian fan knew that Vancouver sprinter Percy Williams, "the World's Fastest Human," had spurned U.S. colleges to train in Canada for his double gold medal performance at the 1928 Olympics, and that the Edmonton Grads had won seventeen consecutive North-American Women's basketball championships against the best the United States could send onto the court. And despite all the hot air about Canadian-American kinship, Canadians clung to their sense of national moral superiority, buttressed with negative stereotypes of the United States. The U.S. political and judicial systems were corrupt, and American society was immoral, violent, and materialistic. English and French Canadians, women and men, children and adults, businessmen and trade unionists shared these stereotypes. The *Canadian Unionist*, the newspaper of the All-Canadian Congress of Labour summed it up succinctly: the United States was a country "where murderers go unhanged . . . where prohibition is the rule and bootlegging has been the practice . . . where child labour laws will not hold water and where negroes may not vote." Viewed through eyes narrowed by such *a priori* reasoning, American mass culture did not inspire pledges of allegiance to the Stars and Stripes. Instead, concluded *Canada and Her Great Neighbor: A Sociological Survey of Opinions and Attitudes in Canada Concerning the United States,* it provided further evidence of things Canadians thought they already knew. American magazines, wire service news, radio programs, and movies left Canadian readers, listeners, and viewers "convinced of the depravity of Americans."[37]

As William Phillips, the first American minister to Canada, soon discovered, the "much-talked-of 'invisible border' was in fact a very real barrier." Exactly where Canada stood was difficult for the few Americans who gave it any thought to understand. Canada had become more autonomous from Great Britain and could be prickly about that autonomy. Yet the British Empire connection manifestly still mattered, and autonomy from Britain did not herald the absorption of the Dominion into the United States. As the short section on "Canadian Relations" in a text on U.S. foreign policy explained, "it is certain that if Canada ever achieves complete independence, it will not be for the purpose of joining the United States." One of the contributors to *Canada and Her Great Neighbor* suggested an answer: "Canadians are determined to be both a North American and a British nation, but above all a nation with a distinctive Canadian personality."[38]

5 Acquaintance to Alliance, 1930–1941

When Vincent Massey and William Phillips left their posts in 1930, modern state-to-state relations between Canada and the United States were firmly in place. Canadian governments had forged an independent diplomatic presence in Washington, and the U.S. legation in Ottawa was—in all but its name—the first foreign embassy in the Canadian capital. But the bilateral relationship extended well beyond this: both countries had shown a preference for conflict resolution outside diplomatic channels and away from the public gaze. During the 1920s, the International Joint Commission had quietly disposed of a dozen potentially thorny boundary waters and pollution issues; during the 1930s, it would resolve two dozen more. But if the means of settling disputes had evolved, the contentious issues themselves had remarkable resilience. The Great Depression struck the United States and Canada more severely than virtually any other countries on the globe, causing new problems and exacerbating old ones. Like economies, U.S.-Canadian relations follow cycles, and the early thirties marked a simultaneous interwar nadir for both. Yet after this low point, the relationship was rapidly restored and broadened in an atmosphere of escalating international tension as Germany, Italy, and Japan challenged the American and British world systems. The Statute of Westminster in 1931 made Canada technically autonomous within the British Empire, but Britain remained a significant third presence in U.S.-Canadian interaction. Canada had evolved from a pawn and a hostage in Anglo-American quarrels to a hoped-for active role as what historian Norman Hillmer describes as "a golden hinge, allowing the Anglo-American relationship to operate smoothly." Although no longer constitutionally bound to do so, Canada joined Britain in the war against Germany in September 1939. During the two years before the Japanese attack pushed America to war in December 1941, the United States and Canada—with Britain's blessing—built a formal alliance to defend the hemisphere. This alliance, like the long relationship from which it grew, was predicated upon geopolitical and economic realities more than cultural affinity.[1]

"Countless Irritations and Pin-pricks," 1930–1933

In June 1930, Canadian journalist Leslie Roberts warned readers of *Harper's Magazine* of an alarming increase in anti-Americanism in Canada, caused by the "thoughtlessness and intolerance of the United States toward its northern neighbor." Prohibition, product of "the bigotry of American die-hard-dries" demonstrated America's "contempt for Canadian feelings." There was grumbling in Parliament and in the press when the King government caved in to the American demand to ban liquor exports without receiving anything in return. "If a country like France or Italy asked us to do so we would refuse, and rightly so," protested Quebec member of Parliament Henri Bourassa; "We do it . . . because of the power of the American government to make good their claims upon us." King's concession did not end binational incidents over booze. The United States refused to agree to arbitrate the *I'm Alone* incident until 1932, claiming that the ship actually belonged to a Boston gangster. The Hoover administration toughened Volstead Act enforcement, so that the *I'm Alone* was joined on a growing list of unresolved problems by the sinking of the *Josephine K,* whose Nova Scotia skipper was killed by the Coast Guard. More provocative even than attacking Canadian ships on the high seas were "United States patrolmen [who] stalk their prey on Canadian soil and shoot to kill." When trigger-happy U.S. agents wounded Ontario bootlegger Arthur "Muskrat" Laframboise on the Canadian side of the Detroit River, newspapers chorused outrage. Canadian policemen, one editorial noted, could "catch rum-runners without firearms."[2]

Congress further offended Canadians in 1930 by imposing on them the same immigration requirements as those on migrants from outside the hemisphere. Accustomed to unregulated movement across the border, Canadians' racist sensitivities were offended when they had to "join Latvia and Japan on the quota list" if they wished to live and work in the United States. Entry to the United States from Canada now had to be made through a formal "port of entry" staffed with guards, customs officials, and immigration officers, all of whom had "the manners of longshoremen." Some fifteen thousand Ontarians who crossed daily to work in Detroit suddenly found themselves unemployed. The U.S. Department of Immigration began to unceremoniously deport those foreign-born who became public charges. Canadians were appalled by reports of naturalized Canadians being deported not to Canada but to their places of birth: in one case, U.S. authorities sent Vancouver journalist Herbert Upjohn from Los Angeles to Shanghai, "handcuffed to sixty Chinese." Over one hundred thousand Canadians returned voluntarily between 1930 and 1936, so that the balance of binational migration turned in Canada's favor. Canadians should have hailed the closing of the border as a demographic blessing: historian Yolande Lavoie estimates that by 1930, 2.75 million Canadian-born had emigrated to the United States, joined by an additional 2 million who came to Canada from Europe and remigrated to America. Allowing for the fertility of these vanished Canadians, Canada would have had a population of 16 million in 1931, rather than the 10.4 million actually counted in the Dominion census. Instead, Canadians lamented the lost opportunities in America. The member of Parliament for Windsor, Ontario, described the new regulations as one of several "serious points of friction" in bilateral relations; he was not the only Canadian to conclude "that our boasts of friendship are very extravagant, [but] in fact, our friendship is not as deep as we . . . are inclined to suggest."[3]

But the most grave of the "countless irritations and pin-pricks" that "Step-Uncle Sam" inflicted on Canada was the "Yankee tariff barriers [which] yearly mount higher and higher." In 1929, new Republican president Herbert Hoover courted the farm vote by promising still higher barriers against agricultural imports. Republican majorities in both houses of Congress happily surpassed the president's pledge: the Smoot-Hawley tariff of 1930 shut Canadian potatoes, beef, butter, and poultry out of United States markets. Before Congress passed the tariff, Prime Minister Mackenzie King quietly sent a series of emissaries to warn Hoover of Smoot-Hawley's serious economic and diplomatic effects. The *Literary Digest* and the *Nation* made the same case to the American public: Canada had replaced Britain as "the best customer of the U.S.A.," two-way trade was the largest between any two nations in the world, and Canada bought one-third more from the United States than it sold to that country. Why jeopardize this with a tariff war? Neither the president nor Congress was impressed; Canada had complained about the Fordney-McCumber tariff of 1922, and yet the 1920s had been a decade of unparalleled prosperity in both countries. Hoover sincerely believed that the United States could enjoy both a high tariff and increased international trade simultaneously.[4]

The president offered the prime minister an exchange: Canada would be exempted from the new tariffs in return for a Canadian promise to cooperate in one of Hoover's pet projects, the St. Lawrence Seaway to open the Great Lakes to oceangoing ships. The seaway would lower transportation costs to and from the U.S. Midwest and keep farmers voting Republican. King had his own domestic agenda, and opposition to a seaway from Canadian railroads and from the province of Quebec might have stopped King from accepting the proposal. But Hoover doomed the deal in advance by leaking the offer to the press. Whatever the president's intention, his clumsy revelation backed the prime minister into a corner. Trading a seaway for a tariff exemption would mean yielding to U.S. pressure before a binational audience. King did not worry when Conservative newspapers called him "yellow" for "scratching the big bird's bald head"; but when a Vancouver newspaper sympathetic to King's Liberal party described the exchange as "a bargain . . . unworthy of the dignity of the Canadian people," the prime minister understood that it was time to cater to his country's psychic need to stand up to Uncle Sam. King rejected Hoover's proposal to link the seaway and trade issues, and retaliated for Smoot-Hawley with countervailing tariff increases and additional levies on steel and on fruits and vegetables. Canada had fired the second shot in the North American theater of the international trade war that exacerbated the Great Depression.[5]

This counterattack did not save King's Liberals from defeat in the Canadian election of July 1930. As in 1911, the opposition Conservatives played the cards of strident economic nationalism and anti-American chauvinism with consummate skill. "Tens of thousands of American workmen are living on Canadian money," Conservative leader R. B. Bennett told his audiences, promising still-higher "red-blooded" tariffs. A Conservative government would stand up to "Mr. Hoover's rum-chasers" and end the indignities caused by prohibition enforcement. One Conservative candidate called Mackenzie King "the right-hand man of the American government" and urged voters to send him "back where he belongs—back to work in New York City for the Rockefeller foundation." Once in office, the new government's first actions were to pass a five-page list of tariff increases and to slam Canada's door against immigrants. The irony of Canadian anti-Americanism was never more obvious, for these Conservative policies were mirror images of Republican protectionism and nativism in the United States.[6]

Prime Minister Bennett proposed to replace vanished trade with the United States with expanded trade within the British Empire. He had scant success, however, in his attempts to reach reciprocal tariff agreements with Britain and the other Dominions. A much-publicized Imperial Economic Conference in Ottawa in 1932 aroused United States fears of a British Empire trading bloc, but its practical results were "pathetically small," economic historian Ian Drummond concludes. The United States need never have worried that its economic influence on Canada would diminish: even as tariff warfare and depression cut the total volume of U.S.-Canada trade in half in the early 1930s, the Canadian economy intertwined with the American. As *Forbes* magazine explained, a high Canadian tariff, even with British Empire preferences, was, "from the American angle . . . not so bad, after all." American exporters could easily out-hustle "the slow-going Britisher" for the Canadian market. "If worst comes to worst . . . , all that United States industry, following hundreds of examples, would need to do, is to establish more branch factories in Canada, get in on the protection to Canadian industry and, incidentally, avail itself of the present or coming policies of preference to manufacturers of any part of the British Empire." Operating in Canada was simplicity itself: "No questions would be asked and no conditions would be imposed" on American capital. Thus the Conservatives' rising tariff escalated the number of U.S. branch plants in Canada from 524 in 1929 to 816 in 1936. Already established branch factories, such as those of Ford, Chrysler, and General Motors, continued to grow without the actual export of capital from the United States. A study in 1940 found that "the Canadian automotive industry has been almost entirely financed by earnings in Canada reinvested under the supervision of the American concerns." The study *Canadian-American Industry,* published in 1936, found that binational direct investment was not all one way. The short chapter "Canadian Industry in the U.S." identified 110 Canadian companies that operated in the United States and emphasized that "in proportion to Canada's wealth and population, her direct investment in the United States is even larger" than U.S. investment in Canada. As a proportion of total investment, however, it was infinitesimal. In Canada, on the other hand, American companies controlled a quarter of manufacturing in Canada, a third of the mining, and two-thirds of the petroleum industry.[7]

That this situation caused no alarm to Canada's Conservative government illustrates the limits of its anti-Americanism. As did every prime minister before him, R. B. Bennett understood the importance of good relations with the United States. As a State Department briefing paper explained to President Hoover before he received the prime minister in Washington in 1931: "for political reasons . . . Mr. Bennett frequently finds it advisable to criticize us despite the fact that he personally is friendly to this country." True to this analysis, Bennett tried to keep his brief meeting with the president almost a secret, refusing the already traditional photographs on the White House lawn; President Hoover's terse press release thanked "Mr. Bennet" for his visit. Hoover's ignorance of and indifference to Canada contributed a dimension of difficulty to U.S.-Canadian relations, as did Bennett's abrasive personal manner, but long-standing circumstances, not personalities, were at the root of bilateral problems. The striking asymmetry of national power was all too conspicuous, and the relationship was infinitely more significant to Canada than to the United States. Canadians were hypersensitive to these facts and Americans oblivious to them. Diplomatic appointments and state visits illustrate this imbalance. Bennett had denounced the opening of a Canadian mission in Washington in 1927 as "separation . . . the end of our connection with the Empire," but in 1931, he appointed his advisor and brother-in-law, William D. Herridge, to replace Vincent Massey as minister to the United States. The political hacks Hoover chose to succeed William Phillips were without discernible competence, an indication of how lightly the White House took the new legation in Ottawa. In 1927, Governor General Lord Willingdon had made an official visit to Washington as Canada's head of state, but neither Calvin Coolidge nor Herbert Hoover found time to accept Ottawa's reciprocal invitation. Offended that Hoover was preoccupied with Latin America yet ignored Canada, the *Ottawa Citizen* advised the president to "look North. If the goodwill of South America is worth cultivating, surely the goodwill of Canada is worth keeping."[8]

There were in fact notable joint initiatives during Hoover's and Bennett's two-year overlap in office. In 1932, at Britain's request, Canada contributed its entire Pacific Fleet of two destroyers to help the United States prop up the dictatorship in El Salvador against a revolution. And on one critical issue on which previous presidents and prime ministers had failed, Hoover and Bennett succeeded: they agreed to build a St. Lawrence seaway. The seaway had been the principal subject of their semisecret discussion in 1931, and a treaty was amicably negotiated and duly signed in July 1932 by W. D. Herridge and American secretary of state Henry L. Stimson. Had the seaway been constructed as a vast antidepression public works project and opened with pomp and circumstance during King George VI's visit to North America in 1939, Hoover and Bennett might be hailed by historians as great architects of binational amity. The collapse of the project illustrates how U.S.-Canadian relations can move beyond the control of individual presidents and prime ministers. The president had to satisfy the Senate, and in 1934 the Seaway Treaty failed to get the necessary two-thirds majority. The power of the provinces within the Canadian federation constrained the prime minister. Bennett ignored Quebec's objections to the seaway but ran aground when Ontario repudiated its pledge to pay part of the Canadian share of construction costs. The seaway languished for another quarter-century, and the historical reputations of Herbert Hoover and R. B. Bennett languished along with it.[9]

New Deal America—No Deal Canada

Like the Americans who voted for him, Canadians didn't at first know what to make of Franklin Roosevelt. "We have little to expect from Roosevelt," editorialized the *Canadian Forum*, "we only knew we could expect nothing at all from Hoover." The month of the inauguration, March 1933, was the pit of the Great Depression, with one-third of the work force out of work in both countries. The new president served Americans an alphabet soup of federal regulatory and welfare agencies: the National Recovery Administration (NRA), the Agricultural Adjustment Administration, the Tennessee Valley Authority, the Federal Emergency Relief Administration. Roosevelt's "New Deal" did not stimulate full recovery, but it redefined the role of the state by broadening the federal government's managerial role in the economy. Through the Works Progress Administration (WPA) and the Social Security Act, the New Deal rooted the modern welfare state in America. In 1933, the United States and Canada lagged far behind western Europe in government acceptance of responsibility for individual citizens; by 1940, the United States had begun to catch up.[10]

The New Deal dealt Canada a mixed hand. Securities regulations interfered with borrowing in U.S. money markets, and Canadian pulp and paper companies had to accept NRA production and pricing rules to maintain access to U.S. newsprint buyers. The Roosevelt experiment also aroused unprecedented interest among Canadians. The Liberal party invited Raymond Moley and Averill Harriman from Roosevelt's "brains trust" to Ontario to explain "the Meaning of the N.R.A.," and British Columbia's Liberal premier proposed a "little New Deal" to the people of his province. The New Deal's specific influence on Canadian public policy is difficult to measure; as Harriman told the Canadian Liberals, "the New Deal is a point of view, not a fully developed social or economic theory." Those Canadians who sighed, "Oh, for a Roosevelt!," were more envious of the president's jaunty activism than of any of his particular programs. W. D. Herridge regularly entertained New Dealers at the Canadian legation in Washington and urged his brother-in-law R.B. Bennett to emulate Roosevelt. Specific legislation did not matter: ordinary Americans did not understand the New Deal "any more than they understood the signs of the zodiac." In January 1935, the prime minister paid the president the sincerest of compliments, that of plagiarism. In a series of radio talks modeled on FDR's "fireside chats," Bennett announced his own New Deal to Canadians. Bennett's conversion was an eleventh-hour attempt to save his depression-doomed government, but he had a larger objective in common with Roosevelt. Both leaders espoused government intervention to save capitalism in North America, and they explained themselves to disgruntled conservatives in identical language.[11]

Their electoral fates, however, could not have been more different. Americans reelected Franklin Roosevelt with the largest majority ever accorded a president; extrapolating for the differences of the parliamentary system, Canadians rejected Bennett equally massively. Instead, they returned to the prime ministership William Lyon Mackenzie King, who had condemned Bennett's New Deal as "Hitlerism, Fascism or Communism." In 1936, while Roosevelt's WPA reduced America's relief rolls with a massive public works program, King set up commissions to investigate the depression rather than agencies to relieve it. In fairness to King, Canada's dilemma was a failure of finances as much as of imagination: the dominion could not afford the expenditures the United States undertook. The most frequently compared programs of America's New Deal and Canada's "no deal" were those for unemployed single men. In the United States, they could join the Civilian Conservation Corps (CCC) and build parkways and campsites; in Canada, they were dispatched to remote relief camps run by the military to dig holes and fill them up again. "While American CCC youths earn a dollar a day and their keep," an article in the *Nation* pointed out that "Canadian camp workers are paid twenty cents a day, less deductions." These national differences could be seen in microcosm in the International Peace Garden that straddled the North Dakota–Manitoba boundary. Dedicated in July 1932, the garden centered around a cairn that read: "We two nations pledge ourselves that as long as men shall live, we will not take up arms against one another." Eight years later, the American side of the International Peace Garden had bloomed because the CCC had built a dam and planted a real garden; the Canadian side remained untended prairie.[12]

North America's modern binational labor movement also flowered during the New Deal after unions barely survived the disastrous decade of the 1920s. On both sides of the border, workers had confronted capital at the end of World War I. It seemed, writes historian David Montgomery, "that a unified movement . . . might be in the offing," an international movement "very different from the American Federation of Labor." In the industrial history of either country, 1919 was the most strike-torn year, and among the 3600 strikes in the United States and the 336 strikes in Canada were general strikes in Seattle, Washington, and Winnipeg, Manitoba. But in both countries, employers and governments joined forces to suppress the labor revolt. The defeat of the attempt to organize the steel industry set the tone for the twenties, as bosses battled unions with the stick of traditional union-busting techniques, combined with the carrot of "welfare capitalism"—benefit programs designed to avert organization. Faced with anti-unionism in various guises, neither the American Federation of Labor (AFL) nor its Canadian affiliate and counterpart, the Trades and Labor Congress (TLC) of Canada, found a way to organize the fastest-growing sector of the North American economy, the technologically advanced mass production industries such as steel and automobile manufacturing. Union membership dropped in both countries during the 1920s, from 5 to 3 million in the United States, and from four hundred thousand to three hundred thousand in Canada; the number of industrial disputes reached forty-year lows. When the American Federation of Labor held its 1929 convention in Toronto, the *Toronto Globe* noted that "the day of the firebrand and the spellbinder is gone" and that "the strike is discredited, except as an absolutely last resort." The *Globe* praised the AFL and the TLC for their political nonpartisanship, the opposite of the British model of an independent Labour party. AFL president William Green's speech to the convention, replete with references to "the imaginary boundary line [with] no standing armies," was as vapid as anything a gathering of Rotarians might have nodded through. Although seven of every ten unionized workers in Canada belonged to AFL unions, convention speakers criticized the independent Canadian unions that had organized the others. "There is no room for two Labor movements in North America," Green made clear.[13]

The explosive growth of industrial unions that started three years later took both the craft-based AFL and businesspeople by surprise. The social movement for unions organized by industry was born on the shop floors of both countries, as workers sought dignity and decent lives in the midst of economic uncertainty. Working-class discontent alone would not have produced the mass industrial insurgency; New Deal labor legislation helped to make the new unions possible. Section 7(a) of the National Industrial Recovery Act, revised and strengthened as the Wagner Act in 1935, outlawed the most effective anti-union techniques of employers as "unfair labor practices" and established a National Labor Relations Board to supervise union certification. As important as the legislation itself was the new legitimacy that such recognition gave the labor movement. "The president wants you to join the union," organizers told workers as they signed their union cards. Union ranks swelled with recruits from the mass production industries until the AFL was unable to contain the crusade to organized the unorganized within its craft union ranks. A rift began during the 1935 AFL convention, which led to the departure of the industrial unions as the autonomous Congress of Industrial Organizations (CIO) in 1938. Under President John L. Lewis of the United Mine Workers of America, the CIO charted new political and industrial directions. In 1936, CIO unions violated a sacred AFL principle by committing money and campaign workers to the Democratic party to ensure Roosevelt's reelection. In 1937, the CIO's United Steel Workers won recognition from U.S. Steel, and its United Auto Workers (UAW) signed a contract with General Motors (GM) after a six-week "sit-down" strike at GM's plant in Flint, Michigan. The GM strike, says historian Sidney Fine, was "the most significant American labor conflict in the twentieth century." The CIO had transformed industrial relations in the United States, but at the heavy price of a profound division within the American labor movement.[14]

The CIO had an instant presence in Canada through the Canadian locals of seven of the founding industrial unions, which left the AFL. As a result, this division was reproduced in the ranks of Canadian labor when AFL president Green ordered the TLC to expel the CIO deviants. Unfortunately for unorganized workers in Canada, the CIO's success did not travel north as completely as did this schism. The CIO was too organizationally overburdened to expand and more inclined to accept Canadian autonomy than the AFL was. "Canada must develop its own leaders if it is to have a sound labor movement," was how Sidney Hillman of the Amalgamated Clothing Workers put it. And Canadian labor did develop its own leaders and win its own victories. The CIO contributions to campaigns in Canada were a handful of organizers and the near-magic power its name inspired in working people. As historian Irving Abella demonstrates, "it was on the assembly lines of Oshawa and Sarnia [Ontario], and not in the union offices of Washington and Detroit, that industrial unionism in Canada was born." That, of course, was also how the CIO worked in America, by helping local insurgents to build their own effective industrial unions. Canada's Flint was Oshawa, where the UAW used conventional tactics rather than the "sit-down" strike to win a contract from GM, and there were other victories in steel in Nova Scotia and in the garment trade in Montreal.[15]

But just as there was no Canadian New Deal, there was to be

no northern carbon copy of CIO success; the Canadian trade union renaissance was on a much smaller scale. Part of the problem was the U.S. connection, which allowed Canadian businesspeople and their political allies to use "the nationalist stick to beat the labour dog." For the CIO struck genuine terror into the hearts of middle-class Canada, shocked by the massive violence of U.S. industrial disputes. Police and militia regularly broke strikes in Canada, but deaths were rare; the eighteen dead at Republic Steel in Chicago in May 1937 simply confirmed Canadians' impression of the brutality of American society. "This country . . . should be grateful that it is not going through such experiences as the United States," commented editorials. The CIO was also denounced as "communist," and editorial cartoons showed John L. Lewis as a comrade of Joseph Stalin. Communists were prominent among CIO organizers in both countries, but those in Canada were homegrown "Reds," not American imports. Prime Minister Mackenzie King complained about "the increasingly aggressive tactics" and the "threats" of "newer industrial unions in the United States," and Maurice Duplessis and Mitchell Hepburn, premiers of Quebec and Ontario, declared war on the CIO. Duplessis used special antiradical legislation to disband the Montreal local of the United Steel Workers. Hepburn, vowing to "fight against the Lewis organization and Communism in general," denounced the United Auto Workers as alien agitators and deployed provincial police against the Oshawa strikers. General Motors had better sense; corporate headquarters instructed the managers of its Canadian branch plant to sign a contract with the UAW virtually identical to that in force in Michigan. The Oshawa strike, wrote labor economist Norman Ware in 1937, "has brought the working people of Canada and the United States closer together." The disparity in CIO fortunes on each side of the border, however, underlines the importance of New Deal labor legislation in making trade unions an accepted part of American economic life. "The crucial difference between Canada and the United States in this period," writes historian Craig Heron, "was the role of the state." In 1940, the CIO had 3 million members in the United States and fewer than fifty thousand in Canada, and the binational gap in overall "union density" reached a new high. Historian David Brody's words describe the situation perfectly: "the two movements came close to having a unitary institutional history, [but] with the Canadians generally marching a half step to the rear."[16]

At the end of the 1930s, the United States was the more advanced welfare state, Canada the backward northern neighbor. America resounded with the vibrant working-class movement, one Canadian workers and their leaders struggled to emulate. In the United States, the success of the New Deal mitigated demands for more radical change; in electoral politics, it incorporated most of the American Left into an amorphous coalition behind Roosevelt and the Democratic party. The bankruptcy of Canadian responses to the depression had the opposite effect and helped to build the Co-operative Commonwealth Federation, a third party with a name borrowed from the American Populist movement that dedicated itself to social democratic solutions to the problems of industrial capitalism. These divergent directions would shape the evolution of the welfare states of Canada and the United States, but their effects lay in the future.[17]

Foundations of Alliance, 1933–1939

One very minor event of the New Deal actually took place in Toronto, where the American Optometric Association drafted its industrywide NRA code in July 1934. The conventioneering optometrists were among millions of American tourists who discovered Canada during the decade. After 1920, the automobile made it possible for people of more modest means to have a northern vacation, and after 1930, the weak Canadian dollar (a U.S. dollar was worth $1.25 Canadian in 1932) made Canada more affordable still. In 1922, 95,000 U.S. cars entered Ontario; in 1932, there were 730,000. "The Dominion is such a glorious vacation country," the *Cleveland Plain Dealer* exulted that same summer. Overall, 8.9 million Americans came to Canada in 1933 in autos, while 417,132 Canadian cars entered the United States. Transborder tourism earned Canada an annual $130 million (CDN)

Nonagricultural Workers in Unions in the United States and Canada, 1900–1990

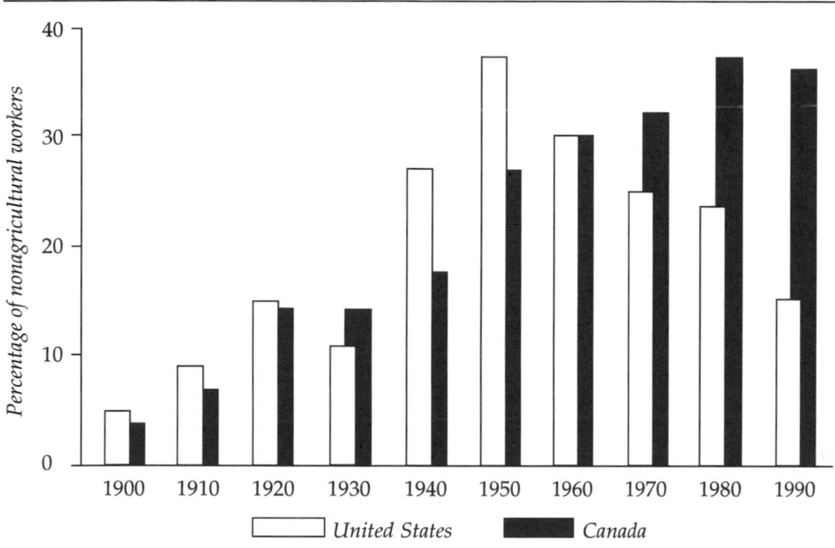

Canadian Membership in International Unions, 1911-1992

Year	*Total Union Membership*	*Membership in International Unions*	*Percentage of Membership in International Unions*
1911	133,132	119,415	89.7
1921	313,320	222,896	71.1
1931	310,544	188,219	60.6
1941	461,681	288,005	62.4
1951	1,028,521	725,613	70.5
1961	1,446,942	1,040,208	71.9
1971	2,210,554	1,371,109	62.0
1981	3,487,231	1,557,792	44.7
1992	4,089,000	1,253,000	30.6

Sources: Data for the years 1900–1990 are from David Arrowsmith, *Canada's Trade Unions: An Information Manual* (Kingston, Ont., 1992), 53–54; 1992, from Canada, Bureau of Labour Information, *Directory of Labour Organizations in Canada, 1992–93* (Ottawa, 1992), xiv.

surplus. In an uncharacteristic moment of humility, Prime Minister Bennett formally thanked the American people for "this welcome traffic." "Most tourism between any two countries in the world" was added to "longest undefended border" and "largest volume of trade" on the list of North American "world firsts" of which every Canadian and virtually no American was aware.[18]

Canada's biggest tourist attractions during the Depression were the Dionne quintuplets, born in May 1934 in the northern Ontario hamlet of Callander. Three million visitors made the long trek north to gawk at the five chubby little girls in their fenced playground at "Quintland." The Americans among them returned to the United States to reinforce the prevailing cinematic image of Canada as a bucolic wilderness where mounties played by Nelson Eddy crooned to passionate French-Canadian beauties played by Jeanette Macdonald, as in *Rose Marie* and *Indian Love Call. The Country Doctor,* Hollywood's version of the Dionne's story, depicted the quints' parents as rustic simpletons, and the physician who delivered them as a "simple soul" who worked "for the pure joy of helping people." Little wonder that most Americans, wrote literary critic Edmund Wilson, thought of Canada as a "gigantic wildlife reserve situated conveniently next door." Canadians complained about American ignorance of their country—"for the love of Mike, are there nothing else in our Dominion but Indians, French Canadian lumberjacks and North West Mounted Police?" Yet they also collaborated in building this innocent image, as the techniques the Ontario government used to market the Dionne quintuplets in the United States attested.[19]

U.S. ignorance nonetheless deeply offended Canadians, each of whom could relate a personal story of an encounter with an uninformed American. To promote better understanding of Canada's importance to the United States, Columbia University professor J. T. Shotwell persuaded the Carnegie Endowment for International Peace to sponsor four "Conferences on Canadian-American Affairs" and to publish the twenty-five-volume series *The Relations of Canada and the United States* between 1936 and 1945. The scholars attracted to the newly invented field of Canadian-American relations were mostly

Canadians or Canadian-born academics in U.S. universities; "the Americans who turned up," complained one of the former, "were second-string men." Yet for all this high-powered Canadian expertise on the United States, an investigation commissioned by the Carnegie Endowment found that "the amount of formal instruction which Canadians received about the United States was extraordinarily slight." Canadians learned almost nothing about America in school; everything, it seemed, came from popular culture or oral tradition. Canadian educators justified their neglect by arguing "that no more attention should be given to the United States than Americans give to Canada." Canadians knew what they thought of the United States and saw no reason to learn anything that might change their minds! An analysis of seven Ontario newspapers from 1921 to 1934 found editorial comments on the United States to be overwhelmingly negative; yet the editorials "expressed no real fear" of the United States, save for their anxiety about American trade unions. When 1,200 Canadian high school students were given a list of adjectives and asked which best characterized Americans, 973 chose "boastful" and only 54 chose "law-abiding." Yet 850 added "friendly."[20]

Canadian-American relations warmed noticeably after Franklin Roosevelt entered the White House in 1933. Toward Latin America his "Good Neighbor Policy" replaced "Dollar Diplomacy" enforced by the "Big Stick." As Secretary of State Cordell Hull told the member countries of the Pan-American Union in December 1933, "no state has the right to intervene in the internal or external affairs of any other." Canada was not among those members, and the United States was cool to the idea of Canada entering the Union: a constitutional monarchy still sentimentally attached to its colonial British parent, did not quite fit in at a gathering of republics born in revolution. It was obvious, however, that Roosevelt and Hull informally intended good neighborhood to extend north within the hemisphere as well as south. Franklin Roosevelt was the first—and is still the only—American president to take more than a passing interest in Canada. Like much about FDR, that interest is difficult to explain. There was a sentimental connection through the Roosevelt summer home on

Campobello Island in New Brunswick. But there was obviously more. The conspiratorially minded might argue that Canada permitted FDR to have an opening to the world that would not alarm the isolationists in Congress, a politically safe route to broader international goals through the seemingly innocuous bilateral relationship. Whatever the reasons for Roosevelt's interest, he became the first American president to be "genuinely popular in Canada," wrote a young historian named C. P. Stacey in 1936, in part because of "the simple fact that he has contrived to make Canadians feel that he is interested in and friendly to their country."[21]

Roosevelt's attention to good relations with Canada began almost with his inauguration. After the "Hundred Days" that launched the New Deal, Roosevelt visited Campobello Island for first time since he had been stricken with polio there twelve years earlier. An enthusiastic welcome from islanders and old Canadian friends among the summer people quickly exorcised painful memories. In the quest of worldwide reciprocal tariff cuts, in April 1933 he welcomed R. B. Bennett, chastened by three years of trade war, to the White House for discussions. Roosevelt so impressed the prime minister that Bennett praised the president's "wide vision, unselfish courage, . . . steady courage, and sincerity" in a speech on the CBS national radio network. Congress gave Roosevelt discretionary power in the Reciprocal Trade Agreements Act in 1934. Discussions begun with the Bennett government moved slowly; the State Department was not about to sign an agreement that might become an issue in a Canadian national election the next year. The U.S.-Canada trade agreement was signed by Cordell Hull and Mackenzie King in November 1935, a month after Bennett's electoral defeat. In return for Canadian "most-favored-nation" treatment of American manufactured goods, which reduced tariffs on almost a thousand items, the United States admitted most Canadian fish, forest, and farm products. The U.S. negotiators had excluded codfish and table potatoes from the deal, so that John D. Hickerson, the State Department's expert on Canada, accurately assessed the treaty as "so favorable to us" that political consequences would be minimal. In Canada, the doomsday criers of annexation were eerily silent. After seventy-five years as an explosive issue, harsh economic reality brought a reciprocity agreement with scarcely a whimper of domestic protest in Canada. Initiated by a Conservative government and concluded with its Liberal successor, the treaty exemplifies the underlying structural continuities and ambiguities of Canada's relationship with the United States.[22]

The world context of that relationship changed fundamentally in the 1930s, as Japanese expansion into China, the Ethiopian adventures of Benito Mussolini's Italy, and Hitler's rise to power in Germany made obvious the League of Nations' inability to control international aggression. The defense question in U.S.-Canadian relations no longer meant protecting the United States from Britain or Canada from the United States, but protecting North America from a threat from Europe or Asia. As historian J. L. Granatstein has pointed out, it was Franklin Roosevelt who injected defense into the bilateral dialog, beginning in July 1936 when he made the state visit no previous president had scheduled. Speaking at the Citadel in Quebec, Roosevelt remembered the "brave French, brave British, and brave American colonists" who had fallen in battle there. Americans and Canadians were not "foreigners" to one another, and amid "the grave problems that face the world today," it was time to "tighten the close bonds which already unite our two peoples." Although the *New York Times* was careful to report that "political alliances were not considered," correspondent John MacCormac described the visit and accompanying confidential discussions as "a mile post in the relations of Canada, the United States and Great Britain." Canadians were thrilled that the president had noticed them; in Montreal, crowds jammed the station, hoping to glimpse him through the window of his railway car. *Saturday Night*—a Canadian magazine that had recently howled for protection against U.S. competition—gushed approval: "President Roosevelt showed a just appreciation of the relationship between his country and ours. . . . There is a common quality of North Americanism which to a large extent overrides international boundaries."[23]

In Quebec, Mackenzie King had contributed the ubiquitous platitude about "the unfortified frontier, the century of peace" and "the message . . . the New World sends to the Old." It was the second time he had met the president, and the beginning of the personal friendship between "Franklin and Mackenzie" that he came to feel so important to understanding between the two countries. It was a friendship never as intimate as King liked to believe—he never screwed up his courage to tell Roosevelt that his few close friends called him "Rex"—but there was a warmth that had never existed before and never has since between a president and a prime minister. King clung tenaciously to the dream of Ottawa's special role as a "linchpin" between Washington and London to build "an alliance of three great democratic groups in the interest of world peace." He hoped to involve the United States in a trilateral scheme of "economic appeasement" of Germany and Italy, and this was his unrealistic goal for the trilateral trade negotiations that soon began. The Canada-U.S.-U.K. agreements that followed in 1938 lowered trade barriers in the North Atlantic triangle, but their contribution to projecting an image of Anglo-American solidarity that could prevent a European war was nil.[24]

Lord Tweedsmuir, governor general of Canada from 1935 to 1940, cultivated trilateral friendship throughout his term. He helped orchestrate Roosevelt's initial visit in 1936 and repaid the president's courtesy the following year. After accepting honorary degrees from Harvard and Yale, Tweedsmuir addressed the graduating class at the naval academy at Annapolis and both houses of Congress. The "regrettable differences of opinion," he quipped, were in the past; now "the future of civilization [lay] in the hands of the English-speaking people." British newspapers praised the visit. "Canada is the natural interpreter of Great Britain and the United States to one another," the *Standard* reported; "Britons turn no jealous eye upon such cordial exchanges between the peoples of Canada and the United States." British diplomats and politicians doubted that Canada could make any real contribution, and London wanted American help only on Britain's explicit terms. U.S.-Canadian friendship could be a useful development in the Anglo-American alliance, so long as it did not become so intimate that Canada was lost as a military resource to the empire.[25]

Lord Tweedsmuir brought up the defense cooperation between the

British Empire and the United States in his address at Annapolis: "Every addition to your navy is an extra addition to the security of the world," he told the midshipmen. Roosevelt and King were slower than Tweedsmuir to acknowledge the military realities now implicit in the bilateral relationship. In August 1938, with the newspapers full of news of German military strength, the president raised the issue in public at Queen's University in Kingston, Ontario. After accepting the inevitable honorary degree, he updated the Monroe Doctrine to the new global situation: "The Dominion of Canada is part of the sisterhood of the British Empire," he told the special convocation assembled in the football stadium. "I give to you the assurance that the people of the United States will not stand idly by if domination of Canadian soil is threatened by any other Empire." King adumbrated the Canadian corollary in less memorable language: Canada understood its reciprocal responsibility to be sufficiently well armed that, "should the occasion ever arise, enemy forces should not be able to pursue their way, either by land, sea or air to the United States, across Canadian territory." The president and prime minister had served notice that Canada and the United States might become active allies, not simply passive friends. In Canada, only the most perfervid British Canadians disapproved, and the cautious enthusiasm in Britain undercut their antagonism. In the United States, the hazy commitments to a benign neighbor were sufficiently vague that isolationist sentiment was not aroused. Why had an American president not said the same thing fifty years ago?, Roosevelt wondered in a letter to Lord Tweedsmuir. The answer should have been obvious: a half-century earlier it would have been unthinkable for America to have made or Canada to have accepted such a pledge.[26]

To Roosevelt, the Canadian connection had offered a politically safe way to use hemispheric security to send a warning that would perhaps "have some small effect in Berlin." To King, the exchange with the president signified that "we have at last got our defence programme in good shape. Good neighbors on one side; partners within the Empire on the other. Obligations to both in return for their assistance. Readiness to meet all joint emergencies." More dispassionate assessments were less optimistic. Canada had not done any strategic planning with Britain, let alone with the United States, and of course none could be contemplated between the United States and Britain. Likely enemies lay outside the hemisphere and, as the Canadian Department of External Affairs reminded King, Roosevelt had said exactly nothing about "military support for other democracies outside the Americas." British prime minister Neville Chamberlain was equally dubious: "It is always best and safest to count on nothing from the Americans but words," he had earlier concluded.[27]

Both King and Roosevelt applauded British appeasement of Germany. After Chamberlain's concession of a third of Czechoslovakia to Hitler at Munich, Roosevelt wrote to King that "We in the United States rejoice with you, and the world at large, that the outbreak of war was averted." British historians Corelli Barnett and Ritchie Ovendale charge Roosevelt and King with complicity in appeasement's conception, blaming Chamberlain's unwillingness to confront Hitler on a lack of firm support from the United States and the senior Dominion. Whatever the personal views of the president and the prime minister, however, domestic political constraints blocked more outspoken foreign policies. Each was watched carefully by isolationists in Congress and Parliament who were determined that their countries not intervene in a European conflict. The Royal Canadian Air Force officers who visited Washington during the Czech crisis to purchase aircraft traveled surreptitiously in civilian clothes. Senator Gerald P. Nye's inquiry into U.S. intervention in World War I seemed to prove that the America had been manipulated into war by "merchants of death" who had sold arms to Britain. Nye inspired the series of neutrality acts between 1935 and 1939 that forbade selling armaments or lending money to belligerent nations. "The United States are acting wisely in this regard," applauded Canadian anti-interventionist Agnes Macphail. Might Canada remain neutral if Britain went to war and take refuge with America within the hemisphere? A month after Munich, an article in the *American Mercury* predicted that Canada's "spirit of Empire . . . would never stand the strain of war." Its author cited migration, trade and investment, and popular culture as integrating influences making Canada "a part of the United States in all save the formal act of transfer." That formal transfer would occur when Britain entered a European war; French-speaking Quebec would withdraw from the federation, and "the remaining provinces will seek admission to the American Union."[28]

For all the obvious cultural evidence of Canada's "Americanization," the two countries remained very different; unlike Americans, Canadians perceived this to be so. Their responses to the European crisis demonstrated this. In the United States, isolationism had a broad popular base and was legitimated by a tradition of "no entangling alliances" that dated back to George Washington. Canadian isolationists were unable to overcome the emotional bond that the English-Canadian majority felt with Britain. To Canada, isolation from Britain meant dependence on the United States, something very few Canadians, and no Canadian political leader, could countenance. Mackenzie King confided to his diary in October 1938: "I do not like to be dependent on the U.S.; change of leaders there might lead to a vassalage so far as our Dominion was concerned. There [is] more real freedom in the B[ritish] C[ommonwealth] of Nations, and a richer inheritance. This I truly believe." In a major European war touched off by fascist aggression, wrote the prime minister, Canada's "self-evident national duty" was to fight at Britain's side.[29]

In May and June of 1939, the Royal Tour of King George VI and Queen Elizabeth put Canada's British connection on continentwide display. An earlier trip planned for George's brother Edward VIII had been canceled by his abdication to marry Baltimore divorcée Wallis Warfield Simpson. Edward had been wildly popular in Canada, and the newspapers his Canadian subjects read universally blamed the wicked Mrs. Simpson for debauching their monarch; such depravity was all too typical of an American. Three million adoring Canadian subjects—almost a third of the population—greeted George and Elizabeth as they visited each of the nine provinces over four weeks. When the blue-and-gold-painted Royal Train turned south to take Their Majesties to the United States for a four-day interlude, Canadians watched carefully for signs of *lèse majesté*. There were few; American crowds were also enthusiastic—"The British Take Washington Again," proclaimed one headline—but George VI reminded them repeatedly that he was Canada's king as well as Britain's. To emphasize this, his first stop at the New York World's Fair was at the Canadian pavilion. When uninformed American editors suggested that the king was part of a dark plot to lure the United States into a British alliance, equally uninformed Canadian editors responded indignantly that "no military plot was being hatched." During an informal day at the president's Hyde Park home, Roosevelt did indeed make some rash promises of support to King George and Mackenzie King, promises that went unreported and unkept. "The King and Queen heaved a sigh of rather satisfied relief when their train crossed back into Canadian territory," according to the *Winnipeg Free Press;* another journal described Their Majesties' pleasure that the "tough-looking American police had been replaced by the scarlet-coated mounties."[30]

Neutral America, Belligerent Canada, 1939–1941

"Alone among the free nations of America," Canada "went to war in 1939 against the Hitlerite tyranny." That the distinguished Canadian historian C. P. Stacey could write with such emotion forty-two years after the fact suggests the mixture of pride and bitterness with which Canadians viewed their country at war and America at peace. No law compelled Canada to join the war against Germany; the Statute of Westminster of 1931 gave each British Dominion the constitutional right to remain neutral. For English Canada, that right existed only in theory, and Canada's sentimental bond to Britain coincided with the country's national interests. Mackenzie King stage-managed the decision to placate French Canadians, so that when Parliament assembled, only four of the 252 members of Parliament spoke for neutrality. The seven-day delay between the British and Canadian declarations allowed Canada to buy munitions and aircraft in the United States before neutrality laws required Roosevelt to add its name to the prohibited list. The King government hoped to avoid a massive contribution of Canadian infantry for Europe, but Hitler unfortunately refused to cooperate with these best-laid plans. The "phoney war" of the winter of 1939–40 ended abruptly when the German Blitzkrieg swept over France in May 1940. A Canadian brigade was among the British troops evacuated from the Continent without their weapons. When France asked Germany for an armistice on 17 June, Canada suddenly found itself promoted to Britain's most important ally! Nothing better illustrated the desperation of the military situation of the British Empire–Commonwealth.[31]

In historical retrospect, U.S. entry into World War II has taken on an air of the inevitable. Roosevelt made his pro-Allied sympathies reasonably transparent and never repeated Woodrow Wilson's admonition that Americans be "neutral in thought as well as deed." He persuaded Congress to bend the neutrality acts to allow "cash-and-carry" purchases, so that the Allies were able to buy $50 million worth of munitions in the first seven months of war on this basis. Public opinion, measured by the new polls conducted by George Gallup, showed that 84 percent of Americans wanted an Allied victory, while only 2 percent cheered for the Axis; 14 percent had no opinion. One history of Canadian-American relations goes so far as to conclude that "after the fall of France US neutrality became an ever more transparent fiction," counting off American actions as if they were part of an inexorable Roosevelt plan to lead America into war with Germany. In August 1940 the president traded fifty old American destroyers for leases on British bases in the Caribbean and in Newfoundland, the British colony Canada coveted as a tenth province. In a fireside chat in December, Roosevelt proposed to make America the "arsenal of democracy," and in March 1941, he signed the lend-lease bill that allowed him to provide Britain with up to $7 billion in arms and supplies. In April, American warships began to guard North Atlantic convoys against submarines, and in August, Roosevelt had his first face-to-face strategy session with British prime minister Winston Churchill.[32]

The difficulty with this neat chronology is that neither Roosevelt, Churchill, Canadian prime minister Mackenzie King, nor anybody else knew what was ahead when France collapsed in June 1940. Americans' distaste for Nazi Germany did not translate directly into support for Britain. Whatever Roosevelt's personal convictions—which were not consistently interventionist—the president could not simply decide to join Britain at war. There was persistent noninterventionist sentiment in Congress and the country, personified in Charles Lindbergh, spokesman for the America First Committee backed by Sears-Roebuck millionaire Robert Woods. In search of his unprecedented third term as president in 1940, Roosevelt guaranteed he would "never send American boys to fight in any European war," and his Republican opponent Wendell Willkie made the same promise. As late as the autumn of 1941, only 41 percent of Americans were prepared without qualification to enter the war.[33]

This context of uncertainty explains the alacrity with which Canadian prime minister Mackenzie King allowed Roosevelt to turn the mutual promises of 1938 into a military alliance. The Ogdensburg Agreement was announced on 18 August 1940—the second anniversary of Roosevelt's speech in Kingston. King traveled at Roosevelt's request to join the president in Ogdensburg, New York, where the president had gone to inspect the American First Army. Eight divisions of American troops so near the border once would have terrified Canadians, but with Britain battling to avert German invasion, the ninety-four thousand soldiers became a reassuring presence. The press did not report that the First Army had no modern weapons, and that trucks armed with lengths of telephone pole played tanks in their maneuvers. King's defense predicament dwarfed Roosevelt's: virtually all of Canada's armed forces stood watch in Britain against the Axis. If Britain fell, the entire force would be lost, yet King and his generals would not consider bringing them home. Roosevelt proposed a partial answer to this dilemma—a Permanent Joint Board on Defence (PJBD) to plan "the defence of the north half of the western hemisphere." Details of defense cooperation were left for the PJBD to work out; it was to be a bilateral institution removed from public view that would suggest action to still-sovereign governments, sort of a military version of the International Joint Commission. Roosevelt pressed King about the possibility of American bases in Canada, but the prime minister demurred by promising "facilities" would be available when necessary.[34]

Through their summit diplomacy, the two leaders had reached an informal executive agreement far more significant than any previous U.S.-Canada treaty, an agreement that was never debated in the U.S. Senate or in Parliament. Although the president's sudden telephone summons left Mackenzie King no time to consult his cabinet, the PJBD reflected precisely the sort of arrangement Canadian strategic planners had hoped to conclude with the United States. Not surprisingly, newspaper comment and public opinion in Canada were overwhelmingly positive, even from the English-Canadian business community, the bastion of anti-Americanism in the Dominion. U.S. minister in Ottawa Pierrepont Moffat reported that "the old fear that cooperation with the United States would tend to weaken Canada's ties with Great Britain has almost entirely disappeared. Instead, Canada believes that such cooperation would tend to bring Britain and the United States closer together." From a U.S. perspective, the board was a "prototype of many subsequent organizations established . . . to increase the efficiency of their crusade against the enemies of civilization." Roosevelt was the leader who ran the political risk by dealing with a belligerent, but Canada was a benign belligerent the president could safely use to make a point; a June 1940 Gallup poll had found that 81 percent of Americans would go to war to defend their northern neighbor. The *Chicago Tribune*, the most outspoken editorial voice of nonintervention, supported the board as "common sense" and as "a contract of limited liabilities" that made it *less* likely "for this nation to engage in any European military adventures." The Roosevelt administration accordingly stressed the defensive nature of the relationship with Canada; Undersecretary of State Sumner Welles contended that the Canadian arrangement paralleled that with the other American republics, simply providing a planning mechanism in the event Canada were attacked by a non-American power. Yet, the United States had now given structure to Roosevelt's pledge not to "stand idly by" if Canada were attacked.[35]

When Mackenzie King got around to explaining Ogdensburg to Parliament in November 1940, he emphasized that the American alliance allowed Canada to funnel men, women, and material to Britain, secure in the knowledge that the United States sheltered the hemisphere. His goal had been not just to protect Canada but "the defence of the British commonwealth of nations as a whole," and "the British government was kept duly informed of what was taking place." This was not strictly true. Churchill had known nothing of Ogdensburg in advance and, on learning of it, wired King that history might judge him more harshly than public opinion in the event that "Mr. Hitler cannot invade us and his Air Force begins to blench under the strain." It was Churchill who judged too harshly. King's U.S. compact was the only course that military circumstance left open to Canada to support the British commonwealth. The prime minister continued to revere the metaphor of Canada as North Atlantic "linchpin" between Britain and America, the exact term Churchill himself used to describe Canada as "the binder-together of the English-speaking peoples." In practical terms, however, this linchpin role was insignificant. King's single contribution was to act as conduit between Roosevelt and Churchill in distasteful discussions over the disposition of the Royal Navy should Hitler conquer Britain. In a broader sense, the linchpin notion was a useful propaganda artifice. Hollywood's *Sherlock Holmes and the Scarlet Claw* (1944) concludes with Holmes extolling to Dr. Watson Canada's value as a bridge across the North Atlantic. As David Reynolds has argued, however, the real basis of eventual British-American cooperation was not "latent cultural unity" but "similar geopolitical and ideological interests" fully acknowledged only during the crisis of 1940–41.[36]

The dollars-and-cents significance behind the high-sounding speeches about the U.S.-Canadian alliance came to the fore in March and April 1941. In peacetime, Canada had balanced its chronic trade deficit with the United States through a trade surplus with Britain and western Europe. War upset this balance; it increased imports from the United States, ended sales to Europe, and turned sales to Britain into credit transactions financed by Canada. In 1940, Canada spent

$744 million (CDN) in the United States and earned only $451 million (CDN). Canada refused to accept United States aid under lend-lease, but the act loomed momentous: by diverting British purchases to the United States, it produced a foreign exchange nightmare for Canada. This time Mackenzie King broached the subject with Roosevelt. After brief discussions at Hyde Park, on 20 April 1941 they announced an agreement to rationalize "mobilizing the resources of this continent." The United States would supply Canada with components for munitions bound for Britain as part of British lend-lease aid and, more important, increase its purchasing in Canada to bring bilateral trade closer to a balance. Mackenzie King exaggerated what had happened at Hyde Park when he told the House of Commons that it was the foundation of a "new world order," but its departure from previous U.S.-Canada economic experience could scarcely be exaggerated. This was no doubt why King repeated six times during the speech that his intent at Hyde Park had been "maximum aid to Britain."[37]

U.S. foreign policy historians ignore or brush past the agreements at Hyde Park and Ogdensburg, but they are conspicuous even in survey textbooks of Canadian history. Nationalist historians excoriate Mackenzie King for selling out Canada's British birthright for Yankee pottage, leading Canada down the American fork to "a continental system dominated by the United States." But Canada embarked on that road that eventually made it a satellite of the United States, not because its leaders loved Britain less but because they loved the mother country more—sometimes more than prudent calculation of national interest might have dictated. It was a case, as J. L. Granatstein reveals succinctly in the long title of a short book, *How Britain's Weakness Forced Canada into the Arms of the United States.* And what safer place could there have been in 1941 than in America's arms?[38]

6 World War to Cold War, 1941–1947

After a century and a half of slowly unfolding familiarity, the United States and Canada moved to the embrace of alliance suddenly between 1938 and 1941. Like the many individual human relationships contracted amid World War II, the binational union was accompanied with professions of timeless attachment. The promise at Ogdensburg, said Mackenzie King, was "the enduring foundation of a new world order, based on friendship and good will." As a "mission of good will," the American Legion chose Toronto for its July 1941 convention. On the Fourth, "side by side the Doughboy and Jack Canuck made the ceremonial rounds . . . as the Union Jack and 'Old Glory' flew side by side in the gentle breeze [of] true democracy." It was "continentalism new style," wrote an American scholar, with "unity and collaboration in place of separateness and independence." As in most wartime romances, however, reality soon intruded on illusion. Once the United States became a belligerent, Canada lost whatever limited utility its leaders imagined it had as a link between American and Britain. For the duration of the conflict, Canada and the United States made the difficult adjustments of actually working as partners in arms—and the smaller partner did most of the adjusting. Economic adjustments worked in Canada's favor, however. War built further economic integration, but it also strengthened Canada's economy relative to that of the United States. War exposed the imbalance and the ambivalence of the bilateral relationship, and in 1945, Canada's ties to Britain still ran far deeper than those to the United States. Their wartime role also gave Canadians a sense that Canada was a significant "middle power" nation with an independent international role to play in the new United Nations. Formal bilateral wartime institutions (the PJBD was the exception) lapsed with the surrender of Germany and Japan in 1945, and postwar expectations were that some of the prewar distance would return to U.S.-Canadian relations. But almost before the shooting war against fascism was behind them, the confrontation with the Soviet Union replaced it as the context for the U.S.-Canadian interaction. Even more abruptly than the world war, this cold war led to a new set of conflicted intimacies.[1]

Big and Little Brothers-in-Arms

"Yesterday, December 7, 1941—a date which will live in infamy—the United States of America was suddenly and deliberately attacked by naval and air forces of the Empire of Japan." Thus began Franklin Roosevelt's war message to Congress after Japan's surprise success against the U.S. Pacific Fleet at Pearl Harbor. Thus ended a decade of growing tensions with Japan over Japanese expansionism in China and southeast Asia. Although historians of U.S. foreign policy debate the degree of commitment the Roosevelt administration had already made to the war effort by late 1941, there is no debate that the attack on Pearl Harbor converged American public and official opinion on a single objective—the defeat of Japan. Pearl Harbor contributed, to use Robert Divine's phrase, to the "triumph of internationalism" in the United States. Within a week, Hitler thrust America directly into the British Commonwealth's war with Germany and Italy by his unnecessary and, in retrospect, illogical declaration of war against the United States. Without Hitler's misjudgment, the Roosevelt administration would have had to focus its fighting power on the Japanese forces in the Pacific and to continue only to supply material to the war across the Atlantic—a course of events that seemed all too likely to the British. Instead, the German declaration evoked the eventual Anglo-American grand strategy: to fight a holding action in the Far East on the premise that Japan could not stand alone, while concentrating Allied forces on the European enemy—Germany.[2]

The Combined Chiefs of Staff—the commanders of the three armed services of Britain and the United States meeting with Roosevelt and Churchill, or their special representatives—did Anglo-American strategic planning. The principal point of friction between the United States and Britain here was over the location and timing of a second front. With the Soviet Union bearing the brunt of the land war in 1941–42 on Germany's eastern front, Roosevelt and his advisors worried about a Soviet collapse or withdrawal from the war, a repetition of the Bolsheviks' unilateral departure from World War I after the October Revolution in 1917. This had to be avoided at all costs, and convoys with American lend-lease supplies continued to flow into the Soviet Union when channels were open. Winston Churchill and other British leaders believed, rightly, that Allied forces were unprepared for a cross-channel push in 1942 or 1943. Instead, they urged an attack on Germany's flanks and a massive strategic bombing campaign to undermine and, if possible, destroy the German military-industrial machine. Thus, Britain and the United States agreed on the North African campaign to contain and destroy Germany's more isolated forces to clear the way for a coordinated invasion of southern Europe through Sicily and Italy in 1943, with a cross-channel invasion of Europe to come later.

These decisions had fundamental importance for Canada: the fates of a million Canadian service people and billions of Canadian dollars hinged on them. Canada's contribution to British grand strategy before 1941 had been negligible, despite the Dominion's indispensability to British survival during two dark years of U.S. neutrality. The Mackenzie King government's impact on Anglo-American grand strategy after Pearl Harbor was nonexistent. King complained to Churchill of Canada's exclusion from the Combined Chiefs, but his objections were not relayed to Washington. General Maurice Pope eventually became a semiofficial Canadian observer and was allowed access to censored documents; he attended exactly one of the two hundred meetings of the Combined Chiefs. Mackenzie King did not participate in any meaningful way even in the two wartime meetings that took place in Quebec City in August 1943 and September 1944. Pressed by his advisors, King quietly requested, again through Churchill, admission to the sessions. Roosevelt rejected the idea instantly; if Canada took part, he argued, Brazil, Mexico, and a dozen smaller allies would demand a place at the conference table. King never asked again. While Churchill and Roosevelt planned Operation Overlord, the Normandy landings of June 1944, King contented himself with the opportunity to be ceremonially photographed sitting between the two men who decided the future of Canada's combatants. Neither of them evidently felt any need for a Canadian "linchpin." As King later recalled privately, his role had been "not so much a participant in any of the discussions as a sort of genial host, whose task . . . was similar to that of the General Manager of the Chateau Frontenac [Hotel]."[3]

Canadian leaders quickly concluded that bilateral Canadian-American wartime cooperation worked better than the trilateral variety because the institutional basis had been established before the United States entered the war. Two-thirds of the PJBD's work had been done in 1940–41, when Canada was at war and the United States at peace. Each country had five representatives: a cochair, an officer from its army, navy, and air force, and a delegate from the U.S. Department of State and the Canadian Department of External Affairs, who reached consensus on draft recommendations to the two governments. "The Canadians had to recognize American power; the Americans had to cater to Canadian sensitivities," wrote Hugh Keenleyside, one of the former. As a result, the PJBD was remarkably successful in working out proposals that were mutually satisfactory to Washington and Ottawa. Nine of the thirty-three recommendations dealt with the nettlesome problem of Newfoundland, which Canada and the United States competed to defend. Canadian board members quickly explained to their American counterparts that there would be no permanent U.S. military bases in Canada; it was to be "a defence board, not a real-estate board," American chair Fiorello LaGuardia remarked in an interview in September. There were two tough decisions. In Basic Plan No. 1, Canada reluctantly agreed to put its forces under U.S. "strategic direction" in the event of an attack on North America. Canada refused to concede this strategic subordination in Plan ABC-22 for action against by joint forces elsewhere on the globe. Although the American military members of the PJBD hated the concept, such a counterattack was to be "effected by mutual cooperation." Thus the board allowed the very junior partner to retain a face-saving degree of its sovereignty. Fortunately for Canadian dignity, no crisis occurred to force the issue.[4]

The Canadian government pressed to expand bilateral ties beyond the PJBD in an effort to expand the Canadian role in strategic and industrial planning. American generals and diplomats firmly resisted such suggestions, wary of creating a Canadian precedent that other nations in the Americas would insist on. The Departments of War and the Navy politely but emphatically rejected a Canadian request in 1941 to establish a Canadian Joint Staff in Washington independent of representation within the British military mission. Secretaries Frank B. Knox and Henry L. Stimson contended that it was adequate to work through the Joint Board and for Canada to have representatives at conferences between American officials and the British Joint Staff Mission on issues "in which Canadian interests are involved." The United States proposed a compromise in which Canada would station its military members of the PJBD in Washington, a compromise Canada rejected. American affronts to Canadian pride continued until July 1942, when the American high command eventually acquiesced and Major General Maurice Pope became chief of a Canadian Joint Staff in Washington. The protracted negotiations left an "undertone of acrimony" that historian Stanley Dzuiban describes as "one of the least happy aspects of the U.S.-Canada World War II relationship."[5]

After the collapse of France, the United States took an increasingly assertive military posture to forestall the Axis from gaining a foothold in the Western Hemisphere. Newfoundland, a British colony not yet part of Canada, was critical as a base for air and naval patrols against German submarines in the North Atlantic. Roosevelt's destroyers-for-bases trade of September 1940 transferred fifty aged U.S. ships to the Royal Navy in return for bases in Newfoundland and elsewhere. Because Canada had tried since confederation to make the British colony a Canadian province, Newfoundland generated political difficulties between Canada and the United States. The Canadian government insisted that its "special concern" with Newfoundland's fate be formally recognized in Anglo-American plans. The American military presence, with its attendant nylon stockings and Hershey bars, cheered Newfoundlanders enough to intensify Canadian concerns about the colony's future. The Canadian garrison in Newfoundland seemed to be there as much to resist peaceful U.S. absorption as to repel Hitler's hordes. The Canadian troops accomplished their twin missions: in 1949, Newfoundlanders chose to join Canada in a bitterly fought referendum. The U.S. bases, however, remained.[6]

German conquest of Denmark and control over Vichy France posed a new security threat from Danish and French possessions in close proximity to vital Atlantic shipping lanes. The Roosevelt administration considered the Danish colony of Greenland to be part of the Western Hemisphere and integral to hemispheric defense. Economic competition was at issue as well: in addition to Greenland's strategic location, the island was a source of cryolite, a mineral used to manufacture aluminum, which was sought aggressively by U.S. and Canadian corporate interests. Britain pressed Canada to occupy Greenland, and Canadian defence minister J. L. Ralston made preparations to do so. U.S. assistant secretary of state Adolf Berle, furious at what he perceived as Canadian interference, accused Canada of "plain grand imperialism on a miniature scale." The United States feared that a Canadian occupation would provide Berlin with an excuse for offensive action against the island. The United States acted to avert either of these possibilities. In April 1940, U.S. Navy ships began to patrol the Greenland coast, and the United States provided the government of Greenland with munitions to protect the essential cryolite mine. Mackenzie King, anxious that Canada not get out of step with the United States, reassured Roosevelt and canceled Ralston's expedition. After this minor unpleasantness, the United States predominated; in April 1941, the Danish minister in Washington agreed to the construction of American air bases in Greenland.[7]

Canada, the United States, and Britain had greater difficulty balancing defensive questions with larger diplomatic policy toward Vichy France and the Free French movement under General Charles DeGaulle. The Vichy governments of Marshal Pétain and Pierre Laval clearly collaborated with Nazi Germany, but the United States wished to keep Vichy officially neutral to cancel the potential damage the French fleet could cause if used by Germany. Winston Churchill sought the same goal with a harder line toward Vichy. Canada's position was complicated by a large French-Catholic minority with some sympathy for Vichy, so that by early 1942, Canada was the only one of the Dominions that retained diplomatic relations with the Vichy regime. The potential security threat of the French islands of St. Pierre and Miquelon off the south coast of Newfoundland focused these conflicting policies toward Vichy and the Free French. The Roosevelt and King governments preferred that there be no formal alteration in the status of the islands, since official U.S. policy toward Vichy was to maintain the status quo of French overseas possessions in the Western Hemisphere. American minister in Ottawa J. Pierrepont Moffat and Mackenzie King concurred that it would be preferable to avoid action by the Free French. When a powerful wireless radio transmitter on St. Pierre aroused Canadian-American concern that it might be used to coordinate submarine wolf-pack operations, Canada and the United States concluded an arrangement under which Canada sent wireless operators to the island to supervise transmissions from the station.[8]

General DeGaulle precipitated a near crisis in Anglo-American-Canadian relations when his Free French Forces captured the tiny islands in December 1941. The United States was furious that DeGaulle's vice-admiral Muselier took the islands with British-supplied ships that sailed from under Canadian military noses from Halifax. DeGaulle's precipitous action crystallized the conflicting trilateral approaches. DeGaulle's intervention dismayed Mackenzie King, but the British seem to have preferred to have the Free French forces in control than Canadian authorities, but the Americans were not prepared to take any action that would compromise their Vichy policy. British ambassador in Washington Lord Halifax stressed that nothing should be done about the occupation, but he did agree that Hull should discuss the possibility of concluding an agreement with King, Vichy, and Churchill in which Churchill would request DeGaulle to withdraw his forces. Hull was enraged by Churchill's 11 December speech in Ottawa defending DeGaulle and criticizing Vichy, and he came close to resignation when Roosevelt failed to support him in a meeting at the White House with Churchill. From Hull's perspective, the Allied goal was to keep Vichy neutral, and DeGaulle's actions had threatened that position. From Churchill's vantage point, the Free French forces in North Africa would be important to the British and Americans as they moved toward the reconquest of Europe. This was a critical issue then and in the course of 1942. Churchill prevailed, and Hull, as was so often the case during the war, had to swallow his pride. Yet, this was a victory for the Free French and Churchill, not for Canadian policy, as some authors contend.[9]

Hull's concern was that the United States not be isolated in its Vichy policy, for the United States could not long continue to recognize Vichy France if Canada and Britain severed their diplomatic ties. In the spring of 1942, Canada recalled its ambassador for consultation but stopped short of breaking relations. Hull was especially distressed by the domestic political damage caused by British anti-Vichy propaganda, which fed an already strong American popular antagonism toward Vichy. What shaped U.S. policy was the neutrality of the French fleet and access to vital French North Africa. Hull took seriously Laval's warnings to American officials that Vichy would defend the French empire against any attack, including Allied landings in French North Africa. By the fall of 1942, after an agreement with Admiral Darlan cleared the way for the Allied invasion of North Africa, both Canada and the United States were able to distance themselves from Vichy. Yet Mackenzie King remained anxious that Vichy might declare war on Canada. Marshal Pétain's promise to restore traditional Catholic values in a rejuvenated France won the Vichy regime sympathy among some French-Canadian Roman Catholics, so that war would have exacerbated King's political problems in a Quebec already alienated from the war effort by the imposition of military conscription.[10]

Such diplomatic wrangles were a diversion from the main task of winning the war against the Axis. Both the German submarine threat on the North Atlantic and the Japanese peril in the Pacific necessitated active Canadian-American military cooperation. Although the

U.S. Navy had been engaged in an undeclared war against Germany in the Atlantic since 1940, two years of battle before Pearl Harbor gave the Royal Canadian Navy (RCN) seniority as battle-hardened veterans. Inevitably, then, there was some resentment when, in September 1941, even before Pearl Harbor, RCN ships operating outside Canadian coastal waters were placed under the command of the neutral Americans. That situation was not altered until May 1943, when it was reversed; for the remainder of the war the Royal Canadian Navy commanded the Northwest Atlantic forces, including American vessels. Throughout the war the Canadian navy was an important factor in protecting not only Canadian coastal and trans-Atlantic shipping but also transports leaving and entering Boston and New York harbors. As Stetson Conn and Byron Fairchild observe in their history of hemispheric defense, "the whole framework of cooperation, naval as well as military" rested as much on Canada as on the United States and Britain.[11]

In the North Pacific, the principal area of Canadian-American joint action was the response to the Japanese occupation of the Aleutian Islands of Kiska and Attu in June 1942. For the next two years, several Canadian naval vessels, air force squadrons, and almost five thousand infantry were stationed in the area. Canadian forces participated in this sector, however, because of the persistence of Canadian officials rather than from any real spirit of bilateral sharing of the military burden. Major General Maurice Pope, chairman of the Canadian Joint Staff in Washington, requested a Canadian role in the Aleutian operations through U.S. chief of staff George Marshall in May 1943. U.S. chief of naval operations admiral Ernest King opposed Canadian involvement, which he argued would simply "complicate" the logistical problems and serve no useful military purpose other than to improve future relations. Thus, when American troops counterattacked the Japanese at Attu in May 1943, they did so alone, suffering high casualties but entirely eliminating the Japanese force. When five thousand Canadian troops combined with the Americans in a joint assault on Kiska in August 1943, they found the Japanese had evacuated the island. Not only were Canadian troops denied a victory; they suffered the additional indignity of an overzealous U.S. customs officer who levied duty on their equipment as they moved into Alaska.[12]

Canada's First Division landed in the invasion of Sicily in July 1943, yet General Dwight D. Eisenhower refused to allow any reference to the Canadian presence in what was billed as an "Allied" or an "Anglo-American" campaign. Eisenhower had sound military reasons for his refusal. German intelligence listened to the radio, so that announcing the presence of the Canadian army would supply the enemy details about troop deployments. But King took the question of recognition so seriously that he telephoned the White House during dinner to arrange for Lester Pearson of the Canadian Mission to see the president. Pearson won a promise that the Canadian involvement would be given due public acknowledgment, once the landings were underway. Such were the demeaning appeals required of a small country that was, as Pearson put it, "uncomfortably squeezed in between" the United States and the United Kingdom. It was all very far from the role of Anglo-American "linchpin" that King had envisioned for Canada in 1940.[13]

After Pearl Harbor, Mackenzie King's personal rapport with Franklin Roosevelt won no special concessions, for leading America to war left the president precious little time to worry about relations with Canada. King's call to the White House about the Italian invasion, for example, was handled by Harry Hopkins. Still, the Roosevelt-King pairing was unique in the U.S.-Canadian relationship. They overlapped in office for a decade, from King's return to power in October 1935 until Roosevelt's death in April 1945. The president and prime minister met for "summit diplomacy" on eighteen occasions, twelve of them after Canada went to war in 1939. Nationalist historians of Canada argue that King deliberately eroded the British connection and turned Canada into an American dependency. Blinded by "the President's easy charm," suggests Donald Creighton, King failed to look out for Canada's interests at these meetings; the outcome, writes W. L. Morton, was that Canada became "so irradiated by the American presence that it sickens and threatens to dissolve in cancerous slime." But the restructuring of the U.S.-Canadian relationship was more the product of historical circumstance than it was of strengths or deficiencies in King's or Roosevelt's personal character. Like every president and every prime minister, the two personified the fearful asymmetry between the United States and Canada. King's options, like those of every other Canadian prime minister, were severely constrained by this asymmetry. King struggled constantly to maintain Canada's freedom of action, and it is difficult to imagine a scenario in which another Canadian leader could have been significantly more successful. Although he never in public acknowledged problems in the U.S.-Canada relationship, in private King was never naive about United States power and was constantly preoccupied with guarding Canada's sovereignty. He knew, however, that "if the Americans felt security required it [they] would take peaceful possession of part of Canada." All he could do was to try to keep that from happening.[14]

North American Arsenals for Democracy

The United States granted Canada a voice in Allied wartime economic councils, although that voice was never as loud as Canadian leaders believed it should have been. Relative national contributions to Allied munitions production illustrate both Canada's frustration and explain Anglo-American unwillingness to share power. From Washington's perspective, Canada's 5 percent of Allied munitions production was much smaller than Britain's 33 percent or the United States' 61 percent; thus Canada had to be excluded from the economic planning boards to justify the exclusion of other small Allied countries. From Ottawa's angle, Canada supplied five times as much war material as did all of those smaller Allies combined, as well as additional vast quantities of food and essential commodities. Canadian remonstrations never won representation on the Munitions Assignments Board, but by November 1942, its protests brought a place on the Combined Production and Resources Board. Canada was at first excluded from the Combined Food Board, despite huge Canadian exports of meat and grain. In this case, the Canadian approach was to maneuver representatives onto seven of the ten Food Board subagencies while negotiating for full membership, which came at last in November 1943.[15]

No American-British-Canadian collaboration had the long-term impact of the production of nuclear weapons. In June 1942, at British insistence, the Combined Chiefs added Canada as a minor third party in a scientific project codenamed "Tube Alloys"; three months later, Tube Alloys became the top secret Manhattan Project to develop an atomic weapon. At Quebec City in August 1943, Roosevelt and Churchill established a Combined Policy Committee of three Americans, two Britons, and Canadian minister of munitions and supply C. D. Howe to supervise the program. Atomic consultation, like most wartime cooperation, was imperfect. Howe was not invited to a Combined Policy Committee meeting until the spring of 1944. But although Howe and Mackenzie King had no part in the decision to drop the atomic bomb, the Canadian leaders were within the small circle who knew what was to happen to the Japanese city of Hiroshima on 6 August 1945.[16]

Atomic weapons development underlined several features of the Anglo-Canadian-American relationship. The first was growing American scientific and technological supremacy, illustrated by the speed with which American scientists pulled ahead of British researchers once the Manhattan Project was initiated. A second was that the United States sometimes depended on imported Canadian resources: Canada was invited to Manhattan because it was one of two major world sources of uranium. A third was that the U.S. government often took Canadian compliance for granted; Washington did not bother to check with Ottawa when it contracted with Consolidated Mining and Smelting in British Columbia to construct a heavy water plant. Yet despite the occasional indignities it endured, Canada derived indisputable benefits from charter membership in the atomic club. Wartime nuclear collaboration constructed the heavy water pile for the production of plutonium at Chalk River, Ontario, and provided Canadian scientists, in historian Donald Avery's words, "a chance to play in the scientific big leagues." These facilities and this knowledge helped to make Canada a world power in the peaceful applications of atomic energy in the postwar years, and allowed Canada's somewhat hypocritical boast that it was the only country with the capacity to build nuclear weapons that chose not to do so.[17]

Less significant in the long term than nuclear cooperation, but more controversial at the time, was the construction of such American military-industrial facilities as the Canol oil project at Norman Wells, Northwest Territories. Initiated in 1942 to supply oil products along the route of the projected Alaska highway and for Alaska-based military aircraft, the project involved the expansion of production at Imperial Oil's Norman Wells facility, the construction of a pipeline to Whitehorse in the Yukon, and the construction of a refinery at Whitehorse to produce aviation gasoline. Under the terms of the U.S.-Canada agreement, the pipeline and refinery would be the property of the U.S. government and would be operated under U.S. authority, but at the end of the war, the Canadian government would be given the first option to purchase the facilities. Canol was highly controversial at the time in U.S. political and military circles, largely because its expense and use of scarce resources in wartime seemed to bear little relationship to the actual military benefit of the project. Canol nonetheless provides an excellent example of a U.S.-Canada bilateral military-industrial project in wartime, as well as an indication of the keen American interest in longer-term oil development prospects for strategic use in the Canadian northwest.[18]

A fifteen-hundred-mile highway through that Northwest to link Alaska to the rest of the United States became the dream of West Coast politicians in both countries during the Depression. British Columbia's premier T. D. Pattullo actually journeyed to Washington in an attempt to promote the project, but Ottawa's fears of a loss of sovereignty forestalled serious discussion. War against Japan brought U.S. military pressure to build the road but, as with the Canol project and U.S. bases, Canadian nervousness remained. In February 1942, Canada reluctantly agreed to the PJBD's recommendation that construction begin. The United States built the road with American labor and bore the entire expense of $148 million (U.S.). "Money didn't mean a fucking thing to them Americans, . . . you never saw such waste," recalled a Canadian truck driver. The highway opened by the end of 1943 and carried thirty million tons of supplies and equipment to U.S. forces in Alaska in 1944. Its military importance declined rapidly thereafter, as the war of attrition against Japan moved to its atomic climax. Certainly construction of the highway undermined Canadian sovereignty in the region—northerners claimed that the U.S. Army answered the telephone with the phrase "American Army of Occupation"—but as with so many other aspects of the U.S.-Canadian wartime relationship, the Canadian government had little option. At war's end, Canada paid the United States for its work (as it did for all U.S. installations in Canada) and ceremonially took control of the highway. Both countries ignored the sovereignty of the native peoples who hunted, fished, and trapped the lands the road traversed. For these First Nations, the Alaska Highway remained a permanent physical and psychological scar across the landscape.[19]

In most respects, Canada fared well in its wartime economic relations with the United States. The Hyde Park Declaration of April 1941 immediately relieved Canada's balance of payments problem that lend-lease had exacerbated. The further arrangement that "each country should provide the other with defence articles which it is best able to produce" meant a substantial increase in American military purchases from Canada. Economic competition was partially set aside to serve the greater cause of Allied victory. Wartime economic expansion brought both economies to near full employment and created more than enough manufacturing orders to go around. There was sudden and unprecedented cooperation in previously competitive areas such as agricultural exports. Canadian farmers gained wartime access to the market their great-grandfathers had lost in the 1860s, as the United States admitted Canadian oats and barley in order to allow U.S. corn farmers to divert acreage to oilseeds that in turn were exported to Canada. Total bilateral trade was nearly $4 billion (U.S.) between 1941 and 1945, moving closer to balance each year until Canada had its first-ever trade surplus with the United States in 1945. Canada was therefore able to avoid what desperation compelled Britain to do: sell overseas assets to meet its payments to the United States or transfer title to territory in return for material assistance, as in the destroyers-for-bases deal of 1940. As historian Robert Bothwell expresses it, Canada became the "exception to the general rule of mendicancy that obtained in the wartime alliance"; alone among U.S. allies, it paid its own way in money as well as in blood. This perhaps explains why, as the Canadian minister in Washington Leighton McCarthy told Prime Minister King, the United States "had given us pretty much all we had asked for" on economic questions.[20]

On 1 January 1944, the two missions established in 1927 officially became embassies, and the ministers were elevated to ambassadorial rank. This redesignation was symbolic; the real wartime transformation was the profusion of bilateral lines of communication beyond traditional diplomacy, the contacts political scientists would later call "trans-governmental bureaucratic relations." Bureaucrats related transnationally on the five economic agencies set up to implement Hyde Park: the Materials Coordinating Committee, the Joint Economic Committees, the Joint War Production Committee, the Joint Agricultural Committee, and the Joint War Aid Committee. In addition, an unprecedented profusion of federal bureaus sprang up in both national capitals to regulate the wartime economies, and each Canadian agency dealt directly with its U.S. analog through an official stationed in Washington. Even Canadian cabinet ministers used extradiplomatic avenues to press policy issues on influential Americans. Minister of munitions and supply C. D. Howe prepared the ground for Canadian membership on the Combined Production and Resources Board during a 1942 fishing trip with Donald Nelson, chair of the United States War Production Board.[21]

Such contacts lead some historians to misjudge the war years as the first stage of an inexorable amalgamation of Canada into a U.S.-dominated continental economy. But as historian R. Warren James concludes, "any tendency to subservience was fiercely resisted by Canadian officials," and the flurry of wartime cooperation created the appearance of a greater degree of industrial integration than in fact took place. Hyde Park did not mean, as *Time* magazine would later claim, that "in effect, Canada had become an economic 49th state." The five joint economic agencies had impressive titles, but only the Joint War Production Committee and the Materials Coordinating Committee actually did anything. The Joint Economic Committees, which had been supposed to plan for the postwar period, produced nothing of any consequence and were disbanded in March 1944. There was no general free trade area, and national tariffs remained in force except on specific defense items. Canada's trade surpluses between 1942 and 1945 were not because of Hyde Park, but because there was a strong demand for Canadian munitions and natural resources. Nor was Hyde Park's goal "that production programs should be coordinated" entirely achieved. Much of Canada's war production continued to be built to British, not American, designs and specifications. For the first time in its history, Canada achieved massive industrial growth without heavy reliance on U.S. direct investment. Public investment made up for its absence, some of it into crown corporations (the Canadian term for government-owned enterprises) and some into private industry—including the American branch plants for ALCOA, Ford, and General Electric. There were few nationalizations: the purchase of a uranium mine at Great Bear Lake to create Eldorado Nuclear was an exception. During World War I, Canada's industrial production had been confined to artillery shells; in World War II, Canada's factories contributed tanks, vehicles, aircraft, naval frigates, and ocean freighters. In his comparative study of the economic effects of World War II, Alan Millward lists Canada as one of two countries for which wartime economic stimulation produced "a permanently effective acceleration of the development process."[22]

The frothy rhetoric of cooperation and the easy informality of transborder contacts gave Americans an exaggerated notion of the degree to which barriers between the United States and Canada had disappeared. U.S. assistant secretary of state Adolf Berle described in his diary an afternoon talk with Hugh Keenleyside, assistant undersecretary in the Canadian Department of External Affairs. Keenleyside, Berle wrote, had told him that "this is now one continent and one economy; that we shall have to be integrated as to finance, trade routes, and pretty much everything else; and in this I so thoroughly agree with him that it is refreshing. We talked long and happily about it—though much lies in the realm of dreams." Keenleyside understood this "dream" very differently: "For war purposes we were prepared to go as far as would be beneficial for our joint effort to defeat the worst threat ever faced by Western civilization." Postwar "industrial cooperation" was not a blueprint for continental integration but "the exact opposite"; through "shared production schemes" Canadian industries would receive "a guaranteed percentage of the American market" and thus would enhance Canadian economic integrity, not diminish it. Hyde Park was an informal agreement, without the force of a treaty; although officials from both countries repeatedly spoke of continuing the Hyde Park "spirit" into the postwar years, actual cooperation temporarily declined. Wartime agencies, except the Permanent Joint Board on Defense, were dismantled, wartime bureaucrats returned to their business careers, and Canadian political anxiety about dependency on the United States reawakened and intensified.[23]

Strangers Beneath the Skin

Effusive declarations about shared democratic values obscured the societal differences that persisted between the two countries. The way in which each country dealt with ethnic diversity furnishes a wartime window onto these contrasts. In the United States, World War II accelerated the cultural assimilation of the French-Catholic "little Canadas" of New England, which 1930s immigration restrictions had begun. As historian Gary Gerstle has shown, wartime propaganda and military service invited once-despised "Canucks" to a new identity as working-class Americans. "The younger generation is turning away from tradition and finds the American way more interesting than the life of their fathers," lamented Jacques Ducharme in 1943; "there is no future in the maintenance of survival." Franklin Roosevelt felt no such sadness. "The French-Canadian elements . . . are at last becoming a part of the American melting pot," he exulted to Mackenzie King, "and most of them are speaking English in their homes." The president proposed "some sort of planning . . . by which we can hasten the objective of assimilating the New England and Canada's French Canadians into the whole of our respective bodies politic." King had no such objective and did not reply; French Canadians were 30 percent of Canada's population. Maintaining the delicate harmony between French and English had been the principal task of his long political career, and the wartime debate over conscription had heightened French-Canadian alienation. The president's suggestion and the prime minister's silence illustrate the difference between a bicultural Canada and an America with one hegemonic culture; that Roosevelt offered such advice shows that even the president who knew Canada best had a fundamental gap in his understanding.[24]

The metaphors of "melting pot" and "mosaic" are often used to depict the two countries' differences with regard to cultural pluralism. The United States is the assimilative "melting pot" that recasts ethnic minorities into uniform English-speaking Americans; Canada is the "mosaic" that encourages the cultural survival of diverse ethnic groups. This melting pot/mosaic metaphor accurately describes Canada's historically greater degree of ethnic diversity, but there is no evidence that this diversity resulted from a greater Canadian appreciation of, or tolerance for, cultural minorities. As historian Allan Smith argues, "circumstances have imposed the pluralist idea" on Canada, and many English-speaking Canadians "have bitterly resented those circumstances." War removed some of the restraints on this resentment. As during World War I, English Canada imposed military conscription on French Canada. U.S. and Canadian wartime policies toward naturalized citizens of German and Italian origin were almost indistinguishable, and in both countries, the caucasian majorities reacted with near-identical racism to the perceived security threat posed by the Japanese minorities of the Pacific Coast states and British Columbia. Even before Pearl Harbor, the Permanent Joint Board on Defense had advocated that "policies of a similar character" be devised to deal with "elements in the population of Japanese racial origin" in the event of war with Japan. Although there is little evidence of a coordinated plan, 125,000 Japanese and Japanese-Americans and 22,000

Japanese and Japanese-Canadians were simultaneously relocated to internment camps away from the coast. Roosevelt's Executive Order 9066 of 19 February 1942 preceded Canada's Privy Council Order 1486 by only five days: in both countries the internees were herded behind barbed wire and deprived of their liberty and their property.[25]

According to historian Roger Daniels, however, after the orders were issued, the Canadian government treated the internees with greater severity. In the United States, the War Relocation Authority tried to "rehabilitate" all "loyal" Japanese Americans into mainstream society as rapidly as possible. Internment camps offered English-language schools and even college extension courses. Thousands of American-born Japanese were allowed to volunteer for military service in Europe, and thousands more were released from internment camps on the condition that they remain off the Pacific Coast. In 1944, the U.S. Supreme Court ruled that this restriction on their mobility was unconstitutional, and large numbers of Japanese Americans returned to California. Canada's B.C. Security Commission made no attempt to reintegrate Japanese Canadians; its camps were simply holding pens. The Canadian armed forces rejected Japanese-Canadian volunteers, and releases from custody came more slowly and carried more restrictions. Canadian courts rejected Japanese-Canadian legal appeals, and the ban on returning to the Pacific Coast continued in force until 1949. The most dramatic measure of these U.S.-Canadian differences, however, were the identical numbers who chose to be voluntarily repatriated to Japan, four thousand from each country, or five times as many proportionately from Canada as from the United States. Daniels attributes the differing treatment of the Japanese-American and Japanese-Canadian minorities not to different attitudes on the part of politicians and publics, which he describes as "almost interchangeable"; it was "the American constitution, with its tradition of judicial review which was largely responsible." Thus the American impulse to assimilate individuals rather than to acknowledge social groups worked to the advantage of Japanese Americans.[26]

Canada seemed so familiar to the American service people stationed there, and yet it was different. Bob Hope, Tallulah Bankhead, and

Shirley Temple came north to entertain them and made appearances to help sell Canadian victory bonds. Hollywood's contribution to cultural unity was the movie *Captains of the Clouds,* in which Canada's air ace "Billy" Bishop pinned RCAF pilot's wings on James Cagney. Young toughs in Toronto sported "zoot suits," although the suits touched off no riots such as those in New York and Los Angeles. But war severed many peacetime cultural connections. The rationing of gasoline, oil, and tires shrank transborder tourism, and travel and immigration restrictions disrupted binational baseball leagues. The *Sporting News* reported that Canadian teams had gone back to the game's "dead-ball" era because the King government's War Exchange Conservation Act banned new Rawlings baseballs as "non-essential" imports. Import substitution created indigenous Canadian replacements. American feature films were joined on Canadian movie screens by the *Canada Carries On* documentaries from Canada's National Film Board, and more radio dials turned to the CBC to hear Canadian war news and war soap operas. American periodicals became harder to find because "pulp magazines" were prominent on the list of restricted imports. Conservative opposition leader R. B. Hanson demanded that "war or no war, the time will never come when Canada will allow these salacious magazines to appear again on the bookstalls of this country."[27]

To the despair of Canadian children and those adults who secretly devoured them, comic books were among the "salacious magazines" excluded. Unlike Britain and Australia, English Canada had developed no indigenous comic strips but imported them from the United States. Canadian comic artists who sought their fortunes on the funny pages migrated south, among them Harold Foster, who drew *Prince Valiant*, and Joe Shuster, creator of *Superman,* the quintessential crusader for "Truth, Justice and the American Way." Canadian youngsters absorbed *The Batman, Captain Marvel,* and *Walt Disney's Comics and Stories* as avidly as their counterparts in the United States. The U.S.-Canada trade agreement of 1935 had removed the tariff, although news stands raised the ten-cent cover price to twelve or fifteen cents. There are no accurate statistics of comic book circulation in Canada, but between 1937 and 1940, the value of magazines imported to

Canada from the United States increased from $2.25 to $6.5 million (CDN). In the winter of 1940–41, Canadian kids found that their favorite comic titles had suddenly vanished from the racks in Canadian pharmacies, tobacco stores, and bus depots.

Shutting out American comic books quickly spurred a domestic Canadian comic industry. *"Wow" Comics #1* reached the news stands in the summer of 1941, and by 1945, four companies were printing comic books for a national market. Because of wartime shortages, the pages were in black and white; only the covers were colored. Between the covers of these "Canadian whites," kids discovered a miniature replica of the familiar American comic panorama: detectives, superheroes, cowboys, secret agents. Some of the characters were transparent "swipes" from the United States. "Captain Wonder," a Canadian boy who doubled as a costumed crime-fighter, was a carbon copy of "Captain Marvel," complete with an ancient mystic and lightning flashes to effect the transformation. But despite such obvious imitations of American material, the Canadian comic books were distinctively Canadian. As patriotic propaganda for the war effort, they outdid the efforts of the government's Wartime Information Board. In every issue, gallant Canadian servicemen (and in one case a servicewoman) such as "The Sea Fury" or "The Invisible Commando" crushed a crude stereotype of a German or a "Jap." "Johnny Canuck," "Canada's answer to Nazi oppression," was drawn by Toronto artist Leo Bachle to "typify the Canadian character." Johnny had no superheroic powers; when he "sent Hitler's generals reeling through the air with a single blow," he used the same human muscles as any other "fine fighting Canuck." His female counterpart was "Nelvana of the Northern Lights," a superheroine in a miniskirt who defended the sovereignty of the Canadian North from the evil "Kablunets." Canada's British connection was a recurring theme. Three comic book war heroes—"Spanner Preston," "Ace Barton," and "Pilot Officer Jimmie Clarkson: The Sign of Freedom"—were Canadians flying in the Royal Air Force. In a strange inversion of the U.S. exclusion of Canada from wartime strategy, readers of these comic books would never have known that the United States was one of Canada's allies.[28]

Below the surface of cooperation, after six years of war lurked Canadian indignation at American self-satisfaction at having "saved the world for democracy." Canadian leaders heartily resented their marginalization within the Allied strategic command, although none publicly complained about it. Ordinary peoples' complaints were also for private Canadian consumption. The memories of *Six War Years* collected by oral historian Barry Broadfoot are replete with bitter anti-Americanisms. A Canadian contractor insisted that the ten-month drama of the Alaska Highway was "balderdash, hoopla . . . generated by public relations types in the American Army." The "real" highway had been built only after the war by Canadians. A construction worker on the project remembered that "there was fighting and knifings and murders, . . . and white soldiers kicking black soldiers off the sidewalks." "We didn't like the Americans," a Canadian soldier commented about his U.S. comrades. "I was always amazed at how many of these fellows showed up drunk, half-drunk or with a hangover," remembered an RCAF officer. "We never wanted the Yanks around us, their air support," claimed a Normandy veteran; "they'd bomb anything that moved, Canadians, British, their own, . . . anything that moved." But although Canadians' stereotypes of the United States remained unaltered, their image of themselves was profoundly reshaped by justifiable national pride in their wartime accomplishments. In addition to its economic and military contributions to victory, during the war years Canada laid the foundations of the welfare state that had been created in America during the Great Depression. National unemployment insurance was implemented in 1941, a Canadian version of the Wagner Act in 1943, and universal family allowances (government grants to parents of children under eighteen) in 1944. Canadians evinced no desire to protect these gains with isolation within North America; almost eighty percent of them wanted their country to be active in postwar preservation of world peace. In World War II, concludes historian J. L. Granatstein, Canada leapt psychologically from "semi-autonomy" to "genuine nationhood."[29]

The United States emerged from four years of war as the most powerful country on the globe. On those infrequent occasions when Americans thought about Canada, they were more uncertain than ever what to make of it. Any understanding of Canada as the third most important military and industrial power in what came to be called the "Free World" discorded sharply with the bucolic northern wilderness depicted in such movies as *Springtime in the Rockies* and in such hit songs as Glenn Miller's "Under Blue Canadian Skies." Was Canada a country or a British colony? "The American," wrote Harvard history professor Crane Brinton in 1945, has "a hard time understanding the fact that, though he sees the face of George VI on Canadian postage stamps, . . . Canada is an independent nation." Even in the minds of America's leaders, wrote Lester Pearson privately from Washington, Canada was "suspended . . . somewhat uneasily . . . between the position of British colony and American dependency."[30]

A New World Order Frozen by Cold War, 1945–1947

The United States and its allies turned their attention to the shape of the postwar order well before the end of hostilities in Europe and the Pacific. With Britain and the Soviet Union, it dominated the transitional process, and its preoccupations tended to determine the context within which lesser nations such as Canada would function in the post-1945 years. The political and economic institutions of the postwar order grew from several major international conferences between 1943 and mid-1945. In Quebec in July 1943, Roosevelt and Churchill cast their thoughts briefly to a vision of a future organization that would succeed the discredited League of Nations. At Moscow in October 1943, Cordell Hull, Anthony Eden, and V. M. Molotov continued on that theme. That autumn in Washington, a more broadly based group of nations established UNRRA, the United Nations Relief and Recovery Administration. In July 1944, more than forty countries met at Bretton Woods, New Hampshire, to establish an International Monetary Fund and a World Bank to stabilize the postwar economic order. Meeting at Dumbarton Oaks, near Washington, from August through October 1944, representatives of the United States, Britain, the Soviet Union, and China talked of a United Nations (UN); the next spring some fifty nations met in San Francisco to adopt the UN Charter.

Where Canada would fit into this postwar international system was not of great concern to anyone but Canadians. American officials found the contribution of Norman Robertson, Canadian undersecretary of state for external affairs, highly constructive, and noted but did not implement his comments about protecting the rights of middle powers. Canada played an important role in the creation of UNESCO, the UN Economic and Social Council, and became a charter member of that council. Canadians in the UN Secretariat also made important contributions. John Humphrey of the Human Rights Division joined Eleanor Roosevelt to draft the UN's Universal Declaration of Human Rights, an achievement he described as a major accomplishment of Canadian-American cooperation. Americans and Canadians shared a strong new commitment to internationalism, a stable world order, and the economic restructuring and collective security that were essential to this new international order. They also came to share a growing disquiet over a perceived threat from "Russia," as the Soviet Union was universally described on both sides of the border. Increasing bipolarism between the Soviet Union and the United States, anxiety about the new ideological ogre of communism, the economic reconstruction of Europe, and conflicts over nuclear weapons: these were the preoccupations that provided the context for the U.S.-Canada relationship during the transition from war to early cold war.[31]

Canada was no more than a vocal bystander in great power debates. As such, Canada did not participate at Quebec, Moscow, or Dumbarton Oaks, except as a diplomatic whisper in the British ear. Nor did Canada have an impact on shaping the terms of the peace settlement. Canadian troops came home rapidly after victory in Europe because Canada was not one of the occupying powers and went unrepresented on the Allied Control Commission. Mackenzie King strongly favored a world rather than regional organization for the postwar era, fearing that a stress on regionalism would result in continued dominance of international debate by a small number of powers; of equal concern was that an emphasis on regional security might enable the United States to slide back into prewar isolationism. On the other hand, Canada played an active role at a May 1943 conference to discuss food and agricultural questions. Lester Pearson ably represented Canada, and he shortly became chairman of both the interim commission and the formal organization that took shape at San Francisco in 1945 as the UN Food and Agriculture Organization.[32]

Well before the United States forced Japanese surrender with atomic destruction, it was evident that East-West tensions would be the aftermath of war. No one, however, could have anticipated the length, severity, and near insanity that came to characterize the cold war. Relations with the Soviet Union began to deteriorate even before the end of the war in Europe, and Roosevelt, although well-disposed toward Stalin, had grown disillusioned before his death. The sources of conflict were diverse: Soviet anxiety for military security on its western borders, the question of war debts and reparations, the contribution of the Soviet Union to the war in the Pacific, the control of atomic weapons and scientific knowledge, Communist parties in western Europe, Soviet espionage activities throughout the West. American and Soviet mutual suspicion also derived from the deep legacy of antiradicalism in the United States, and from Soviet animus at the unsuccessful 1919 American and British intervention (abetted by a contingent of Canadian troops) in the Bolshevik revolution. These differences emerged at international conferences at Yalta in February 1945, before Roosevelt's death, at the UN founding meetings in San Francisco, and at Potsdam in July–August 1945. By that time, the more acerbic Harry Truman was president and Clement Attlee was British prime minister; Mackenzie King, alone among the wartime leaders of the North Atlantic triangle, remained in power in Canada.

Although Canada was less inclined to confront the USSR, preferring negotiation and accommodation, Canadian and American officials shared fundamental assumptions about the Soviet Union and the threat it posed to the West and acted accordingly in the establishment of a military alliance. English- and French-Canadian newspapers lauded Truman's Navy Day speech in New York in October 1945, which defined American goals as a peaceful international open world order but qualified them by the refusal to recognize any government "imposed on any nation by the force of any foreign power." The views expressed by Canadian under-secretary for external affairs Lester Pearson toward the Soviet Union resonated with those advanced by George Kennan of the U.S. State Department, later published under the pseudonym "X" in a *Foreign Affairs* article that circulated within the Canadian External Affairs Department. Pearson had just returned from his ambassadorial duties in Washington, where he seems to have imbibed from the well of growing anti-Soviet sentiment. He wrote King: "My own view . . . is that without some fundamental change in the Soviet state system and in the policies and views of its leaders, the U.S.S.R. is bound to come into open conflict with western democracy. This, of course, does not mean that war is inevitable, because changes and collapse do take place. But without them . . . the end must be conflict. The Russian leaders themselves insist on this." Pearson was less strident than Kennan, who argued that "we have here a force committed fanatically to the belief that with US there can be no permanent *modus vivendi.*" In a major Moscow address in February 1946, Stalin had declared that international accommodation was impossible while capitalism and imperialism still guided Western policies. Stalin's words rang in the ears of Western officials as they counseled Truman to escalate his "get tough with the Russians" policy.[33]

Revelations of Soviet espionage in Canada fed such anxieties. In September 1945, Igor Gouzenko, a cipher clerk at the Soviet embassy in Ottawa, defected to Canada with details about a spy network that extended through Canada to the United States. His spymaster was Colonel Nikolai Zabotin, the military attaché. Zabotin had enlisted Canadians into his web, as well as British scientists who had come to Canada for wartime atomic research. To facilitate catching the spies and to avoid rupturing relations with the USSR, Canada, Britain, and the United States agreed to keep Gouzenko's revelations secret for as long as possible. Someone leaked: on 4 February 1946, journalist Drew Pearson released the news to the millions of Americans who tuned in to his national radio show. The most likely source of Pearson's exclusive was FBI director J. Edgar Hoover, afraid that the Canadians would fumble an opportunity to demonstrate the menace of the tiny Communist parties of Canada and the United States. Hints of the involvement of a senior State Department official further hardened East-West lines and thus the full-scale onset of cold war by 1948. In a message to Congress in March 1947, President Truman moved from the rhetoric to the policy initiative that would later be described as the Truman Doctrine. He asked Congress for $400 million to confront what he assured them was Communist-inspired insurgency in Greece and threatened Soviet aggression in Turkey: "It must be the policy of the United States," Truman intoned, "to support free peoples who are resisting subjugation by armed minorities or by outside pressures."[34]

Although United States officials still sometimes viewed Canada as a colonial fragment of the British Empire, the Truman State Department considered Canada "of the first order." The magnitude of the economic relationship combined with the reality of geographic proximity to emphasize Canada's importance to American policy makers—when they were not preoccupied with the Soviet Union or their own internal affairs. Mackenzie King and his ministers shared Truman's concern about communism, but in five meetings between King and Truman from 1945 to 1947, the prime minister resisted any more concrete military alliance. The Truman administration pressed for definitive steps to improve continental defense, including the establishment of weather stations, training facilities, and bases in the Canadian Arctic and the adoption of American weapons and training in lieu of British. The best that Truman could wrest from King was a vague "Joint Statement for Defense Collaboration" issued in February 1947 on the eve of the Truman Doctrine address to Congress. The Joint Statement proposed "to increase the familiarity of each country's defense establishment with that of the other" by exchanging observers and the "encouragement" of standardization of arms and equipment. Compared to the fulsome language of Ogdensburg and Hyde Park, the document was cautious and noncommittal. "Permanent" and "quickly" had been replaced with "limited" and "gradual," and the last sentence was an escape clause: "either country may at any time discontinue collaboration."[35]

In this transitional period, when the cold war had yet to freeze solid, Canada sought acceptance for the role of a "middle power" ("small power" did not fit with Canada's new self-image) in the Great Power shaping of world events, and it was in Canada's self-interest to avoid provoking the Soviet Union. Any conflict between the United States and the Soviet Union would inevitably involve Canada. As C. P. Stacey suggests, however, that objective remained illusory in the uncertain aftermath of World War II. "A so-called 'middle power' might make a loud noise . . . or take the line of quiet diplomacy . . . ; it came in the end to the same thing, and that was very little." World War II had altered the world balance of power, but Canada's foreign policy was still guided by the need to maintain familial relations with Great Britain and neighborly relations with the United States, with the Soviet Union complicating both relationships.[36]

7 Canada in the New American Empire, 1947–1960

The modern U.S.-Canadian relationship dates from the intensified cold war that began in 1948. Britain's military and economic weakness, made painfully obvious in 1946–47, created new dilemmas for the other two sides of the "North Atlantic Triangle." Canada lost its historic British counterweight to the United States, and the United States was forced into Britain's old imperial role. With dizzying rapidity, the American-led struggle against the Communist specter brought a degree of intimacy between Canada and the United States that the war against Germany had never demanded. Both countries became charter members of the multilateral North Atlantic Treaty Organization (NATO) in 1949, and a year later, Canada followed the United States into a shooting war in Korea. Soviet nuclear bombs and long-range bombers made Canada indispensable to continental defense against transpolar air attack and prompted a peacetime U.S. presence in the Canadian Arctic and the bilateral North American Air Defense Agreement (NORAD) in 1957. A series of Defense Production Sharing agreements seemed the logical corollary to military merger, and America's cold war quest for raw materials security further encouraged economic integration. Unlike earlier periods, U.S. direct investment in Canada and bilateral trade increased simultaneously. America's domestic cold war "Red scare" echoed across the border in attempts to purge alleged Communists from the civil service, politics, the arts, and the labor movement. New cultural tidal waves of television and rock music rolled north as well. During the 1950s, Canada became as integral a part of the new American Empire—more integral, grumbled nationalists—as it had been of the old British Empire. The main motif in Canadian-American cold war relations was U.S. pressure for cooperation and conformity and an understated Canadian countereffort, not always vigorous, for an independent voice. This contest was an unequal one. By 1960, some Canadians came to feel that they had lost it.

The United States, Canada, and the Origins of the Cold War

The only certainty about the origins of the cold war is that historians will continue to debate them passionately. Historic geopolitical rivalries, prewar ideological conflicts, and strains within the wartime alliance with the Soviet Union perhaps made East-West tension inevitable. Post-1945 contingencies, however, gave momentum to the cycle of measure and countermeasure that launched the cold war in earnest in 1948. The Truman Doctrine, write historians Lawrence Aronsen and Martin Kitchen, "let loose the genie of anti-communism and it was never possible, nor even deemed desirable, to get it back into the bottle." Thomas G. Paterson has shown how coercive United States programs for European economic reconstruction contributed further to ill will, and Gar Alperovitz how the United States monopoly of atomic weapons fueled Soviet suspicion of America's intentions. Twenty million Soviet casualties in the "Great War Against Fascism" determined Soviet leadership to secure their borders against invasion by creating puppet regimes in eastern Europe; a Communist coup backed by Soviet military force unseated the pluralist government of Czechoslovakia in February 1948. In June, the Soviet Union closed the land corridor through Soviet-occupied Germany to Berlin. The West answered with a year-long airlift of essential supplies until the Soviets lifted the blockade. After his narrow electoral victory over Republican Thomas Dewey in 1948, President Truman made "meeting the Communist threat" the centerpiece of his program, even if it required the occasional deliberate exaggeration of that threat. His 1949 inaugural address described the North Atlantic Alliance and the Marshall Plan as the foundations of U.S. foreign policy, and Truman won swift congressional approval of the Mutual Defense Assistance Act, which provided billions of American dollars for the military buildup of the "free world." As if on some perverse cue, the Soviet Union detonated its first atomic weapon that same year, and China "fell" to communism when Mao Zedong's Red Army drove the discredited Chinese government of Jiang Jieshi into exile on Taiwan.[1]

In Washington, a powerful bureaucracy with a vested interest in demonizing the Soviet Union swiftly emerged. The National Security Act of 1947 created the unified organizational structure with which the United States fought the cold war: the integrated Department of Defense, the Central Intelligence Agency, and the National Security Council. The official assertion of American strategic thought was NSC-68 (National Security Document 68), which was submitted to the president in April 1950. With the demise of Japan and Germany, the decline of the British and French empires and the emergence of the Soviet Union and United States as the main "aspirants to hegemony," the historical international system had become a world of polarized powers. The Soviet Union, "animated by a new fanatic religious faith, antithetical to our own," sought "to impose its absolute authority over the rest of the world" through military conquest and subversion "by infiltration and intimidation." NSC-68 outlined the United States response to this Soviet threat: to "contain" the Soviet Union and to reject isolation and "develop a healthy international community" within the inter-American system and a rehabilitated western Europe. To continue to carry out this program, the United States needed overall military superiority alone and in concert with "other like-minded nations."[2]

Canada was inevitably among these "other like-minded nations." The ideology of NSC-68 became the keystone in the cold war arch that bridged the forty-ninth parallel, and its strategic and political assumptions the context of Canadian-American relations. There was apprehension in Washington about the strength of Canadian commitment to the cold war crusade. Canada's leaders talked anticommunism, but their lack of action troubled the State Department. "The menace to freedom has never been greater or more insidious," Mackenzie King told the graduating class at William and Mary University in May 1948; "freedom is threatened not only by military force but by an organized conspiracy to establish a tyranny over the human mind." A month later, however, King's cabinet unanimously refused to send Royal Canadian Air Force planes or crews to Germany for the Berlin airlift. Combined with the persistent unwillingness to accept an expanded American military presence in Canada, to the United States this suggested a lack of real resolution on Canada's part. Very few American officials understood the logic that underlay Canada's caution. Following bilateral defense discussions in Ottawa in 1946, George Kennan, head of the Policy Planning Staff in the State Department and one of the architects of containment, stressed the need to convince Canadian leaders that the United States was taking Canada into its confidence on defense issues; but concerns about the degree of Canadian commitment continued. The counselor in the U.S. embassy, for instance, fretted that "military apathy, together with the traditional isolationism of the French Canadians and an apathetic desire to return to more conservative government spending in every field, have prevented so far the public formulation of a long-range national defense policy."[3]

Americans confused the Canadian quest for a policy distinct from, and more cautious than, that of the United States with a lack of policy. Canada stayed out of the Berlin airlift, for example, because it was not a member of the Allied Control Commission for the occupation of Germany. "The Russians" might make Canadian planes "the actual occasion for an incident which led to war." Moreover, wrote Defence Minister Brooke Claxton, Canada had "no say whatever in determining the policy"; the RCAF would "in fact have no status in the matter except as the subsidiary or paid help of the United Kingdom or of the United States." In retrospect, however, any American concerns about Canada's cold war reliability seem groundless. Canada regularly voted with the American bloc at the United Nations, and despite occasional deviations on specific issues, such as Communist China, Canadian governments never embarked on dramatically different foreign policy courses from those of the United States. Militarily, the Canadian shift in the 1950s from a defense strategy based on Britain to one tied to the United States was very clear and very rapid. Canadian governments, Liberal or Conservative, were always sensitive to the threat to

Canadian sovereignty inherent in the expansion of their military relationship with the United States during the Truman and Eisenhower presidencies. Yet despite their caution, American radar networks soon spanned Canada's North, and Canada's military forces were consolidated under American command through NATO and NORAD, and armed with standardized American weapons. This strategic merger was so complete that in 1960 a Canadian colonel could observe ironically that "Canadians are obliged to accept a larger measure of dictation on defense matters from Washington than they were ever willing to take from London."[4]

Canada was drawn into the cold war dynamic of U.S. foreign policy for complex reasons, one of which was genuine dread of Soviet expansionism. Historian Denis Smith frames Canada's acquiescence to U.S. leadership within what he calls "the politics of fear." Canadian policy makers were desperately anxious that the United States step forward in defense of western Europe and North America—"discharge her international responsibilities" was Lester Pearson's phrase. They were more afraid that the United States would reject the military and economic burdens of this role than they were of the problems a "Pax Americana" would cause for Canada. But the Canadian Department of External Affairs image of the Soviet Union was not identical to that of the State Department. Canadian officials agreed that "a fundamental cleavage inevitably exists" between East and West, but some argued that "it is a mistake to cast all the blame for the present tension on the Soviets." Canada's own history predisposed Canadians to the conclusion that "both the Soviet Union and the United States are expanding powers." As Lester Pearson explained, communism alone was not the problem, but that its "crusading and subversive power" had been "harnessed by a cold-blooded, calculating . . . Slav empire." Hume Wrong, Canada's ambassador to the United States, deplored "the blinding unbalanced fear and hatred of Russia and communism prevalent in [the United States that] unfortunately seems to have penetrated the State Department."[5]

But this more nuanced explanation of Soviet behavior did not yield an alternative policy. And if Canadian anticommunism was kinder,

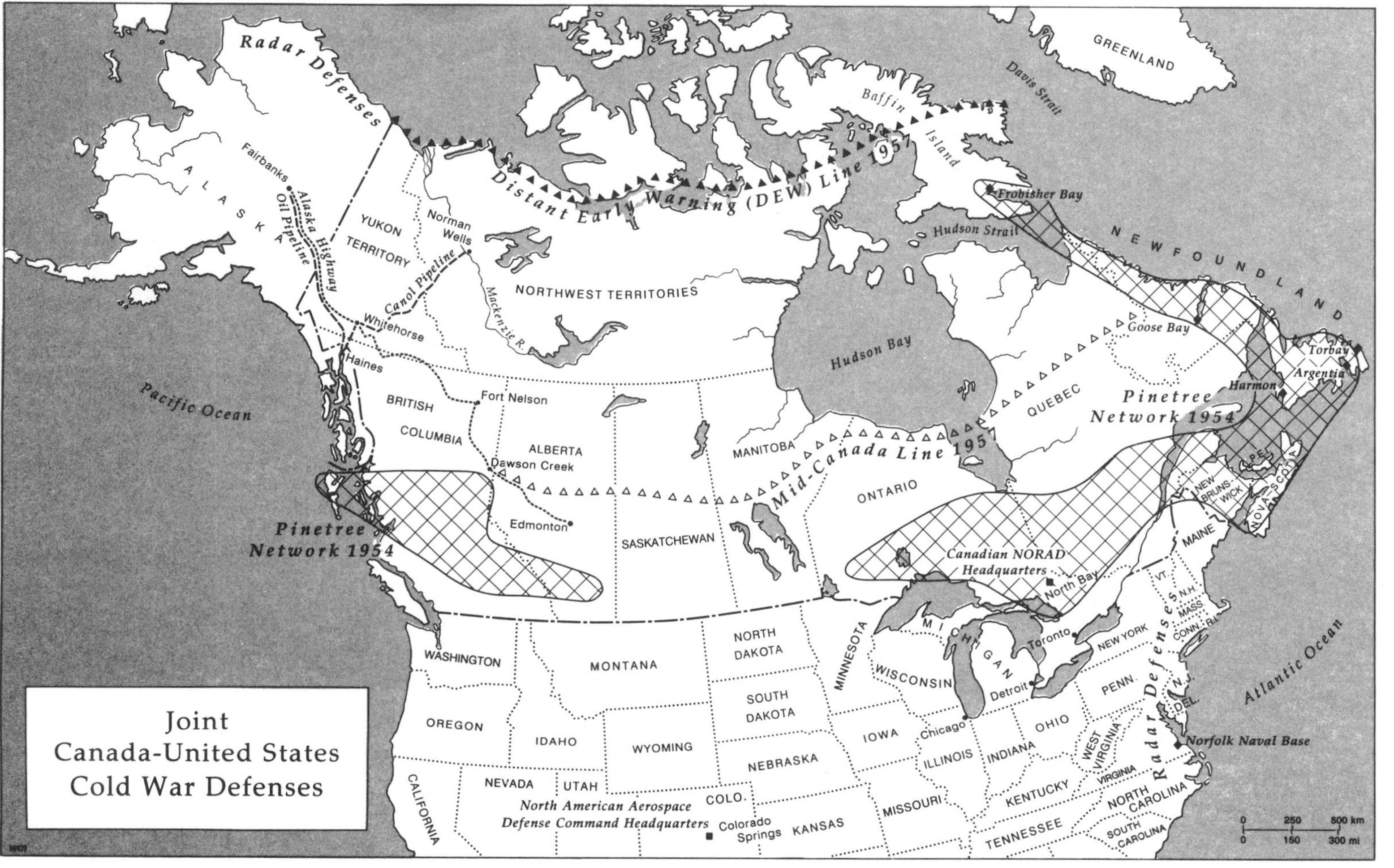
Joint
Canada-United States
Cold War Defenses
Radar Defenses
Distant Early Warning (DEW) Line 1957
Mid-Canada Line 1957
Pinetree Network 1954
Pinetree Network 1954
Radar Defenses
GREENLAND
Davis Strait
Baffin Island
Frobisher Bay
Hudson Strait
NEWFOUNDLAND
Goose Bay
Torbay
Argentia
Harmon
Hudson Bay
QUEBEC
ONTARIO
MANITOBA
SASKATCHEWAN
ALBERTA
BRITISH COLUMBIA
NORTHWEST TERRITORIES
YUKON TERRITORY
ALASKA
Fairbanks
Alaska Highway
Oil Pipeline
Canol Pipeline
Norman Wells
Mackenzie R.
Whitehorse
Haines
Fort Nelson
Dawson Creek
Edmonton
Pacific Ocean
Atlantic Ocean
Canadian NORAD Headquarters
North Bay
Toronto
Detroit
Chicago
P.E.I.
NOVA SCOTIA
NEW BRUNS-WICK
MAINE
VT.
N.H.
MASS.
CONN.
R.I.
NEW YORK
N.J.
DEL.
PENN.
OHIO
WEST VIRGINIA
VIRGINIA
NORTH CAROLINA
SOUTH CAROLINA
KENTUCKY
TENNESSEE
INDIANA
ILLINOIS
MICHIGAN
WISCONSIN
MINNESOTA
IOWA
MISSOURI
NORTH DAKOTA
SOUTH DAKOTA
NEBRASKA
KANSAS
MONTANA
WYOMING
COLO.
Colorado Springs
North American Aerospace Defense Command Headquarters
IDAHO
UTAH
NEVADA
WASHINGTON
OREGON
CALIFORNIA
Norfolk Naval Base
0 250 500 km
0 150 300 mi

gentler, and less histrionic than the American variant, it was equally uncompromising. King and the prime ministers who followed him, Louis St. Laurent and John Diefenbaker, were unyielding anti-Communists, as were their ministers of external affairs, St. Laurent, Lester Pearson, Sidney Smith, and Howard Green. None of these men questioned America's containment strategy; they quibbled only about tactics. They agreed with "the policy of firmness and containing the Soviet Union" but worried lest it "be pushed too hard and too fast." They had no doubt where Canada stood in a showdown between the United States and the Soviet Union. Canada might reject sending planes for the Berlin airlift, but as Mackenzie King confided to his diary, a real "fight against Communism" would be a very different matter: "it was quite certain that if war broke out . . . Canada would wish to come in instantly. . . . [T]here could be no two views on that score."[6]

In continental defense, Canadian leaders followed America's lead out of fiscal reality as well as ideology. In the new world of bipolarism and long-range bombers, Canada had become a buffer state between the United States and the Soviet Union. If Canadians would not or could not defend themselves, the United States would perforce step in to do it for them. Minister of Defense Brooke Claxton told Prime Minister Mackenzie King in early 1947 that although Canada should strive to accomplish as much on its own as was possible, limited economic resources and common sense dictated cooperation with U.S. defense objectives and operations. Four years later, Claxton put it more bluntly: "It may be very difficult indeed for the Canadian Government to reject any major defence proposal which the United States Government presents with conviction as essential to the defence of North America." Economics impelled Canada into junior membership in America's cold war club. As a capitalist nation, dependent on international trade, the benefits were obvious. Defense cooperation with the United States was much cheaper than unilateralism. Canada could perhaps have stretched its capacity to the limit to create on its own the military infrastructure that would have made American bases on Canadian soil and a cooperative system of air defense unnecessary.

But Canadians did not have the political will to spend their money this way. Canada had been a colony protected in part by a parent country for most of the 350 years that Europeans had lived there; it did not require too extensive a rationalization to enjoy from the United States the security they had formerly accepted from France and Britain. Security did not come without an ultimate cost, however, as Canadians had twice learned in world wars and would learn again in Korea.[7]

Proud to March at America's Side

Canada and the United States were "present at the creation" in 1949 of the first major regional security alliance, the North Atlantic Treaty Organization. NATO emerged from the early recognition that the UN would be unlikely to fulfill a collective security role in the aftermath of the inaction that accompanied the Soviet takeover in Czechoslovakia. The initiative came from Europe, where Britain, France, and the Benelux countries had united in the Brussels Pact, and from Canada, where diplomat Escott Reid had been putting words in the mouth of External Affairs Minister Louis St. Laurent about the need "for the free nations of the world to form their own closer association for collective self-defense." The first stage was secret "security conversations" among the United States, Britain, and Canada, and in the summer of 1948, U.S. undersecretary of state Robert Lovett met in Washington with the ambassadors of Canada and the Brussels Pact countries. Talks broadened to produce the North Atlantic Charter, in which twelve countries (the United States, Canada, Britain, France, the Benelux nations, Denmark, Iceland, Italy, Portugal, and Norway) pledged "that an armed attack against one or more of them in Europe or North America shall be considered an attack against them all."[8]

NATO meant something very different to Canada than it did to the United States. For America, it was a dramatic departure from the tradition of "no entangling alliances," which had been an article of faith and practice since George Washington's Farewell Address. The idea of permanently stationing an army on European soil would have been unthinkable before the cold war, but Michigan senator Arthur Vandenberg, a Republican with impeccable isolationist credentials, provided critical congressional support to the NATO treaty because he believed that it would deter Soviet aggression so that American troops might be kept out of Europe. Truman and his new secretary of state Dean Acheson had no such illusion: they perceived NATO as integral to the policy of containment already in operation, the military counterpart of the Marshall Plan for the economic reconstruction of Europe. Canadian ties to Europe were deeper, emotionally and militarily, but NATO was entered neither lightly nor as a decision made in Washington. To the contrary, the treaty offered the prospect of a multilateral counterpoise to U.S. influence. As Lester Pearson later suggested, in NATO Canada sought safety in numbers in the alliance precisely to avoid "seduction" by its southern neighbor. As Escott Reid, a diplomat who worked closely with Pearson, explained, Canada had to "avoid being left alone with the United States . . . because of the great disparity in power between the two countries." NATO, along with the UN and the British Commonwealth, offered an opportunity "to redress the balance in North America." Canada also wanted NATO to be more than "an old-fashioned military alliance." St. Laurent spoke of "an overwhelming preponderance of *moral* force" as well as economic and military power. Article II of the charter, inserted at Canada's request, called on the signatories to "contribute toward the further development of peaceful and friendly international relations by strengthening their free institutions, by bringing about a better understanding of the principles on which those institutions are founded, and by promoting conditions of stability and well-being."[9]

After hints from Dean Acheson, Canada nominated U.S. general Dwight D. Eisenhower to be NATO's first Supreme Allied Commander, Europe (SACEUR). The "future of western civilization," said the new SACEUR, depended on NATO's success. But any hope that the alliance might enhance that civilization rather than simply permit it to survive died quickly, as the U.S. cold war agenda swamped other voices, and NATO's military dimension overshadowed its other objectives. Secretary of State Acheson thought Canadians incurably inclined toward moralizing in foreign policy and utterly naive about international power politics. Although the NATO charter specifically gave each member nation the right to determine "as it deems necessary" its own military contribution, the United States pressed Canada to station troops in Europe, and in 1951, the St. Laurent government complied. Canada also followed the United States in an unprecedented rearmament. Although Canadian defense expenditures never reached U.S. proportional levels, between 1948 and 1953 they leapt from 6.8 to 43 percent of Canada's budget, and from 1.3 to 7.5 percent of the gross national product (GNP). Yet the conventional nonnuclear forces—the only forces Canada maintained—were overshadowed in NATO strategy by the nuclear weapons the United States would use in "massive retaliation" against Soviet attack. By 1955, NATO had so little concern for the ideals of "free institutions" that at U.S. insistence, Canada shared NATO membership with a rearmed Germany and with such "democracies" as Greece and Turkey.[10]

World events of course catalyzed NATO's shift to a purely military emphasis: the creation of the Warsaw Pact, the USSR's mirror-image; the Soviet detonation of a "nuclear explosion" (President Truman's announcement avoided the words "atomic bomb"); and most dramatically, the Korean War. "NATO owes the fact that it has built up its strength to the communist aggression in Korea," Brooke Claxton later remembered; "Korea came along and saved us" was Dean Acheson's more trenchant description. A former Japanese colony, the Korean peninsula had been partitioned between the USSR and the United States along the Thirty-eighth Parallel in 1945. Canada was injected into Korean affairs in 1948 when the UN General Assembly elected Canada to its supervisory commission. The King government had been at first unwilling to serve, but the United States, Canada's nominator, pressed the matter. After a direct appeal from President Truman to Prime Minister King, Canada reluctantly consented. The commission was a failure, and the UN's planned reunification never took place. Instead, a communist People's Republic of Korea formed in the North and an unstable quasi democracy in the South. In June 1950, 110,000 North Korean soldiers with Soviet arms swept across the

Thirty-eighth Parallel to drive the weaker South Korean forces before them toward Seoul and the sea. Although no one in Washington had any illusions about South Korean president Syngman Rhee's dedication to democracy in Korea, the Truman administration was shocked by the attack and reversed its previous inclination to treat South Korea as outside the American strategic perimeter in the Pacific. To the surprise of the world, Canada included, the United States decided on military intervention at once. Dean Acheson immediately brought the issue before the UN Security Council, which (in the absence of the Soviet Union) condemned the North Korean invasion and authorized the use of force to repel it. Within five days, U.S. munitions flowed to the South Korean army, U.S. jets struck at the North Korean advance, the U.S. Seventh Fleet interposed between mainland China and Taiwan, and General Douglas MacArthur embarked American troops for Korea from bases in Japan.[11]

There was no formal congressional declaration of war. Korea was described as a UN "police action," even if it was an essentially American conflict. Had the early fighting progressed well for South Korean and American troops, the multilateral dimension of the war might never have developed; but the American forces fared badly, and the Truman administration soon appealed in general for UN assistance and specifically for Canadian forces. For Canada, the UN imprimatur and America's anticommunist cause left no doubt, despite memories of the domestic crises caused by two world wars and apprehension that Korea would broaden into a wider conflict involving China and the Soviet Union. Canada was also limited by the forces available to it, for its rearmament program remained in its early stages. The Canadian contribution, made gradually throughout 1950, eventually totaled 25,000 troops, three Royal Canadian Navy destroyers, and an RCAF transport squadron. Their symbolic significance meant more to the United States than their military import: 821,000 American GIs served in Korea. The Canadians fought well—the Second Battalion of Princess Patricia's Canadian Light Infantry won a U.S. unit citation for covering an American withdrawal through a dusty Korean pass. Canadian troops remained in Korea until 1957, four years after an armistice ended the futile conflict where it began—with a polarized Korea divided at the Thirty-eighth Parallel. Throughout these years, Ottawa heard a constant refrain from Washington that Canada was not carrying its share of the cold war military burden. In Korea, unlike the two world wars, morbid calculus supported the United States argument: 34,000 dead Americans were proportionately more than the 406 Canadians who never re-crossed the Pacific.

Canadian leaders feared throughout that the Korean conflict was the wrong war at the wrong time, and that the USSR had drawn UN forces into a costly, unwinnable quagmire that would allow Soviet gains in other sectors of the globe. Canada repeatedly urged the United States to seek a negotiated settlement, but always did so quietly and confidentially. Many Canadian policy makers had private reservations about the resolution that authorized UN forces to attack across the Thirty-eighth Parallel, but Minister of External Affairs Lester Pearson voted in favor of it in the UN General Assembly. As General MacArthur's advance rolled northward, Pearson entreated the United States to respect its assurances to Canada that "when the United Nations forces were approaching the Chinese border, the United States would follow a very prudent and unprovocative course of action . . . so that the Government in Beijing would have no excuse for committing their forces in North Korea." The Canadian cabinet shared Truman's fury when MacArthur crossed the Yalu River, triggering massive Chinese intervention. On 2 April 1951, in a speech in Toronto, Pearson described MacArthur's behavior as "a threat to the unity of the free world," and the Canadian government was delighted when the president finally ordered General Omar Bradley to "fire the son of a bitch" two days later, although there is no evidence of a direct connection. Even after General Matthew Ridgeway replaced MacArthur, however, Canadian officials worried "that there was hardly a substratum of truth" in reports from the American high command. After a visit to Korea, Defence Minister Brooke Claxton "came to have less and less confidence" in the U.S. Army's claim that they "had killed and wounded so many Chinamen for each hour or bomb." Concern over what they felt was American irresponsibility in

Korea colored later Canadian attitudes to American escalation of the nuclear debate and to further adventures in Asia.[12]

But their concern did not scare Canadians out of the cold war. They feared the arrogance and overconfidence of American power but simultaneously fell victim to a peculiarly Canadian form of hubris, bred of two centuries of feeling morally superior to the United States. Canadian leaders rationalized the necessity of their satellite status in the new American empire into a virtue. Because Canada had a "special relationship" with the United States (no one observed aloud that Britain and Australia also claimed "special relationships" with America), Canada had a unique ability to shape American policy behind the scenes. If Canada seldom criticized U.S. international initiatives in public, no matter how strongly it opposed those policies, that did not mean that Canada was an American client-state. To the contrary: through "quiet diplomacy" conducted in confidence, Ottawa was using its "special relationship" to restrain Washington from even more dangerous decisions. In the Korean example, Canadians credited their influence with constraining the United States from full-scale war with China and from that greatest of horrors, dropping the atomic bomb. That this myth was completely impossible to prove—or disprove—only added to its attraction. In the words of an academic apologist, political scientist Peyton Lyon: "Even when Washington persists in policies that many Canadians consider misguided, it remains entirely possible that the Americans would have pursued these policies with greater vigor, or launched other misguided policies, without Canadian representation." The more difficult the international crisis, the more important Canada's quiet, constraining voice became. With nuclear weapons and long-range bombers to deliver them, the Americans might blow up the world at any minute.[13]

Those same military technologies made Canada's North critical to American cold war defense strategy. U.S. officials anticipated that any strike against the United States would come by air over the North Pole; hence the first line of strategic defense had to be a cooperative one in the Canadian Arctic. Although Canadian military planners were skeptical of the importance and imminence of any direct attack on North America, that was the conclusion of the Joint Military Cooperation Subcommittee of the Permanent Joint Board on Defense in 1946. Korea and the Soviet nuclear bomb gave the situation greater urgency and made the establishment of a largely U.S. defense system on Canadian territory a major element of the bilateral relationship. The three air defense radar systems that went up in Canada between 1950 and 1957 illustrate how rapidly changing U.S. perceptions of defense requirements could arouse Canadian political sensitivity, and how that sensitivity could in turn frustrate the United States. Each radar network was constructed at American insistence, and each raised questions of financing and control. After protracted negotiations, the Pinetree Network, which ran just north of the Canadian population centers along the U.S. border, became a joint enterprise. Press releases delicately skirted the fact that the United States paid two-thirds of its cost. When U.S. air defense strategists insisted on another line farther north, Canada used its own "McGill Fence" radar technology and paid for, staffed, and named this Mid-Canada Line on its own. But when the National Security Council (NSC-139 and NSC-159/4) concluded that the threat of a Soviet nuclear attack necessitated a Distant Early Warning (DEW) Line across the Arctic, Canada conceded American financing and operation. The DEW Line highlighted Canada's dilemma: although the U.S. cold war strategy was unvarying, the details of United States tactics were subject to change without consultation and with little advance notice. It was impossible for Canada, even if it chose to, to make itself secure enough to eliminate the Pentagon's pressure for American bases, troops, and equipment on Canadian soil.

The Canadian position on continental defense was consistent: defense cooperation with the United States was desirable and inevitable, but the United States should be granted no long-term rights of occupation to defense sites. Facilities should be joint enterprises under Canadian command whenever possible, and the presence of American troops on Canadian soil should be avoided when feasible and phased out quickly when it was not. These objectives were easier to set than to achieve—there were fifteen thousand U.S. servicepeople stationed in Canada by the mid-1950s. Canada's goal shifted to retaining as much control over this American presence as it could. U.S. troops were governed by the Visiting Forces Act, passed by Parliament in 1947. The act granted U.S. commanders the right to enforce military discipline on their troops while on Canadian soil. Any violations of Canadian law, however, came under the jurisdiction of Canadian courts. Matters were complicated when Newfoundland joined the confederation in 1949, and Canada became the landlord for the U.S. leases signed by the British that still had ninety years to run. These bases might have been in North Carolina rather than Newfoundland. The Internal Revenue Service collected taxes, the U.S. Post Office delivered the mail, and U.S. law governed even Canadian civilian employees, who were forbidden to join labor unions and were uncovered by workmen's compensation or unemployment insurance. On more than one occasion, U.S. Military Police had stood off Newfoundland policemen at gunpoint. "We can only imagine," confided a Canadian cabinet minister, "what the attitude of the United States would be if the position were reversed." In November 1949, *Maclean's* magazine revealed the "national shame" that "the Yanks rule a part of Canada." To the chagrin of the Canadian government, however, the United States was unimpressed by Canada's discomfiture. To renegotiate leases with Canada would set a dangerous precedent for U.S. bases in other countries. Washington refused to alter the Newfoundland leases without a *quid pro quo*—a base for the Strategic Air Command at Goose Bay, Labrador. In 1952, after hard-nosed bargaining carried out through the PJBD, the legal status of the Newfoundland bases changed to reflect the Visiting Forces Act, and U.S. B-29 bombers were in readiness in Labrador for an atomic offensive against the Soviet Union. This was the only long-term lease the United States bullied Canada to grant, however; Goose Bay reminded Canadian leaders, writes historian David J. Bercuson, of "the need to protect Canada's sovereignty not only from Soviet attack, but from American encroachment as well."[14]

When U.S. officials thought about it, Canadian sensitivity irritated them as much as American insensitivity infuriated Canadians. American ambassador to Canada Stanley Woodward complained on his retirement in 1953 that Canadian nationalism complicated defense cooperation, and when President Dwight Eisenhower visited Ottawa that November to meet with Prime Minister St. Laurent, the defense of North America against nuclear attack overshadowed the rest of their agenda. Air defense integration had been the subject of extensive discussions of the Permanent Joint Board on Defense, and at PJBD recommendation, Canada had conceded the right of U.S. interceptor flights over Canada. The eventual solution to air defense cooperation was to merge it in NORAD, the North American Air Defense Command. NORAD came into being because the Royal Canadian and U.S. air forces wanted it. The Royal Canadian and U.S. armies and navies, each steeped in hoary tradition, retained a degree of aloofness from each other despite NATO and the integration of their weapons. But the RCAF and the USAF, the youngest services, moved to easy familiarity. Under their new "system of integrated operational control," NORAD's American commander in chief and his Canadian deputy would coordinate "mutual self-defence" of "the Canada–United States region." NORAD evolved slowly because triservice rivalry meant that the United States had no single system of its own until the mid-1950s; "integration of the Canadian and American air defense systems," writes historian Joseph T. Jockel, "brought Canada into what had been a purely American state of confusion." As a result, official Canadian approval on 24 July 1957 came from the new Conservative government of John Diefenbaker. Subsequent events revealed that Diefenbaker and his cabinet had only the vaguest idea how much of Canada's national sovereignty they had signed away.[15]

Integrating Affluence

Junior membership in America's cold war club also proved indispensable to Canadian economic self-interest. Canada was a capitalist country—a "free enterprise" country in the new rhetoric of anticommunism—and more dependent on international trade than the United States. Just as Britain's military weakness ordained a U.S.-Canada defense alliance, Britain's financial problems dictated closer Canadian economic ties to the United States. Before 1939, Canada had sold more to Britain and Europe than it bought from them, a trade surplus that allowed Canadians to buy more from the United States than they sold there. Peace did not restore this happy situation; instead western Europe's postwar economic plight reduced purchases of Canadian grain, fish, and lumber at the same time as Canadian demand soared for consumer goods from U.S. factories. It was a currency problem rather than a trade imbalance; Canada's transatlantic customers could not pay for what they bought in U.S. dollars, nor could their currencies be converted into them. As a result, 1946 to 1947 turned into a reenactment of the economic crisis of 1940–41: Canada faced a massive shortage of American dollars to cover its debts in the United States. In November 1947, the Canadian government imposed emergency controls on imports and outflows of currency and unhappily considered further constraints. These restrictions to trade displeased the U.S. government, but it obligingly ignored the fact that Canada had contravened the 1938 U.S.-Canada trade agreement and loaned Canada $300 million (U.S.) to help meet the emergency. Alternative longer-term solutions, however, were obviously necessary. Canada had hoped for increased multilateral trade as a way out of its dilemma, and its representatives accordingly had worked hard for the General Agreement on Tariffs and Trade (GATT) signed in Geneva that same November. But Europe remained too economically weak to offer any real answers; more plausible resolutions to Canada's problems lay in Washington.[16]

Canada's first request was to be sheltered beneath the wing of the U.S. European Recovery Program announced by Secretary of State George Marshall in June 1947. Canada did not itself request aid from the Marshall Plan, but if European recipients were allowed to spend their Marshall Plan money on Canadian exports, Canada's shortfall of American dollars would be greatly reduced. Canada appealed for justice rather than charity. Its dollar crisis had been caused in large part by $2 billion dollars (CDN) loaned to western Europe in 1946 and 1947. As C. D. Howe pointed out, Canada had spent "more per capita to assist European recovery" than had the United States. The Truman administration conceded Canada's principle, and in return, Canadians did their best to aid administration attempts to sell the Marshall Plan to Congress and the American public. In his speech to Congress, the president specifically cited Canadian generosity to Europe as a justification for the Marshall Plan, and as a reason why it "should not be restricted to purchases within the United States." This "off-shore purchasing" was singled out by congressional critics such as Ohio Republican senator Robert Taft, and Canadian diplomats, politicians, and businessmen waited anxiously while the legislation dragged through Congress. In April 1948, the plan and the provision for purchases from Canada were finally approved. "We should give Canada a lot of credit for this," Truman's assistant secretary of state Willard Thorp later commented; "Canada is forgotten; nobody remembers that Canada had anything to do with the Marshall Plan [yet] Canada made a substantial contribution." Canada was not forgotten financially, however. Historian J. L. Granatstein estimates that during the first two years of its operation, the Marshall Plan put $1.155 billion (U.S.) into Canadian coffers.[17]

Canada's second goal was to bring its trade with the United States closer to a balance. After cautious probing, Canadian emissaries made a startling proposition in October 1947 for "a comprehensive agreement involving, wherever possible, the complete elimination of [customs] duties." As the State Department account of the undisclosed meeting explained it, "they feel that Canada must either integrate her economy more closely with that of the United States or be forced into discriminatively restrictive policies involving greater self sufficiency . . . with corresponding danger of friction with the United States, if not economic warfare." Not even the fact that discussions were underway was disclosed to the press, and the secret negotiations moved swiftly. State Department trade officials felt that a sector-by-sector trade agreement would die in Congress, and countered with a broader offer of "substantially free trade between the two countries" in which "each [country] would retain its separate tariff vis-à-vis third countries." This assuaged Canadian anxiety about their historic relationship with Great Britain, so that by March 1948 all but the details had been roughed in. Apart from quotas on agricultural products, which were essential to domestic politics in both countries, the draft agreement abolished all tariffs between them. A State Department memo described it as "a unique opportunity of . . . knitting the two countries together—an objective of United States foreign policy since the founding of the Republic."[18]

The 1948 U.S.-Canada free trade agreement never reached either legislature. Congressional opposition would perhaps have doomed the agreement; in the Canadian Parliament, the huge Liberal majority would eventually have forced it through, but only after a rancorous debate. Mackenzie King's initial enthusiasm for free trade wore through as he weighed the likely political side effects. He thought back to the Liberal party's 1911 electoral disaster over reciprocity; this new and more far-reaching agreement "would be twisted into a final endeavor to bring about economic union with the United States, which would mean annexation and separation from Britain." On further reflection, he wondered if this might not be perilously close to the truth. The "long objective of the Americans," he wrote in his diary, "was to control this continent [and] to get Canada under their aegis. If I was an American, I would have the same view specially considering Russia's position." King abruptly decided to break off discussions, and free trade evaporated from the binational agenda for another forty-six years.[19]

Despite this, the volume of U.S.-Canada trade, already the largest two-way commodity trade in the world, became larger still. Canada's imports from the United States reached about 70 percent of total imports during World War II and remained there after the war. The dramatic postwar change was the increase in the percentage of total Canadian exports now destined for the U.S. markets. Between 1946 and 1951, Canadian exports to the United States more than doubled in real terms (from $888 million CDN to $2,298 million CDN) The United States absorbed 38 percent of Canada's total exports in 1946 and 59 percent in 1951. Canadian exports to Britain stagnated (from $598 million CDN to $631 million CDN) and declined in proportional terms from 26 percent of total Canadian exports in 1946 to only 16 percent in 1951. This precipitous decline of Anglo-Canadian trade was not a Canadian decision or a "sell-out" of Britain, as some Canadian nationalists murmured. Despite millions in Canadian aid, Britain simply could not afford to buy very much from Canada, leaving its former colony, in historian Bruce Muirhead's words, "no choice other than to exploit the one reliable market it did have, the United States." The United States thus achieved one of the historic goals of its Canadian policy—"knitting the two countries together" and detaching Canada from a British Empire preferential trading system—without any comprehensive free trade agreement.[20]

American demand for Canadian resources fueled a resource boom of greater dimensions than that of the 1920s. In the 1920s, raw materials had been shipped south to manufacture consumer products; in the 1950s, U.S. consumer demand was augmented by the military needs of America's new role as global policeman. Canada was a nearby and reassuringly stable foreign supplier in a turbulent world; as a Department of Defense research report explained it to President Eisenhower, critical resources produced in Canada were "almost as good emergency insurance as resource production in [the] continental United States." The best example of trade directly linked to military demand was the hundredfold increase in the value of American uranium imports from Canada between 1948 and 1959, but the value of imports of aluminum, copper, lead, nickel, zinc, and iron ore had surpassed their World War II peaks by 1950, doubled by 1955, and increased again by half by 1960. Much of their production was controlled by U.S. mining multinationals: lead and zinc, for example, came from American Smelting and Refining and from American Metal Corporation.[21]

Among the most profitable commodities the United States sent north was popular culture, for which Canada continued to be the most important single external market. Canadians bought 40 percent of all the American books and 80 percent of all the American magazines sold abroad and were the second largest absolute (after Britain) and by far the largest per capita consumers of American movies. Two new technologies spurred mass cultural exports after 1945: vinyl 33 and 45 RPM records, which brought rock 'n' roll to a vast teenage audience, and television, in which the United States gained continental and world programming leadership as it had with cinema and radio. As before, there were large percentage profits in Canada for U.S. cultural industries; once a cultural product has been produced, language and geography made the marginal cost of exporting it to Canada minimal, and Canadians bought pop culture at prices that were "slightly higher in Canada." Unlike the 1920s, after 1945 Canadian governments made no use of protectionism to achieve cultural sovereignty. After Canada's intelligentsia vented its dismay about the menace of American mass culture through the Royal Commission on National Development in the Arts, Letters, and Sciences (the Massey Commission) in 1951, Canada followed the commission's recommendation of state promotion of high culture and the continued support of the public infrastructure such as the CBC and the National Film Board (NFB). This cultural promotion, as before, was never a serious threat to the U.S. firms exporting cultural products. NFB documentaries would not reduce consumption of Hollywood's feature films. Canada's new public television service, far from being a threat, actually bought programs from U.S. networks: "I Love Lucy" and "I Was a Communist for the FBI" came to Canadian screens via the CBC![22]

On the two occasions on which Canada pondered restricting sales of American culture, U.S. entertainment exporters did not need Washington's help to neutralize Canadian cultural sovereignty policies that threatened their interests. Beginning in 1943, American magazines skirted Canada's periodical tariff by printing "Canadian editions" in Canada with minimally different editorial content and advertising aimed at Canadian consumers. *Time* used its Canadian subsidiary to dissuade the St. Laurent and Diefenbaker governments from discriminatory tax changes that would have made this ruse uneconomic. In 1947, faced with controls on Canadian distribution because of the currency crisis, and with the possibility that the NFB would begin feature film production, the Motion Picture Association of America sold the Canadian government on the so-called "Canadian Co-operation Program." This transparent flimflam promised to display Canada to the world through the work of Hollywood studios. Producers were to be "encouraged" to use Canadian locations whenever appropriate, Canadian news in the newsreels was to be increased, and scriptwriters promised that Canada would be mentioned as frequently as possible in the dialog of features made in Hollywood! The wonder is not that the plan achieved no results, for Hollywood did not intend it to, but that this bizarre scheme took in such an otherwise hardheaded Canadian as C. D. Howe.[23]

Hollywood's recourse to this deceit demonstrated that economic relations would never be trouble-free. From the Canadian perspective, two historic problems continued: how to ensure continued access to their American market during outbreaks of congressional protectionism, and how to deal with byzantine U.S. customs procedures. During the early 1950s, for example, the U.S. Tariff Commission and Congress toyed with protection against a variety of Canadian agricultural products, against fish fillets, and against lead, zinc, and oil. The Eisenhower administration addressed potential friction points promptly and continued the long-standing preference to work quietly and informally through special bilateral institutions rather than engage in open diplomatic wrangling. Within a year of taking office, Eisenhower had cooperated with the St. Laurent government to establish a cabinet-level Joint U.S.-Canada Committee on Trade and Economic Affairs. As the State Department explained, such institutions afforded an opportunity not only to resolve existing problems but also to anticipate and head off emerging issues.[24]

Economic questions received broader consideration by a commission chaired by Clarence B. Randall, head of the U.S. Council on Foreign Economic Policy. Personally involved in iron ore development in Canada, Randall persistently advocated the economic integration of the two countries, undaunted by the failure of free trade in 1948. His committee's 1954 report touched on all of the critical postwar economic issues: foreign aid and economic assistance, foreign investment, agriculture and raw materials, trade policy, labor standards, and currency convertibility. In spite of disagreement from

Congress with the report's proposed aggressive trade liberalization, Eisenhower recommended and Congress approved an extension of the Trade Agreements Act, which cut tariffs on specific items up to 15 percent, simplified customs procedures for imports, and provided income tax incentives to encourage American private foreign investment.[25]

Not that American capital needed much encouragement to invest in Canada. The foundations of an American branch-plant economy had been laid there much earlier by, among other things, Canada's "national policy" of protective tariffs. Until 1940, the tariff had created a crude inverse relationship between trade and foreign investment: higher Canadian tariffs reduced American exports but increased American investment in Canada; lower Canadian tariffs increased exports and reduced U.S. investment. In the melodramatic words of historian Stephen Scheinberg, Canada "could only choose the gravedigger, to be buried by American exports or by American branch plants." During the 1950s, however, both trade and the American economic presence in Canada expanded rapidly at the same time. The State Department calculated that U.S. direct foreign investment in Canada grew from $3.58 billion (U.S.) in 1950 to $8.33 billion by the end of 1957, an increase more significant than that of U.S. direct foreign investment in Latin America over the same period. The bulk of that investment was in manufacturing ($3.51 billion) followed by oil ($2.15 billion) and mining and smelting ($1 billion). Canadian estimates set the value of total American investment, direct and portfolio, at $16.72 billion at the end of 1960. This represented 75 percent of all foreign investment in Canada, as compared to 60 percent in 1939. British investment had fallen from 36 to 15 percent over this same period.[26]

Defense production was a fundamental element of economic integration: as it became truly continental in scope during the 1950s, parts of the Canadian economy became northern extensions of what President Eisenhower would later call "the military-industrial complex." The Statement of Principles of Economic Cooperation, signed in October 1951, was the first of a series of industrial defense accords that brought U.S. capital and technology to Canada on a far larger scale than had the Hyde Park Declaration during World War II. The United States interpreted its Buy-American Act so as to permit military purchases in Canada. Defense procurement was one area in which the American government and industry were strongly supportive of the Canadian concern: not only official Washington but also the U.S. Chamber of Commerce recommended the "highest practicable degree of standardization and coordination in the production of military equipment and in defense planning." A series of Defense Production Sharing agreements, the first in 1958, extended this arrangement and permanently exempted Canada from the Buy-American Act. By 1960, eight of Canada's fifteen most important defense contractors were subsidiaries of American corporations, among them Pratt & Whitney, Westinghouse, General Motors, and General Electric. General Dynamics named its aircraft subsidiary in suburban Montreal "Canadair," but the interceptors it turned out were U.S. F-86 Sabre jets.[27]

"No other nation as highly industrialized as Canada has such a large proportion of industry controlled by non-resident concerns," two political economists reported to a gathering of Canadian academics in 1956. Observing this fact was much easier than accounting for it. Economist Peter Kresl argues that lack of opposition to foreign ownership was caused by a labor movement dominated by U.S.-based unions. Certainly the 1950s marked the apex of this tendency: more than a million Canadian workers, 72 percent of organized workers in Canada, belonged to unions headquartered in the United States. Although union density—membership as a percentage of the nonfarm labor force—crept toward U.S. levels, the Canadian working class seemed destined to continue to march a half-step behind its American counterpart. A year after the American Federation of Labor and the Congress of Industrial Organizations reunited in 1955 as the AFL-CIO, in Canada the Trades and Labour Congress and the Canadian Congress of Labour suddenly found each other. The only outspoken left-wing critic of U.S. investment in Canada was Tim Buck, leader of the Communist party. Canadian Communists had been spared the harassment heaped on their U.S. comrades by the House Committee on Un-American Activities, but Communist advice was no more likely to be listened to in Canada.[28]

Mainstream analyses of the significance of the high level of U.S. direct investment remained a decade in the future. When these analyses came, they pointed out potential problems: U.S. firms might make decisions not in Canada's best interest; they would be subject to extraterritorial U.S. laws; they would do all their research and development in the United States; they would concentrate primary extraction in Canada and manufacturing in the United States. In the 1950s, however, most Canadians remained complacent about the extent of U.S. ownership of their economy. In the continental prosperity of the 1950s, Canada's postwar economic problems seemed long in the past. For seven years of the decade, the dollar with Queen Elizabeth's portrait was actually worth several cents more than the bill that after 1957 was emblazoned with the phrase "IN GOD WE TRUST."

At the State Department, Clarence Randall continued to press for U.S.-Canada free trade. In the light of the 1990s debate over a North American Free Trade Area, his ideas have a remarkably "modern" ring to them. Randall understood the political impediments that had checked free trade in the past but insisted that circumstances had altered; with Europe moving toward a common market that could include Britain, North American economic integration might prove essential. The advantages of free trade with Canada would outweigh the disadvantages to some sectors of the U.S. economy, and these would be mitigated if integration with Canada were phased in over a twelve- to fifteen-year period. In 1957, Randall persuaded the department to conduct a study of economic integration between the two countries. But Secretary of State John Foster Dulles put an abrupt damper on Randall's prescient enthusiasm. It would be "inappropriate now for the United States to propose an economic integration," Dulles warned Randall in July 1957. Canadians were "rightly proud of their national independence and are eager to control their own destiny. . . . There might be Canadian concern that the economic integration of both countries would in effect subject Canada to preponderant United

States economic influence. Therefore, . . . any initiative [for free trade] should come from Canada." Better to deal with areas of friction as they arose, such as Canadian concern over the "voluntary" import restrictions President Eisenhower imposed on oil, or the PL-480 program, which dumped U.S. agricultural surpluses on international markets to the anguished protests of Canadian farmers. Washington also rebuked Canada for its trade with "Red" China (as the People's Republic of China was universally known in the period), specifically as it involved sales by U.S. subsidiaries in Canada. This last was an ominous portent for the 1960s and Canadian commerce with Castro's Cuba, but in the 1950s, quiet diplomacy on both sides kept it out of the headlines.[29]

Canada Falls Out of Step, 1958–1960

By the time President Eisenhower made his second official visit to Ottawa in July 1958, Secretary of State Dulles had warned him that the Conservative government of John Diefenbaker was "strongly nationalistic" and inclined more to Britain than to the United States. NORAD had further institutionalized defense cooperation, but Eisenhower requested assurance from Diefenbaker that the high level of cooperation that had characterized the Liberal years—for the Liberals had held power in Canada continuously since 1935—would continue under the Tories. A fundamental question soured U.S.-Canada defense relations during Diefenbaker's prime ministership: whether there should be nuclear weapons in Canada and who should control them. During his first two years in office, Diefenbaker clearly moved toward an acceptance in principle of Canada's nuclear role. Perhaps no one anticipated how strong the political backlash would be on this issue when it reached public debate in 1959 and 1960. What triggered the debate was a series of decisions related to the strategic defense of Europe and North America and Canada's military role in that defense. In late 1957, NATO, confronted with the reality of significantly superior numbers of Warsaw Pact ground forces, decided to rely on nuclear weapons. The Canadian role as part of a strike force in the event of war required that its American-designed CF-104 Starfighters carry nuclear warheads. The Canadian forces, however, did not order nuclear warheads for the missiles carried by the CF-104s.[30]

The issue of nuclear weapons became more volatile when Prime Minister Diefenbaker in February 1959 announced to Parliament that his government had "reluctantly" decided that, for reasons of strategic necessity and to fulfill Canadian obligations under NORAD, nuclear weapons would have to be based in Canada. His government negotiated with the United States over the placement of nuclear weapons at American Harmon Air Force Base and Goose Bay in Newfoundland. A major difficulty over the potential placement of U.S. nuclear weapons on Canadian soil was that the U.S. Atomic Energy Act stipulated that American nuclear weapons abroad had to be under control of American forces; to circumvent this, there were discussions of a "two key" or joint control program, in which the use of the weapons would have to be approved by both countries.[31] At the same time, the Diefenbaker government canceled its contract with the A. V. Roe Company to manufacture a "Canadian" interceptor, the CF-105 Avro Arrow. Diefenbaker's decision about the Arrow project reflected an unhappy realization that Canada could not afford to build military aircraft without the hope of foreign sales, and that none of Canada's allies—certainly not the United States—was going to buy the Arrow. The Arrow cancelation was a major blow to the aircraft industry in Canada and to the expectations with which Canada had greeted the postwar era; it cost the economy of Ontario, Canada's largest provincial economy, almost twenty-five thousand jobs. In its place, the government substituted U.S. Voodoo interceptor jets; renaming the RCAF Voodoos the "CF-101" did nothing to stem a nationalist backlash. The new interceptor was to be armed with Genie air-to-air missiles and supplemented in the air defense system by American Bomarc ground-to-air missiles. Both the Genies and the Bomarcs compounded Diefenbaker's nuclear dilemma, for they required nuclear warheads to be effective. Even with their nuclear tips, however, neither the Genie nor the Bomarc missile would be any use against the ICBMs—Inter-Continental Ballistic Missiles—that now supplemented the Soviet Union's force of manned bombers.

The ICBMs were a constant reminder that there was still a cold war, and Diefenbaker remained personally strongly committed to it. His distaste for the burgeoning nonaligned movement more than matched that of the Eisenhower administration. In 1958, Canada had supported the president's invasion of Lebanon, the first test of the "Eisenhower Doctrine," in the UN Security Council. Diefenbaker's speech to the General Assembly in 1960 was a perfervid denunciation of the Soviet Union and of Nikita Khrushchev's role at the United Nations. The prime minister was discouraged that the Soviet downing of a U.S. U-2 spy plane collapsed the Paris summit in May, by escalating East-West tensions over Berlin, and by the Communist advances in Laos and the growing crisis in the Congo. Diefenbaker seems to have shared neither the growing disquiet in the Canadian Department of External Affairs about American overreliance on nuclear weapons nor his diplomats' reservations about the American hard line toward Cuba. Instead, Diefenbaker was troubled by Castro's tilt toward the Soviet Union and spoke of the dangers of a Communist foothold in the Western Hemisphere. In meetings in Montebello, Quebec, in July 1960, American officials were stunned by the fervor of Canadian criticism of American policies in Cuba. But arms sales to Canada were still on target, and Diefenbaker had expressed his personal appreciation to Eisenhower for ensuring that the U.S. defense budget in mid-1960 included a $244 million allocation for Bomarc-B missiles. The signals were mixed and confusing.[32]

Diefenbaker was confronted by a combination of public backlash and lack of consensus within his own government and civil service, with the opposition to nuclear weapons being led by his new minister of external affairs Howard Green (Sidney Smith, his predecessor, died suddenly in March 1959) and the undersecretary, Norman Robertson, who had been Canadian ambassador in Washington in 1957 and 1958. Opposition within the government and from the public led to a lengthy debate over these apparent decisions and ultimately to the refusal of the Diefenbaker government to implement the North American dimensions of agreements he had undertaken without sufficient thought. Although the State Department perceived a deterioration in relations with Canada, Diefenbaker still announced after his June 1960 visit to Eisenhower that the two countries shared the "same ideals and objectives." But he and other Canadian officials had suddenly become much more interested than the Eisenhower administration in discussing the discontinuation of nuclear weapons testing and eventual disarmament. On the eve of the Washington meetings, Christian Herter, who had become secretary of state on Dulles's death in 1959, expressed his concern to the president. But Eisenhower seemed not to want to be bothered with the visit from "merely a Prime Minister," even from such a close neighbor. Nonetheless, Herter believed it important to influence Diefenbaker to ensure continued strong and united Canadian-American defenses. In that connection, Eisenhower and Herter worked hard, but without success, to avert Canada's cancelation of a planned joint air defense exercise euphoniously alliterated as "Sky Shield." It all seemed very distant from Louis St. Laurent's declaration in 1953 that "Canada has been proud to march at the side of the United States, and to recognize the leadership this great country is providing for the free and independent nations."[33]

What had happened to cloud the sunny feelings of that day only a year earlier when President Eisenhower and Prime Minister Diefenbaker had opened the St. Lawrence Seaway together? In fact, nothing represents the bilateral relationship during the cold war better than that seaway. In 1951, Canada, determined to have the long-sought link between the Atlantic and the Great Lakes, threatened to construct it unilaterally. The Eisenhower administration, like those before it, favored the venture for commercial reasons, but economic logic had never been enough to persuade Congress. After it had languished in political impossibility for a half-century, the administration suddenly resurrected the seaway as an indispensable infrastructure for American national security. The two hundred miles of channels and locks would move strategic raw materials, most notably iron ore from Labrador and northern Quebec, into the industrial heartland of the

United States. In 1954, President Eisenhower played this defense card to trump the congressional shills for competing railroad and Atlantic port interests, and the project sailed ahead. The president and Queen Elizabeth II opened the seaway in June 1959 with a glittering ceremony at St. Lambert, Quebec. The *Montreal* Star reported "scattered, hesitant applause" for Eisenhower's single halting sentence in French, and hearty cheers for the Queen's fluency. "We like you, but we all fell in love with the Queen, Ike," boomed a voice during a quiet moment. Nothing could better capture Canada's different attitudes to its new and its old imperial allies. The Royal yacht *Britannia* cruised up the seaway so that Queen Elizabeth could repeat the ceremony with Vice President Richard Nixon at Massena, New York. The seaway, the vice president told the crowd sweating beneath a blazing sun, was "a symbol of a united past and a hopeful sign for the future." Then, just as the Massena High School Band hit the final note of "The Star Spangled Banner," its bass drummer fainted dead away. Was this portent meant for Nixon, for the U.S.-Canadian relationship, or for both?[34]

8 The Moose That Roared, 1960–1968

The cinematic surprise of 1959 was the British comedy *The Mouse That Roared*. In the movie, an infinitesimal European kingdom named the Grand Duchy of Fenwick, governed by Peter Sellers in multiple roles, attacks the United States. It must have seemed to the American government at that time as if Canada had borrowed the Grand Duchy's tactics. From Washington's perspective, a sudden and perplexing pattern of confrontation supplanted fifteen years of Canadian accommodation to America's wishes. Prime Minister John Diefenbaker and his Conservative colleagues were, alas, much less amusing company for Americans than Peter Sellers. The Canadian "moose" roared about nuclear weapons, about relations with Cuba and China, and about U.S. foreign investment; there were even reverberations of long-dormant cultural nationalism. Unlike the movie, the showdown did not end when Canadian voters rolled the credits on the Diefenbaker government and replaced them with Lester Pearson's Liberals, or when bullets in Dallas recast Vice President Lyndon Johnson in the part of President John F. Kennedy. Instead, a U.S. war in Southeast Asia was added to the script of Canadian-American problems, which loomed larger than the individual actors in Ottawa and Washington. On the movie screen, incredibly, the Grand Duchy of Fenwick accomplished its strategic objective of winning American aid, and Fenwickers and Americans lived happily ever after. But Canada and the United States had to cope with each other in the real world, not on the screen.

Kennedy, Diefenbaker, and the Cold War

In the 1960 presidential campaign, John F. Kennedy outplayed the leading cold warrior of his generation. The shop-worn pieties of Republican Richard Nixon contrasted poorly with the new politics of the young Democratic senator from Massachusetts. The Republicans, Kennedy charged, had allowed the Soviet Union to seize nuclear missile superiority and yet had failed to maintain adequate conventional armed forces. Kennedy painted the now-traditional picture of East-West relations as a struggle between two conflicting ideologies: "Freedom under God versus ruthless godless tyranny." But the new and improved cold war he sold the electorate in four television debates promised that the "Communist tide" could be not just halted but rolled back: "I ran for the presidency because I do not want it said that . . . the years when our generation held political power . . . were the years when America began to slip [and when] the balance of power began to turn against the United States and the cause of freedom."[1]

Historians dispute the balance between the individual and the broad impersonal force in shaping history. The causes of the increasing strain on the U.S.-Canada relationship in the early 1960s are a case in point: how much can be attributed to the reciprocal antipathy that developed between John F. Kennedy and John G. Diefenbaker? It has become a Canadian cliché to contrast the confident, cosmopolitan, Harvard graduate who was president with the insecure, teetotaling, small-town Saskatchewan lawyer who was prime minister. Matinee idol Cliff Robertson portrayed Kennedy the war hero in the movie *PT 109*; a film about Diefenbaker's career (such an unlikely production is difficult to imagine) would have featured an unknown character actor. From their first meeting, the two men held each other in hearty contempt. Despite his Germanic surname, Diefenbaker was a sentimental British-Canadian nationalist; he believed that the new president had inherited a "hatred" for Britain from his father, "anti-British buccaneer" Joseph P. Kennedy. Diefenbaker's strident Soviet-bashing at first glance seemed common ground with Kennedy, but Diefenbaker was content to have the cold war remain a rhetorical battle. He would have much preferred Richard Nixon in the White House. During his June 1960 visit to Washington to discuss the U-2 crisis, Diefenbaker had advised the Republicans to cancel the television debates because "there was no advertising value in it for Nixon." Diefenbaker's inexperience in international affairs, a weakness of which Liberal Opposition leader Lester Pearson often reminded him, made him hesitant and indecisive. Kennedy displayed the same machismo in both his international and his interpersonal relations.[2]

But a policy as well as a personality gulf separated Kennedy and Diefenbaker. The Kennedy administration's altered understanding of the bipolar balance of power was far more decisive in shaping U.S. foreign policy—and thus U.S.-Canadian relations—than their personalities. The transition in Canadian-American relations in the early 1960s is understandable only from this perspective. In the thirty-five months Kennedy held office before his assassination in Dallas, he demonstrated that his gut appeal to American nationalism, pride, and anticommunism was more than campaign bombast. The administration believed that the Soviet Union and its satellites were moving into a new, more aggressive phase. Communism could no longer simply be contained: it had to be confronted everywhere and rooted out where possible. Weapons and space were the only programs to receive significant budget increases: Kennedy tripled the power of the U.S. nuclear arsenal, and expanded and reequipped conventional forces to prepare for a "flexible response" across the globe. Kennedy centralized the foreign policy-making process in the White House, the National Security Council (NSC), and the Pentagon, with a corresponding shift of power away from the State Department. This trend toward the "imperial presidency" had been under way since the late 1930s, but it was intensified by both the style of the Kennedy administration and the crises that engulfed it in the early 1960s. These institutional shifts enhanced the authority of Robert McNamara at the Department of Defense, and of McGeorge Bundy and his successor Walt W. Rostow at the National Security Council; they diminished the influence of Dean Rusk and the State Department, which had been traditionally knowledgeable about, and more sensitive toward, Canadian concerns. The structural changes were of course made without any thought to Canada, but as happened with more frequency, such changes influenced the course and nature of U.S.-Canada relations.

The first two meetings between Kennedy and Diefenbaker, in Washington in February and in Ottawa in May 1961, revealed the Kennedy administration's world view and where Canada fit into it. Most of the foreign policy issues that the two governments would face surfaced during those initial discussions: bilateral defense, nuclear weapons, Berlin, Fidel Castro in Cuba, insurgencies in Southeast Asia, and North American aid to what had come to be called the "Third World"—less-developed nations aligned behind neither the United States nor the Soviet Union. Some Canadians, most notably Minister of External Affairs Howard Green, had criticized the United States as excessively hostile to the USSR, blind to opportunities to negotiate with the Communist bloc, and too quick to label social and political unrest in the Third World as Communist-inspired. In its intelligence estimate "Trends in Canadian Foreign Policy," the CIA suggested that Diefenbaker's Conservative government might take Canada in a divergent direction. Canada had entered a new phase of increased "sensitivity" to American influence in its cultural, economic, and military affairs. The CIA anticipated that Canada would continue to seek a more independent foreign policy, pressing for disarmament, arms control, and a nuclear test ban, and for an end to the U.S. blackball of Communist Chinese membership in the United Nations. Canada would maintain its basic commitments to NATO and NORAD, the CIA predicted, but the Conservatives would exploit the latent anti-American sentiments among the Canadian public for electoral advantage. A Liberal return to power in Ottawa might soften the Canadian resistance to the storage of nuclear weapons on Canadian soil.[3]

Kennedy and his senior advisors saw the Diefenbaker government, Howard Green in particular, as willfully oblivious to the threat posed by Nikita Khrushchev's expansionist Soviet regime. Khrushchev, they lectured the Canadians, had been emboldened by the success of the Soviet orbital space flights, by Communist gains in Laos, and by Castro's success in Cuba. Between the first and second U.S.-Canadian meetings, the spectacular failure at the Bay of Pigs of an American-backed invasion of Cuba presumably emboldened Khrushchev still further. The wily Russian, Kennedy and Rusk warned Diefenbaker and Green, would entertain disarmament discussions for propaganda purposes while he stepped up pressure around the vulnerable periphery of the "free world": guerrilla war in Southeast Asia, destabilization efforts in Iran, and continued manipulation of East Germany to force the West's hand on Berlin. The Canadians did not seem to listen. Diefenbaker's aide from External Affairs, Basil Robinson, suggests that the prime minister had formed an "irrational prejudice" against Kennedy and Dean Rusk before they arrived in Ottawa for their second meeting in May 1961. Kennedy, preoccupied with his scheduled June summit with Khrushchev in Vienna, was patronizing and dismissive of Canadian concerns. The Bay of Pigs disaster in April 1961 should have taught the president caution. Instead, Kennedy blamed the fiasco on the State Department and resolved never again to let this irresolute foreign-policy bureaucracy embarrass him. "The message of Cuba, of Laos, of the rising din of Communist voices in Asia and Latin America," Kennedy told an assembly of newspaper editors, was that "the complacent, the self-indulgent, the soft societies are about to be swept away with the debris of history." The United States, "in concert with all the free nations of this hemisphere," had to take a more realistic look at the Communist menace.[4]

Kennedy expected Canadians to take a "realistic look" at Cuba, where the administration did not want them to take an accommodationist stance. Diefenbaker and Kennedy were more of one mind on Cuba than any other item on their agenda. The prime minister supported the American-backed filibuster into the Bay of Pigs and condemned Cuba as a "bridgehead of international communism" in the hemisphere, an anti-Castro posture at odds with that recommended by his own Department of External Affairs. Howard Green opposed any further American intervention in Cuba, fearing complications throughout Latin America. The Kennedy administration rebuffed as "unhelpful" Green's suggestion that Canada mediate between the United States and Cuba; instead, it asked Canada to help by joining the U.S. economic boycott. After securing a large reserve of his favorite Havana cigars, Kennedy had cut off Cuba from U.S. markets with the Trading with the Enemy Act. As they had in regard to China, Canadian leaders refused American requests to cut off trade relations with Cuba. Again, however, the Canadian government could not always stop U.S. extraterritorial trade laws, specifically the control regulations for foreign assets, from discouraging Canadian subsidiaries of U.S. parent companies from doing business with Cuba. Over the next twenty years, paradoxically, Canadian trade representatives in Havana proved valuable to the United States, for they informally gathered intelligence useful to the CIA. They had no direct part, however, in fantastic CIA covert operations to remove Castro by lacing his cigars with LSD or by blowing him up with explosive clamshells while he swam in the Caribbean.[5]

Kennedy also pressed Canada to expand its aid to Latin America to parallel his Alliance for Progress program, and to join the Organization of American States (OAS). This departure from long-standing U.S. opposition to Canadian membership was directly linked to the cold war and to Cuba: the president hoped that Canada would assist U.S. attempts to rally hemispheric solidarity against Castro. Formerly restricted to "republics," the OAS charter had been amended at U.S. insistence to read "states" so that a constitutional monarchy such as Canada could be eligible. President Eisenhower had discussed participation confidentially with Diefenbaker, but Kennedy delivered his invitation to become partners "against the encroachment of international communism in this hemisphere" in a speech to the Canadian Parliament. The prime minister had been seriously considering the idea, but the president's public appeal left him no room for maneuver: if he agreed, Diefenbaker would be seen to have surrendered to American coercion. The most that Canada would concede was to send an observer to the meetings of the OAS Economic and Social Council.[6]

Southeast Asia posed further problems for the bilateral relationship. To Canada, which had firsthand experience, Vietnam seemed like a hotter and less hospitable Korea. When the French colonial regime in Vietnam had fallen in 1954, the Geneva accords had divided that unhappy country at the seventeenth parallel. Ho Chi Minh's Communist-nationalist coalition controlled the north, with what increasingly emerged as an American client state under Ngo Dinh Diem in control to the south. The Geneva accords, to which the United States was not a signatory, established a three-member International Commission for Supervision and Control (ICSC) for Vietnam, whose task was to establish the division at the seventeenth parallel, supervise a cease-fire and oversee elections in 1956 that would lead to eventual reunification. Without prodding from the United States, Canada joined the ICSC as the "Western" representative on the commission to balance Soviet bloc Poland and nonaligned India. The elections never took place, and the Canadian ICSC representatives became at best apologists for and at worst accomplices to an expanding American presence in South Vietnam. The Diefenbaker government had strong reservations about Kennedy's increases in United States military involvement in the region. Even the military advisers the president sent were a possible violation of the 1954 Geneva agreements. The Kennedy administration saw this as further evidence that the Canadians seriously underestimated the Soviet threat. Vice President Lyndon Johnson minced no words after his fact-finding mission to Indochina: the "battle against Communism must be joined in Southeast Asia with strength and determination to achieve success."[7]

Kennedy hoped to make further progress on an agreement for the storage of U.S. nuclear weapons at U.S.-leased military bases in Newfoundland. The United States was willing to accept an agreement for U.S. custody and joint control, the system used at bases in Great Britain, in return for definitive Canadian agreement to at last arm its air defense missiles with nuclear warheads. Canada needed the warheads not simply to fulfill its agreed-on obligations to NORAD and NATO but also to allow the weapons to function at all. Diefenbaker, along with his minister of defense, Douglas Harkness, personally favored this course but still refused to act. To the prime minister, Canada's nuclear role was a domestic political problem more than an issue in Canadian-American defense relations. He was sensitive to public complaints about Canada's defense partnership with America, the most articulate and influential of which was a book by James M. Minifie, CBC correspondent in Washington. First published in February 1960, *Peacemaker or Powdermonkey* went through five printings in its first year and remained in print throughout the decade. Minifie argued that Canada's vision of NATO as the foundation of a "North Atlantic Civilization" had been "betrayed and prostituted," and that Article 2 of the NATO charter had "become the deadest letter in the diplomatic cemetery." NORAD, he pointed out, did not protect Canadians from Soviet attack; instead it guarded the bombers of U.S. Strategic Air Command, the instrument of "massive retaliation," a policy in which Canada had no say. Minifie's alliterative title stated his solution: Canada had to stop acting as America's "powdermonkey" in NATO and NORAD, and assert itself as a world "peacemaker" through the United Nations. Within the cabinet, several ministers, Green the most outspoken, remained adamantly opposed to a nuclear role for Canada as long as there was any hope of an international disarmament agreement. Diefenbaker hoped that if he dissimulated long enough, the problem would go away. Kennedy knew that it would not. The president planned no serious progress toward disarmament in Vienna and wanted to enhance defense capability in a forward area along the route of a Soviet air attack on the United States.[8]

Neither United States nor Canadian officials were pleased with the nonresults of the bilateral Kennedy-Diefenbaker encounters. Two sessions of summit diplomacy had yielded no meeting of minds on nuclear weapons, Latin America, or Southeast Asia. To the Kennedy administration, Canada's foot-dragging on storage and acquisition of nuclear warheads was an obvious dereliction of its duty to NATO and NORAD. Howard Green's prattle about disarmament, East-West negotiations, and Communist China's place in the world community all undermined America's cold war strategy. These policy differences were exacerbated when, after the second meeting, Kennedy carelessly left behind a memo written by NSC Advisor Walt Rostow. In "What We Want from Ottawa Trip," Rostow spoke of the need "to push the Canadians" toward a series of U.S. positions in Latin America and Asia. After he discovered it in his wastebasket, an infuriated Diefenbaker complained to United States ambassador Livingston Merchant that good neighbors did not "push" each other into anything. To Washington, the prime minister's petulant reaction confirmed that a once-dependable cold war ally was now a question mark in American diplomacy. Had Canada become one of the "soft" nations destined for the "debris of history"?[9]

Berlin, Cuba, and the Nuclear Weapons Debate

Kennedy had warned Diefenbaker to expect a "Berlin crisis" before the end of 1961, and after his unsatisfactory discussions of German reunification with Khrushchev in June, the president decided that Berlin would be the "great testing ground of Western courage and will." To demonstrate his courage, Kennedy increased the defense budget, mobilized military reservists, and began a major fallout shelter construction program. Khrushchev responded to this saber-rattling with barbed wire, land mines, machine gun emplacements, and finally a cement barrier to block the flow of refugees from East to West Berlin. The Berlin Wall stood for the next thirty years as the concrete symbol of the cold war and of Kennedy's overreaction. The Berlin crisis sharpened the urgency of U.S.-Canada defense discussions. Diefenbaker continued to perplex the United States: he announced that "Canada stood firmly beside its NATO allies" and imitated Kennedy's bomb shelter program with the "Diefenbunker," and yet he continued to refuse nuclear weapons. Washington's bewilderment was an accurate reflection of what was going on in Ottawa, where the antinuclear Department of External Affairs vied with the prowarhead Department of National Defence. Diefenbaker seemed to have sided with the latter, until a White House leak of Kennedy-Diefenbaker correspondence again made it seem that he was bending to American pressure. When bullying miscarried, Kennedy tried flowers and candy: the United States agreed to purchase Canadian-built F-104Gs for European NATO allies through the U.S. Military Assistance program, a $200 million deal for the Canadian aircraft industry. But the prime minister remained coy, and Canada's nuclear virginity continued intact.[10]

The Berlin situation was compounded by the Soviet military buildup in Cuba during the summer of 1962. Then, on 16 October, United

States U-2 reconnaissance flights photographed Medium Range Ballistic Missile sites under construction along the north coast of the island. The subsequent Soviet–United States confrontation, remembered as the Cuban missile crisis, brought nuclear catastrophe closer than at any moment during the cold war years. Kennedy at once formed an ad hoc executive committee to plan and implement his administration's response. The strongest voices on the committee included Defense Secretary McNamara, National Security Adviser McGeorge Bundy, Kennedy's brother Robert, and Joint Chiefs of Staff Chairman General Maxwell Taylor; Secretary of State Dean Rusk was conspicuously silent. Rusk's invisibility reflected the State Department's limited impact on the decisions, and that in itself foretold problems for Canada. In a television address on 22 October, Kennedy announced a U.S. naval blockade to prevent nuclear warheads from reaching Cuba and called on Khrushchev to remove the missiles. American warships scoured the Caribbean, turning back Soviet naval vessels and boarding one freighter. On 28 October, Khrushchev agreed to remove the missiles in return for an American pledge not to invade the island.[11]

The biggest questions of the Cuban missile crisis—why use an ultimatum rather than negotiations; were the missiles in Cuba a real threat to the United States or only to the president's prestige—are largely irrelevant to the impact of the crisis on relations with Canada. What mattered to America's allies was Kennedy's choice of a unilateral response, and his thoughtless (there is no evidence of malice) disregard for their opinions. As America's partner in NORAD as well as in NATO, Canada had a double claim to consultation. Instead, the Canadian ambassador in Washington Charles Ritchie remained unsummoned to the State Department until literally the eleventh hour. Diefenbaker, Howard Green, and Douglas Harkness saw the photographic evidence and received a perfunctory briefing in Ottawa from former U.S. ambassador to Canada Livingston Merchant only after the president's television address had already been scripted and scheduled. Millions of American viewers (and Canadians, for the CBC carried the address) would know as much two hours later. Kennedy followed up Merchant's synopsis with a message promising that he would try to keep the prime minister informed. As Diefenbaker wrote years later, he "knew the difference between consultation [and] the presentation of something which is, or which is about to become, a *fait accompli.*" Britain had no role in shaping American policy, but its ambassador to the U.S. David Ormsby-Gore was a Kennedy friend, and British prime minister Harold Macmillan received personal telephone calls from the president early in the crisis. Some "special relationships" were more special than others. The United States ignored Canada, its closest ally, during what it believed to be the gravest crisis of the cold war. The situation, however urgent, allowed more time for consultation than there would have been in the event of imminent nuclear attack, but there is no evidence that Kennedy ever considered consultation. His only communication with Diefenbaker before the last-minute Livingston Merchant mission to Ottawa was a letter of 19 October excoriating Canada for supporting a UN resolution calling for a moratorium on nuclear testing. This was, the president claimed, "tantamount to Canada's abandoning the Western position." Canadian policies were tilting in the wrong direction, and the "action intellectuals" who ran Washington had no time to listen to dissenting voices.[12]

Other U.S. allies were infuriated by Kennedy's unilateralism—France's Charles DeGaulle empathized with Diefenbaker—but all remained silent until well after the confrontation ended. Canada was the lone ally to delay instant cooperation with American defense requests. The United States asked Canadian forces to move, in the grotesque acronymic language of the military, from DEFCON (Defense Condition) 5 to DEFCON 3—DEFCON 0 was nuclear holocaust. Although he had left Livingston Merchant with the impression that he was "on side," Diefenbaker neither refused this request nor cooperated with it—he simply did nothing. His indecision made little difference to Western readiness to repel Soviet attack: Minister of Defense Harkness quietly ordered the Canadian Chiefs of Staff into readiness, and Canada's NORAD forces that were integrated with the USAF had already automatically moved to DEFCON 3. The chief of naval staff on his own initiative ordered Canada's Atlantic fleet to sea. Two days later, Diefenbaker authorized the Canadian armed forces to join their American counterparts in DEFCON 2. Although Diefenbaker hoped for a multilateral negotiated settlement of the crisis that would be less provocative of the USSR, he was never openly critical of the United States. After Kennedy's address, Diefenbaker proposed that a UN commission visit Cuba to determine the "facts." This was interpreted in Washington as disbelief in U.S. evidence, but Diefenbaker described the evidence he had seen as "ample" and argued that the Soviet Union had "reached out across the Atlantic to challenge the right of free men to live in peace in this hemisphere."[13]

Like Kennedy's brinkmanship, Diefenbaker's indecision is easier to explain than to defend. As did the American public, Canadians gave the president's Caribbean cowboy drama the highest ratings; when Diefenbaker's two days of delay were disclosed, almost 80 percent of them disapproved in a Gallup poll. In retrospect, it is interesting that the prime minister's assessment of Kennedy now comes closer to the historical consensus. Diefenbaker feared that Kennedy was too determined to erase the Bay of Pigs and the rumors that he had been routed by Khrushchev at Vienna and on Berlin. Kennedy, he wrote, "was perfectly capable of taking the world to the brink of thermonuclear destruction to prove himself the man for our times, a courageous champion of Western democracy." Yet Diefenbaker himself was too preoccupied with image, too determined to demonstrate that Canada was not "a satellite state at the beck and call of an imperial master."[14]

The Cuban missile crisis snapped American patience on the unresolved issue of nuclear weapons for Canada. The U.S. campaign to convince the Diefenbaker government to accept warheads for its missiles had been handicapped by multipartisan resistance to nuclear arms in the Canadian Parliament. The New Democratic party, social democratic successor to the Cooperative Commonwealth Federation (CCF), and the Liberal party were, if anything, more opposed to nuclear weapons than the governing Conservatives. Although Diefenbaker's mail ran two to one against nuclear arms, opinion polls showed a majority in favor. Canada's antinuclear posturing had a strong element of hypocrisy in it—Canada was, said critics, a "nuclear dope peddler" who had earned millions selling the United States uranium used to build its nuclear arsenal. The Cuban missile crisis had demonstrated the total impracticality of the Diefenbaker notion of storing critical nuclear components in the United States until the actual need to fire the missiles occurred. However much debate there was about the effectiveness of a nuclear-tipped Bomarc, Genie, or Honest John missile for its intended military purpose, no one could seriously deny that Canada had agreed to acquire the weapons for its NORAD and NATO forces. On 3 January 1963, U.S. general Lauris Norstad, NATO's supreme commander, said as much at a press conference in Ottawa. A week later, the Liberal party "rethought" its position on nuclear weapons—"flip-flop" was the word the other parties used.

The Kennedy administration could now escalate its pressure on Diefenbaker. Defense Secretary Robert McNamara ended further negotiations with Canada. The prime minister still refused to budge and instead announced that Kennedy had assured him that in the future NATO would increase conventional forces and rely less on its nuclear deterrent. On 30 January, a bombshell press release dropped from the highest levels of the State Department and the NSC. George Ball and McGeorge Bundy flatly affirmed that Canada's weaponry was valueless without nuclear warheads, asserted that the Diefenbaker government had no practical alternate solutions for North American defense, and charged that Diefenbaker had distorted the nature of recent secret defense discussions with President Kennedy. The prime minister of Canada, in other words, was a liar. In a press conference the following day, Dean Rusk unapologetically reinforced the American position. All of the evidence suggests that the Kennedy administration hoped to help Pearson and the Liberals topple Diefenbaker's Conservative government, but the president himself was allegedly furious at Ball and Bundy for using the blunt instrument of a press release rather than a diplomatic note. Kennedy supposedly feared that such an overt public rebuke from Washington would instead solidify Diefenbaker's position and hinder U.S. efforts to destabilize his government.[15]

Ball and Bundy were vindicated by the reaction from Canada. Canadian ambassador Charles Ritchie was recalled as a diplomatic protest (the first time this had happened in the bilateral relationship), but State Department reports showed that after an anticipated sudden flurry of nationalistic outrage at the U.S. incursion into Canadian affairs, both the newspaper editorials and the "man on the street" accepted the American argument. Canadian political cartoonists pilloried Diefenbaker rather than the United States, and the *Globe and Mail* and the *Toronto Telegram,* ordinarily pro-Conservative, supported the acquisition of nuclear weapons and criticized the Diefenbaker government for failing to honor its obligation. Canadian opinion swung quickly and decisively against Diefenbaker. Within a week, his minister and his associate minister of defense, Douglas Harkness and Pierre Sévigny, resigned from the cabinet to protest the prime minister's unwillingness to accept the warheads. Parliamentary governments can survive their allotted five years only as long as they command a legislative majority: the Kennedy administration thus got near-instant gratification. Less than a week after the State Department press release, Lester Pearson's nonconfidence motion deflated the Diefenbaker government and forced a national election in Canada.[16]

American ambassador Walton Butterworth reported that Diefenbaker seemed "a man determined to take his party as well as himself into political oblivion," but the election on 8 April did not turn out exactly as planned by Pearson or, presumably, by the Kennedy administration. In addition to the defense debacle, Diefenbaker had given Canadians many reasons to vote against his Conservatives: he had handled the economy with equal maladroitness. Once the campaign started, however, Diefenbaker adeptly exploited his difficulties with Washington to obscure his dismal domestic record. The Conservatives revived their anti-American campaigns of 1891 and 1911. One Conservative minister accused the United States of treating Canada like "a Guatemala or something" (which drew a protest from the Guatemalan ambassador) and warned "don't push us around, chum." Diefenbaker argued that refusing nuclear weapons showed courage, not cowardice: "Canada was in both [World] wars a long time before some other nations were." What the American embassy characterized as "outrageous histrionics" seemed to work—hecklers shouted "Yankee lover" at some of Pearson's rallies. Diefenbaker's 1963 campaign embodied the eerie Canadian ambivalence about the United States. Anti-Americanism was his ever-present text, yet he compared his role as "underdog" to that of President Harry Truman in 1948. Just like Truman, he told whistle stop audiences, "Everybody's against me but the people." Enough voters were with Diefenbaker that the Liberal party won only a plurality rather than a majority in Parliament. Lester Pearson's minority government would have to depend on the support of other parties to govern and would be vulnerable to sudden parliamentary defeat just as the Conservatives had been. The warmth of President Kennedy's congratulatory telegram was nonetheless striking.[17]

Southeast Asia and North America

The day after his government took office, Prime Minister Pearson announced that Canada would acquire nuclear weapons for its forces. By August, the two countries had reached agreement on the delivery of nuclear warheads to the Canadian forces, and by October, there was agreement on the storage of nuclear weapons by the U.S. forces at American bases in Canada. A dispute that had endured for half a decade had been resolved in favor of the U.S. position. "The welshing and double-dealing which characterized our relations with our partners" had ended, wrote Canadian columnist Pierre Berton; "anti-Americanism is finished as a political issue." This, of course, was nonsense, which is why journalistic profundities become such fun for historians. Liberal minister of external affairs Paul Martin later recalled that he and Pearson had chosen nuclear weapons for Canada with a "heavy heart."[18]

And their colleague Walter Gordon, minister of finance, was already at work on a budget that would become a bilateral economic incident. Between 1955 and 1957, Gordon had chaired a Royal commission to consider "Canada's Economic Prospects." The investigation revealed a (to Gordon) alarming degree of U.S. control of Canadian manufacturing, mining, and petroleum extraction. The Diefenbaker government had buried the Gordon report—a sign that there were limits to Diefenbaker's dislike of the United States. Gordon now made the report's conclusions the basis for proposed tax legislation that discriminated against corporate and individual foreign investors, including a 30-percent "take-over tax" on shares in Canadian corporations sold to nonresidents. Wall Street exploded, as did its echoes in Montreal and Toronto, Bay and St. James streets. After formal U.S. protest, the take-over tax was withdrawn and the other changes modified. Far from restricting U.S. foreign investment, Gordon found himself shortly thereafter in Washington begging successfully that Canada be exempted from Kennedy's proposed restrictions on foreign borrowing in the United States. When the National City Bank of New York attempted to purchase the Mercantile Bank of Canada, however, Gordon accomplished one economic nationalist goal in the form of legislation forbidding foreign control of Canadian chartered banks.[19]

But Diefenbaker was gone, and Gordon at worst was a minor irritant. With Lester Pearson in charge up north, Americans could readjust to their habitual image of Canada (if they had one) as "the great-out-of-doors where some millions of squatters have unaccountably settled, a museum of old-fashioned qualities miraculously frozen in ice." Canada was a nice, nearby respite from the stress of American life, perfectly captured in lyrics of Andy Williams's hit "Canadian Sunset": "a weekend in Canada, a change of scene." After his return from one of many such weekends, Dean Acheson wrote to a friend that things were "all very relaxed as Canada usually is." The retired secretary of state joked that Gordon's "boner on the Budget" had been "as stupid a performance as the Bay of Pigs." Canadians, he concluded, were "as Walt [Butterworth] said, a tribal society, naive, terribly serious about the wrong things and not at all aware of their real problems. . . . Their best move would be to ask us to take them over; and our best move would be to say, no."[20]

But the most corrosive public issue within America in the 1960s soon brought painful division to the U.S.-Canada relationship as well.

On the deepening and tragic involvement of the United States in Vietnam, Canada proved a most ambivalent ally. In September 1963, two months before his assassination, Kennedy starkly defined American policy: "We want the war to be won, the Communists to be contained, and the Americans to go home." Kennedy had increased military aid to the South Vietnamese and twice increased American forces. The Americans killed in action during the Kennedy years died as "advisers," but there were sixteen thousand such advisers in Vietnam by the time of his death. Canada's attitudes and behavior with regard to U.S. policy in Southeast Asia remained contradictory. The Pearson government sympathized with U.S. anticommunist aims, but Canadian leaders were skeptical whether Vietnam represented an unambiguous case of external communist aggression. As a putative middle power, Canada preferred strong international organizations and negotiated settlements; Canada's limited direct involvement in Vietnam was consistently premised on a belief in the value of negotiation and de-escalation of military conflict. From the Canadian perspective, it was critical that the war not escalate to involve China and the Soviet Union in a wider war in which Canadians would have to participate. Canadian diplomats ran messages between the United States and North Vietnam, a secret revealed when Rand Corporation analyst Daniel Ellsberg turned the *Pentagon Papers* over to the *New York Times* in 1972. Canadians grew publicly critical of U.S. military tactics and took in more than fifty thousand American "draft dodgers" or "war resisters"—the term one chose made an immediate political statement. The differences over Vietnam that alienated Prime Minister Pearson and President Johnson underline the greater importance of political structure and national interest than of personality in foreign relations. American leaders had been strongly supportive of "Mike" Pearson for years; although he never for a moment sacrificed his conception of Canada's interests, no international figure of his generation had been as good a friend toward the United States. Yet within two years, newspaper cartoons would show Lyndon Johnson berating the Canadian leader for his intrusive statements about the United States war in Vietnam.[21]

Like U.S. domestic opposition to the Vietnam War, U.S.-Canada division over Southeast Asia emerged slowly. When Pearson met with Kennedy at Hyannis Port in 1963, he empathized with the president's dilemma of how to extricate the United States from Vietnam but offered little advice save caution. Kennedy did not live long enough to make the fatal mistakes on Vietnam that would have blighted his career; his legacy to Lyndon Johnson was not an easy one. Lyndon Johnson continued what he believed were Kennedy's policies and kept Kennedy's team virtually intact: Kennedy became one of America's most revered presidents, and in Canada he is remembered in the names of streets and schools across the country. Lyndon Johnson is among those presidents most detested. It is difficult for anyone under forty years of age to recall that Johnson was not always uncelebrated in either country: his Great Society program and his populist facade caught imaginations on both sides of the border. In January 1964, Pearson met the new president in Washington to put the finishing touches to a Columbia River Treaty and an international park at Roosevelt's summer island of Campobello. The two leaders amicably explored world issues ranging from China and Southeast Asia to Cuba and the Congo, and inched closer to an agreement to rationalize North American automobile production. "We have no problems that cannot be solved," enthused Johnson, ". . . no future that cannot be shared." Pearson was less effusive. "The days of easy and automatic relations," he warned, "are over . . . I know that in the future we are going to have problems and difficulties." The prime minister described the binational connection in the universal male discourse of the era; it was like a man's relationship with his wife: "At times it is difficult to live with her. At all times it is impossible to live without her."[22]

The two leaders next met in September 1964 in Great Falls, Montana, as Johnson flew to Vancouver and Seattle to look at the Columbia River development—significantly, it was his first trip outside the United States as president. Pearson again spoke of neighborly ties and the mutual desire to keep the fence between them in good repair. Johnson caught on in Vancouver: he suggested that cooperation such as the Columbia River project was possible because "we respect our differences." That was exactly what the Agreement Governing Trade in Automotive Products (the Autopact) did—guarantee respect for national differences. "Canadian" cars were American cars made behind a protective tariff in Windsor, Oakville, or Oshawa, Ontario, by Chrysler, Ford, or General Motors of Canada. Workers in the industry belonged to one international union, the United Automobile Workers—*les Travailleurs unis de l'automobile* in Quebec. Although the agreement was touted as a sectoral step toward free trade, it was in fact an experiment in managed trade such as those hoped for by Canadian planners immediately after World War II. Autopact carved up the North American market so that each country manufactured something close to the same percentage of total automobile production that it consumed. Parts and accessories could be shipped either way free of duty. The deal from the outset favored the smaller Canadian automobile industry and offset what had been the major component of Canada's unfavorable balance of trade with the United States. The question becomes why the United States agreed to it. The answers are intricate: the big three automakers liked it because it permitted plants to specialize and eliminated small production runs; parts manufacturers were pleased that it stopped Canada from subsidizing their Canadian competitors; the State Department pretended it was a step toward ultimate free trade. Lyndon Johnson professed not to like it and later accused Canada of "screwing" the United States. He supported it, however, because Lyndon Johnson paid his political debts; the president owed Lester Pearson for sending Canadian soldiers to Cyprus as a UN Peace Force to keep Greece and Turkey from tearing up NATO with their blood feud over the island. Democratic senator Vance Hartke of Indiana, an opponent of the automobile agreement, later charged that it was "a direct trade-off": in return for Autopact, Canada promised to "come and involve themselves in the war in Vietnam."[23]

If so, it was an implicit promise quickly broken. By the time Johnson and Pearson signed the Autopact at the president's Texas ranch in January, the cruel cycle of American engagement in Vietnam had been set in motion. The political and military situation had deteriorated, the

South Vietnamese army had proven ineffective, and the United States had increased the number of advisers and begun to drop American commando saboteurs into the North. In the spring of 1964, Secretary of State Dean Rusk requested and received the services of Blair Seaborn, the Canadian member on the International Control Commission, to make contact with North Vietnamese leaders. Seaborn, explained Rusk to Henry Cabot Lodge, the U.S. ambassador in Saigon, was to find out "what is on Ho Chi Minh's mind" and to "get across to Ho and his colleagues the full measure of U.S. determination to see this thing through." Ultimately, Seaborn made five visits to Hanoi, three in 1964 and two in 1965. The message Seaborn delivered in June 1964 warned that, although the United States had no desire to overthrow the Democratic Republic of Vietnam (DRV), it regarded the Vietcong guerrillas in South Vietnam as under DRV control and would use the military means necessary to confine the DRV north of the seventeenth parallel set in the 1954 Geneva accords. The North Vietnamese response Seaborn brought back was ominous: its action south of the parallel would cease when the United States withdrew and when a neutral government in line with the National Liberation Front program was in power in Saigon. "It would be unwise at this stage," Seaborn advised the State Department, for the United States to expect to bring the North Vietnamese to heel by military or economic means. If anyone in Washington heard this, no one heeded it. In August 1964, reported attacks by North Vietnamese torpedo boats on American destroyers propelled the Gulf of Tonkin Resolution through Congress. The resolution gave President Johnson carte blanche "to take all necessary measures to repel any armed attack" through executive action.[24]

Canadians "breathed a concerted sigh of relief" at Lyndon Johnson's landslide electoral victory over conservative Republican Barry Goldwater that November. "Johnson . . . hides one of the most finely trained minds in American public life beneath a Texan veneer," commented the *Winnipeg Free Press;* affairs in Southeast Asia would be sorted out by a responsible president. In March 1965, "responsible" Lyndon Johnson launched Operation Rolling Thunder—punitive bombing attacks against North Vietnam. Johnson seemed to leave the door ajar for negotiation; the alleged purpose of the bombing was to bring the North Vietnamese to the table, and the State Department continued to seek Seaborn's services as a go-between. This was the backdrop against which Pearson accepted Temple University's World Peace Award in Philadelphia in April. His speech was sympathetic to the United States. He described the war in Vietnam as among those "spurious 'wars of national liberation' which are really wars of Communist domination"; America's "motives were honorable; neither mean nor imperialistic. Its sacrifices have been great." Bombing, alas, had not produced "the desired political response from Hanoi." Almost hesitantly, Pearson suggested that "a suspension of air strikes against North Vietnam *at the right time*"—the words were underlined in his speech—might allow Hanoi to save face and begin negotiations. The proposal was the quintessence of Canadian cold war advice to the United States. Pearson had, however, challenged the foundation of American policy through a decade of war under Johnson and Richard Nixon—that Hanoi would never negotiate in good faith unless it was being "bombed into the stone age," as General Curtis LeMay liked to put it.[25]

The speech stung Johnson. It was the location more than the content of the criticism that offended the president. The antiwar movement would not achieve truly national political influence until after the bloody Vietcong Tet Offensive in 1968, but in April 1965, it was gaining momentum in Congress and on campuses. Chairman of the Senate Foreign Relations Committee J. William Fulbright and his colleague senator Wayne Morse were consistent critics, and the first university teach-in took place at the University of Michigan only a month before Pearson's speech at Temple. President Johnson had been working hard to "domesticate" this dissent, and now that "oh so clever Canadian" Pearson had come "into your own backyard and tell us how to run the war." Pearson had deliberately failed to clear his remarks with Bundy or Rusk, knowing in advance that they would disapprove. "You pissed on my rug!" the president bellowed the next day at Camp David, grabbing the prime minister by the shirtfront.

"All those details," writes journalist Richard Gwyn, "have passed into Canadian folklore, enshrining the memory of Johnsonian coarseness and Pearsonian bravery." Pearson's bravery in this instance is apocryphal. After Johnson's tongue-lashing, the prime minister told the press that Canadians "would want to continue supporting the United States effort to bring peace to the people of Vietnam." Even safe in Canada, he thanked the president for "speaking to me so frankly" and pronounced Johnson's "exposition of the American case for planned and limited air retaliation . . . reassuring and impressive." But Pearson also warned Johnson that Canadian public opinion was turning against U.S. policy in Southeast Asia, and that "a minority Government, cannot merely brush off these criticisms . . . Canada is . . . anxious that its leaders do not appear to be merely echoes of the United States." In his diary, Pearson noted that Johnson was being absorbed by Vietnam, and worried that Johnson might prove to be unequal to the challenge.[26]

Pearson's Temple speech was not the cause of Johnson's decision later that year to stop the bombing temporarily. Yet the president wanted to keep the prime minister onside. Before the United States resumed air attacks in 1966, he assured Pearson that it was only because Hanoi had showed no willingness to talk and that only military targets would be attacked. Pearson was unpersuaded. Like Senator William Fulbright, he had little confidence in a military victory and less in the viability of a South Vietnamese state. Because Pearson feared a general Asian war, the Canadian government attempted a diplomatic contribution independent of Washington. Minister of External Affairs Paul Martin selected retired diplomat Chester Ronning, Canada's senior China expert, to sound out Hanoi about peace. Born in China, Ronning had contacts no American diplomat could match: he knew both Ho Chi Minh and China's Chou En-lai personally. To the U.S. State Department, this diminished rather than augmented his credentials, as did Ronning's outspoken advocacy of China's admission to the United Nations. Although the Canadian Department of External Affairs did not know it, the United States already had a secret line of direct contact with Hanoi; the use of Ronning was superfluous from the U.S. perspective. Dean Rusk was especially displeased by Martin's decision to send Ronning to meet with officials in Saigon (including American ambassador in Saigon Henry Cabot Lodge) as well as in Hanoi. Canada's evenhandedness implied that there might be wrongs on both sides. The Canadian government was excited when North Vietnamese prime minister Pham Van Dong hinted to Ronning that Hanoi would negotiate if the American bombing ceased. But Washington was unimpressed and refused to believe North Vietnam could be sincere. Nor did a second Ronning mission in June 1966 produce any results; the North Vietnamese told him bluntly that Canada's pressure for a peace offensive was pointless at a time when the United States was stepping up its attacks. The State Department described both of the Ronning missions as "negative." Its own use of Blair Seaborn as a conduit for belligerent messages to Hanoi was one thing, but independent Canadian attempts to be diplomatically helpful were quite another. In Vietnam as in Cuba, Canada had yet to find a course of action that did not involve prudent consideration of U.S. objectives and regular consultation with Washington officials.[27]

Responding to both political pressure and personal conviction, the Pearson government took a more critical line against the war. In May 1966, Pearson called for a cease fire and a phased withdrawal by both North Vietnam and the "forces of other governments." Over the next year, Paul Martin traveled to Tokyo, Warsaw, and Moscow in a fruitless effort to promote peace negotiations. To his frustration, the Poles and the Soviets imagined that Canada had Johnson's ear; they asked repeatedly why Canada had not used its influence in Washington to end the fighting. In April 1967 in California, Pearson again suggested a bombing halt, and his government began to nag the Johnson administration about a negotiated settlement. It took no action, however, to reduce the flow of Vietnam-bound war material produced in Canada under the Defense Production Sharing Agreements. Between 1959 and 1970, the U.S. Department of Defense contracted $2.65 billion (CDN) worth of military equipment in Canada. Napalm, the petroleum-based explosive that symbolized Vietnam's obscenity to the U.S. antiwar movement, was manufactured in a plant in Quebec;

the men of the Special Forces, who epitomized the American martial spirit to the war's champions, wore green berets knitted in Ontario. There could be no more ironic illustration of the complexity of the Canadian-American relationship.[28]

As in the United States, Canadian public protest against Lyndon Johnson's war mounted rapidly in 1967 and 1968. There are petitions against the war in the Johnson papers from Canadian individuals, groups, and schools. "Can you rest easily being a part of the brutal machine that America has unleashed . . . in South-East Asia?," a college classmate in Toronto wrote to Johnson's press secretary Bill Moyers. This protest rooted itself in traditional Canadian images of American corruption and violence. Like everything else in Canada, however, the Canadian antiwar movement was tinged by cultural proximity to the United States. Chants of "Hey, Hey, LBJ—How many kids did you kill today?" reverberated at McGill and the University of Manitoba, just as they did at Columbia and the University of Michigan. In May 1967, when the president made an unannounced whirlwind tour of Montreal's World's Fair "Expo '67," the couple who shouted "Johnson, assassin" during his speech were hustled out. The man who countered with "All the way with LBJ" was allowed to remain. As in the United States, by no means all Canadians opposed the war in Vietnam, as the estimated twenty-seven hundred Canadian volunteers who joined the U.S. Marines during the decade bore testimony.[29]

Johnson helicoptered to the prime minister's summer home at Harrington Lake to listen to yet another Canadian proposal "for breaking the Vietnam deadlock." Crafted by Minister of External Affairs Paul Martin, the plan called for both sides to cease active hostilities and retreat to create a demilitarized zone; the provisions of the 1954 Geneva accords would apply while a negotiated settlement was worked out in "Big Four" talks among the United States, the Soviet Union, Britain, and France. Johnson and Rusk were polite enough to return to their helicopter without puncturing Pearson and Martin's pathetic attempt to revive Canada's dream of being a linchpin among the great powers. The *New York Times* dismissed the plan in one sentence. The Johnson administration is "giving careful consideration to halting the bombing," Pearson reported to Parliament. "If so, that's news to Washington," commented the *Washington Post*. The next day a "State Department spokesman" announced that the United States had "doubts about [the plan] because it would place the prestige of the President dangerously on the line" if he accepted these terms and North Vietnam rejected them. "Unless [the peace proposal] proves to have some effect," editorialized the *Toronto Globe and Mail*, "Mr. Pearson's much-touted 'quiet diplomacy' will appear even more ineffective than it does at present." Absolutely nothing came of the plan, of course. For Canadians, the "special relationship" with Washington would soon have less credibility than stories of the Rocky Mountain Sasquatch.[30]

As much as they may have disagreed on Vietnam and whatever their personal assessments of one another, Pearson and Johnson kept the lines of communication open. Pearson's assessment of Johnson's Vietnam dilemma was as astute as any other at the time. Pearson wondered, wrongly, if Johnson really had control over the American military, or if he had decided to let the military have its way in Vietnam in the (mistaken) belief that this would permit his domestic program to win in the United States. When in March 1968 Johnson announced both a cessation of bombing of North Vietnam and his own decision not to seek reelection, Pearson wrote the president warmly endorsing his decision on the bombing.[31]

In the Johnson-Pearson 1960s, Canadian-American relations returned to the equilibrium that had characterized the years before Kennedy and Diefenbaker. The Liberal government had managed for the moment to diffuse Canadian nationalist complaints about the American economic presence in Canada. Vietnam, on the other hand, not only occasioned friction both between the United States and Canada but also generated domestic dissent against the established orders in both countries. Intergovernmental differences over the Vietnam War before 1968 should not be exaggerated, however. There were strong and legitimate voices in both countries who saw American policy as militaristic and imperialistic, and who blamed the Johnson administration for this. But the Pearson government shared the ideological assumptions of its southern neighbor, and the differences between the two were more tactical than fundamental and stemmed essentially from the different interests of a middle power such as Canada and a major world actor on the world stage such as the United States. Given the differing levels of power involvement in the world, there would always be a distinction in the national interests of the two countries. Given that power reality, in conflict, American policy would always prevail.

The Warfare State and the Welfare State

On the surface, the 1960s were the decade of North American, even of worldwide, cultural convergence. For Canada, "convergence" meant moving toward an American norm; it went without saying that Canada was not going to assimilate the United States. To nervous Canadian cultural elites, ominous evidence of convergence was everywhere, but broadcasting was most foreboding because of its influence on the young. Beyond the fact that the seventy percent of Canadians who lived close to the border could pick up American broadcasts over the air, most "Canadian" entertainment broadcasting was of American origin. On AM radio, English-Canadian teenagers listened to Elvis and the Everly Brothers, and French-Canadians to Quebec singers covering direct translations of American rock. After the "British invasion" in 1964, Canadian kids watched their Commonwealth cousins, the Beatles, on the "Ed Sullivan Show," telecast every Sunday evening by the Canadian Broadcasting Corporation just before "Bonanza." The state-owned CBC vied with the private CTV to see which network would pay more to purchase the rebroadcasting rights to these and other popular U.S. programs: when the CTV bought up baseball's World Series, the CBC countered with NFL football. Even Canada's "anti-imperialist youth," whose goal was "national self-determination and independence from the American Empire," borrowed their style and their strategies from the civil rights and antiwar demonstrations they watched on television.[32]

Canada mirrored the United States, but as Alice found out, a mirror can do strange things to images. Viewed from thirty years distance, the 1960s stand out as the decade of greatest Canadian domestic divergence from the United States. It was between 1960 and 1970 that three of the characteristics that today most distinguish the two countries were set in place: the launching of the New Democratic Party, a social-democratic political party of the labor movement and the left that challenged the Liberals and the Conservatives; the development of a more extensive Canadian welfare state, complete with a national medical insurance plan; and the official national legislative recognition of Canada's bicultural English-French nature. The last of these phenomena has everything to do with Canadians' definition of themselves as being different from Americans, but a detailed discussion of the Official Languages Act of 1969 is inapropos in a book on U.S.-Canada relations. The former two occurrences, however, were interrelated and are of great relevance to that relationship. How did it come about that post-1960 Canada developed a viable labor-left band within the legitimate political spectrum and a comprehensive welfare state at precisely the moment that both of these hopes died in America? William H. Chafe summarizes the literature on the United States effectively: "the Vietnam war assuredly destroyed Lyndon Johnson's dream of a united America committed to a 'Great Society.'" The hot war in Asia completed the work of the cold war in fragmenting the American left: the AFL-CIO stood staunchly behind President Johnson, while others "who began as true believers in liberal reform became skeptics instead, alienated from their society and committed to revolutionizing its central values and structures." In Canada, these same people enlisted as New Democrats or remained in the strong left wing within the Liberal party. Nudged from inside and out, the Liberal government of Lester Pearson between 1963 and 1968 gave Canada universal pension and national health systems—the Canada Pension and Medicare. The latter came from the example of the New Democratic provincial government of one of the prairie provinces; the relevant chapter in Granatstein's *Canada, 1957–1967* is entitled "Medicare: Saskatchewan Moves the Nation."[33]

Historians of each country have written about the strange death of liberal America and the curious creation of social-democratic Canada in splendid isolation, as if these things occurred on different planets. The only study to explore them comparatively is Seymour Martin Lipset's *Continental Divide: The Values and Institutions of Canada and the United States* (1990). Lipset attributes the differences primarily to the ideological foundations laid by the American Revolution, which assigned to the United States an "American Whig Ideology" with its "emphases on individual success and equality of opportunity, rather than of results," and to Canada a "Canadian Tory Identity" with its "greater emphases on the state and communitarianism." In Professor Lipset's words, "The United States, set in a classically liberal-Whig mold, stands out among developed countries in the relative lack of involvement of its governments in fields such as . . . welfare, health care, and urban amenities." "Tory Canada," on the other hand, Lipset argues, has throughout its history had both a more active national state and a more vibrant political left than has the United States. Readers who have reached this chapter of *Ambivalent Allies* will know that this conclusion is inconsistent with the histories of the two countries: until the 1950s, Canada was America's backward neighbor in both regards. Historian Robert Bothwell's conclusion that "Lipset's contrast of a classically Liberal U.S. society with a . . . Tory Canadian counterpart is . . . somewhat overdrawn" is a gentle way of suggesting that Lipset's argument is incomplete.[34]

A more convincing explanation for U.S.-Canadian differences in these regards is the huge contingency of the cold war and the massive emotional and fiscal resources the United States expended to fight it. American Liberals expended their reforming energy defending New Deal liberalism from McCarthyite smears but were unable to hold back the right-of-center consensus that created what historian Stephen J. Whitfield calls "The culture of the cold war." By the 1960s, a "military-industrial complex" had fastened its grip so tightly on the United States that its antidemocratic implications came to disturb President Eisenhower.[35]

Canada fought the cold war, too, complete with a red scare, a northern Joe McCarthy (George Drew, Diefenbaker's predecessor as leader of the Conservative party), and branch plants of General Dynamics. But the Canadian experience of these things was different from that of the United States. Canadians went to Reds-under-the-bed movies such as *My Son John,* watched television programs such as "I Was a Communist for the FBI," or read comic books such as *Walt Disney's Uncle Scrooge,* in which Scrooge defeated Asian insurgencies led by cartoon Communists named "Wahn Beeg Rhat" or "Hassan Ben Jaild." But they had been inundated in American pop culture for half a century, long enough to learn to pass it through their national perceptual filters. Many things about cold war America repelled them. They were annoyed to learn that the U.S. Immigration Service had thousands of Canadian names among the 250,000 on its inventory of aliens to be denied entry to the United States because of radical political connections, and they exploded when Herbert Norman, Canada's ambassador to Egypt, took his own life after the U.S. House Un-American Activities Committee revealed his youthful Communist indiscretions. And just as Canada lacked such amenties as M&Ms, Hershey Bars, and Fritos Corn Chips, it did not have a full-scale American-style "military-industrial complex." Its military was proportionately smaller and had less status and influence. Because of Canada's subordinate roles in planning the world wars and Korea, there were no Canadian Douglas MacArthurs. There were no Canadian "Dr. Strangeloves" either, or at least none in Canada, because there were no "Think Tanks" such as the Rand Corporation to nurture them. Canada's national security bureaucracy was small, and without the U.S. separation of powers between the legislature and the executive to hide behind, it was constrained by legislative supervision. Most important, defense industries were smaller, both in absolute terms and relative to the overall economy. Canada enjoyed a lucrative trade in component parts for U.S. weapons, but after the cancelation of the Avro Arrow interceptor, its defense industries were a profitable sideline but never the engine of the country's manufacturing economy. Tourists from both countries saw what this meant when they visited Seattle, Washington, and Vancouver, British Columbia, only 148 miles apart. A defense-based economy gave Seattle a completely different urban geography and made the two cities "distant neighbors." The percentage of the Canadian national budget devoted to defense declined steadily after 1955, and the share of GNP spent on the military fell even faster. In the United States, the opposite occurred. By the end of the 1960s, America was spending 59 percent of its national budget, and almost 10 percent of its GNP, on defense, as compared to Canada's 18 percent of its budget and 2.45 percent of GNP. Canada, safe (if nervous) under the American nuclear umbrella, bought a social security instead of a national security state. America battled the Communist threat around the globe and, in the process, built a warfare state instead of a welfare state.[36]

9 The Ambivalent Ally, 1968–1984

Pierre Elliott Trudeau was prime minister of Canada longer than any other save Sir John A. Macdonald and William Lyon Mackenzie King. With Trudeau as its leader, the Liberal party held power in Ottawa for fifteen years, broken only by the brief Conservative interregnum of Joe Clark in 1979 and 1980. The parliamentary system permits longer political careers; after Franklin Roosevelt successfully defied the two-term tradition, American presidents were constitutionally limited to eight years in office. Trudeau served opposite five presidents: Lyndon Johnson, Richard Nixon, Gerald Ford, Jimmy Carter, and Ronald Reagan. None of them liked him very much except Carter. That there were so many presidents declared how difficult these years were for the United States, and accordingly, how difficult they were for the U.S.-Canada relationship. Canadians (English Canadians, that is) discovered that it was much less fulfilling to be America's junior partner than it had been to be Britain's, and that the "bonds of sentiment and loyalty" were missing on both sides. Partnership with America offered the material benefits of selling armaments and automobiles to the United States; it brought the spiritual poverty of continued complicity in America's war in Vietnam. A strident new Canadian nationalism demanded that Trudeau's government act to stop the Americanization of Canada, and obtained action to control U.S. investment and to block American popular culture. When Trudeau retired and Ronald Reagan was elected to his second term in 1984, the "special relationship" was something only for historians to ponder.[1]

Distinct Societies

At no time in their twentieth-century histories have Canada and the United States seemed so divergent as when America was "coming apart at home" over race and Vietnam. Canadians, of course, had always considered their country fundamentally different from the United States, but numerous events of the late 1960s and early 1970s buttressed their national narcissism about small differences and their long-standing conviction of moral superiority. American social critics offered confirmation. "Society in the United States is close to disintegration," a Michigan trade unionist told an Ontario audience in February 1968, "because of its failure to deal with the problems of poverty and urban life." Events of the next few months bore him out, as violence swept the United States in the wake of the murder of Martin Luther King, Jr. The Washington correspondents of Canadian newspapers reported in detail both the rioting and looting by "gangs of Negro youths . . . within a few blocks of the White House" and the brutal treatment meted out to them if "policemen wearing riot helmets equipped with plastic visors, waving rifles, shotguns and pistols" arrived to stop them. Canadian editors rushed to pour out their preconceptions: "The American people claim to be the most democratic in the world," wrote Montreal's *Le Devoir*, "but this great military and economic power is a sick nation [which] tolerates systematic injustice, hatred, [and] poverty." The United States "has never reached that state of civilization in which its people were prepared to commit their security to the rule of law," observed the *Toronto Globe and Mail*. Canadian editors tendered lofty condescension. "The writing has been on the wall for many years," the *Winnipeg Free Press* offered; "Congress must not procrastinate any longer either on civil rights or . . . strict controls on the sale of firearms." The only chance for Americans to escape "the smoldering hell they have built with racial prejudice," contributed the *Toronto Globe and Mail*, was to "spend billions . . . and end the Vietnam war to make the spending possible." "America has, since its beginnings, been characterized by a unique tradition of violence," wrote journalist Claude Ryan after an assassin claimed Robert Kennedy two months later. "We thought this tradition was over. The events of recent years have proved unfortunately that is not the case." Canadian rocker Burton Cummings howled his critique of the Republic: "I don't need your war machine, I don't need your ghetto scene—American woman, stay away from me."[2]

Some Americans felt the same way. Cummings's song bulleted to number three on the U.S. pop charts, and for the first time since the early nineteenth century, Americans migrating to Canada began to outnumber Canadians moving to the United States. Since the end of World War II, prosperity and U.S. immigration controls had reduced the net migration of Canadians to the United States; between 1946 and 1957, 293,000 Canadians emigrated south while 78,000 Americans moved to Canada. The professionals who could qualify for an United States "Green Card," however, formed a higher proportion of the people Canada lost. Throughout the 1950s, this "brain drain" siphoned off, for example, the equivalent of about 20 percent of Canada's engineering graduates each year. In the 1960s, the Vietnam War and U.S. urban violence helped Canada to hold its own people and absorb some its neighbor's. Young, single Canadian males in the United States were liable to the draft after one year's residence, which no doubt helped many choose Halifax over Houston. Between 50,000 and 125,000 (estimates vary that widely) American men of that same generation chose Canada as well. If the higher number is closer to accurate, these war resisters (or draft dodgers) accounted for all of Canada's net migration advantage of 250,000 to 150,000 over the period from 1965 to 1975. Half of Canadians, according to a 1968 poll, wished that the war resisters would stay home; this percentage was more a negative comment about the United States than a statement of support for the Vietnam War. America's problems made Canadians feel better about themselves and their country. Even those disinclined to nationalism or anti-Americanism, such as historian Michael Bliss, observed in 1970 that Canada "is a more attractive country vis-à-vis the United States than it has ever been."[3]

Apart from their differences of opinion over wartime expatriates, Canadians liked the fact that Americans were taking favorable notice.

The 6 million U.S. visitors in the centennial year of 1967 found that Canada had clean, safe cities with skyscrapers, and that not all Canadians wore stocking caps and checked jackets. Montreal's World's Fair—"Expo '67"—drew a host of admiring U.S. comment. Extolling "the good new buildings" and "the shining new subway," the *New York Times* concluded that Americans could "learn about other things than fairs from this Canadian jewel city." Two years later, Montreal landed a major league baseball team, appropriately nicknamed the "Expos." That decision showed how little Americans understood about Canada: the barons of baseball would have been far more shrewd to award the first foreign franchise to Toronto, Canada's financial capital and coming metropole; Montreal was about to be convulsed by Québecois ethnic nationalism in search of an independent Quebec. Canada dealt with the Quebec independence movement with both carrot and stick. An Official Languages Act in 1969 made French and English equal in national institutions; and in October 1970, massive military repression crushed the cells of the Front de libération du Québec (the Quebec Liberation Front), who had carried out two political kidnappings. During this "October Crisis," the Canadian government suspended the civil liberties of 21 million Canadians to catch a handful of terrorists—without significant domestic protest. The contrast between Canadian and American approaches to dissent was instructive: Canadians, expatriate U.S. intellectual Edgar Z. Friedenberg noted, were remarkable for their "deference to authority."[4]

The stirrings of Canadian nationalism exploited by John Diefenbaker and encouraged by Walter Gordon became an anti-American whirlwind by 1970. Even somnolent academic seminars on U.S.-Canadian relations could be shaken awake by its gusts. At Columbia University in November 1970, a former Canadian cold warrior recanted at gale force. Professor James Eayrs of the University of Toronto eloquently summarized the case of Canada's new nationalists. NATO, NORAD, and the PJBD endured, but "the spirit of Ogdensburg ha[d] long since evaporated" and "the identity of basic aims shattered." The United States had betrayed Canada's trust, wearing anticommunism as "a protean disguise . . . behind which American oilmen as well as American airmen could go about their stealthy business." Canada had become nothing more than "a continental chore-boy for the Strategic Air Command," a place for SAC pilots to "practice their bomb runs." Eayrs posited that "the main strategic threat to Canada comes not from our north but from our south," from "a new generation of American imperialists." Canada's duty, he concluded, was to break off its American alliance in order to provide moral support to "the millions of Americans trying to compel a change of policy" in Vietnam, to say "goodbye to good neighborhood in the interests of us all. Otherwise a future president of the United States—perhaps some young opponent of the [Vietnam] war now in Canada or jail—will say to a future prime minister of the neighbor still unknown: 'Where were you when we needed you?' " Twenty Canadian journalists rushed to file their stories; the one American journalist who covered the seminar appears to have missed Eayrs's speech.[5]

Sleeping with an Elephant

Pierre Elliott Trudeau had no patience with nationalist passions. The Liberal party chose him to replace Lester Pearson because he promised an answer to the Quebec question, and in June 1968, the electorate gave him a majority government—155 of the 263 seats in the House of Commons—for that same reason. The new prime minister was not going to give in to Canadian nationalism any more than he was to the Québecois variant. Trudeau questioned all of the foreign-policy myths of post-1945 Canada: "Quiet Diplomacy," the "helpful fixer" role, the "linchpin" function, the "special relationship." Nothing was sacred. Former Washington ambassador Charles Ritchie, reassigned to London, found "the climate in Ottawa very anti-NATO" and heard "a great deal of talk of neutrality for Canada based on the Swedish model." Even "the 'British connection' seems to be receding out of view. Only the crown remains." Trudeau did not cherish Canada's diplomats, either. He eviscerated the Canadian Department of External Affairs much as John F. Kennedy had done to the U.S.

State Department a decade earlier. In quest of an imperial prime ministership, he concentrated authority in the prime minister's office and made use of Ivan Head, his special advisor who came with him from his previous portfolio in the justice department. The resulting "denigration of External Affairs" (to use Kim Nossal's term) undermined the department that had handled the bilateral relationship from its beginnings. Trudeau was a relentless rationalist who subjected every aspect of Canada's external policy to review. The result was a six-pack of booklets issued jointly as *A Foreign Policy for Canadians* in 1970, which proposed that Canada refocus its trade and international ties beyond North America toward Europe, Asia, and Latin America. Those Canadians who read the series of light discussion papers—not a very demanding intellectual task, historian J. L. Granatstein has commented—were struck by the "curious absence" of a paper on Canadian-American relations. The feeble response was that *all* the papers, to some degree, were about Canadian-U.S. relations! "Seventy percent of Canada's foreign policy is predetermined by the Canadian-U.S. relationship," Trudeau had once commented. Canada's goal, he argued, "should be to maximize freedom of movement with regard to the remaining thirty percent."[6]

Lame-duck Lyndon Johnson was spared Pierre Trudeau. Instead, new Republican president Richard Nixon welcomed him to Washington in March 1969, continuing what had become a tradition that the first foreign leader greeted at the White House would be the Canadian prime minister. The two men managed their profound dislike for each other remarkably well. The Watergate tapes revealed that Nixon's private term for Trudeau was "that asshole"; what Trudeau called Nixon remains hidden from the historian: it would have been no more complimentary, but surely would have been expressed more elegantly. Otherwise, president and prime minister spoke frankly from the first: Trudeau opened two defense subjects assumed to be unpleasant. In Europe, Canada would halve its NATO contingent to five thousand (he did not tell the president that his cabinet had considered leaving NATO altogether); in North America, Canada objected to the new Safeguard Anti-Ballistic Missiles being sowed in the fields of North

Dakota and Montana. A missile system to destroy missiles, Trudeau argued, would escalate an East-West arms race that seemed to be slowing down and postpone Canada's goal of nuclear disarmament. And Canada intended to recognize formally the People's Republic of China.

Nixon's nonreactions surprised the prime minister. The president understood the need for NATO reductions—he wanted American troops back in the United States as well. Safeguard would go ahead, with Canada getting regular reports of "plans and developments in the ABM field" in the hope that Canadians would come to appreciate its strategic necessity. On China, Nixon had already accepted the advice of his national security advisor Henry Kissinger (Nixon brought Secretary of State William Rogers out only for ceremonial display) that recognition was inevitable and desirable. Kissinger's business contacts on the Trilateral Commission had favored recognition since 1963, but the Vietnam War and the Cultural Revolution had impeded it. Canadian recognition might smooth the way for a United States opening to Beijing; in any event, what Canada did was of no great consequence. Nixon pressed one issue of his own—the United States plan for a continental oil policy. That already existed, Trudeau responded disingenuously. Western Canada provided parts of the United States with oil and natural gas; eastern Canada imported an equal amount pumped by U.S. companies in Venezuela. It was after this visit that Trudeau made his famous—to Canadians, that is—remark that "Living next to you is in some ways like sleeping with an elephant; no matter how friendly and even-tempered is the beast, one is affected by every twitch and grunt."[7]

Although he made no secret of his distaste for America's Asian war, Trudeau never nagged Nixon to make peace, as Pearson and Paul Martin had done with Johnson. No Canadian should have had any illusions that friendly counsel from Canada would bend Nixon on the war. In quest of international stature in his undeclared campaign for the Republican nomination, Nixon had made a major speech to Toronto's Empire Club (the name derived from the British "Empire," but was nonetheless apt) in which he affirmed his faith in the "domino theory" and bluntly stated that "the future of Canada as well as the

United States is tied to the creation of a free and prosperous empire in Asia." Trudeau understood that Americans themselves would have to confront their president. The United States antiwar movement had intensified since Pearson's Temple University address. There was now an articulate congressional opposition, and antiwar protest turned to the active resistance graphically displayed in the streets of Chicago during the 1968 Democratic convention. Grassroots connections between Canadian and American opponents of the war proliferated as a sort of underground railroad (the comparison was made often) led draft evaders north. There were Canadians among the protestors in Chicago, and on Canadian university campuses students denounced Canadian complicity in providing arms to the United States. Trudeau gave them little satisfaction. His protests were symbols, such as his speech to a delegation of Mennonites in Winnipeg that Canada should be "a refuge from militarism" for draft resisters. This pleased no one—ultra-left antiwar pickets that same day passed out leaflets reading "Death to Trudeau."[8]

As part of his policy of "Vietnamization," President Nixon reduced American ground forces from half a million to fewer than one hundred thousand, but stepped up the U.S. air offensive in search of "peace with honor." With Henry Kissinger assuring them that this goal was "at hand," American voters gave Richard Nixon resounding reelection over the "acid, amnesty and abortion" Democrat George McGovern in November 1972. Trudeau was less fortunate: a week earlier, Canadian voters had reduced his government to a minority. It was time, he was persuaded, to speak out on Vietnam: the new Parliament resolved against the war in January 1973, infuriating the Nixon administration and relegating Canadian diplomats in Washington to the "shit list" with such neutral countries as Sweden. Canada came off the list some weeks later when it agreed to be America's designate on a new international commission to supervise a proposed cease-fire. For four months, Canada kept a staff of 290 in Vietnam who did important work supervising exchanges of prisoners of war. But the commission, described as a "masquerade" and a "charade," had no success in its larger assignment of supervising the cease-fire: North Vietnam was not about to stop fighting on the eve of victory. Canadians came home in frustration on 31 July; the last American troops followed shortly thereafter. Without its American strings, the puppet government in Saigon collapsed in twenty months.[9]

In Ottawa, the fate of Trudeau's minority government dangled on the parliamentary votes of the nationalist New Democratic Party. The long-awaited position paper on Canadian-American relations had been issued just before the election, provoked by a change in U.S. economic policy that is the subject of the next section. *Canadian-American Relations: Options for the Future* made clear that "the United States is Canada's closest friend and will remain so," but the paper continued to suggest that Canada reduce its dependence on the United States. Minister of External Affairs Mitchell Sharp (in Trudeau's cabinets, the position was a revolving door) gave the policy a name: the "Third Option." The Third Option repackaged the long Canadian search for counterbalances to the United States begun in the 1940s. Pearson and St. Laurent had tried multilateral international organizations such as the United Nations and NATO; Diefenbaker had offered the chimera of a revitalized British connection; now Trudeau and his ministers of external affairs offered the world. There were no more discernable results; nor was the United States particularly discomfited by the attempt. As NSC advisor Brent Scowcroft commented to two Canadian historians years later, Washington simply thought, "there go the Canadians again." American economic realities, not Canadian foreign policy illusions, brought about the bilateral conflicts of the Nixon-Trudeau years.[10]

Canadian Economic Nationalism

Canadian economic nationalism predated Pierre Trudeau—in truth, the prime minister thought it a nuisance and a distraction from the things he really cared about. Until the mid-1950s, Canadian economic nationalism took the form of protective tariffs against imported American manufactured goods; thereafter, although protection remained important, economic nationalists fulminated against U.S. foreign investment. There was a enchanting illogic in this: it was the protective tariff that had brought United States direct investment to Canada in the first place. The reaction against U.S. direct investment, which began in the late 1950s, built to a nationalist crescendo in the "Waffle movement" of 1969, so-called because its members demanded that the New Democratic Party "waffle" to the left, away from the political center. Young "Wafflers" (one of the authors among them) wore two campaign buttons. One bore the label of a popular ginger ale overprinted with the phrase "Nixon Drinks Canada Dry"; the second called for "An Independent Socialist Canada." Not many Canadians agreed with the Waffle's prescription, but by 1972, two-thirds of them accepted its diagnosis of the disease.[11]

Historians who point to the irony that nationalist reaction occurred when the *proportion* of foreign ownership in Canada was at a historic low miss the point. There had been a immense absolute increase in U.S. direct investment during the postwar resource boom; in earlier periods, foreign investment had been more diverse in its origins, and a substantial proportion was British portfolio investment, which English Canadians did not regard as "foreign." Just as the 1960s exploded the myths of Canadian foreign policy, they shattered the fantasy that foreign investment was a phase that Canada would pass through, as the United States once had. The nationalists had two good arguments: Canada's branch plants manufactured largely for the Canadian domestic market, and did little "R&D" (research and development) in Canada. This would mean fewer high-skill jobs as the demographic waves of the baby boom broke on Canada's economic beach in the 1970s and 1980s. The national revulsion against U.S. foreign investment was also indivisible from the more general nationalist anti-Americanism and, like it, was born of confidence rather than despair. During the 1960s, as Canadians grew richer selling automobiles and armaments to Americans, their median income moved to U.S. levels for the first time in the country's history.[12]

The Liberal government at first fell back on the trusty Canadian method of investigating intractable problems. In 1968, Walter Gordon had prodded the Pearson government to set up a task force headed by University of Toronto economist Mel Watkins to investigate foreign ownership in the Canadian economy and to suggest ways to encourage Canadian ownership. The resulting report reflected Gordon's contention that Canadians had to choose either colonial status vis-à-vis the United States or economic independence, but in 1967, such strong views were not welcome within the Liberal party. Gordon's successor as finance minister, Mitchell Sharp, buried both Gordon's ideas and the Watkins report. The only new economic institution created in the 1960s that could be considered nationalist was the Canadian National Energy Board, the objective of which was to establish more national controls over exploration, development, and the export marketing of petroleum and natural gas. In 1970, the House of Commons Standing Committee on External Relations commissioned economist Ian Wahn to report on foreign investment; he recommended a target of 51 percent Canadian ownership for Canadian industry. Minister of National Revenue Herb Gray now pressed his advantage, preparing for cabinet discussion in early 1971 yet another analysis of the deleterious impact of foreign investment on Canada.[13]

Richard Nixon's New Economic Policy did more than any of these reports to demonstrate to Canadians the dangers of dependence, and to inspire economic nationalism and the Third Option. The world, Canada included, had gained economic ground on the United States in the 1960s, as America confirmed the long-term impossibility of a "guns *and* butter" economic strategy. By 1970, the United States faced major balance of payments difficulties and the paradox of rising unemployment, economic stagnation, and high inflation. In August 1971, the president announced an increase in the dollar value of gold and the suspension of the gold convertibility of the dollar, thus effectively devaluing the U.S. dollar. Nixon served notice to all trading partners that the United States would improve its trade balance through a 10 percent surtax on all imports. The U.S.-Canada Autopact had shifted the balance of trade in the industry by $800 million in Canada's favor: only rapid action by the State Department kept Secretary of the Treasury John Connally from including Autopact's cancelation in the president's speech. These actions were taken without significant (in the case of Canada, without any) international consultation within the world economic order established at Bretton Woods and in the GATT (General Agreement on Trade and Tariffs). Congress seemed even more protectionist than the administration, so that for Canada, confrontation appeared unavoidable. "Economic power will be the key to other kinds of power in . . . the last third of this century," Richard Nixon told an audience in Kansas City. The "elephant" had rolled over on the "mouse."[14]

Canadian finance minister Edgar Benson and minister of external affairs Mitchell Sharp, neither a nationalist, believed that the "special relationship" had died. But a pilgrimage to Washington by Trudeau in December and Nixon's official visit to Canada in April 1972 offered some damage control. Trudeau's personal intellectual interest in Henry Kissinger went a long way to moderate the prime minister's reaction to the policies of the Nixon administration. National Security Adviser Kissinger's pragmatic approach to foreign policy, his influence in the White House, and the high degree of White House control over foreign policy in the Nixon administration aided reconciliation. Canada cajoled from the Americans an understanding that the import surtax would not be applied to Canada (it was short-lived in any event) and that Canada would not be penalized if the now-floating dollar began to sink, thus improving the position of Canadian exports in the United States.[15]

Such developments, and the Trudeau government's minority position in Parliament, played into the hands of advocates of a nationalistic economic policy. Walter Gordon's dream to "buy Canada back" through a Canada Development Corporation (CDC), a government-initiated holding company that would mobilize Canadian investment capital, came into being that same year. The Crown corporation exemplified exactly the type of "discriminatory" policy that troubled Washington. Over the next decade, the CDC made substantial investments in mining, chemical, and pharmaceutical companies operating in Canada, even though the Canadian government eventually divested itself of its majority holding in the corporation. The Third

Option of enhancing trade with Asia and Europe also gained impetus. Almost unnoticed by the Nixon administration was the Canadian creation in 1974 of the Foreign Investment Review Agency (FIRA) to "screen" foreign acquisitions of Canadian corporations to determine if they were "in the national interest." The CDC and FIRA were examples of economic nationalism's capitalist dimension, premised on the notion that, given a jump start by government, Canadian entrepreneurs could retake the economy through the private sector. Economic nationalism's socialist dimension came to the fore when Canadian nationalism fused with the energy crisis generated by the 1973 Arab-OPEC oil embargo to create Petro-Canada. This Crown corporation launched the Canadian government into the petroleum industry—traditionally a sector about two-thirds U.S.-controlled.[16]

Canada's choice of more nationalistic energy policies probed a sensitive nerve in the United States. Every American administration since World War I had been committed to national oil security, because U.S. dependence on foreign oil kept increasing. By 1970, the U.S. armed forces obtained 40 percent of their supplies from foreign sources. Between 1960 and 1975, total U.S. energy consumption doubled, with the use of oil and natural gas growing fastest; imports multiplied from 23 percent to 39 percent of this demand. Canada's contribution was significant and growing: U.S. oil imports from Canada more than tripled to 18.7 percent in 1967, when imports from Canada exceeded those from the Middle East. This took place despite U.S. import barriers to Canadian oil that in 1968 kept wells in Alberta shut down for want of access to the American market. The Nixon administration believed that national security in oil production could be achieved if the northern Canadian tar sands were developed and pipeline facilities expanded for delivery of crude oil to the American market. The Nixon administration knew that American national oil security also depended on the availability of oil to its allies—Japan and western Europe. Canada, it concluded, was more reliable than any other foreign supplier because of its political stability, its degree of economic interdependence with the United States, and the relative invulnerability of means of transport. Canadian imports should thus be treated as part of domestic U.S. production. The Pentagon was especially anxious that consideration be given to the post-1980s, when it was anticipated (wrongly, as it turned out) that production in the Western Hemisphere would decline. The Arab-OPEC oil embargo in 1973 and 1974, sparked by U.S. support for Israel in the Egyptian-Syrian-Israeli war, pushed Washington to act. Nixon's National Energy Policy of April 1973 included a continuing search for secure world supplies, an end to import controls, and the establishment of a National Energy Office. The crisis assigned Canada an expanding importance in American thought as an oil producer in the 1970s: a Senate investigation of the geopolitics of energy concluded that in spite of the major political obstacles involved, "an energy effort in Canada" seemed to be "an obvious priority."[17]

But Canada had its own energy problems of which Washington was oblivious. During the Arab-OPEC embargo, Canadian oil exports to the United States increased substantially, but Canadian imports from Saudi Arabia had increased by a greater percentage. After the Canadian election of July 1974, Trudeau regained his parliamentary majority and was no longer dependent on the nationalist New Democratic Party; desire to assure its own energy self-sufficiency, not simple anti-Americanism, was the impetus behind Canadian consideration of an embargo on oil exports to the United States. A U.S. Senate Foreign Relations subcommittee urged the importance of "persuad[ing] the Canadian Government to delay implementation of its announced objective of curtailing exports to the United States"; Canada relented on an embargo but imposed a tax increase on oil exports and border price increases on natural gas exports, over U.S. objections. The dramatic increase of $14.4 billion in U.S. expenditures on oil imports during the first eleven months of 1974 underlined the vulnerability of the United States to imported energy. For Third World nations to challenge United States plans neither surprised nor unduly alarmed American policy makers; when Canada began, at least from Washington's perspective, to move in a similar direction, the surprise and disapproval was immediate. Yet Canadian economic nationalism escaped worse wrath from the United States because the Nixon administration's economic woes were compounded by the crisis brought on by its political corruption. A bungled burglary of Democratic party headquarters during the 1972 presidential campaign began to prove too difficult to cover up. Soon President Richard Nixon was drowning in Watergate, a political crisis that left little time to be angry with Canada. The crisis ended only with the president's resignation in August 1974, one step ahead of impeachment; when Vice President Gerald Ford took charge in the White House, he and Secretary of State Henry Kissinger immediately established the Strategic Petroleum Reserve to store crude oil for emergency use.[18]

Closing the "Candy Store"

Canada's most successful novel of 1973 was a thriller by retired Major General Richard Rohmer. In *Ultimatum*, a Canadian government refuses American demands to surrender vast quantities of natural gas; after a heroic resistance, Canada is militarily overwhelmed and annexed to the United States. The astonishing thing about *Ultimatum*'s success was not that a novel with a preposterous plot, cardboard characters, and wooden dialog could top the best-seller list—in that respect, Rohmer's book was no worse than any of Tom Clancy's or Robert Ludlum's; what was surprising was that a *Canadian* rather than an American novel could lead Canada's best-seller list. Sixty percent of the books sold in Canada that year were American books and about 25 percent Canadian. Most of the latter were textbooks, cookbooks, and how-to books: less than one percent of the mass-market fiction sold in Canada had been written there. Lobbyists for Canada's other cultural industries—magazines, film, television, recorded music—could cite similar figures. If the United States determined 70 percent of Canada's foreign policy, how much more completely did America set Canada's cultural agenda? Cultural exports were critical to a U.S. economy with balance-of-payments difficulties: by the 1970s, popular culture had become America's second largest export income-earner after agricultural trade. Canada was critical as a market. Its three-quarters English-speaking population and its geographic proximity made it the cheapest foreign market for American popular cultural industries to produce for and to deliver to, and profit margins were accordingly very high. As a *Time* executive told a reporter in 1975, "they don't call Canada the candy store for nothing."[19]

Canada's concern about cultural "Americanization," as always, had two faces. One was the sincere concern of an alarmed nationalist intelligentsia that had grown larger as the baby boomers poured into colleges and universities. The other face was the economic self-interest of cultural entrepreneurs who wanted to produce movies, record music, own sports franchises, publish magazines and books, and earn a living at it. All demanded, and some received, the support of Canada's government. Government policy also had two sides, one promotional and the other protectionist. These two techniques were not exclusive and could be applied simultaneously, as in magazine publishing, where domestic publishers could receive special postal privileges and tariff protection at the same time. But in the new Canadian nationalism of the 1960s and 1970s, the balance swung in favor of protection. Again as before, the U.S. government usually ignored promotion but retaliated swiftly against protection, usually at the behest of an American cultural industry that cried foul at Canadian government interference with access to its "candy store."[20]

The attempt of Canadian magazine publishers to eliminate the competition of the "Canadian editions" of *Time* and *Reader's Digest* was a well-picked bone of bilateral contention. By the 1970s, the controversy had spun around the Canadian-American cultural sovereignty cycle—agitation, investigation, legislation, retaliation, and Canadian capitulation—three times over two decades. Canadian magazines would protest, with justice, that *Time* and *Reader's Digest* had an unfair advantage. Then a government investigation would conclude that the Canadian publishers had a solid case: given the vast sales of the two magazines in the United States, the unit cost of the editorial content was tiny. By adding a few pages—exactly four, in *Time*'s case—they were allowed the same tax treatment as entirely Canadian magazines. The Canadian government would draft legislation to end this privilege, *Time* and *Reader's Digest* would complain to Washington, the United States would threaten countermeasures, and the Canadian government would shrug its shoulders. But the issue refused to go away, and in 1975, the Trudeau government's Bill C-58 gave the two "Canadian editions" a choice: to "Canadianize" with 75 percent Canadian content or join the dozens of U.S. periodicals that circulated freely in Canada without tax exemptions for their advertisers. *Reader's Digest* chose to stay and become a model cultural corporate citizen; after it became obvious that the Ford administration could not save it, *Time* published its last "Canadian edition" in March 1976.[21]

The Broadcasting Act of 1968 was another attempt by the Trudeau government to "safeguard, enrich and strengthen the cultural, political, social and economic framework of Canada." Although every radio and television station had to be Canadian-owned to receive a broadcasting license, Canada's mixed public and private radio and television system was itself the principal purveyor of American recorded music and programming to Canadian audiences: like *Time* magazine, broadcasters found it cheaper, and thus more profitable, to purchase what they transmitted in the United States rather than to incur the costs of its production themselves. By buying and retransmitting U.S. programs, said nationalist critics, private TV broadcasters in Canada did not have broadcasting licenses so much as "licenses to print money." The public television network, the CBC, did this not in the name of profits but in order to compete for viewers with the private networks and with U.S. stations close to the border. Ratings showed that, given a choice, Canadians preferred U.S. entertainment programs to their Canadian counterparts. The Broadcasting Act of 1968 created a new federal regulatory body, the Canadian Radio and Television Commission (CRTC), to enforce "Canadian content" rules that required all stations, public and private, to offer "programming . . . of a high standard, using predominantly Canadian creative and other resources and predominantly Canadian in content and character." The CRTC had teeth: it could deny license renewal to violators of its "CanCon" rules. On AM and FM radio, 30 percent of the songs played had to meet criteria for "Canadian-ness" that were sometimes confusing: Mick Jagger recorded in Toronto could be "Canadian," and Neil Young recorded in New York "foreign." For television, the CRTC insisted on 60 percent Canadian content with 50 percent in the "prime time" evening hours. "Canadian content," however, was loosely defined: both the Superbowl and the World Series were considered to be of sufficient interest to Canadians to qualify.

Thus, although the CRTC's CanCon rules denied air time to U.S. programs and recordings, they did not do enough damage for Washington to take serious notice. The expansion of Cable TV, however, led to a most flagrant use of "cultural sovereignty" to pick American pockets and to line those of Canadian broadcasters. Canadian cable companies simply stole and retransmitted the signals of U.S. stations to Canadians who paid them for this stolen property. To compound this theft, a section of Bill C-58 required Canadian cable operators to "strip" the ABC, CBS, or NBC broadcast of a program and "simulcast" the Canadian rebroadcast in its place. Canadian viewers could watch "Dallas" or "Mork and Mindy," but their "cultural sovereignty" to watch Canadian rather than U.S. commercials was carefully guarded. Because Bill C-58 had also laid *Time* to rest, it became the most controversial cultural irritant in U.S.-Canada relations.

The Trudeau government's promotional policy for Canadian feature films, on the other hand, rang no alarm bells in Hollywood and brought no diplomatic notes from Washington. The Canadian Film Development Corporation (later Telefilm) provided public money to film Canadian features and was accompanied with generous tax credits to induce parallel private investment and with a liberal set of rules to define what could be considered a "Canadian" feature film. In 1979, $160 million (CDN) of public money was spent to produce sixty-seven "certified Canadian features," ten times as many as a decade earlier. Cultural nationalists called it the "Second Golden Age" of Canadian film, overlooking the fact that there had not been a first one. For their money, Canada's taxpayers got poor imitations of Hollywood, movies made, wrote film critic Martin Knelman, "in the shadow of the American eagle, or of the MGM lion, or of Mickey Mouse." To guarantee sales in the United States, the filmmakers imported U.S.

stars, selected stories that would appeal to American audiences, and disguised locations as "Anywhere, USA." Some of the movies were Hollywood projects that producers found a way to "Canadianize" to earn tax breaks and subsidies. The best picture nominees for the 1979 Genie Awards (Canada's attempt at a northern Oscar) are instructive. *The Changeling* was a haunted-house thriller starring special effects and George C. Scott. *Meatballs* was fun at summer camp with Bill Murray; the camp was supposed to be anywhere in the United States, but certainly not in Ontario, where it was actually filmed. Reviewers described *Jack London's Klondike Fever,* which starred Rod Steiger as London, as "a pathetic piece of bad historical fiction"; it was embarrassingly like the movies Hollywood had made about Canada in the 1930s and 1940s, except that the Canadian taxpayers paid for it themselves. Only one feature actually starred a Canadian actor: Christopher Plummer played Sherlock Holmes in *Murder by Decree,* filmed in London with an international cast. The final film made the other four look like *Casablanca. Yesterday* was a tear-jerker about an American hockey player at Montreal's McGill University during the Vietnam War era and his Québecoise girlfriend. The English-Canadian McGill students were beer-swilling racist boors, the professors stuffy old Englishmen, and the French Canadians hot-headed, bomb-throwing separatists. Rather than building a Canadian popular culture, wrote a critic, such movies confirmed that Canada was a "land of mediocrity, habitat of sycophants to a cut-rate U.S. dream." Hollywood had no reason to protest to Washington about the CFDC: the American film community simply went to Canada and stuck its snout in the public trough.[22]

Did these attempts to assert "cultural sovereignty" change anything? The death of *Time* allowed the Canadian news magazine *Maclean's* to absorb its readers. For television, cultural lobbyist Paul Audley grumbled that "Canadian content" was "very loosely defined," but the content regulations were strictly enforced, so that the quantity of Canadian television production showed an impressive increase. Canadian news and public affairs programs and childrens' shows won praise from American commentators. The most obvious broadcasting failure was English-Canadian television drama, which was almost nonexistent. In 1978, 91 percent of the news English-speaking Canadians watched was domestic, but 89 percent of their TV entertainment was American. Even French Canadians watched U.S. entertainment shows, sometimes dubbed in French, for 60 percent of their TV viewing. For Canadian music, the CanCon regulations for air play combined with an old-fashioned protective tariff on imported tapes and LP records to launch a domestic industry and the individual careers of dozens of Canadian singers: Anne Murray, Bryan Adams, k.d. lang. Some critics sniffed haughtily, however, at "filling the airwaves with undistinguished rock-and-roll—acceptable as long as it is played by a band from Sudbury or Winnipeg, but not if it comes from Des Moines." Feature films remained Canada's vast wasteland; critics lampooned the "reel estate boom" of the late 1970s created by CFDC dollars. The cultural sovereignists replied truculently to all charges: "Sure, it's junk, but at least its *our* junk." To argue that these policies had established "cultural sovereignty" required a leap of faith that not even they could make. But the fact that the ultimate goal remained elusive did not persuade the Trudeau government to eliminate the policies. As an academic observed in 1976, "there are indications that U.S. tolerance levels are not as high as they were a few years ago." This put the problem in the mildest terms possible; what are referred to as "irritants" by professional trade negotiators were festering sores to the members of Congress who spoke for the U.S. cultural exporters afflicted by them.[23]

"Donkeys Are Much More Companionable Beasts"

The Trudeau-Carter years should have been relatively free of conflict: no president ever worked harder to understand the issues in U.S.-Canadian relations. During the now-traditional first visit from the Canadian prime minister, Carter showed that he had done his homework with an analogy to Trudeau's 1969 elephant joke. The elephant was the symbol of the Republicans, he noted, but now "the donkeys are here, and donkeys are much more companionable beasts."

Carter's ambassador to Canada, Kenneth Curtis, was a former governor of Maine with a firsthand understanding of Canada. Edmund Muskie, secretary of state later in the Carter presidency, was from the same border state. Carter's single term is additional evidence of how much of U.S.-Canada relations was beyond the influence of individual presidents and prime ministers. There were no pivotal new problems between 1976 and 1980, but he and Trudeau were unable to translate goodwill into bilateral bliss. U.S.-Canada relations did not become significantly worse, but neither did they become significantly better. It was a case, wrote Lawrence Martin, Washington correspondent for the *Toronto Globe and Mail*, of "shattered expectations."[24]

Each leader faced domestic obstacles. Trudeau's were posed by the provinces, in particular Quebec, where an *indépendantist* provincial government under René Lévesque was elected a week after American voters chose Carter. Lévesque did his best to demonstrate that an independent Quebec was no threat to American economic or military security; he reassured investors and promised Washington, which had not asked, that contrary to official *Parti québécois* policy, an independent Quebec would join NATO and NORAD. The State Department kept "an eagle eye" on Quebec and gave independence no encouragement. Carter's problems came from Congress, caused by the post-Watergate weakness in the presidency and Carter's own outsider status in Washington. As an example, when diplomats drafted an Atlantic fisheries agreement in 1979, the president lacked the legislative influence to push it through the Senate. As always, things that made good bilateral relations with Canada could interfere with U.S. domestic goals. Carter never doubted that the "acid rain" that Canada complained about was in part from coal-fired electric generating plants in the midwestern states, but the goal of U.S. energy self-sufficiency led him to support a plan to convert oil-fired plants to coal.[25]

America's massive energy demand meant that no president could escape this pressing concern. The administration counted on Canadian electric power and natural gas, and Carter promised Americans he would work closely with Mexico and Canada to develop complementary energy policies. He and Trudeau approved in 1977 a pipeline from Alaska that would enable Alaskan and Canadian natural gas to displace an estimated seven hundred thousand barrels of imported oil a day by 1985. The overthrow of the Shah of Iran in 1979 complicated U.S. energy security still further and helped ensure Carter's electoral defeat. The Iranian revolution also temporarily thrust Canada into American headlines. On the morning of 4 November 1979, armed Iranian supporters of the fundamentalist leader Ayatollah Khomeini seized the American embassy in Teheran—the visible symbol of the Shah's link to the West. Sixty-six American hostages remained in their hands until 20 January 1981, after Ronald Reagan's inauguration. What is important to U.S.-Canada relations was the role played by Canada's ambassador to Iran, Kenneth Taylor. With his staff, he engineered the escape of five American diplomats who evaded capture in the onslaught on the embassy. It was the highest point of Conservative prime minister Joe Clark's brief minority government. Minister of External Affairs Flora MacDonald agreed to provide false Canadian documents to the Americans and arranged to evacuate the embassy. Disguised as Canadians (eh!), they left Teheran with the last of the Canadian diplomats in January 1980. The public response in Ottawa and Washington was predictably ebullient. The daring rescue came too late to save either Clark or Carter from political defeat; but it made Canadian ambassador Kenneth Taylor a hero and brought him the post of consul general in New York City. U.S.-Canada relations enjoyed a rare moment of euphoria.[26]

Tweaking the Eagle's Beak

The escalation of bilateral conflict between 1968 and 1980 had been gradual and low-key; after Trudeau's reelection in February 1980 and Ronald Reagan's inauguration, it became more rapid and more public. Reagan's conservative ideology and his commitment to restore American prestige in the world made a clash likely; Canada made it certain by taking a stronger position on energy controls. In October 1980, Trudeau's finance minister Allan MacEachen made the National

Energy Policy (NEP) part of his budget. World oil prices had sharply increased in the course of the 1970s, and Canadian producers hoped to reap the windfall, but the NEP established a price differential between domestic and international sales and between "old" and "new" oil. For old oil, sources developed before 1973, prices could not exceed 75 percent of world levels. Only the price for new oil, or oil produced by expensive innovative technologies, was allowed to rise to world levels. The NEP also included export controls, production taxes, and a petroleum incentives program, which subsidized oil and gas exploration and development by Canadian firms. In an effort to encourage frontier development, the NEP established a royalty system, which favored the operations of Canadian firms in frontier regions, and restricted licenses for frontier projects to those firms with a minimum of 50 percent Canadian equity. The NEP coincided with the objectives of the Foreign Investment Review Agency, the Canada Development Corporation, and Petro-Canada: to increase the level of Canadian ownership in the oil and gas industry. The target (which would surely have seemed modest to an American if the shoe had been on the other foot) was 50 percent by 1990. To that end, Petro-Canada purchased the Canadian subsidiaries of several foreign-owned firms, including Petrofina Canada and BP Canada, in 1981 and 1982.[27]

The NEP drew fire from Alberta, the principal oil-producing province, from the American firms that operated in Canada and from the Reagan administration. It touched off what political scientist Stephen Clarkson described as a crisis in Canadian-American relations, and demonstrated the difficulty Washington often has in distinguishing between specific bilateral issues with Canada and the broader open-door objectives of U.S. foreign policy. What especially troubled the U.S. Congress and sectors of the American business community was that the NEP appeared to be linked to hostile takeover attempts by Canadian firms against U.S. interests, such as Seagram's pursuit of Conoco. It was in that context that the House of Representatives Committee on Government Operations discussed the establishment of an American equivalent to FIRA.[28]

Immediately after the budget address, Carter's ambassador Kenneth

Curtis expressed his concern to new minister of external affairs Mark MacGuigan—the fifth to hold that position in a Trudeau cabinet. In March 1981, the Reagan Department of State, directed by ham-fisted Alexander Haig, formally protested the NEP and implied that there might be retaliation against Canadian investments in the United States. Cooler heads withdrew the implications, but the context was not favorable for Reagan's visit to Ottawa that month. The president pointedly stressed that the direction of U.S. economic policies was toward deregulation of the private sector, not increased state intervention. Responding to a journalist's question about Canada's new energy policy, Reagan touched on the real issue from Washington's perspective—energy security. "The proper goal for us must be energy independence in the United States," said the president, "not that we would take advantage of either of our neighbors there with regard to energy supplies," he added carefully. In the course of the year, comments from the Reagan administration and the American oil industry were less circumspect. Myer Rashish, undersecretary of state for economic affairs, referred to the NEP as "discriminatory . . . favoring domestic investment." He emphasized that it was the national security implications of any restrictions on American private foreign investment in energy resources that was the problem. In September 1981, Robert Hormats, assistant secretary of state for economic and business affairs, told the Economic Policy Council of the United Nations Association that the United States had to combat efforts on the part of other nations to increase their intervention in the investment area in the interest of short-term objectives. On Canada, he was blunt: "I am frankly surprised that a major developed country, provider, and host for so much international investment would adopt such nationalistic and short-sighted policies. . . . Such policies, if unchallenged, are likely to encourage other countries to adopt . . . similar measures."[29]

Canadian officials denounced the Rashish speech—somewhat unfairly, given that it had been Rashish who had persuaded Haig to withdraw his original threatening note of protest—but the Reagan administration stood by his remarks. The *Toronto Globe and Mail* contended in front-page coverage that the speech was "sweeping public condemnation of Canadian-ownership programs." Lawrence Eagleburger, assistant secretary of state for economic affairs, convinced that Canadian-American relations had reached a watershed, told a meeting in New York of the Center for Inter-American Relations that such reactions in Canada were "unconstructive"; the United States did not challenge the NEP goal of "Canadianization" but the means used to achieve it. He was also at pains to sensitize his primarily American business audience to the reality of American domination of corporate Canada. From the perspective of the Reagan administration, Canada was a First World nation that had adopted the mentality and policies of the Third World. Such views were encouraged by the very real differences between Trudeau and Reagan over relations with the Soviet Union and the Third World and a more genuine Canadian tolerance for nonalignment than existed in official Washington during the Reagan years.[30]

Under pressure from several American officials, from newly appointed ambassador Paul Robinson through trade representative William Brock and Treasury Secretary Donald Regan, the Trudeau government back-pedaled slightly on the NEP in areas that were critical to the Reagan administration. The Reagan administration's success owed something to Robinson's insistence that the United States should be nonconfrontational in its response to the NEP: evidently the U.S. challenge to the NEP before a GATT panel was not considered "confrontational." In his fall 1981 budget speech, MacEachen assured that the Canadianization provisions of the NEP would not be applied to other sectors of the economy and that, contrary to the government's first Speech from the Throne, FIRA would not be made stronger. Instead, FIRA procedures and criteria were relaxed: only firms with more than two hundred employees would be subject to a full FIRA review. After little more than a year of the Reagan presidency, the NEP and other outstanding issues had plunged the relationship between the two neighbors to its lowest point since the Diefenbaker-Kennedy years, epitomized most graphically by the sinister likeness of Trudeau that graced the 25 June 1982 cover of William F. Buckley, Jr.'s *National*

Review, one of the few magazines President Reagan had been known to read. George Schultz's replacement of the abrasive Haig and Allan MacEachen's shift to External Affairs produced some improvement. Schultz's business connections made him personally familiar with the Alberta oil industry, although the views he heard from Alberta in 1982 would scarcely have inclined him favorably toward Trudeau or Ottawa![31]

There were other issues, though they loomed small next to United States concern for energy security. U.S. policy toward Latin America in the years that Pierre Trudeau was prime minister lurched from crisis to crisis, but Canada remained peripheral to the inter-American system, neither a member of the Organization of American States nor a signatory to the Rio Treaty of Mutual Security. Canadian investments in Latin America, while important in the Commonwealth Caribbean and Brazil, paled by comparison with those of the United States. There was no Canadian inclination to challenge the U.S. claim to Latin America as its own sphere of influence. Until after 1984, Mexico remained in a highly nationalist phase with its back turned to North America. Thus Canadian access to the region was tenuous. Canadian policy diverged from that of the United States in the region only in the Canadian opposition to the American use of military force. The Canadian government remained as anxious as the U.S. government professed to be to promote democratization of political regimes, open-market economies for trade and investment, and regional stability. With the cold war still in full stride, and Cuba continuing to be a player in regional politics, Canada remained more loyal to its cold war commitments in Latin America than elsewhere. The Socialist government of Salvador Allende in Chile (1970–73) received little support from Canada when faced with destabilizing economic pressure from the United States and from the CIA-supported internal opposition. During the military coup that murdered Allende, the Canadian ambassador to Chile worried only about Canadian-owned Bata Shoes, although junior officials in the Canadian embassy provided sanctuary to Chileans who sought refuge from the military terror. The Canadian assessment of Allende's overthrow paralleled the authorized American version—that Allende had lost control of government, creating the danger of a more radical initiative from the extreme left.[32]

Canadian interest in Latin America increased when the Central American crisis escalated after 1980. Some Canadian voices—like some American voices—raged against the American-supported Contras' attempt to depose the Sandinista government of Nicaragua, and objected to the failure of the United States to restrain the El Salvadoran army and its military-linked death squads. But as on Vietnam a decade earlier, in his official statements Trudeau walked the tightrope between anticommunism and condemnation of American policy in Central America. In 1980, following the murder of Archbishop Romero and the rape-murder of four American missionaries, the Trudeau government supported a UN resolution condemning human rights violations by the El Salvadoran government and called for an end to military aid. Canada later sponsored a UN resolution condemning human rights abuses in the U.S. client-state of Guatemala. Secretary of State for External Affairs Allan MacEachen urged his American counterpart George Schultz to avoid a military solution to the deepening Central American crisis, and Trudeau himself in a press conference in April 1983 expressly criticized American policy and distanced Canada from the U.S. approach. There is no evidence that Canadian criticism had the slightest moderating effect on the Reagan administration's Latin American policy.[33]

Canada was not forewarned of the U.S. decision to invade the tiny island of Grenada in October 1983. Grenada symbolized for many Canadians the Reagan administration's foreign policy extremism and its amplification of the cold war. The Caribbean island of barely one hundred thousand in population had a Marxist government in power that had friendly relations with Cuba. Cubans were in Grenada in a variety of capacities. Their construction of an airstrip, which the Reagan administration claimed was designed to be used by Cuban and Soviet aircraft (a claim that the British engineers on the project flatly rejected) and the alleged danger to a thousand American students on the island from Marxist factional conflict were the justifications for the invasion. Whatever the truth of the claims from both sides, Canada officially condemned the United States in the United Nations for the use of force. The invasion was not, in the view of Canadian UN ambassador Gérard Pelletier, a "legitimate exercise of the right of self-defence. . . . Nor that it was consistent with the principle of the prohibition of the use of force in international relations."[34]

Canada kept up its cold war military commitments, at least on paper, but Trudeau subjected Canada's Department of National Defense to the same "denigration" he meted out to the Department of External Affairs. In reality, wrote an unreconstructed Canadian cold warrior in a play on the words to Canada's national anthem, it was the "True North *not* strong and free." The Trudeau government renewed NORAD, now renamed the North American *Aerospace* Defense Command. It retained its NATO membership despite reductions in personnel and equipment to its armed forces; Canada's per capita expenditures for NATO were the lowest of any member of the alliance. Despite domestic pressure not to do so, the Trudeau government allowed the United States to test its new cruise missile in Canada—the Canadian North made a good surrogate for Siberia, and providing a test range for U.S. missiles was a much cheaper way to show defense solidarity than actually buying weapons.[35]

Trudeau had observed that Canadian spending on defense could not win America's ear to alter the cold war agenda; his final foreign policy endeavor was therefore something completely different—his so-called "peace initiative" in 1983 and 1984. The Reagan administration had from the outset taken a hard line against the Soviet Union, the "Evil Empire." The Strategic Defense Initiative ("Star Wars") was designed as much to beggar the USSR, should it attempt to emulate it, as it was to improve U.S. defenses. Most independent scientists regarded the project with derision, but the SDI held out the opportunity, if it worked, of making Soviet heavy ICBMs obsolete and favoring America's more flexible arsenal of land-, air-, and sea-based missiles. It also threatened to undermine the framework of nuclear deterrence. The Soviet shooting down of Korea Airlines Flight 007 triggered massive world reaction, in Canada as well as the United

States, and Trudeau was genuinely worried that East-West relations would continue to deteriorate.[36]

Trudeau's peace initiative was not a one-shot, precipitous, or unplanned endeavor. The prime minister was genuinely committed to nuclear nonproliferation and arms reduction; he had spoken eloquently on the latter issue in 1978 at the United Nations special session on disarmament and had courted Western officials who shared his concern. Against the advice of senior members of the foreign and defense policy establishment in Canada, in September 1983 Trudeau established a formal working group in the government to produce a policy initiative. The target date was 27 October, when Trudeau delivered the university address "Strategies for Peace and Security in the Nuclear Age." Trudeau's conclusions in the speech were undeniable: there was "acrimony" in East-West relations, there was fault on both sides, a "vision of a world transformed" was indeed absent. Few could have questioned the need for improved communication between Washington and Moscow. Trudeau was not soft on the Soviets: he asked the Soviet Union to reform itself and to "modify its own objectives towards the West." His sincerity fell on cynical ears in Washington, where Lawrence Eagleburger summarized the State Department's view of Trudeau with the remark that the prime minister seemed like "a leftist high on pot." As Canadian ambassador Allan Gotlieb observed, the Reagan administration bitterly resented Trudeau's "habit" of giving "moral equivalence" to the United States and the Soviet Union. Without strong support from Washington, the peace initiative was meaningless; Washington was not merely unreceptive but dismissive. The Soviet Union and China were no more encouraging. In Moscow, Secretary Andropov lay dying; in Beijing, Trudeau received a lengthy lecture from Chairman Deng Xiaoping on the aggressive policies of Moscow and Washington. There was encouragement only from such countries as East Germany and Romania; were these Canada's real international peers? From the perspective of Reagan's Washington, Trudeau had received a lesson in realpolitik. Only one of the Trudeau initiatives bore fruit—the call for a NATO foreign ministers conference, which met in Stockholm in early 1984. The most damning assessment came from former Canadian ambassador to Moscow Robert Ford, who stated the obvious: the Canadian government lacked the power to effect change in either East or West.[37]

It was humiliating proof of Canada's irrelevance. For whatever reason, Trudeau's Third Option had gone from tragedy to farce. Economically, Canada was tied as tightly to the United States as ever, but its never-easy relationship with the United States had become more difficult than ever. As historian John English has stated, Trudeau had "enjoyed tweaking the eagle's beak"; he had also learned how difficult it was for Canada to move beyond range of the eagle's talons.[38]

10 Republicans and Tories, 1984–1993

In the 1980s, U.S.-Canadian relations underwent a revolutionary shift toward ideological and political convergence and a remarkable accommodation on a wide range of divisive issues. It was a revolutionary decade that began with an escalation of the cold war and ended with the toppling of the Berlin Wall and the collapse of the Soviet Union. The United States and Canada moved from discomfort with each other to the conclusion of a free trade agreement and Canadian membership in the Organization of American States in 1989. There was a new military partnership. The Mulroney government endorsed the Bush administration's invasion of Panama in December 1989, and Canada was America's enthusiastic junior partner in the U.S.-led alliance in the Gulf War against Iraq in 1991. The 1993 North American Free Trade Agreement among Canada, the United States, and Mexico, would have been unthinkable in the Canadian political environment a decade earlier.

The United States and Canada in a Changing Global Context

The tensions over the Trudeau government's National Energy Policy and Canadian screening of foreign investment had eased by the time that Pierre Trudeau left office in 1984. His replacement, Liberal finance minister John Turner, held office for only weeks before Brian Mulroney's Tories drove the Liberals from power in Ottawa. Mulroney's arrival and Reagan's second mandate were part of a more general international trend toward the political right. Even Mexican president Miguel de la Madrid, far from being a conservative, was drawn toward neoliberal economic policies in the new North American environment. This new conservatism portrayed its dedication to market economics as nonideological, at the same time that it intensified the rhetoric of the cold war. This incongruity was heightened by Mikhail Gorbachev's ascendance in the Soviet Union, which brought détente, internal economic reform, and eventually the demise of the Soviet system.

Ronald Reagan had entered office in 1981 pledged to restore America's international prestige after what he portrayed as years of extended humiliation for the United States: the defeat in a "noble cause" in Vietnam; the embarrassment of the Iranian hostage-taking; the Soviet invasion of Afghanistan; another oil embargo; the fear of economic decline; and the perception that communism had won a new foothold in the hemisphere with the Sandinista victory in Nicaragua, all in 1979. The Reagan administration brought a Hollywood-style vision of world struggle between the forces of good and evil, with rhetorical references to the Soviet Union and its allies as the "evil empire." Anti-Sandinista mercenaries in Nicaragua ludicrously came to be called "freedom fighters"; Oliver North of the National Security Council, who ran the scandalous Iran-Contra operation, was described by the president as a national hero. By 1985, the president had articulated what came to be known as the Reagan Doctrine. Not unlike Truman, with his cold war pledge four decades earlier, Reagan promised to support anti-Communist movements anywhere in the world who resisted Soviet and Soviet-surrogate forces. Reagan boosted the military budget and expanded U.S. forces stationed abroad at the same time that his administration reduced foreign aid. George Ball, under secretary of state in the Kennedy and Johnson administrations, suggested that Reagan's message to the poorer countries of the world could be characterized "by a cartoon of the Thomas Nast genre showing a bloated millionaire descending from his limousine to tell a group of ragged urchins: 'Why don't you do as I did, utilize the free market and you'll all be rich.' "[1]

The sense of American decline did not originate with Reagan, however: it brought him to office. In a television address in 1979, President Carter had warned Americans against "a crisis of confidence . . . that strikes at the very heart and soul and spirit of national will." The Reagan Republicans exploited this fear that the United States was in decline, giving way to Japan and the European community. U.S. debt had mushroomed; the American share of world trade seemed threatened, and the United States appeared to have lost international leadership in technological innovation. The economic and political world order established under U.S. hegemony at the end of World War II was in disarray, but America could no longer dictate the outcome of international deliberations. American-authored global solutions gave way to trading blocs and regional organizations. The Uruguay round of GATT negotiations fragmented repeatedly as Europe and Japan rejected the U.S. insistence on an end to agricultural and other production subsidies.[2]

The Reagan administration defined its international agenda for the 1980s as "principled realism." That foreign policy agenda altered little when former vice president George Bush succeeded Reagan in 1989. Indeed, it is important to recognize the continuity between the Reagan-Bush era and the long-standing goals of U.S. foreign policy. *National Security Strategy of the United States,* a White House document released in 1990, stated those goals forthrightly: the safety of the nation and its "way of life"; the creation of an "international environment of peace, freedom and progress"; the admission that "the flourishing of democracy in America did not require a completely democratic world," coupled with the conviction that "it could not long survive in a largely totalitarian one"; a commitment to the "prosperity of the free market system" and an "open international economic system." This list was entirely consistent with the world view of Woodrow Wilson, Herbert Hoover, or Franklin Roosevelt.[3]

Brian Mulroney's Conservative government was much more comfortable within this context than its predecessors had been. The Trudeau Liberals had seemed to threaten the foundation of American foreign policy—an open door world. Foreign investment review and a national energy policy challenged American corporations'—and thus America's—access to raw materials, sources of energy, and markets at a time of crisis. Days after the Tory victory in September 1984, Prime Minister-elect Mulroney announced in New York that "good relations, super relations with the United States, will be the cornerstone of our foreign policy." As proof, the Conservatives promised that the National Energy Policy would be scrapped, and that the Foreign Investment Review Agency would become "Investment Canada": a government agency to encourage foreign investors. Canada, said its new chairman of the board, was "open for business again."[4]

The two conservative governments shared an ideological compatibility that bridged the forty-ninth parallel. U.S. policy did not change in the course of the 1980s; Canadian policy accommodated itself to it. The improvement in Canadian-American relations during the decade derived from the ideological orientation of the Tory government, not from the imposition of U.S. official views on a hesitant Ottawa. Both Republicans and Tories accepted the older assumptions of the cold war, although "middle power" Canada continued to prefer multilateral solutions to international problems. Both spoke of arms control. Both professed a commitment to balanced budgets, and to trade liberalization, privatization, and deregulation. Both pursued the final three goals with considerably more zeal than they pursued fiscal prudence. This policy compatibility extended to president and prime minister: Reagan and Mulroney liked each other personally. Reagan was one of the few presidents who actively sought a closer relationship with Canada, and who consistently made improved trilateral North American relations and liberalized trade a priority of his administration.

The new prime minister made a brief visit to Washington in September 1984 and welcomed the reelected president formally to Canada at Quebec City in March 1985. This "Shamrock" Summit, so-called because it spanned St. Patrick's Day, recaptured an amity missing since the 1950s. Mulroney joined the president in a corny rendition of "When Irish Eyes Are Smiling," "a public display of sucking up to Reagan" that a nationalist historian of Canada suggests "may have been the single most demeaning moment in the entire political history of Canada's relations with the United States." Their agenda recalled the 1950s, as Mulroney and Reagan signed an agreement to spend $1.5 billion (U.S.) on an expansion of the northern air defense system, costs to be shared on a 60/40 United States/Canada basis. Both affirmed their commitment to the Defense Development and Production Sharing Agreements that had been part of cold war military-industrial integration, and agreed to further reduce trade barriers on defense products. The darkest storm cloud on the bilateral horizon, the sensitive environmental question of acid rain pollution, was deferred until "further study" by "special envoys" from each country. The "new partnership" at the Quebec City summit was a conscious dismissal of the conflicts of the previous two decades.[5]

The following year, meeting in Washington, Reagan and Mulroney renewed the NORAD agreement for another five years. NORAD renewal, once routine, suddenly became a contentious issue in Canada. The acronym now stood for the North American *Aerospace* Defense Command, and renewal would involve Canada in the Reagan administration's Strategic Defense Initiative—the plan to station antiballistic missile laser weapons in space, known popularly as "Star Wars." Prominent members of the American scientific and defense establishment criticized SDI, arguing that it would destabilize Soviet-American relations, undermine efforts to conclude a meaningful reduction in nuclear armaments, and lead the Soviet Union to further weapons buildup. The proposed space weapons violated U.S. obligations under the Strategic Arms Limitation Treaty (SALT) of 1972, and seemed to contradict President Reagan's announced intention to pursue Strategic Arms Reduction Talks (START) with the Soviets. In this charged political atmosphere, consensus in the Canadian Parliament was impossible. A joint Canadian Senate–House of Commons committee report supported the need for the United States to undertake basic research on SDI technology but expressed serious reservations about the implications of SDI for Soviet-American relations. The decision was a very Canadian compromise between the "hawks" who shared the Reagan perspective and the members of Parliament who regarded the president's approach as provocative and irresponsible. The best Mulroney could provide Reagan was a telephone call encouraging him to press on with research without Canadian participation and promising that Parliament would not overtly prohibit the involvement of Canadian companies in SDI.[6]

The prime minister's telephone call to the White House was evidence that the channels of communication were more visibly open between the two countries than they had been since the difficult years of the Diefenbaker-Kennedy relationship. One of the features of the new relationship was the greater frequency of high level meetings. Mulroney and Reagan pledged to meet annually to review outstanding issues. Reagan's secretaries of state and Mulroney's ministers of external affairs met even more frequently; George Schultz and Joe Clark conferred six times in 1985. The improved relationship also owed a good deal to the energy and diplomatic skills of Allan Gotlieb, Canadian ambassador to Washington from 1981 to 1989. Gotlieb's most original contribution was to court Congress, understanding that nothing could be accomplished in the area of trade policy or environmental controls without active congressional support and that a hostile and protectionist Congress could do infinite damage to Canadian interests. Tories and Republicans worked so well together that by January 1986, Ronald Reagan could boast to a radio audience that he had achieved his promised "renewed spirit of friendship and cooperation with Mexico and Canada," and that the "most productive period in Canadian-American friendship" was at hand.[7]

Environmental Impasse

For Canadians unhappy with the "new partnership" between their country and Reagan's America, "Star Wars" made the defense issue appear extraterrestrial, and concern about foreign investment seemed outmoded. Pollution affected people's lives every day, so that the issues that aroused the most widespread Canadian concern were those relating to the environment. By the early 1980s, a chapter with such a title as "Binational Responsibilities for a Shared Environment" had become *de rigueur* in edited collections on Canadian-American relations. One such chapter explained the new interest: "opinion surveys . . . indicate a growing disposition, especially among the well-informed and educated, increasingly to accept elements of the ecological perspective." The most disputatious environmental issue was that of airborne sulphur dioxide and nitrous oxides from automobiles, heavy industry, and coal-fired generating plants in the U.S. Midwest, pollutants that fell on the northeastern states and the Canadian provinces with each shower, poisoning lakes and forests, eroding buildings, damaging human health. "The subject of acid rain engaged passions like no other," Ambassador Allan Gotlieb remembers of his eight years in Washington. But the Reagan administration had already circled the wagons against the environmentalist attack, and denied that a problem existed. In 1983, two Canadian National Film Board documentaries on acid rain were declared "foreign propaganda" by the U.S. Information Agency.[8]

At their Shamrock Summit, Reagan and Mulroney had appointed Drew Lewis, former U.S. secretary of transportation, and William Davis, former Ontario premier, to study acid rain—an inexpensive sop to Canadian and New England concerns. A year later, the prime minister met the president with the envoys' conclusion in hand: "acid rain imperils the environment in both countries." A jaunty Reagan promised action and a jubilant Mulroney showed off Canada's new influence in Washington, announcing that acid rain had become "a front-burner issue." "After Mulroney left Washington," the *Washington Post* quipped twenty months later, "the burner was turned off." The Reagan administration was unwilling to enforce the legislation in place since the Nixon administration—the Clean Air Act of 1971—let alone take the initiative against transboundary air pollution. Administration spokespersons blamed congressional opposition from industrial and coal-producing states, notably Ohio, Michigan, and West Virginia, which had a vested economic interest in blocking action. One outspoken Ohio representative, Charles Lukens, demanded the expulsion of Ambassador Gotlieb because the Canadian ambassador had challenged a vitriolic Lukens speech blaming acid rain on Ontario. Canada did not, Gotlieb admitted, "have clean hands," but Canadian governments were attempting to resolve the problem, while the United States had actually moved backward. Canada paid former White House staffer Michael Deaver a six-figure salary to lobby for new legislation, again without result. Vice President George Bush journeyed to Ottawa to absorb parliamentary criticism, but the visit was a public relations gesture, rather than a sign of action in Washington. As Gotlieb concluded, the acid rain experience demonstrated that Canada was like any other foreign country: its diplomats could accomplish little unless the administration were prepared to take a firm, positive stand.[9]

The Conservatives changed tactics. "You are a major part of our problem," Prime Minister Mulroney told the Americas Society in New York in March 1988, warning the United States to stop "polluting your neighbor's property with destructive wastes." The *Toronto Globe and Mail*'s correspondent observed cynically that "Mr. Mulroney's rebuke, a tacit admission that Canada can make no headway with the Reagan Administration, nevertheless serves to trumpet the Canadian cause to voters back home." The urge to stand up to Uncle Sam often grips Canadian governments in election years, and the Prime Minister's political theater answered nationalist nervousness that Canada had conceded too much to America. Mulroney refused suggestions that his government make an acid rain treaty a *quid pro quo* for agreement on another issue the Reagan administration cared about—free trade or the SDI—lest the United States propose similar "linkages" of its own. In the absence of a U.S.-Canada treaty, the Ontario government took unilateral measures to reduce sulphur dioxide emissions from the province's industries by 66 percent by the mid-1990s. Mulroney and George Bush ("the environmental President") promised in a 1991 accord to enforce their own countries' existing air quality laws—hardly a bold step toward "binational responsibility for a shared environment." Five years later, despite reductions in sulphur dioxide emissions on both sides of the border, acid rain remained at issue. In September 1996, the Canadian co-chair of the International Joint Commission resigned to protest U.S. failure to invoke the Clean Air Act against increased pollution from midwestern power plants.[10]

The lack of answers to the environmental dilemma of the Great Lakes, the world's largest source of "fresh" water, is equally disheartening. Anxiety about the lakes was almost a century old, but Lake Erie had to be pronounced "biologically dead" before the Nixon and

Trudeau governments could conclude the Great Lakes Water Quality Agreement in 1972. The agreement was renewed by Carter and Trudeau in 1978, with the added pledge that "zero discharge" of toxins would be permitted. But as with the acid rain accord, each country was to act in parallel, subject to its own laws rather than to a treaty binding under international law. Parallel domestic laws had not only to be enacted but also to be enforced, and the binational Great Lakes Water Quality Board (GLWQB) that supervised the agreement observed virtually no progress in this regard. Each year's report revealed new pollutants and expanded problem areas within the "Not So Great Lakes" system, and environmental lobby groups accused both governments of "only paying lip service to [their] cleanup promises." In 1989, even this lip service stopped. The U.S. co-chair of the GLWQB described zero discharge of toxins as "unrealistic," and his Canadian counterpart suggested that because the rate of deterioration of the lakes had slowed, "the light at the end of the tunnel" was in sight. "That light . . . may be a radioactive lamprey [eel] or a hunk of phosphorescent material," wrote a disillusioned editorialist; "we enter the nineties with the depressing prospect of confronting monsters more numerous than those we set out to vanquish."[11]

Another Carter initiative met a fate similar to the Great Lakes Water Quality Agreement. In 1979, a Carter-Trudeau East Coast Fisheries Agreement that contained potentially effective provisions for managing fish stocks passed Parliament easily but failed in the U.S. Senate. Despite the president's personal plea that delay "would be detrimental to the conservation of the fishery resources," the New England fishing lobby prevailed, and its senators defeated the treaty and its resource management proposals. Ronald Reagan made no attempt to revive it, and Canada petulantly dispatched destroyer escorts and even a submarine to drive New Englanders from the scallop beds of Georges Bank. At a time when their governments professed to be uniquely attuned to each other, the United States and Canada were unable to work out a mutual response to the problem of managing the fish resources of the Atlantic Coast. As on other critical environmental issues, the "new partnership" between the United States and Canada yielded a meager result. The suspicion lingered that perhaps, given the broader agenda of the Republicans and Tories, no more was intended.[12]

The Free Trade Debate

No bilateral issue of the past half-century evoked in Canadians such strong personal and political emotions as the debate over free trade with the United States. Americans who paid any attention to Canadian affairs were bemused by the passions that the Canada-U.S. Free Trade Agreement (FTA) aroused in the "Great White North." Canada as early as 1983 had first suggested free trade. The objective of the Canadian government and businesspeople who exported to the American market was not so much to expand trade as to maintain security of access to the United States. Congress was inclined toward protectionism, and an Omnibus Trade Act loomed in Washington, recalling the days of the Fordney-McCumber and Smoot-Hawley tariffs.[13]

The first impetus for free trade came from studies by think tanks such as Canada's C.D. Howe Institute; then important national magazines and newspapers, such as *Maclean's* and the *Toronto Globe and Mail,* became cautiously supportive of the idea. The Canadian Chamber of Commerce and the Canadian Federation of Independent Business came aboard as major lobbyists in favor of an accord. Free trade acquired bipartisan respectability in Canada when the Royal commission on the Canadian economy, chaired by former Liberal finance minister Donald Macdonald, concluded that an agreement with the United States would injure only a small number of the industries that his commission had studied. Free trade was the best long-term policy for Canada's economic future, said Macdonald; all that was necessary to achieve it was for Canadians to take "a leap of faith."[14]

Brian Mulroney was a late convert to this new religion. Campaigning for the Conservative leadership in 1983, he had told reporters that Canada "could not survive with a policy of unfettered free trade." At the Shamrock Summit, however, Mulroney and Reagan agreed quietly (it was not mentioned in the official statement) to examine reducing trade barriers. In the summer of 1985, a joint statement of both houses of the Canadian Parliament recommended that Canada explore free trade with the United States and introduced the phrase "comprehensive trade agreement" into the discourse. The Mulroney government's free trade feelers were strongly and warmly endorsed by Ronald Reagan, quite in contrast to the position Reagan took on bilateral environmental problems. The severe U.S. trade deficit with Canada explained Reagan's alacrity: $7.3 billion in 1981, $13.1 billion in 1982, $14.3 billion in 1983, and $23.3 billion in 1986.

In May 1986, Ottawa and Washington announced "wide-ranging talks" between Simon Reisman on the Canadian side and Peter Murphy on the American. For sixteen months, news of negotiations filled Canadian newspapers and appeared every now and then in the business pages of the *New York Times* and the *Washington Post.* Just hours from the deadline at which the talks would have broken off in failure, Reisman and Murphy reached a draft agreement. On Monday, October 5, 1987, U.S.-Canada relations made America's front pages for the first time since the Iran hostage escape. The agreement was much too complex for small United States dailies to summarize easily; most of them simply reprinted "U.S., Canada to Try Free Trade" from the *New York Times.* The tiny Durham, N.C., *Morning Herald* looked deeper into the draft agreement, however. "CANADA TO HAVE ACCESS TO ALASKAN OIL," the *Herald* warned readers who, like the headline writer, were oblivious to the fact that Canada exported millions of barrels of oil to the United States annually.[15]

Neither the United States nor Canada regarded the detailed free trade agreement in 1988 as a complete success. It eliminated over a ten-year period tariffs in commodity trade in industry and agriculture; liberalized Canadian controls on foreign investment; provided national treatment for American firms operating in Canada; and provided limited bilateral access to government procurement contracts in each country. Most important to Canada was the establishment of bilateral dispute settlement panels to circumvent the political vagaries of United States trade laws. Cultural industries proved especially contentious: the first paragraph of article 2005 exempts Canada's cultural industries from the FTA, but the second paragraph reserves the U.S. right to retaliate against Canadian cultural protectionism. Canadian concern that Canada's social programs might be defined as unfair trade subsidies remained unresolved, as exactly what constituted an "unfair subsidy" under the terms of the FTA was left (and remains in 1996) undefined.[16]

The Reagan administration's understanding of the agreement was evident in its *Statement of Administrative Action* that accompanied the presentation of the agreement for Senate approval. The administration anticipated few modifications in American law to implement the FTA; significantly, the administration promised to pursue further liberalization of Canadian investment controls and to extend the agreement to energy and cultural industries, and to eliminate technology transfer requirements and other performance requirements not barred by the FTA. For the steel industry, the administration assured Congress that nothing in the FTA precluded reaching agreement with Canada to reduce Canadian steel exports. In the area of government procurement, although the agreement liberalized competition, there were major exceptions on the American side. The Defense Appropriations Act and the Berry Amendment were left unchanged; these require the Department of Defense to purchase solely from U.S. suppliers all textiles, clothing, shoes, food, stainless steel flatware, certain specialty metals, buses, ships, and components. As well, chapter 13 of the FTA did not alter the 50 percent differential in favor of domestic U.S. suppliers for all procurement of hand tools.[17]

The Canadian energy industry was as anxious to consolidate and expand its market access to the United States as the American government and U.S. industry were determined to ensure guaranteed access to Canadian resources. The main impediments to U.S. investment and trade had been Canadian government controls such as FIRA and the National Energy Program. Thus, the FTA stipulated that Canada could not establish a higher price for its energy exports than the domestic price, and in the event of Canadian desire to conserve resources and reduce exports, Canadian suppliers were required to maintain exports to the United States at a level that was proportionate to "Canadian total export shipments of that commodity in relation to total Canadian supply." Canada had insisted that the FTA leave the basic conditions of the automobile industry untouched, so that U.S.-Canada trade continued to be governed by the Autopact of 1965, despite continuing criticism from the "Rust Belt" of northern de-industrializing states, whose governors and congressional delegations believed that the Autopact had worked only to the advantage of Canadian auto producers. Not all Canadian industries were winners, of course. Textile producers and the garment industry, traditionally highly protected, feared FTA provisions that stipulated that textiles and apparel would not be considered products of either Canada or the United States unless they underwent a double transformation in either or both countries. A garment had to be produced in Canada or the United States from fabric produced in either country.[18]

Canadian business was thus not monolithic in its endorsement of the FTA. Support in Canada for the FTA came, naturally enough, from industries that were already well established in the United States markets and feared their loss through American Congressional protectionism, like the oil and natural gas industries. Textiles and the garment industry, boot and shoe manufacturers, the furniture industry, wine and liquor producers, brewers, and farmers all had serious reservations about their capacity to compete with American producers. Commercial bankers disliked the specific provisions that opened banking in Canada to United States competition, although in general they were supportive of a bilateral agreement. In spite of this sectoral business opposition, provincial Liberal governments in Quebec and Ontario, home to more than half of Canada's population, endorsed the free trade agreement with the United States, the former enthusiastically and the latter grudgingly. The New Democratic Party opposed the FTA; the Ontario NDP promised to ignore it if they were elected, although following their provincial victory in 1990 these promises went unfulfilled.

"Free trade was one of the most significant policy issues in the life of the Canadian nation," write Bruce Doern and Brian Tomlin, "and Canadians had to look deep into their national soul to decide where they would stand." Most did such soul-searching: a survey in February

1988 found that 90 percent of Canadians had an opinion on the five-month-old FTA then before Parliament and Congress. No issue better illustrates the disproportionate relative importance of the U.S.-Canada relationship to the publics of each country: only 39 percent of Americans interviewed were aware of the agreement. There were two visions of the Canadian-American relationship involved in the debate as well as two divergent visions of the nature of Canadian society, one nationalist, one continentalist, one market-driven and the other based on the conviction that what had made Canada distinct from (and superior to) American society was the role of the state in shaping a more harmonious, egalitarian society in which there was a more equitable distribution of social services. Critics of the agreement felt that far more had been lost in the autumn of 1988 than simply tariff and nontariff barriers to trade with the United States. They cited the considerable evidence that a profound restructuring of Canadian society was among the goals of free trade's advocates, and that Canada's more generous social programs would be scaled back to create a "level playing field" for economic activity in the two countries. Toronto multimillionaire Conrad Black expressed precisely the perspective on the FTA that terrified opponents of Canadian-American economic integration. The Canadian "quest for an identity independent of the Americans," Black contended disapprovingly, was the source of all of Canada's problems. "[It] has given us a prime rate five points above that of the United States; top tax rates almost 20 points higher; a sharply higher price index; a growing and proportionately much larger public sector deficit despite the American defence burden; and only seventy percent of the U.S. standard of living. We are wedded to a redistribution of money between regions and individuals which makes excessive taxation and public sector insolvency almost inevitable."[19]

As the debate developed, the polarization between Canadian proponents and antagonists of free trade with the United States intensified. Proponents contended that new global realities dictated that Canada had to make a major break with the "National Policy" mentality of the nineteenth century; without free trade and international economic competitiveness the Canadian economy would stagnate, they argued.

Free trade advocates portrayed their opponents as wild-eyed radicals, nationalist-isolationists out of touch with the "real world," gray-bearded relics from the long-defunct "Waffle" wing of the NDP. The American market was too important to the Canadian economy, they maintained, to risk its loss to congressional protectionism. The opponents of the FTA were in fact more diverse, and their arguments more subtle. On one hand were those who argued that Canada's long-term interests would be better served by expanding Canada's trade with the rest of the world, rather than hitching the Canadian economic wagon to the United States. This restated Canada's hope for multilateral alternatives, last expressed in Trudeau's "Third Option." The traditional concern remained that the FTA would diminish economic sovereignty, leaving power in the hands of U.S.-based corporate head offices. The most ubiquitous denunciations of the free trade deal focused on the potential dangers to Canadian identity posed by still-greater economic integration with the United States. In the 1980s this argument had a dimension not present in 1891 or 1911: the fear that the FTA was part of a conservative corporate agenda to "harmonize" Canada and the United States by undermining Canada's more generous social programs, from national medical care to unemployment insurance. *Montreal Gazette* political cartoonist "Aislin" depicted the free trade agreement as a salivating Uncle Sam, bib tucked securely under his chin, about to indulge in the culinary delight of roast Canadian beaver.[20]

At the FTA signing ceremony in the White House Rose Garden on 28 September 1988, President Reagan remarked that the open Canadian-American border had become a "symbol for the future," and was no longer an "invisible barrier of economic suspicion and fear." In Canada, however, the issue was far from resolved: emotions and rhetoric mounted to a crescendo in the Canadian national election that November. The opposition Liberal and New Democratic Parties made rejection of the FTA, and suspicion and fear of the United States, the focus of their electoral campaigns. The victory of the Tories decided the fate of the agreement. The Mulroney Conservatives earned only 43 percent of the popular vote, but the distortions inherent in a multiparty

parliamentary system gave them 60 percent of the seats in the House of Commons. Their opponents of free trade with the United States claimed a moral victory, but the election committed Canada to the accord.[21]

Domestic Politics and Bilateral Relations

The "new partnership" so happily pronounced by Reagan and Mulroney in 1985 began to unravel in the economic recession of the early 1990s, just as it had in hard times in the past. After the Gulf War euphoria had faded, the United States returned to its economic and social realities, and Americans increasingly found the Bush administration's performance wanting. Even before the American people chose Democrats Bill Clinton and Al Gore to lead them in November 1992, President Bush had been forced to get tough with Canada on trade policy. Harassed from the right in the primaries by "America Firster" Patrick Buchanan, an erstwhile continentalist who dreamed of adding English

Canada to the union, the Bush administration refused to accept the Canadian preference for binding arbitration through the GATT of several outstanding trade disputes, and vigorously investigated a series of Canadian exporters for alleged dumping or other unfair trading practices. Despite Prime Minister Mulroney's "vaunted friendship with Mr. Bush," noted a Canadian journalist, the president "has not exerted any detectible pressure to block recent U.S. trade complaints about steel and beer." It was, he concluded, "a useful reminder of an eternal truth: foreign allies are nice, but re-election is vital. The choice between friendship and survival is an easy one." Bush did not, of course, survive.[22]

Turbulent Canadian domestic politics contributed a new dimension to renewed bilateral tension. Canada resumed its perennial debate about national unity following the failure of the Meech Lake Constitutional accord in June 1991. The unsettled waters of Canadian confederation received further disturbance in the rise in western Canada of the Reform Party, led by Albertan Preston Manning. Manning was seen by some as a Canadian equivalent of Ross Perot, unsuccessful third party candidate for the American presidency in 1992. Almost the only legitimate similarity was the ability of both men to capitalize on widespread alienation and frustration with government and mainstream political parties, and a deep-rooted hostility to elites in Ottawa and Washington. In Quebec, resurgent nationalism manifested itself in increased support for the provincial *Parti québécois* and for a new federal party called the *Bloc québécois,* both dedicated to the creation of an independent Quebec state. Significantly, both the *québécois* nationalists and the Reform Party displayed enthusiastic friendship toward the United States and were highly supportive of the free trade agreement and of closer economic ties to America. A constitutional agreement that would be palatable to Quebec, the other nine provinces, and the Canadian national government continued to be elusive. In October 1992, Canadians decisively rejected one such proposal in a national referendum.

The referendum defeat prompted Brian Mulroney's resignation, his popularity at a historic low for a Canadian prime minister. The *New*

York Times praised Mulroney as "a good friend to the U.S., a close ally on global issues and a strong partner in demolishing trade barriers." Canadian editorialists censured him for precisely those same things: "Mulroney's bosses too often seemed to be Presidents Reagan and Bush," offered the Sherbrooke, Quebec, *Record.* "He seemed to cozy up much closer to U.S. leaders than most Canadians want." One particularly cruel editorial cartoon showed President Clinton offering the Prime Minister a job on the White House kitchen staff. If the specter of a fragmented Canada on their northern border unsettled Americans, however, they gave few visible signs. Humorist Calvin Trillin suggested that Canadians resolve their constitutional crisis by forbidding all discussion of it, requiring that "the tougher saloons in Toronto display signs that say 'No spitting, fighting or constitution talk.'" On the eve of the constitutional referendum that threatened to "tear the upper half of the continent apart, . . . creating serious potential problems for U.S.-Canadian relations," a Knight-Ridder correspondent reported that "the soul-rending Canadian vote [was] hardly noticed" in the United States. The defeat of the Mulroney proposal was widely reported. But once it became clear that even if Canada were indeed to break up, it would be at a maddeningly slow Canadian pace, journalists remembered the newsroom maxim that "No one cares about Canadian politics."[23]

The event of 1992 that most revealed the enduring ambivalence of the U.S.-Canadian relationship was neither the defeat of George Bush nor the departure of Brian Mulroney, but the victory of the Toronto Blue Jays in baseball's World Series—a triumph repeated a year later. When major league baseball expanded to Montreal and Toronto in 1969 and 1977, the most crotchety among Canada's cultural nationalists decried the Expos and the Blue Jays as further evidence of their country's "Americanization." But Canadian baseball fans remained delightfully untroubled by the American cultural Trojan Horse in their midst. Instead, Canadians made baseball their own: millions of them felt the pain of wounded national pride when the Expos and the Jays four times fell short in their league playoffs. Although the Blue Jays team that confronted the Atlanta Braves nominally represented the "Ameri-

At pregame ceremonies during the 1992 baseball World Series in Atlanta, a confused Marine color guard flew the Canadian flag upside down. AP/Wide World Photos.

can" League, the twenty-five United States- and Latin American-born players on their roster were understood to represent Canada as surely as twenty-five Canadians could have done. "All Canadians are taking this seriously," reported a United States correspondent; "up there, it's them against Uncle Sam." At pregame ceremonies in Atlanta, a confused Marine color guard flew the Canadian maple leaf flag upside down, and an equally confused country singer butchered the tune and lyrics to "O Canada": Canadians had televised confirmation of their national angst about American ignorance and arrogance. They savored the outpouring of American apologies, President Bush's among them, as "the greatest mass acknowledgement of Canada's existence by Americans since former Ambassador Ken Taylor helped spring the [Iran] hostages." And when the series came to Toronto, there was no counter demonstration, no booing of the "The Star-Spangled Banner." Canadians forgave their neighbor, further proof of their own moral superiority, and the Jays' six-game triumph was doubly sweet on that account.[24]

Incorporating Mexico

Ronald Reagan's dream of a North American economic area dwarfed the nightmares of Canadian opponents of free trade. The president envisioned including not only Canada but also Mexico and the Caribbean; his Caribbean Basin Initiative was followed by the Bush administration's Enterprise for the Americas Initiative. The signatures seemed barely dry on the bilateral Canada-U.S. agreement before Canada joined the United States and Mexico in negotiations for the completion of a trilateral North American free trade agreement. The Republican free enterprise agenda for hemispheric trade and economic development, although vaunted as a new departure, in some ways echoed the development ideology and tactics of the Eisenhower administration in the 1950s.

The North American Free Trade Agreement (NAFTA) initiative came from Mexico, encouraged by Reagan administration overtures.

The new Mexican government of Carlos Salinas de Gortari took power in 1989, anxious to expand and protect Mexican markets in the United States and elsewhere, to attract foreign investment to Mexico, and to resolve some of the political, social, and diplomatic problems in Mexican-American relations. Whatever the Mulroney government might have preferred, it decided in the fall of 1990 that it had no real choice: although Mexican economic and political ties to Canada were minimal, preservation of the perceived gains of the Canada-U.S. bilateral accord required that Canada enter the trilateral negotiations.[25]

In late August 1992 George Bush, Brian Mulroney, and Carlos Salinas announced the conclusion of a NAFTA, subject to ratification by the legislatures of each country.[26] Support for this trilateral North American agreement within Canada was less vigorous than it had been for the Canada-U.S. FTA two years earlier, but opposition forces were correspondingly less apocalyptic in their resistance. Had the U.S.-Canada FTA been seen as an unqualified success, some of the opposition to a NAFTA might have been mitigated; but there was a widespread perception in business and academic circles as well as among the general public that the loss of several hundred thousand jobs in Canadian industry during the Canadian recession that began in 1990 could be attributed to the impact of the FTA. From the point of view of Canadian exporters the FTA had proved to be no panacea in resolving cross-border trade disputes. Harassment of Canadian exporters of softwood lumber, Honda automobiles, steel, and beer, by U.S. protectionist lobbies and their allies in Congress, the International Trade Commission, and the Department of Commerce, soured many Canadian producers.[27]

NAFTA furthered the objectives of the Reagan and Bush administrations, in spite of the facts that Mexico had initiated the negotiations and that Canada had voluntarily joined the talks. The NAFTA agreement provided for the elimination of tariff barriers to trade among the three countries over a period of ten to fifteen years. It substantially liberalized investment regulations in Mexico in such areas as the pharmaceutical and oil and natural gas service industries and provided for gradual liberalization of tariffs in the agricultural sector. Mexico held the line against American pressure to open its oil and gas industry to direct investment in exploration and development. Canada sought to protect its agricultural marketing boards and once again successfully exempted cultural industries from the agreement. Canada lost its battle to retain more liberal access for its textile and apparel industry to non–North American yarns: NAFTA stipulated that the fibers from which yarn derived also had to be from North America. In the auto sector, Autopact was once again spared by the agreement, although a change in rules of origin made it more difficult for non–North American manufacturers to enter the North American market from Canada. All three governments placed considerable importance on NAFTA provisions for a wider coverage of cross-border trade in services, including transportation, professional services, management, accounting, engineering, and legal services in Mexico. Both Canada and the United States believed that opportunities for their telecommunications firms were substantial.[28]

Business groups in Canada, the United States, and Mexico coordinated their lobbying efforts trilaterally to secure legislative passage of the NAFTA. Opposition to the accord came from the Canadian Labour Congress and the Quebec-based Confederation of National Trade Unions, in the United States from the AFL-CIO, and from several independent union federations in Mexico. But unlike the business supporters of NAFTA, its trade unionist opponents were unable to coordinate a transnational alliance. The official Mexican trade union movement, linked to the ruling Institutional Revolutionary Party (PRI) supported free trade. The division among auto workers — the Canadian Auto Workers in 1985 had separated from their American parent, the UAW — illustrated the inability of the Canadian and U.S. labor movements to respond in concert to NAFTA. Both the CLC and the AFL-CIO contended that free trade with Mexico would undermine wages and increase unemployment as jobs moved south to take advantage of low-wage Mexican labor. Organized labor argued that NAFTA would further accelerate the trend toward industrial restructuring, corporate takeovers, large-scale plant closures, and a shift of capital to Mexican *maquiladoras* (in bond border factories). In an effort to assuage organized labor in each country, negotiators quickly tacked on a side agreement to maintain existing labor standards, primarily in Canada and the United States.[29]

Environmental groups also added their critique to a trilateral free trade agreement, before and following the conclusion of the accord in August 1992. The legal counsel for the Canadian Environmental Law Association contended before the Canadian Parliamentary Committee on External Affairs and International Trade that when principles of deregulated trade are negotiated by institutions that have no mandate or experience and little real interest in environmental issues, "the results of such agreements are often disastrous insofar as they enshrine economic principles that are at odds with the objectives of environmental protection and resource conservation." NAFTA paid lip service to the concerns of environmentalists in both the general provision that no country could lower its environmental standards in order to attract investment, and in another "side accord" that created a trilateral Commission for Environmental Cooperation.[30]

In Mexico, with the power of the PRI behind him and a compliant media on his side, President Salinas won ratification for NAFTA without difficulty. The Canadian parliamentary system similarly assured an easy passage in Ottawa, as Mulroney's Conservative majority in the House of Commons steamrollered the Liberal and NDP opposition. In the more complex world of U.S. politics, NAFTA faced the stiffest test: winning congressional approval required Democrat Bill Clinton to put his young presidency on the line and to rely heavily on Republican support. The U.S. opponents of NAFTA were strange bedfellows: organized and unorganized labor, environmentalists, consumer groups, the protectionist left, and the populist right of Texas billionaire Ross Perot variously denounced the agreement as a big business plot to exploit cheap Mexican labor and lax Mexican environmental standards. Americans would hear, Perot warned, a "giant sucking sound" as their jobs drained south to Mexico. Yet the agreement gained support from archconservative broadcaster Rush Limbaugh, corporate icon Lee Iacocca, and liberal Democratic New Jersey Senator Bill Bradley. In November 1993, NAFTA squeaked through the U.S. Senate and House by three votes: in January 1994, the United States, Canada, and Mexico formally embarked on their trilateral experiment in North American economic integration.

Epilogue: "Plus ça change . . ."

Few national neighbors can claim the success and mutual prosperity of the relationship that has evolved between the United States and Canada over the past two hundred years. The two countries share not only a continent but also a cultural, political, and economic heritage, which, although divergent in fundamental ways, has striking similarities. In *Canada and the United States: Ambivalent Allies,* we have tried to go beyond traditional diplomatic history and to consider the political, economic, and especially the cultural and social considerations that inform the bilateral relationship. The history of the U.S.-Canadian interaction cannot be written any other way; it is impossible to confine U.S.-Canadian relations within the framework of a traditional diplomatic narrative. Thus, this volume has sought to explore the bilateral relationship in all in its interwoven dimensions.

One of those dimensions, of course, is military and diplomatic. Presidents and prime ministers now praise the border that they share as "undefended," but for the first century and a quarter, the U.S.-Canadian boundary was anything but undefended. The British used Canada as the base for an attack upon their rebellious American colonists, and the Americans invaded Canada twice, from 1775 to 1776, and again from 1812 to 1814. There has been no subsequent invasion, unless one dignifies the Fenian terrorists, but war seemed likely at other times and imminent at least twice, after the Canadian rebellions and during the U.S. Civil War. As the United States ascended to world might, and Canada became more autonomous from Great Britain, war was relegated to the imaginations of army staff officers. After 1900—probably after 1871—continentalism did not involve overt annexationism among significant groups on either side of the border. With the boundary firmly in place after the Alaska dispute, U.S. ambitions toward Canada were limited to securing strategic advantage, guaranteeing access to natural resources or the security of U.S. investment in

Canada, and assuring that Canada did not become a gap in American hemispheric security.

American predominance also colors ("colours," for Canadians) the economic and social dimensions of the relationship. The peoples of the two countries have crossed the shared border in both directions, but four Canadians have emigrated south for every American who has moved north. In the 1990s Canadian immigration to the United States has reemerged as a significant phenomenon. Social movements in the United States have often been mirrored in parallel, even dependent, institutional developments in Canada: the North American labor movement, crusades for social reform, scholarly societies and service clubs, professional sports. During the twentieth-century American popular culture has rolled across English and French Canada like a tidal wave. Since the late nineteenth century, U.S. capital has exploited Canadian natural resources and U.S. manufacturers have built branch plants and sought markets in Canada.

Canadian concern about dependence on the United States has constantly shaped the articulation and implementation of Canada's national policies, far beyond any impact that Canada may have had on the United States. The election of Bill Clinton as president inspired a profusion of Canadian analyses of how the change would effect Canada, analyses that went beyond obvious bilateral issues like trade, the environment and defense. "Will the Clinton contagion cross the border and change the shape of Canadian politics, . . . as is so often the case with American fashions?" asked *Maclean's,* Canada's English-language news weekly. Like Clinton's Democratic administration, the Liberal government of Jean Chrétien, elected in October 1993, moved right to appropriate the conservative agenda of free trade, balanced budgets, and a diminished welfare state.[1]

This is to contend neither that the influence has been in only one direction nor that dependence is not tempered by interdependence. U.S. commentators regularly praise or vilify Canada's public national health care system. In per capita terms, Canadian investment in the United States (much of it in Florida and Arizona real estate) is in fact greater than American direct investment in Canada. Canadian natural resources and Canadian territorial integrity are critical to American economic viability and national security. Ironically, despite the divisive debate over NAFTA within both the United States and Canada, the issue in many ways drew Americans and Canadians together, mobilized by their common concerns about the environment and potential job losses to Mexico. Yet, neither the worst fears nor the most optimistic predictions about the pitfalls or benefits of NAFTA materialized in the first three years of the agreement.[2]

Canadians continue to protest U.S. indifference and ignorance, like the "Longtime Reader in Edmonton" who wrote to "Dear Ann Landers" to complain that "most Americans . . . have very little knowledge of Canada and no curiosity to learn." But Canadians continue to interpret the United States in terms of archaic stereotypes that have their roots in the nineteenth century. Routinized anti-Americanisms drip from editorial cartoonists' pens or flow from the keyboards of newspaper columnists, like that of the *Globe and Mail* sportswriter who explained that Canadian college football lacks fans because it is too "wholesome": "were Canadian university football as odious as U.S. college football — which is thoroughly laden with corruption and moral decay — general interest undoubtedly would surge." But if there is arrogance and ignorance on both sides, the power relationship has been overwhelmingly one-sided, as one would expect given America's greater population, military and economic power and international influence.[3]

The shared cultural heritage of English Canadians and Americans early on created shared consciousness on a wide range of issues, and similarities are abundant and apparent. Both the United States and Canada, as Robin Winks has noted, are "imagined nations," invented in a remarkably short span of world history. Both countries are made up of immigrants, who seized what was in some senses a common western frontier from native North Americans. There were differences in the process of "civilizing" those frontiers, but neither country treated native peoples in a manner that can be cause for pride in the 1990s. Both are capitalist countries grounded in the free market, even though the state has historically played a larger role in Canada than in the

United States. Both enjoy liberal-democratic political systems, and in both countries ordinary citizens grumble about the difficulty of penetrating the political apparatus to make politicians listen to their voices. Both countries are prosperous relative to the rest of the globe, and if the United States has been shaped by a self-consciousness as a "people of plenty," there is no reason to assume that such an awareness has not tinged the Canadian body politic over the last half-century.[4]

But the differences between the United States and Canada are not insignificant, although Americans underestimate and Canadians overstate them. Canada was born, if not of counterrevolution, at least out of a conscious decision not to break the British connection. That decision was fundamental to what followed. Though it has more to do with Canada's difficult northern geography and her fear of the United States than with any collectivist ideology, Canada has been more inclined to accept an enhanced state role in the private sector, from foreign investment review through national health care and the creation of public corporations. It is significant, for instance, that the United States, deeply wedded to the ideology of free enterprise, is the only major oil-producing nation in the world never to have had a state oil company.

In politics, the Canadian system has left more room for divergence from accepted truths; third parties have played a more significant, if never dominant, role. The Canadian national election of 1993 returned members of five parties to the House of Commons, whereas in the United States even the strong popular challenge of independent Ross Perot for the presidency in 1992 made no impact on congressional representation. As elastic as the Republican and Democratic parties have been, it would be preposterous to contend that the two-party system has prevailed, and third parties died, primarily because Americans of any political persuasion could find an ideological home within one of the two umbrella parties. Alexis de Tocqueville commented on the quest for conformity of belief and behavior in American society, whether in the democratic orientation of clothing noted by historian Daniel Boorstin, or in the fear of expressing views that might be taken to be beyond the prevailing consensus. This tendency toward

"Who Are Those People Upstairs?" Oliphant © 1995 Universal Press Syndicate.

homogenization rather than diversity, in spite of the profound belief in American exceptionalism and individualism, sustains one of the paradoxes in United States history. Recent scholarship in ethnic studies has demonstrated that the English-speaking majorities of both countries pressed immigrants to conform and assimilate, and that despite this pressure, those immigrants manifested remarkable cultural resilience north and south of the forty-ninth parallel. But scholarship little affects national identities: the United States understands itself as a "melting pot" nation, while Canada has constitutionally enshrined its "cultural mosaic."

The most distinctive tile in that "cultural mosaic" is, of course, the province of Quebec, and the survival and growth of a French-speaking minority stands out as the single most significant difference between the Canadian and the American experiences. The electoral successes of political parties committed to an independent Quebec—the *Bloc québécois* won three-quarters of Quebec's seats in the Canadian parliament in 1993, and the *Parti québécois* became the government of Quebec in 1994—raise the question of how much longer the Canadian experiment of two nations cohabiting a single nation-state will continue. Quebec voters rejected a vaguely worded version of "sovereignty" by the narrowest of margins in an October 1995 referendum which attracted unprecedented U.S. interest. U.S. political scientist Charles Doran speculated to a congressional hearing that Quebec's departure might cause Canada to "unravel" into "a series of small, isolated, weak entities," and that "the United States may find that on the threshold of the twenty-first century, its relations with Canada are far from exceptional."[5]

In terms of U.S. foreign policy, however, what is striking about relations with Canada is how *un*exceptional the so-called special relationship has in fact been. American policy toward Canada conforms to, rather than diverges from, American policy toward the rest of the world. There are undoubtedly unique features to the bilateral relationship, most notably the abundance of "clearly discernable, mainly non-governmental, continental subsystems" (to borrow John H. Redekop's jargon) in categories ranging from entertainment to education, and the establishment of bilateral institutions such as the International Joint Commission or the Permanent Joint Board on Defense. But the latter may be less unique than Canadians suppose: the United States has long participated in, indeed led, hemispheric defense organizations, and has had joint agreements with its other immediate neighbor, Mexico. The basic pattern of United States foreign policy since the early nineteenth century has been self-consciously liberal, capitalist, internationalist and anticolonial—in the sense that policy makers and political culture have preferred to avoid the formal acquisition of colonies whenever possible. The American approach to Canada has been entirely consistent with these maxims of U.S. policy. For more than two centuries, America has balanced a rational consideration for northern strategic security with its desire for an open door for capital and trade in Canada. When Canada has seemed less than secure, or when there has been any perceived threat to that open door policy, relations have been fractious, as for instance during the Kennedy-Diefenbaker and Johnson-Pearson years over Cuba, nuclear weapons, Vietnam, and the cold war. Similarly, America responded sharply to Canadian economic nationalist policies during Trudeau's years in power. But the United States never attempted direct colonial control: the integration of Canada into the American system after World War II was, by the standards of international relations, a gentle seduction. Thus, the history of the past two centuries suggests a higher degree of similarity between America's Canada policy and the general characteristics of United States foreign policy more than it does any "special relationship."[6]

The U.S. adoption in 1996 of the Helms-Burton law (officially titled the Cuban Liberty and Democratic Solidarity Act) is but the latest evidence of this. Sponsored in the U.S. Senate by North Carolina's Jesse Helms, the legislation attempts to crush Fidel Castro by punishing the citizens of any country that does business with Cuba. The act permits U.S. nationals with claims to property expropriated by Cuba during the revolution to bring suit in U.S. courts against any person who "traffics" ("transfers, distributes, dispenses, brokers or otherwise disposes of . . . ; or improves or invests in or begins to manage, lease, possess, use or hold an interest") in such confiscated property. The act excludes third country nationals from the United States if they violate the law. NAFTA membership did not earn Canada (or Mexico) an exemption from Helms-Burton: seven Canadian executives of Sherritt International Corporation were barred from the United States shortly after the act came into force. President Clinton signed the bill into law with little hesitation: the prospect of winning a larger share of the critical Cuban-American vote in Florida and New Jersey far outweighed any concern about possible damage to U.S.-Canada relations. Helms-Burton demonstrates that any administration may be confronted with congressional initiatives that run counter to presidential preferences in foreign policy, and that Canada can never be "special" enough to earn exemption from U.S. political realities.[7]

Nonetheless, certain distinguishing rituals continue to characterize the bilateral relationship. Canada's prime minister, for example, remains the first foreign leader invited to meet with a new president.

Such rituals have little substance, however. In February 1993, Bill Clinton welcomed Prime Minister Brian Mulroney with hoary platitudes about "the world's longest undefended border," phrases that could have come from the mouth of William Howard Taft. Mulroney in response emphasized the subtle differences between Canadian and United States policies toward Eastern Europe, and as the *Washington Post* put it, "gently chided" the President "to show more leadership in resolving the Balkans conflict." These too are ritual phrases; with an appropriate crisis from another era substituted for "Balkans," the speaker could have been Mackenzie King or Lester Pearson.[8]

Because of such rituals, however, the degree to which Canada is just like any other country to the United States seems not to have been understood by most policy makers or the general public on the Canadian side. The lack of understanding of this basic truth has been the source of confusion, uncertainty, and wounded sensibilities on the part of Canadians when Canadian policy has either failed to meet a desired American standard or when Canada has seemingly or actually challenged a U.S. position. Pierre Elliott Trudeau's oft-quoted metaphor of sharing a bed with an elephant continues to resonate, but it misleads by suggesting that it is only the power relationship between the two that is unequal. Rather, as this study has attempted to suggest, there are fundamental differences that transcend issues of raw power between the two nations. Some social scientists suggest an increasing convergence in values among all three North American countries. Any apparent tendency toward convergence, however, must be viewed through the lens of the past divergence and ambiguity. Two centuries of ambivalence inhibit even the most sanguine historian from the conclusion that the conservative years of the 1980s and 1990s herald a new consensus and convergence between Canada and the United States.[9]

Notes

Abbreviations

ARCS	*American Review of Canadian Studies.*
CHCD	Canada, House of Commons, *Debates.*
CHR	*Canadian Historical Review.*
DCER	*Documents on Canadian External Relations.*
DDE	Dwight David Eisenhower Presidential Library.
FRUS	United States Department of State, *Foreign Relations of the United States.*
Globe	*Toronto Globe.* (After 1936, the *Globe and Mail.*)
HSTL	Harry S. Truman Presidential Library.
JFK	John Fitzgerald Kennedy Presidential Library.
LBJ	Lyndon Baines Johnson Presidential Library.
NAC	National Archives of Canada.
NYT	*New York Times.*

Unless specified otherwise, all translations from French are by the authors, and all statistics are drawn from *Historical Statistics of Canada,* second ed. (Ottawa, 1983), and from *Historical Statistics of the United States* (New York, 1976).

Introduction

1. S. F. Wise and Robert Craig Brown, *Canada Views the United States: Nineteenth-Century Political Attitudes* (Seattle, 1967), 18–19.

1. A Revolution Repeatedly Rejected, 1774–1871

1. A. R. M. Lower, *Colony to Nation,* cited in George A. Rawlyk, *Revolution Rejected, 1775–1776* (Scarborough, Ont., 1968), 9.

2. Hamilton cited in H. L. Keenleyside, *Canada and the United States* (New York, 1929), 9; Philip Lawson, *The Imperial Challenge: Quebec and Britain in the Age of the American Revolution* (Buffalo, 1989).
3. Jefferson to John Randolph, 29 November 1775, in P. L. Ford, ed., *The Writings of Thomas Jefferson*, vol. 1 (New York, 1892), 492; for a similar expression about Nova Scotia, see R. H. Lee to William Lee, 14 May 1778, in E. C. Burnett, ed., *Letters of Members of the Continental Congress*, vol. 3 (Washington, D.C., 1921–34), 236–37; Adams to James Warren, 3 November 1778, in Burnett, *Letters of Members*, 476–77; congressional letters are discussed and quoted in Reginald C. Stuart, *United States Expansionism and British North America, 1775–1871* (Chapel Hill, 1988), 11–13, and in Keenleyside, *Canada and the United States*, 15–18.
4. For accounts of the reaction to both the American Revolution and the Quebec Act, see: Hilda Neatby, *Quebec: The Revolutionary Age, 1760–1791* (Toronto, 1966), 142–55; Fernand Ouellet, *Histoire Economique et sociale du Québec, 1760–1850* (Montreal, 1966), 99–124; Donald Creighton, *The Commercial Empire of the St. Lawrence* (Toronto, 1937); Washington quoted in Stuart, *United States Expansionism*, 13; Generals Wooster and Schuyler quoted in Keenleyside, *Canada and the United States*, 27–28; Bourassa cited in H. Blair Neatby, "Canadianism—A Symposium," Canadian Historical Association *Report* (1956), 74; Gustave Lanctot, *Le Canada et la Révolution américaine* (Montreal, 1965).
5. The best account of religion and other contacts between Nova Scotia and Massachusetts is George Rawlyk, *Nova Scotia's Massachusetts: A Study of Massachusetts—Nova Scotia Relations, 1680–1784* (Montreal, 1973); Gordon Stewart and George Rawlyk, *A People Highly Favoured of God: The Nova Scotia Yankees and the American Revolution* (Montreal, 1972); J. B. Brebner, *The Neutral Yankees of Nova Scotia: A Marginal Colony During the Revolutionary Years* (New York, 1937).
6. The most useful account of the negotiations remains Samuel Flagg Bemis, *Diplomacy of the American Revolution* (New York, 1935). The quotations from Adams are from A. L. Burt, *The United States, Great Britain and British North America: From the Revolution to the Establishment of Peace After the War of 1812* (New Haven, 1940), 48–53.
7. The estimate of the total number who had Loyalist sympathies is from Paul H. Smith, "The American Loyalists: Notes on Their Organizational and Numerical Strength," *William and Mary Quarterly* 25 (1968): 259–77; the estimate of sixty thousand émigrés is from Robert C. Calhoon, *The Loyal-*

ists in Revolutionary America, 1760–1781 (New York, 1981), 501; the estimate of one hundred thousand émigrés is from Wallace Brown, *The Good Americans: The Loyalists in the American Revolution* (New York, 1969), 192; Roger Daniels, *Coming to America: A History of Immigration and Ethnicity in American Life* (New York, 1990), 111; Neil MacKinnon, *This Unfriendly Soil: The Loyalist Experience in Nova Scotia* (Kingston and Montreal, 1986), 57–65; W. H. Nelson, *The American Tory* (New York, 1960), 88–91.

8. Loyalist characterizations of America quoted in MacKinnon, *This Unfriendly Soil*, 159; Cartwright quoted in Jane Errington, *The Lion, the Eagle, and Upper Canada: A Developing Colonial Ideology* (Montreal, 1987), 33; Winslow quoted in Ann Gorman Condon, *The Envy of the American States: The Loyalist Dream for New Brunswick* (Fredericton, 1984), 173–74.
9. Seymour Martin Lipset, *Continental Divide: The Values and Institutions of the United States and Canada* (New York, 1990), 1–18; "Loyalist Myth" discussed in Jo-Ann Fellows, "The Loyalist Myth in Canada," *Canadian Historical Association Historical Papers* (1971), 94–111, and in Murray W. Barkley, "The Loyalist Tradition in New Brunswick: A Study in the Growth and Evolution of an Historical Myth, 1825–1914," *Acadiensis* 4 (1975): 3–45; Wise and Brown, *Canada Views the United States*, 22.
10. Tavern sign described in Stuart, *United States Expansionism*, 33; Marcus Lee Hansen and J. B. Brebner, *The Mingling of the Canadian and American Peoples* (New Haven, 1940), 81–86; George Rawlyk, "The Federalist-Loyalist Alliance in New Brunswick, 1784–1815," *Humanities Association Review* 27 (1976): 142–60; Errington, *The Lion, the Eagle*, 38–39.
11. H. G. Nicholas, *The United States and Britain* (Chicago, 1975), 11; the claim is made in Edelgard E. Mahant and Graeme S. Mount, *An Introduction to Canadian-American Relations* (Scarborough, Ont., 1989), 290; Hamilton quoted in Bradford Perkins, *The First Rapprochement: England and the United States, 1795–1805* (New York, 1955), 31, 33–34, 40. Richard White, *The Middle Ground: Indians, Empires and Republics in the Great Lakes Region, 1650–1815* (Cambridge, 1991), is a prize-winning study of the place of eastern Indian groups between French and British empires, then between the United States and British North America.
12. A synthesis of the traditional consensus is Marshall Smelser, *The Democratic Republic* (New York, 1968), 138–50; revisionist views include: Clifford Egan, "The Origins of the War of 1812: Three Decades of Historical Writing," *Military Affairs* 38 (April 1974): 72–75; J. C. Stagg, *Mr. Madison's War: Politics, Diplomacy and Warfare in the Early American Republic, 1783–1830*

(Princeton, 1983); Donald R. Hickey, *The War of 1812: A Forgotten Conflict* (Chicago, 1989); Steven Watts, *The Republic Reborn: War and the Making of Liberal America, 1790–1820* (Baltimore, 1987); Reginald Horsman, "The War of 1812 Revisited," *Diplomatic History* 15 (Winter 1991): 115–24; Calhoun quoted in Hickey, *A Forgotten Conflict*, 44.

13. Quotes from Lewis Hacker, "Western Land Hunger and the War of 1812: A Conjecture," *Mississippi Valley Historical Review* 10 (March 1924): 370, and Julius W. Pratt, *Expansionists of 1812* (New York, 1925), 88 (both authors of the thesis).
14. White, *Middle Ground*, 482–83; Stuart, *United States Expansionism*, 54–65; *National Intelligencer*, 8 November 1815.
15. James D. Richardson, ed., *A Compilation of the Messages and Papers of the Presidents*, vol. 2 (Washington, D.C., 1899), 484–90; Burt, *U.S., Great Britain and B.N.A.*, 206–316.
16. Jefferson in Richard W. Van Alstyne, *The Rising American Empire* (Chicago, 1960), 88; on the identification of America with Napoleonic France, see Errington, *The Lion, the Eagle*, 80–81, and Condon, *Envy of the American States*, 204–5.
17. A good account of the Anglo-American diplomacy of the period is Bradford Perkins, *Castlereagh and Adams: England and the United States, 1812–1823* (Berkeley, 1965); Brian W. Dippie, *The Vanishing American: White Attitudes and U.S. Indian Policy* (Middletown, Conn., 1982), 10–11.
18. For treatment of the War of 1812 treaties and aftermath, see Perkins, *Castlereagh and Adams;* Charles S. Campbell, *From Revolution to Rapprochement: The United States and Great Britain, 1783–1900* (New York, 1974).
19. On Perry, see Hickey, *A Forgotten Conflict*, 133; New Orleans campaign description from John William Ward, *Andrew Jackson: Symbol for an Age* (New York, 1955), 6, 16–27; S. F. Wise, "The War of 1812 in Popular History," in Arthur Bowler, ed., *War Along the Niagara: Essays on the War of 1812 and Its Legacy* (Youngstown, N.Y., 1991).
20. James A. Henretta et al., *America's History* (Chicago, 1987), 298–303.
21. The most complete discussion of these American influences in British North America is Fred Landon, *Western Ontario and the American Frontier* (Toronto, 1941), 59–143, 193–204.
22. Allen P. Stouffer, *The Light of Nature and the Law of God: Antislavery in Ontario, 1833–1877* (Montreal, 1992), 216–17; Ryerson quoted in Susan Houston, "Politics, Schools, and Social Change in Upper Canada," *CHR* 53, no. 2 (1972): 263; Bruce Curtis, "Schoolbooks and the Myth of Cur-

ricular Republicanism: The State and the Curriculum in Canada West, 1820–1850," *Histoire sociale/Social History* 16 (1983): 305–30; Taché quoted in Jacques Monet, *The Last Cannon Shot: A Study of French-Canadian Nationalism, 1837–1850* (Toronto, 1969), frontispiece; Yolande Lavoie, *L'Emigration des Canadiens aux Etats-Unis avant 1930* (Montreal, 1972), 21, 69–71.

23. William H. Goetzmann, *When the Eagle Screamed: The Romantic Horizon in American Diplomacy, 1800–1860* (New York, 1966), 75, 91; Goetzmann, *Exploration and Empire: The Explorer and the Scientist in the Winning of the American West* (New York, 1966).
24. Mackenzie cited in Wise and Brown, *Canada Views the United States,* 33; David Mills, *The Idea of Loyalty in Upper Canada, 1784–1850* (Montreal, 1988), 32–51, 93–110; Colin Read, *The Rebellion of 1837 in Upper Canada* (Ottawa, 1985); J. E. Rea, "William Lyon Mackenzie—Jacksonian?," *Mid-America* 50 (July 1968): 223–35.
25. Fernand Ouellet, ed., *Papineau: Textes choisis* (Quebec, 1958), 17, 21, 53–58; Wise and Brown, *Canada Views the United States,* 30–32; Jacques Vallee, ed., *Tocqueville au Bas Canada* (Montreal, 1973), 112–13.
26. O'Sullivan and Albany newspaper quoted in Stuart, *United States Expansionism,* 128, 130; Arthur and Palmerston quoted in Kenneth Bourne, *Britain and the Balance of Power in North America, 1815–1908* (Berkeley, 1967), 80, 86; Albert B. Corey, *The Crisis of 1830–1842 in Canadian-American Relations* (New Haven, 1941), 27–43; Kenneth R. Stevens, *Border Diplomacy: The Caroline and McLeod Affairs in Anglo-Canadian-American Relations, 1837–1842* (Tuscaloosa, Ala., 1989).
27. Campbell, *From Revolution to Rapprochement;* Howard Jones, "Anglophobia and the Aroostook War," *New England Quarterly* 17 (December 1975).
28. Polk in Richardson, *Messages of the Presidents,* 4:398. For comprehensive analyses of the role of the Pacific Northwest in Anglo-American diplomacy, see Frederick Merk, *The Oregon Question: Essays in Anglo-American Diplomacy and Politics* (Cambridge, 1967) and Norman Graebner, *Empire on the Pacific* (New York, 1955).
29. Manifesto cited in L. B. Shippee, *Canadian-American Relations, 1849–1874* (New Haven, 1939), 2; Wise and Brown, *Canada Views the United States,* 46–73; Stuart, *United States Expansionism,* 93–97; support for annexation to offset Southern political power was expressed by Henry Dearborn to Daniel Webster, 1830, cited in Charles M. Wiltse, ed., *1830–1834,* vol. 3 of *The Papers of Daniel Webster* (Hanover, 1977), 18; Garrison, July 1848, cited in W. Merrill, ed., *1841–1849,* vol. 3 of *The Letters of William Lloyd*

Garrison (Cambridge, 1971), 577; Donald F. Warner, *The Idea of Continental Union: Agitation for the Annexation of Canada to the United States, 1849–1893* (Lexington, Ky., 1960), 19–32.

30. D. C. Masters, *The Reciprocity Treaty of 1854* (Toronto, 1963 [1938]); J. M. S. Careless, *The Union of the Canadas, 1841–1857* (Toronto, 1967), 132–49; Senator Jacob Collamer cited in Shippee, *Canadian-American Relations, 1849–1874*, 88; A. R. M. Lower et al., *The North American Assault on the Canadian Forest: A History of the Lumber Trade Between Canada and the United States* (Toronto, 1938), 123–47; for the role of American interests in Upper Canadian railroad development, see Peter Baskerville, "Americans in Britain's Backyard: The Railway Era in Upper Canada, 1850–1880," *Business History Review* 55, no. 3 (Autumn 1981): 314–33.

31. Colborne cited in Robin Winks, *The Blacks in Canada* (Montreal, 1971), 155, whose view of Canada's reception of African Americans contrasts with that in John Hope Franklin, *From Slavery to Freedom: A History of American Negroes* (New York, 1947), 361–71; Jason H. Silverman, *Unwelcome Guests: Canada West's Response to American Fugitive Slaves, 1800–1865* (Millwood, N.Y., 1985); Joseph Taper to Joseph Long, 11 November 1840, Long Papers, Special Collections, Duke University Library; Fred Landon, "Canadian Negroes and the John Brown Raid," *Journal of Negro History* 6 (April 1921): 174–82; Howe quotations from L. E. Richards, ed., *Letters and Journals of Samuel Gridley Howe*, vol. 2 (Boston, 1906–9), 447, cited in Winks, *Blacks in Canada*, 270; editor quoted in Wise and Brown, *Canada Views the United States*, 71.

32. "The Fugitive Slave Case in Canada," *Harper's Weekly*, 9 February 1861, 82; Robin Winks, *Canada and the United States: The Civil War Years* (Baltimore, 1960), 228–29; John A. Williams, "Canada and the Civil War," in Harold Hyman, ed., *Heard Round the World: The Impact Abroad of the Civil War* (New York, 1969), 257–98; Macdonald cited in W. L. Morton, *The Critical Years: The Union of British North American, 1857–1873* (Toronto, 1964), 93; McGee quotation from Hyman, *Heard Round the World*, 283.

33. Palmerston quoted in Bourne, *Britain and the Balance of Power*, 213; Brian Jenkins, *Britain and the War for the Union*, vol. 1 (Montreal and London, 1974), 40–43.

34. On "skedaddlers," Hansen and Brebner, *Mingling*, 148–49; Campbell, *From Revolution to Rapprochement*, 110; on the St. Alban's raid, see Jenkins, *War for the Union*, vol. 2, (1980), 357, 359–60.

35. British strategists quoted in Bourne, *Britain and the Balance of Power,* 218–47; on the Trent affair, see David P. Crook, *The North, the South and the Powers, 1861–1865* (New York, 1974), 122–47; Palmerston quotation is from Gordon Warren, *Fountain of Discontent: The Trent Affair and Freedom of the Seas* (Boston, 1981), 135.
36. *Tribune* cited in the *Toronto Globe,* 17 January 1866, 2; W. C. Ford, ed., *A Cycle of Adams Letters, 1861–1865,* vol. 2 (Boston, 1920), 254; Potter quoted in Warner, *Idea of Continental Union,* 47.
37. Leon O'Broin, *Fenian Fever: An Anglo-American Dilemma* (New York, 1971); Hereward Senior, *The Fenians and Canada* (Toronto, 1978) and *The Last Invasion of Canada: The Fenian Raids, 1866–1870* (Toronto, 1991).
38. C. P. Stacey, "Fenianism and the Rise of National Feeling in Canada at the Time of Confederation," *CHR* 12, no. 3 (1931): 238–61; W. L. Morton, "British North America and a Continent in Dissolution, 1861–1871," *History* 47 (1962): 139–56; F. H. Underhill, *The Image of Confederation* (Toronto, 1964), 4.
39. Grant's message to Congress is from *The State of the Union Messages of the Presidents, 1790–1966,* vol. 2 (New York, 1967), 1210; Donald Creighton, *John A. Macdonald II: The Old Chieftain* (Toronto, 1955), 74–102; Goldwin Smith, [Jr.], *The Treaty of Washington, 1871: A Study in Imperial History* (Ithaca, N.Y., 1941). For Grant and U.S. expansionist ideas toward Canada, see also William McFeely, *Grant* (New York, 1981), 347–48.

2. Canada in the Shadow of Industrial America, 1871–1903

1. The world systems model originated with Immanuel Wallerstein, *The Modern World System* (New York, 1974), *The Capitalist World Economy* (Cambridge, 1979), and, with Terence K. Hopkins, *World-Systems Analysis: Theory and Methodology* (Beverly Hills, 1982); Cardwell quoted in Bourne, *Britain and the Balance of Power,* 303–4.
2. "The Fourth of July," *Globe,* 5 July 1876; "Dominion Day," *Globe,* 3 July 1876.
3. NAC, Sir John A. Macdonald Papers, Charles Tupper to Macdonald, 1 December 1888; Henry James's review of Francis Parkman's *The Old Regime in Canada,* in the *Nation,* 15 October 1874; Shippee, *Canadian-*

American Relations, 1849–1874, 476–77; *Congressional Globe*, 40th Congress, 2d session, 3659; Richard A. Preston, *The Defense of the Undefended Border: Planning for War in North America, 1867–1939* (Montreal, 1977), 41–43.

4. *Montreal Evening Star*, 3 July 1876; Douglas Owram, *The Promise of Eden: The Canadian Expansionist Movement and the Idea of the West, 1856–1900* (Toronto, 1980); George F. G. Stanley, *The Birth of Western Canada* (London, 1936) and *Louis Riel* (Toronto, 1963).
5. Donnelly quoted in Warner, *Idea of Continental Union*, 115; W. L. Morton, ed., *The James Wickes Taylor Correspondence* (Winnipeg, 1968); Alvin Gluek, Jr., *Minnesota and the Manifest Destiny of the Canadian Northwest* (Toronto, 1965).
6. Allan Nevins, *Hamilton Fish* (New York, 1937), 388–90; lieutenant quoted in Morton, *Critical Years*, 244.
7. Boat song quoted in Margaret Ormsby, *British Columbia: A History* (Toronto, 1958), 142; California resolution in Warner, *Idea of Continental Union*, 135; David Shi, "Seward's Attempt to Annex British Columbia, 1865–1869," *Pacific Historical Review* 47, no. 2 (1978): 217–38.
8. Charles John Fedorak, "The United States Consul in Victoria and the Political Destiny of the Colony of British Columbia, 1862–1870," *BC Studies* 79 (1988): 8–15; Barry Gough, *The Royal Navy and the Northwest Coast of North America, 1810–1914* (Vancouver, 1971); poem in the *Victoria British Colonist*, 1870, cited in Walter N. Sage, "British Columbia Becomes Canadian, 1871–1901," *Queen's Quarterly* 52, no. 2 (1945): 170.
9. Roger D. McGrath, *Gunfighters, Highwaymen and Vigilantes: Violence on the Frontier* (Berkeley, 1985); Paul F. Sharp, "Three Frontiers: Some Comparative Studies of Canadian, American, and Australian Settlement," *Pacific Historical Review* 24 (1955): 373; Stanley D. Hansen, "Policing the International Boundary Area in Saskatchewan, 1890–1910," *Saskatchewan History* 19, no. 2 (1966): 73; Desmond Morton, "Cavalry or Police: Keeping the Peace of Two Adjacent Frontiers, 1870–1900," *Journal of Canadian Studies* 12, no. 2 (1977): 27; Pierre Berton, *Klondike: The Life and Death of the Last Great Gold Rush* (Toronto, 1963); David Breen, *The Canadian Ranching Frontier and the Prairie West* (Toronto, 1983); *Harper's Weekly*, 5 August 1876, 630–31.
10. Robert M. Utley, *Frontier Regulars: The United States Army and the Indian, 1866–1891* (New York, 1973), 55–56; Chester Martin, *Dominion Lands Policy* (Toronto, 1938); Garrick Mallory, "The Indian Systems of Canada and the United States," *Nation*, September 1877, 148; Hana Samek, *The Blackfoot*

Confederacy, 1880–1920: A Comparative Study of Canadian and U.S. Indian Policy (Albuquerque, 1987), 33; Mills in John Jennings, "The Plains Indians and the Law," in Hugh Dempsey, ed., *Men in Scarlet* (Calgary, 1974), 53–54.

11. R. C. Macleod, *The North West Mounted Police, 1873–1919* (Ottawa, 1978), 3; L. H. Thomas, *The Struggle for Responsible Government in the Northwest Territories, 1870–1897* (Toronto, 1978), 4–5, 60–61; Samek, *Blackfoot Confederacy*, 29–31, 105–22.
12. S. W. Horrall, "Sir John A. Macdonald and the Mounted Police Force for the Northwest Territories," *CHR* 53, no. 2 (1972): 179–200; Pliney Earle Goddard, "The Indian Problem in Canada," *The Red Man*, Dec. 1911, 134; Wallace Stegner, *Wolf Willow: A History, a Story and a Memoir of the Last Plains Frontier* (New York, 1962), 101; Douglas Owram, " 'White Savagery': Some Canadian Reaction to American Indian Policy, 1867–1885" (M.A. thesis, Queen's University, 1971); *Nation*, 6 September 1877, 148.
13. The controversy surrounding Sitting Bull is the subject of Gary Pennanen, "Sitting Bull: Indian Without a Country," *CHR* 51, no. 2 (1970): 123–40; Christopher C. Joyner, "The Hegira of Sitting Bull to Canada: Diplomatic Realpolitik, 1876–1881," *Journal of the West* 16 (1974): 6–18; and Joseph Manzione, *"I Am Looking to the North for My Life": Sitting Bull, 1876–1881* (Salt Lake City, 1991).
14. Lord Dufferin, governor general of Canada, to Sir Edward Thornton, British minister in Washington, 14 Feb. 1878; R. W. Scott, secretary of state of Canada, memorandum, 11 Feb. 1878; James F. McLeod, commissioner, Northwest Mounted Police, to Generals Terry and Lawrence, Sitting Bull Commission, Fort Walsh, 17 Oct. 1877; Evarts to Sir Edward Thornton, 17 June 1878, U.S. Department of State, *FRUS* (1878), 344–45, 349–50; Evarts to Thornton, 27 May 1879, *FRUS* (1879), 496–98; Thornton to Evarts, 15 Nov. 1979, *FRUS* (1880), 498; *Herald*, 23 Oct. 1877, and Fort Benton [MT] *Record* 28 Jul. 1881, cited in Joyner, "Sitting Bull," 14, 16.
15. Hansen and Brebner, *Mingling;* Stuart, *United States Expansionism*, 260–61; Lipset, *Continental Divide*, 172–92; Donald G. Godfrey, " 'Canada's Brigham Young': Charles Ora Card, Southern Alberta Pioneer," *ARCS* 18, no. 2 (1988): 224–34.
16. The most accessible sources for migration statistics are Leon E. Truesdell, *The Canadian Born in the United States, 1850–1930* (New Haven, 1943), and R. H. Coats and M. C. Maclean, *The American-Born in Canada: A Statistical Interpretation* (New Haven, 1943), but the best analysis of those statistics

is Lavoie, *Emigration;* Goldwin Smith, *Canada and the Canadian Question* (Toronto, 1891), 233; "Boston Is the Promised Land of Canadians," *PEI Magazine* 1 (1899): 82; Bruno Ramirez, *On the Move: French-Canadian and Italian Migrants in the North Atlantic Economy* (Toronto, 1991), 21–33; Hugh Dempsey, *Big Bear* (Lincoln, Neb., 1984), 95–105, 112, 122.

17. Lavoie, *Emigration,* 69–71; Yves Roby, "Un Québec emigré aux Etats-Unis," in Claude Savary, ed., *Les rapports culturels entre le Québec et les Etats-Unis* (Montreal, 1984), 106, 109; *Toronto Globe* 2 July 1892; P. N. Facktz, *Canada and the United States Compared* (Toronto, 1889), 13–14; "bone and sinew" in John Carr, *Pioneer Days in California* (Eureka, Calif., 1891), cited in Hansen and Brebner, *Mingling,* 133; "The New President of Cornell University a Canadian," *Toronto Globe,* 23 May 1892, 1.

18. *Annual Report of the Massachusetts Bureau of Statistics and Labor,* 1881, cited in Gerard J. Brault, *The French-Canadian Heritage in New England* (Hanover, N.H., 1986), 68; Yves Roby, *Les Franco-Américaines de la Nouvelle Angleterre, 1776–1930* (Sillery, Que., 1990).

19. *The Canadian-American, The Western British-American,* and *The Mining Journal* [Marquette, Mich.], 3 Jul. 1880, cited in Hansen and Brebner, *Mingling,* 205–6, 215 n. 129; naturalization rates in Alejandro Portes and Ruben G. Rumbaut, *Immigrant America: A Portrait* (Berkeley, 1990), 120–22; Bernice Webb, *The Basketball Man, James Naismith* (Lawrence, Kans., 1973). Interesting preliminary work by Gordon Darroch and Lee Saltow using manuscript census data suggests that both English- and French-Canadian farmers who migrated to Ohio in the 1860s were less prosperous than all other migrant groups in the state.

20. J. M. S. Careless, *Brown of the Globe,* vol. 2, *Statesman of Confederation* (Toronto, 1963), 312–22. Allan Nevins, *Hamilton Fish,* vol. 2 (1937; repr., New York, 1957), 412–13; also Fish to Ambassador Thornton, 11 Feb. 1875, *FRUS* (1875), 653; P. B. Waite, *Canada, 1874–1896: Arduous Destiny* (Toronto, 1971), 79–80.

21. Macdonald "coin" comment quoted in C. C. Tansill, *Canadian-American Relations, 1875–1911* (New Haven, 1943), 381 n. 37; speech in *CHCD,* 14 May 1879; *Canadian Monthly and National Review,* May 1876; Tilley story in Waite, *Arduous Destiny,* 101.

22. Michael Bliss, "Canadianizing American Business: The Roots of the Branch Plant," in Ian Lumsden, ed., *Close the 49th Parallel, etc.* (Toronto, 1970), 26–42; *Monetary Times* cited in Herbert Marshall, Frank Southard, Jr., and Kenneth W. Taylor, *Canadian-American Industry* (1935; repr.,

Ottawa, 1976), 11–16; on INCO, see Michael Bliss, *Northern Enterprise: Five Centuries of Canadian Business* (Toronto, 1987), 286–87, 302–5; relative DFI estimate from Scott Nearing and Joseph Freeman, *Dollar Diplomacy* (1925; repr., New York, 1966), 12; Hugh G. J. Aitken, *American Capital and Canadian Resources* (Cambridge, Mass., 1961); an excellent overview of American corporate expansion abroad is Mira Wilkins, *The Emergence of Multinational Enterprise: American Business Abroad from the Colonial Era to 1914* (Cambridge, Mass., 1970).

23. Graham D. Taylor, "Charles F. Sise, Bell Canada, and the Americans," *CHA Historical Papers* (1982), 18, 28–30; the classic revisionist accounts are Walter LaFeber, *The New Empire* (1963), and William A. Williams, *The Tragedy of American Diplomacy* (1962) and *The Roots of the Modern American Empire* (1969). William Becker disputes the export paradigm in *The Dynamics of Business-Government Relations: Industry and Exports, 1893–1921* (1982). On American finance and overseas investments, see Paul Abrahams, *The Foreign Expansion of American Finance, 1907–1921* (1976), and Wilkins, *Emergence of Multinational Enterprise.*

24. Tansill, *Canadian-American Relations, 1875–1911*, 385–411; NAC, Sir Wilfrid Laurier Papers, G. Amyot to Laurier, 5 August 1887, vol. 2; Ian Albert Hodson, "Commercial Union, Unrestricted Reciprocity and the Background to the Election of 1891" (M.A. thesis, University of Western Ontario, 1952), 129; Richard Cartwright, "The United States and Canada: Speech to the . . . Board of Trade . . . of New York," 21 February 1890.

25. Goldwin Smith, *The Political Destiny of Canada* (Toronto, 1878), "Canada and the United States," *North American Review* (July 1880): 14–25, *Handbook of Commercial Union* (Toronto, 1888), and *Canada and the Canadian Question* (1891; repr., Toronto, 1971); trade statistics from U.S. Department of Commerce, Bureau of the Census, *Historical Statistics of the United States: Colonial Times to 1970* (Washington, D.C., 1976), part 2; Robert Craig Brown, *Canada's National Policy, 1883–1900: A Study in Canadian-American Relations* (Princeton, 1964), 232–35; first Blaine quotation in *Manitoba Free Press*, 20 Feb. 1890, 4.

26. Macdonald's speech reported in *Toronto Empire*, 18 February 1891; "crisis" in *Halifax Morning Herald*, 9 February 1891, and *Regina Standard* 12 February 1891, both quoted in Patricia Katharine Wood, " 'Under Which Flag, Canadian?': Anti-Americanism and the Election of 1891" (M.A. thesis, Queen's University, 1991), 1, 50.

27. Carl Berger, *The Sense of Power: Studies in the Ideas of Canadian Imperialism,*

1869–1914 (Toronto, 1970), 4, 153–76, with the Smith quotation on page 98; P. N. Facktz, *Canada and the United States Compared: With Practical Notes on Commercial Union, Unrestricted Reciprocity, and Annexation* (Toronto, 1889), 39–42; Brown, *Canada's National Policy*, 252–56; Warner, *Idea of Continental Union*, 234–41; "Excited Canadians Tear Up Minister's Flag," *NYT*, 3 July 1892, 1.

28. Margaret Beattie Bogue, "To Save the Fish: Canada, the United States, the Great Lakes, and the Joint Commission of 1892," *Journal of American History* 79, no. 4 (1993): 1429–55.
29. Quotation from *Montreal Evening Star*, 3 July 1876; Alvin C. Gluek, "Canada's Splendid Bargain: The North Pacific Fur Seal Convention of 1911," *CHR* 63 (June 1982): 179–201.
30. Brown, *Canada's National Policy*, chapters 2, 4.
31. For the abrogation proclamation, see U.S. Department of State, *FRUS* (1885), 466–69; Stacey, *1867–1921*, vol. 1 of *Canada and the Age of Conflict*, 35–38.
32. H. G. Nicholas, *The United States and Britain* (Chicago, 1975), 46; Olney to Thomas F. Bayard, London, 20 July 1895, *FRUS*, vol. 1 (1895), 558; Preston, *Defence of the Undefended Border*, 124–41; *Canadian Military Gazette*, 1 January 1896, quoted in Preston, *Defence of the Undefended Border*, 126; Stacey, *Canada and the Age of Conflict*, 48–51.
33. Mahan quoted in Foster Rhea Dulles, *America's Rise to World Power, 1898–1954* (New York, 1954), 27; Graeme S. Mount, "Friendly Liberator or Predatory Aggressor?: Some Canadian Impressions of the United States During the Spanish-American War," *North/South: Canadian Journal of Latin American Studies* 22 (1986): 59–76; "impérialism" in *La Verité*, 21 May and 18 June 1898, quoted in Pierre Savard, *Jules-Paul Tardivel, la France et les Etats-Unis* (Quebec, 1967), 363–405; on U.S. expansionism, see LaFeber, *New Empire*, and Robert Beisner, *From the Old Diplomacy to the New, 1865–1900*, 2d ed. (Arlington Heights, Ill., 1986).
34. Canadian expansionism is discussed in Norman Penlington, *Canada and Imperialism, 1896–1899* (Toronto, 1965), Robert Page, "Canada and the Imperial Idea in the Boer War," *Journal of Canadian Studies* 5 (February 1970): 33–49, and Carl Berger, *Imperial Relations in the Age of Laurier* (Toronto, 1969). See also chapter 2 in Robert Craig Brown and Ramsey Cook, *Canada, 1896–1921: A Nation Transformed* (Toronto, 1974).
35. William R. Morrison, *Showing the Flag: The Mounted Police and Canadian Sovereignty in the North, 1894–1925* (Vancouver, 1985), 34–35.

36. On Canadian access, Sir Julian Pauncefote, British minister to the United States, to John Day, 18 April 1898, *FRUS* (1899), 320; Bradford Perkins, *The Great Rapprochement: England and the United States, 1895–1914* (New York, 1968), 168–69; Roosevelt to Arthur Lee, 24 April 1901, cited in Calvin D. Davis, *The United States and the Second Hague Peace Conference: American Diplomacy and International Organization, 1899–1914* (Durham, N.C., 1975), 65, 62–70; George B. Courtelyou to Secretary of War Elihu Root, 27 March 1902, Root Papers, Library of Congress; for the proclamation and terms of the agreement, see *FRUS* (1903), 488–92; Roosevelt to Root, Lodge and Turner, 17 March 1903; Roosevelt to Holmes, 25 July 1903, cited in George Mowry, *The Era of Theodore Roosevelt and the Birth of Modern America, 1900–1912* (New York, 1958), 163; for the appointment of the American commissioners, see John Hay to Sir Michael Herbert, 5 March 1903, *FRUS* (1903), 494.
37. Final settlement described in *FRUS* (1905), 478–79; Canadian opinion on the Alaska boundary decision reprinted in *Literary Digest* 26 (1903): 279.
38. *Toronto Globe*, 2 July 1892; Laurier in *Manitoba Free Press*, 4 July 1906.

3. Beginning a Bilateral Relationship, 1903–1919

1. Fisher quoted in Samuel F. Wells, Jr., "British Strategic Withdrawal from the Western Hemisphere," *CHR* 49, no. 4 (1968): 348; Carman Miller, *The Canadian Career of the Fourth Earl of Minto* (Waterloo, Ont. 1980), 131–55; C. P. Stacey, *1867–1921*, vol. 1 of *Canada and the Age of Conflict* (Toronto, 1984), 121; Bryce quoted in John Hilliker, *Canada's Department of External Affairs* (Montreal, 1990), 30–34.
2. The most important works that discuss this tendency in the United States are Robert Wiebe, *The Search for Order, 1877–1920* (New York, 1968); Alfred Chandler, Jr., *The Visible Hand: The Managerial Revolution in American Business* (Cambridge, Mass., 1977); and Ellis Hawley, "The Discovery and Study of a Corporate Liberalism," *Business History Review* 52 (Autumn 1978). These insights have been applied to U.S. foreign policy history by Michael Hogan in "Revival and Reform: America's Twentieth Century Search for a New Economic Order Abroad," *Diplomatic History* 8 (Fall 1984). For Canada, see Tom Traves, *The State and Enterprise: Canadian Manufacturers and the Federal Government* (Toronto, 1979), and Paul Craven, *"An Impartial Umpire": Industrial Relations and the Canadian State* (Toronto, 1980).

3. *Joint Report upon the Survey and Demarcation of the International Boundary Between the United States and Canada* (1918).
4. The text of the treaty establishing the IBC is in *FRUS* (1908), 384–97; Bryce quoted in A. C. Gluek, Jr., "The Passamaquoddy Bay Treaty, 1910: A Diplomatic Sideshow in Canadian-American Relations," *CHR* 47, no. 1 (1966): 18; *Joint Report upon the Survey and Demarcation of the Boundary Between the United States and Canada from the Source of the St. Croix River to the Atlantic Ocean* (1934). See also "Treaty Between the United States and Great Britain Relating to the Boundary Line in Passamaquoddy Bay," *FRUS* (1910), 540.
5. For the treaty, see *Treaties and Agreements Affecting Canada*, 312–19; *DCER*, vol. 1, 1909–18 (Ottawa, 1967); N. F. Dreisziger, "Dreams and Disappointments," in Robert Spencer, John Kirton, and Kim Richard Nossal, eds., *The International Joint Commission Seventy Years On* (Toronto, 1981), 9, 11; for negotiations, see Peter Neary, "Grey, Bryce, and the Settlement of Canadian-American Differences, 1905–1911," *CHR* 49, no. 4 (1968): 357–79, and Harriet Whitney, "Sir George C. Gibbons, Canadian Diplomat, and Canadian-American Boundary Water Resources, 1905–1910," *ARCS* 3, no. 1 (1973): 66–71.
6. See the *Annual Reports* of the IJC, and for specific examples, see T. J. Streiter to SS, 6 July 1915, and W. S. Hammond to SS, 10 July 1915, *FRUS* (1916), 296.
7. C. Joseph Chacko, *The International Joint Commission* (New York, 1932), 375; P. E. Corbett, *The Settlement of Canadian-American Disputes* (New Haven, 1937), 51–59; Holmes cited in Spencer et al., *The International Joint Commission*, 4; J. L. Granatstein and Norman Hillmer, *For Better or for Worse: Canada and the United States to the 1990s* (Toronto, 1991), 40–42; R. Douglas Francis and Donald B. Smith, *Destinies: Canadian History Since Confederation* (Toronto, 1988); Thomas G. Paterson, J. Garry Clifford, and Kenneth J. Hagan, *American Foreign Policy: A History to 1914*, 3d ed. (Lexington, Mass., 1988).
8. Preston, *Defense of the Undefended Border*, 142–43; Alvin C. Gluek, "The Invisible Revision of the Rush-Bagot Agreement, 1898–1914," *CHR* 60 (December 1979): 466–84.
9. The best account is Alvin C. Gluek, Jr., "Programmed Diplomacy: The Settlement of the North Atlantic Fisheries Question, 1907–1912," *Acadiensis* 6 (1976): 43–70; Taft's acceptance of arbitration in his message to Congress, 7 December 1909, in *Presidential Addresses and State Papers of William*

Howard Taft, vol. 1 (New York, 1910), 447–49; Calvin D. Davis, *The United States and the Second Hague Peace Conference* (Durham, N.C., 1975), 315–16; Minutes of Conferences in Washington, January 1911, *FRUS* (1911), 271–73.

10. Stacey, *Age of Conflict*, 1:105n; Neary, "Settlement of Canadian-American Differences," 379–80; A. C. Gluek, Jr., "Pilgrimages to Ottawa: Canadian-American Diplomacy, 1903–1913," *CHA Historical Papers* (1968): 64–83; Gibbons to Laurier, 21 December 1907, cited in Whitney, "Gibbons," 69.
11. Marvin McInnis, "Migration," *Addressing the Twentieth Century, 1891–1961*, vol. 3 of *Historical Atlas of Canada* (Toronto, 1990), plate 27; Lavoie, *Emigration*, 64.
12. Harold Troper, *Only Farmers Need Apply: Official Canadian Government Encouragement of Immigration from the United States, 1896–1911* (Toronto, 1972); Paul F. Sharp, "When Our West Moved North," *American Historical Review* 55, no. 2 (1950): 286–300; Grant MacEwan, *Charles Noble: Guardian of the Soil* (Saskatoon, Sask., 1983); Karel Denis Bicha, *The American Farmer and the Canadian West* (Lawrence, Kans., 1968); David C. Jones, *Empire of Dust: Settling and Abandoning the Prairie Dry Belt* (Edmonton, 1987).
13. Janet E. Schulte, "'Proving Up and Moving Up': Jewish Homesteading Activity in North Dakota, 1900–1920," *Great Plains Quarterly* 10, no. 4 (1990): 240–41; Victor Peters, *All Things Common: The Hutterian Way of Life* (Minneapolis, 1965), 41–49; letter to DuBois in Harold Martin Troper, "The Creek-Negroes of Oklahoma and Canadian Immigration, 1909–11," *CHR* 52, no. 3 (1972): 286; R. Bruce Shepard, "Diplomatic Racism: Canadian Government and Black Migration from Oklahoma, 1905–1912," *Great Plains Quarterly* 3, no. 1 (1983): 12–13.
14. H. V. Nelles, *The Politics of Development: Forests, Mines and Hydro-electric Power in Ontario, 1849–1941* (Toronto, 1974), 48–107, 307–47; investment statistics from Herbert Marshall et al., *Canadian-American Industry* (1936; repr., Ottawa, 1976), 299; Wilkins, *Emergence of Multinational Enterprise*, 135–48.
15. Leon Fink, *Workingman's Democracy: The Knights of Labor and American Politics* (New York, 1983); Gregory S. Kealey and Bryan D. Palmer, *Dreaming of What Might Be: The Knights of Labor in Ontario, 1880–1900* (Cambridge, 1982); Fernand Harvey, "Les Chevaliers du Travail, les États-Unis et la société québécoise, 1882–1902," in *Le mouvement ouvrier au Québec* (Montreal, 1980).
16. Miner quoted in Bryan D. Palmer, *Working-Class Experience: The Rise and*

Reconstitution of Canadian Labour, 1800–1980 (Toronto, 1983), 149; Gompers and *Herald* quoted in Robert H. Babcock, *Gompers in Canada: A Study in American Continentalism Before the First World War* (Toronto, 1974), 36, 110.

17. Jacques Rouillard, *Les Syndicats nationaux au Québec de 1900 à 1930* (Quebec, 1979), 74–83; Babcock, *Gompers in Canada*, 210–16.

18. Craig Heron, "Labourism and the Canadian Working Class," *Labour/le travail* 13 (1984): 45–76; Carlos Schwantes, *Radical Heritage: Labor, Socialism and Reform in Washington and British Columbia, 1885–1917* (Seattle, 1979); Canada, Senate *Debates*, 22 July 1903, 683–91; the bill failed in the House of Commons.

19. Allan Smith, "The Continental Dimension in the English-Canadian Mind," *International Journal* 31, no. 3 (1976): 442–69; *CHCD* (1907–8), 6989; Lemieux quoted in A. D. Gilbert, " 'On the Road to New York': The Protective Impulse and the English-Canadian Cultural Identity, 1896–1914," *Dalhousie Review* 58, no. 3 (1978): 410; reformers cited in John H. Thompson, "American Muckrakers and Western Canadian Reform," *Journal of Popular Culture* (1972): 1063–66; Sir Andrew MacPhail, *Essays in Politics* (New York, 1909), 85; Samuel E. Moffett, *The Americanization of Canada*, introduction by Allan Smith (repr., Toronto, 1972), 9, 114.

20. André Seigfried, *The Race Question in Canada* (1907; repr., Toronto, 1968), 95–103; Wilhelm Cohnstaedt, *Western Canada 1909* (Regina, Sask., 1976), 32; John Foster Fraser, *Canada as It Is* (London, 1905).

21. Laurier quoted in Paul Stevens, "Reciprocity 1911: The Canadian Perspective," in A. R. Riggs and Tom Velk, eds., *Canadian-American Free Trade: Historical, Political and Economic Dimensions* (Halifax, N.S., 1987), 2; *Free Press* quoted in D. C. Masters, *Reciprocity, 1846–1911* (Ottawa, 1965), 17.

22. A. K. Weinberg, *Manifest Destiny: A Study of Nationalist Expansionism in American History* (Baltimore, 1935), 367–81; Kendrick A. Clements, "Manifest Destiny and Canadian Reciprocity in 1911," *Pacific Historical Review* 42, no. 1 (1973): 32–52; L. E. Ellis, *Reciprocity 1911: A Study in Canadian-American Relations* (New Haven, 1939), 15, 85–86, 137–38, 191; Richard Gwynn, *The 49th Paradox: Canada in North America* (Toronto, 1985), 37; Robert E. Hannigan, "Reciprocity 1911: Continentalism and American *Weltpolitik*," *Diplomatic History* 4, no. 1 (1980): 3; Paul Wolman, *Most Favored Nation: The Republican Revisionists and U.S. Tariff Policy, 1897–1912* (Chapel Hill, 1992), xiii–xv; *NYT*, 26 February and 7 March 1911.

23. Robert Craig Brown, *Robert Laird Borden, A Biography*, vol. 1, *1854–1914*

(Toronto, 1975), 173–95; Toronto Eighteen Manifesto in *Canadian Annual Review* (1911), 48–49; Foster in *CHCD*, 14 February 1911, 3560–61.

24. Clark in *Congressional Record*, 61st Congress, 3d session, 14 February 1911, 2520; "bosh" in *NYT*, 28 April 1911; Taft to Roosevelt, 11 January 1911, in Henry F. Pringle, *The Life and Times of William Howard Taft*, vol. 2 (New York, 1939), 588; Canadian reaction to release of the letter in 1912, quoted in *Literary Digest*, 18 May 1912, 1029–30.
25. John English, *The Decline of Politics: The Conservatives and the Party System, 1901–1920* (Toronto, 1977), 59–60; Borden, Women's League and election speech quoted in W. M. Baker, "A Case Study of Anti-Americanism in English-Speaking Canada: The Election Campaign of 1911," *CHR* 51, no. 4 (1970): 432, 435; *Le Devoir*, 1 February 1911, 2.
26. Roosevelt in Lawrence Martin, *The Presidents and the Prime Ministers: The Myth of Bilateral Bliss, 1867–1982* (New York, 1982), 75–76; Professor O. D. Skelton cited in John W. Dafoe, *Clifford Sifton in Relation to His Times* (Toronto, 1931), 374; *Varsity* cited in J. Murray Beck, *Pendulum of Power: Canada's Federal Elections* (Scarborough, Ont., 1968), 126; Borden statement in *Canadian Annual Review* (1911): 266.
27. White in *Canadian Annual Review* (1913): 247; Gluek, "Programmed Diplomacy," 69–70.
28. Brown, *Borden*, 1:230–32; Robert Bothwell, "Loring Christie: The Failure of Bureaucratic Imperialism" (Ph.D. dissertation, Harvard University, 1972), 59–60; White and Walker in *Canadian Annual Review* (1913): 247, 666, 743–45; Donald Page, "Canada as the Exponent of North American Idealism," *ARCS* 3, no. 2 (1973): 34–36.
29. Laurier in *CHCD*, Special War Session (1914), 10.
30. Arthur S. Link, *Woodrow Wilson and the Progressive Era, 1910–1917* (New York, 1963), 148 n. 9; Keenleyside, *Canada and the United States*, 372; NAC, Maj. H. J. Woodside Papers, MG 30, I 11, vol. 15, W. H. Gamble to Woodside, 3 February 1916.
31. "German Organizations in the United States," *Canadian Annual Review* (1916): 221–27; Martin Kitchen, "The German Invasion of Canada in the First World War," *International History Review* 7, no. 2 (1985): 245–60; Gaddis Smith, *Britain's Clandestine Submarines, 1914–1915* (New Haven, 1964); on the U-Deutschland and U-53 incidents, Michael L. Hadley and Roger Sarty, *Tin-Pots and Pirate Ships: Canadian Naval Forces and German Sea Raiders, 1880–1918* (Montreal, 1991), 133–78; *Globe*, 11 October 1916, 6.

32. On American neutrality and entry into the war, see Robert H. Ferrell, *Woodrow Wilson and World War I* (New York, 1985); Ross Gregory, *The Origins of American Intervention in the First World War* (New York, 1971); "Wilson—Democracy's Hope," *Nutcracker* [Calgary], 16 February 1917; Gompers visit in *Canadian Annual Review* (1918): 291–93; Hadley and Sarty, *Tin-Pots and Pirate Ships*, 235–38, 258–64; R. D. Cuff and J. L. Granatstein *Canadian-American Relations in Wartime: From the Great War to the Cold War* (Toronto, 1975), 3–67; Granatstein and Hillmer, *For Better or for Worse*, 56–59.
33. Borden's letter is in *DCER*, vol. 1, 1909–18, 24–25; Spring Rice to Governor General, 31 January 1918, *DCER*, vol. 4, 1909–18, 30–32; Stacey, *Canada and the Age of Conflict*, 1:230–31.
34. Michael Bliss, "A Canadian Businessman and War: The Case of Joseph Flavelle," in J. L. Granatstein and Robert Cuff, eds., *War and Society in North America* (Toronto, 1971), 34–36; Hearst incident in *Canadian Annual Review* (1918), 260–61; Bryan incident in *NYT* and *Globe*, 1 March 1918; Borden in *Globe*, 2 March 1918; Keenleyside, *Canada and the United States*, 362, 372.

4. The New Era, 1919–1930

1. Joan Hoff Wilson, *American Business and Foreign Policy, 1920–1933* (New York, 1971).
2. Preston, *Defense of the Undefended Border*, 213–33; L. H. Larsen, "The U.S. Army's 1919 Contingency Plan to Defend North Dakota Against an Unspecified Invader from Canada," *North Dakota History* 43, no. 4 (1976): 22–27.
3. Arthur S. Link, ed., *The Papers of Woodrow Wilson* (Princeton, 1990), vol. 65, 505; Wilson to Gompers, 20 June 1919, *Papers of Woodrow Wilson*, 61:39; Ralph A. Stone, *The Irreconcilables: The Fight Against the League of Nations* (Lexington, Ky., 1970), 134–35.
4. Borah and Rowell quoted in John Herd Thompson with Allen Seager, *Canada, 1922–1939: Decades of Discord* (Toronto, 1985), 54–56.
5. Dafoe to Sifton, 18 May 1921, in Ramsay Cook, ed., *The Dafoe-Sifton Correspondence*, vol. 2, *1919–1927* (Altona, Man., 1966), 70.
6. John S. Galbraith, "The Imperial Conference of 1921 and the Washington Conference," *CHR* 29, no. 2 (1948): 145–47; Stephen Roskill, *Naval*

Policy Between the Wars (London, 1968); Michael Hall, "Anglo-American Naval Relations, 1919–1930" (Ph.D. dissertation, McGill University, 1990); Granatstein and Hillmer, *For Better or for Worse*, 77–78; Stacey, *Canada and the Age of Conflict*, 1:348–55.

7. Sifton to Dafoe, 29 October 1921, in Cook, *Dafoe-Sifton Correspondence*, 2:84; John S. Galbraith, *The Establishment of Canadian Diplomatic Status at Washington* (Berkeley, 1951), 69–77; Colby to President Wilson, 30 and 13 April 1920, in Link, *Papers of Woodrow Wilson*, 65:182, 237; Robert Bothwell, "Canadian Representation at Washington: A Study in Colonial Responsibility," *CHR* 53, no. 2 (1972): 141–48.
8. King in *CHCD* 2 (1920), 2456–60; John Hilliker, *Canada's Department of External Affairs*, vol. 1, *The Early Years, 1909–1946* (Montreal, 1990), 93–95.
9. *NYT*, 13 July 1922; King in Roger Frank Swanson, *Canadian-American Summit Diplomacy, 1923–1973: Selected Speeches and Documents* (Toronto, 1975), 7–10.
10. Philip G. Wigley, *Canada and the Transition to Commonwealth: British-Canadian Relations, 1917–1926* (Cambridge, 1977), 175; Hughes quoted in R. MacGregor Dawson, *William Lyon Mackenzie King: A Political Biography*, vol. 1, *1874–1923* (Toronto, 1958), 434; John A. Schultz, "Canadian Attitudes Toward the Empire, 1919–1939" (Ph.D. thesis, Dalhousie University, 1975), 82–84.
11. Massey appointment in Privy Council Order, 10 November 1926, *DCER*, vol. 4, 1926–30, 13–14; Vincent Massey, *What's Past Is Prologue: The Memoirs of Vincent Massey* (Toronto, 1963), 121–32, 144–47; Peter C. Kasurak, "American 'Dollar Diplomats' in Canada, 1927–41," *ARCS* 9, no. 2 (1979): 57; William Phillips, *Ventures in Diplomacy* (London, 1955), 64–70.
12. Andrew Sinclair, *Era of Excess: A Social History of the Prohibition Movement* (New York, 1962); quotations from Thompson with Seager, *Canada, 1922–1939*, 63–69.
13. *DCER*, vol. 3, 1919–25, and *DCER*, vol. 4, 1926–30, are replete with documents on prohibition disputes; *Journal* quoted in Michael R. Marrus, *Mr. Sam: The Life and Times of Samuel Bronfman* (Toronto, 1991), 133; Richard Kottman, "Volstead Violated: Prohibition as a Factor in Canadian-American Relations," *CHR* 43, no. 2 (1962): 114–23.
14. Quotations from M. Paul Holsinger, "The *I'm Alone* Controversy: A Study in Inter-American Diplomacy, 1919–1935," *Mid-America* 50, no. 4 (1968): 305–13.

15. Hoover quoted in Arthur M. Schlesinger, Jr., *The Crisis of the Old Order, 1919–1933* (New York, 1957), 89.
16. J. A. Guthrie, *The Newsprint Paper Industry* (Cambridge, 1941), 30–59; Carl Weigman, *Trees to News* (Toronto, 1953), 101–12; Trevor J. O. Dick, "Canadian Newsprint, 1913–1930: National Policies and the North American Economy," *Journal of Economic History* 42, no. 3 (1982): 659–87.
17. E. S. Moore, *American Influences in Canadian Mining* (Toronto, 1941), 104; Marshall et al., *Canadian-American Industry*, 87–102.
18. Studebaker quotation in Traves, *State and Enterprise*, 103.
19. Robert E. Ankli and Fred Frederikson, "The Influence of American Manufacturers on the Canadian Automobile Industry," *Business and Economic History* 10 (1981): 101–13; Provincial Archives of Ontario, William Gray Papers, undated clipping (1923?).
20. Mira Wilkins, *The Maturing of Multinational Enterprise: American Business Abroad from 1914 to 1970* (Cambridge, Mass., 1974), 60–63; Coke in Richard S. Tedlow, *New and Improved: The Story of Mass Marketing in America* (New York, 1990), 63–65.
21. Definitions from Kari Levitt, *Silent Surrender: The Multinational Corporation in Canada* (Toronto, 1970), 58–59; *Journal of the Canadian Bankers' Association* 28, no. 3 (1921): 367; Irving Brecher and S. S. Reisman, *Canada-United States Economic Relations* (Ottawa, 1957), 100–101.
22. Cf. Gordon Laxer, *Open for Business: The Roots of Foreign Ownership in Canada* (Toronto, 1989); Jose Igartua, " 'Corporate' Strategy and Locational Decision-Making: The Duke-Price Alcoa Merger, 1925," *Journal of Canadian Studies* 20, no. 3 (1985): 97; Peter Kresl, "Before the Deluge: Canadians on Foreign Ownership, 1920–1955," *ARCS* 6, no. 1 (1976): 93–96; Michael Bliss, *A Canadian Businessman: Sir Joseph Flavelle, 1858–1939* (Toronto, 1978), 431–32; *CHCD*, 1928, I, 637; Yves Roby, *Les Québécois et les investissements américains, 1918–1929* (Quebec, 1976), 81–118; Neil F. Morrison et al., *The Dominion of Canada* (Toronto, 1937), 275–76; *Leader* in Gwenn Ronyk, "The United States in the Twenties as Seen by the Western Canadian Press" (M.A. thesis, University of Regina, 1979), 189–90; Harding in *Canadian Annual Review* (1923), 83–84.
23. Taschereau in Roby, *Investissements américains*, 141; G. E. Jackson, "Emigration of Canadians to the United States," *Annals of the American Academy* 107 (1923): 28; *HSUS*, series C88-114; Lavoie, *Emigration*, 21.
24. *Canadian Forum*, July 1929; A. R. M. Lower, "The Case Against Immigration," *Queen's Quarterly* 37 (1930): 573; W. A. Irwin, "Can We Stem the

Exodus?," *Maclean's,* 15 May 1927; Hansen and Brebner, *Mingling,* 253–62; Carl Berger, *The Writing of Canadian History* (Toronto, 1976), 142–43.

25. IODE cited in Henry F. Angus, ed., *Canada and Her Great Neighbor* (New Haven, 1938), 236; Thompson and Seager, *Canada, 1922–1939,* 175.
26. Mary Vipond, "Canadian Nationalism and the Plight of Canadian Magazines in the 1920s," *CHR* 58, no. 1 (March 1977): 43–63.
27. John A. Schultz, "Whose News: The Struggle for Wire Service Distribution, 1900–1920," *ARCS* 10 (1980): 27–35; Paul Rutherford, *The Making of the Canadian Media* (Toronto, 1978), 38–76.
28. S. F. Wise and Douglas Fisher, *Canada's Sporting Heroes* (Don Mills, Ont., 1974), 28–32.
29. Gallico cited in Neil D. Isaacs, *Checking Back: A History of the NHL* (New York, 1977), 63–64; Charles H. Good, "Will U.S. Cash Cripple Hockey?," *Maclean's,* 1 March 1925, 13, 55–56.
30. Allan Smith, "Canadian Culture, the Canadian State, and the New Continentalism," *Canadian-American Public Policy,* 3 October 1990, 10–20; Frank W. Peers, *The Politics of Canadian Broadcasting, 1920–1951* (Toronto, 1969), 3–29.
31. Citations from Thompson and Seager, *Canada, 1922–1939,* 180–83.
32. John Egli O'Brien, "A History of the Canadian Radio League, 1930–1936" (Ph.D. thesis, University of Southern California, 1964), 58–69; quotations from Margaret Prang, "The Origins of Public Broadcasting in Canada," *CHR* 46, no. 1 (1965): 9–31; Kenneth C. Dewar, "The Origins of Public Broadcasting in Comparative Perspective," *Canadian Journal of Communication* 7, no. 2 (1982): 40–43; Merrill Denison, "Radio in Canada," *Annals of the American Academy of Political and Social Science* (1935): 53–54.
33. Lary May, *Screening Out the Past: The Birth of Mass Culture and the Motion Picture Industry* (New York, 1980), 163–66; Peter Morris, *Embattled Shadows: A History of Canadian Cinema, 1895–1939* (Montreal, 1978), 57–93; Ian Jarvie, *Hollywood's Overseas Campaign: The North Atlantic Movie Trade, 1920–1950* (Cambridge, Mass., 1992), 25–42.
34. R. Laird Briscoe, "What the Censor Saves Us From," *Maclean's,* 1 November 1925; George Drew, "Have British Films a Chance?," *Maclean's,* 15 October 1931, 12.
35. Emily Rosenberg, *Spreading the American Dream: American Economic and Cultural Expansion, 1890–1945* (New York, 1982), 7–8; "Canadian Culture," *NYT,* 7 March 1923, 14; Michael Hogan, *The Marshall Plan* (Cambridge, Mass., 1987), 4–5; Jarvie, *Hollywood's Overseas Campaign,* 50–57, 279.

36. Richard Lowitt, "Ontario Hydro: A 1925 Tempest in an American Teapot," *CHR* 49, no. 2 (1968): 267–74.
37. Robert Ayre, "The American Empire," *Canadian Forum*, January 1927, 105–6; *Unionist* cited in Angus, *Canada and Her Great Neighbor*, 225–48; Guildo Rousseau, *L'Image des Etats-Unis dans la littérature québécoise, 1775–1930* (Sherbrooke, Que., 1981).
38. Phillips, *Ventures in Diplomacy*, 70; Randolph Greenfield Adams, *The Foreign Policy of the United States* (New York, 1926), 428; Angus, *Canada and Her Great Neighbor*, 53.

5. Acquaintance to Alliance, 1930–1941

1. Norman Hillmer, "Ties with the United States," *Historical Atlas of Canada*, vol. 3, *Addressing the Twentieth Century, 1891–1961* (Toronto, 1990), plate 57. This plate beautifully depicts IJC decisions.
2. Leslie Roberts, "Step-Uncle Sam: A Canadian Looks Across the Border," *Harper's Monthly Magazine*, June 1930, 20–27; Bourassa in *CHCD*, 24 March 1930, 888; on the *Josephine K*, see *DCER*, vol. 5, 1931–35, 117–27, 152–54; on Laframboise, *Globe*, 4–5 February 1930.
3. "600 Entry Ports Sought," *NYT*, 7 January 1930, 1, 11; Upjohn case in Roberts, "Step-Uncle Sam," 26–27; Lavoie, *Emigration*, 76–79; Paul Martin in *Proceeding of the Conference on Canadian-American Affairs* (Boston, 1937), 130–31.
4. "Tariff Panic Along the Canadian Border," *Literary Digest*, 27 April 1929, 15–16; Drew Pearson, "High Tariff Diplomacy," *Nation*, 27 February 1929, 250–51; Richard N. Kottman, "Herbert Hoover and the Smoot-Hawley Tariff: Canada, A Case Study," *Journal of American History* 62, no. 3 (December 1975): 609–35.
5. Newspapers quoted in *Literary Digest*, 27 April 1929, 15–16, and in Kottman, "Hoover and the Smoot-Hawley Tariff," 618; H. Blair Neatby, *William Lyon Mackenzie King*, vol. 2, *1924–1932* (Toronto, 1963), 282–89.
6. Quotations in Thompson with Seager, *Canada, 1922–1939*, 202.
7. Ian M. Drummond, *Imperial Economic Policy, 1917–1939* (Toronto, 1974), 191–94, 219–89; Charles Bishop, "Canadian Elections and U.S. Business," *Forbes*, 1 July 1930, 45; branch plant statistics in Wilkins, *American Business Abroad*, 189–90; O. J. McDairmid, "The Canadian Automobile Industry,"

Canadian Journal of Economics and Political Science 6, no. 2 (1940): 267; Marshall et al., *Canadian-American Industry*, 173–75.

8. Swanson, *Summit Diplomacy*, 27–29; Richard N. Kottman, "The Hoover-Bennett Meeting of 1931: Mismanaged Summitry," *Annals of Iowa* 42 (1974): 205–21; *Citizen* quoted in Kottman, "Hoover and Canada: Diplomatic Appointments," *CHR* 51, no. 3 (1970): 295.
9. Harvey Levenstein, "Canada and the Suppression of the Salvadorean Revolution of 1932," *CHR* 62, no. 4 (1981): 451–69; Richard N. Kottman, "Herbert Hoover and the St. Lawrence Seaway Treaty of 1932," *New York History* 56, no. 3 (1975): 314–46; William R. Willoughby, *The St. Lawrence Waterway: A Study in Politics and Diplomacy* (Madison, Wisc., 1961), 133–59.
10. "Canada and the U.S. Election," *Canadian Forum*, December 1932.
11. W. J. McAndrew, "Canada, Roosevelt and the New Deal" (Ph.D. thesis, University of British Columbia, 1973), 84–90; Harriman in *The Liberal Way* (Toronto, 1933), 169, 249–50; NAC, Bennett Papers, Herridge to Bennett, 12 April 1934; Roosevelt in E. S. Greenberg, *Capitalism and the American Political Ideal* (Armonk, N.Y., 1985), 95, and Bennett in Alvin Finkel, "Origins of the Welfare State in Canada," in Leo Panitch, ed., *The Canadian State* (Toronto, 1977), 351.
12. King quoted in Thompson with Seager, *Decades of Discord*, 273; James H. Gray, "Canada Flirts with Fascism," *Nation*, 9 October 1935, 407; J. A. Stormon, "A History of the International Peace Garden," *North Dakota History* 31, no. 4 (October 1964): 205–15; William E. Leuchtenburg, "The Great Depression," in C. Vann Woodward, *The Comparative Approach to American History* (New York, 1968), 308.
13. David Montgomery, *The Fall of the House of Labor* (Cambridge, Mass., 1987), 427–30; *Globe*, 7, 9, 10, 12 October 1929; AF of L, *Report of the Forty-Ninth Annual Convention* (Washington, D.C., 1929), 2, 8, 357–59. For general accounts of labor history in this period, with good bibliographies, see Robert H. Zieger, *American Workers, American Unions, 1920–1985* (Baltimore, 1986), and Palmer, *Working-Class Experience*.
14. Sidney Fine, *Sit-Down: The GM Strike of 1936–37* (Ann Arbor, Mich., 1969), 341.
15. Irving Abella, "Canadian Labor: Some Myths and Realities," in R. A. Preston, ed., *The Influence of the U.S. on Canadian Development* (Durham, N.C., 1972), 209, Hillman quoted 214.
16. "Labour Organization," in *Proceeding of the Conference on Canadian-American*

Affairs (Boston, 1937), 168–95; "Terror in the Wake of the CIO," *Globe,* 1 June 1937, 1; King in *DCER,* vol. 6, 1936–39, 158; Irving Abella *Nationalism, Communism and Canadian Labour,* 1–22, Hepburn quoted 17; Norman Ware, *Labor in Canadian-American Relations* (New Haven, 1937), 70; Craig Heron, *The Canadian Labour Movement* (Toronto, 1989), 74; David Brody, "The Breakdown of Labor's Social Contract: Historical Reflections, Future Prospects," *Dissent,* Winter 1992, 34–36.

17. For a mid-1930s comparison of the two countries, see League for Social Reconstruction, *Social Planning for Canada* (Toronto, 1935), 56, 125, 204–8.
18. *Plain Dealer* and statistics quoted from Canadian Bank of Commerce *Monthly Letter,* no. 47 (May 1933), and no. 59 (May 1934); Bennett in Swanson, *Summit Diplomacy,* 33.
19. Pierre Berton, *The Dionne Years: A Thirties Melodrama* (Toronto, 1977), 115, 191–97; Wilson in Gwynn, *The 49th Paradox,* 43; complaint cited in Morris, *Embattled Shadows,* 232.
20. Carl Berger, "Comments on the Carnegie Series on the Relations of Canada and the United States," in Preston, *Influence of the U.S.,* 32–50; Arthur Lower, *My First 75 Years* (Toronto, 1967), 196–97; survey data in Angus, *Canada and Her Great Neighbor,* 105–8, 272–89.
21. C. P. Stacey, *The Military Problems of Canada* (Ottawa, 1936), 29.
22. Campobello visit in Lawrence Martin, *The Presidents and the Prime Ministers* (Toronto, 1982), 116–17; Bennett in Swanson, *Summit Diplomacy,* 36; Richard N. Kottman, "The Canadian-American Trade Agreement of 1935," *Journal of American History* 52, no. 2 (1965): 288–96; Marc T. Boucher, "The Politics of Economic Depression: Canadian-American Relations in the Mid-1930s," *International Journal* 41 (1985–86): 3–36, Hickerson quoted 35.
23. *NYT,* 1 August 1936, 1, 5; *Saturday Night,* 8 August 1936, 1.
24. King in Swanson, *Summit Diplomacy,* 48–50, and in *Canadian Annual Review* (1937–38), 49–52; Richard Kottman, *Reciprocity and the North Atlantic Triangle, 1932–1938* (Ithaca, N.Y., 1968), 266–73.
25. Tweedsmuir in *NYT,* 2 April 1937; *Evening Standard* [London] 1 April 1937; Victoria M. Wilcox, "Prime Minister and Governor General: Mackenzie King and Lord Tweedsmuir, 1935–1940" (M.A. thesis, Queen's University, 1977), 65–79, 94–98; David Reynolds, *The Creation of the Anglo-American Alliance, 1937–41* (Chapel Hill, N.C., 1982).
26. Speeches in Swanson, *Summit Diplomacy,* 52–62; Chandler Bragdon, "Canadian Attitudes to the Foreign Policy of the United States, 1935–1939"

(Ph.D. thesis, University of Rochester, 1961), 163–69; letter to Tweedsmuir in Robert Dallek, *Franklin D. Roosevelt and American Foreign Policy* (New York, 1979), 162–63.

27. Frank Friedel, *Franklin D. Roosevelt: Rendezvous with Destiny* (Boston, 1990), 300; *The Mackenzie King Diaries* (Toronto, 1973), 20 August 1938; *DCER*, vol. 6, 1936–39, 606–7; Chamberlain quoted in Ritchie Ovendale, *"Appeasement" and the English Speaking World* (Cardiff, U.K., 1975), 317.
28. Roosevelt to King, 11 October 1938, in Elliott Roosevelt, ed., *FDR: His Personal Letters, 1928–1945*, vol. 2 (New York, 1950), 816–17; Corelli Barnett, *The Collapse of British Power* (London, 1970), 218–27, and Ovendale, *"Appeasement,"* 319–20; RCAF visit in Eayrs, *Appeasement and Rearmament*, vol. 2 of *In Defence of Canada* (Toronto, 1965), 148–52; Macphail in *CHCD* (1937), vol. 1, 254; Richard W. Scott, "Anschluss with Canada?," *American Mercury*, October 1938, 158–65.
29. David Lenarcic, "The Nye Committee Visits the Fire-Proof House: A Comparison of Canadian Non-Interventionism and American 'Isolationism' Between the Wars" (Ph.D. thesis, York University, 1990); *The Mackenzie King Diaries* (Toronto, 1973), 28 October and 13 September 1938, in J. L. Granatstein and Robert Bothwell, "'A Self-Evident National Duty': Canadian Foreign Policy, 1935–1939," *Journal of Imperial and Commonwealth History* 3, no. 2 (1975): 222.
30. Gordon Beadle, "Canada and the Abdication of Edward VIII," *Journal of Canadian Studies* 4, no. 3 (1969): 33–36; *Winnipeg Free Press*, 10, 13 June 1939; Gordon Young, *Voyage of State* (London, 1939), 217–60, mounties on 260.
31. Stacey, *Canada and the Age of Conflict*, vol. 2, *1921–1947* (Toronto, 1981), 269; Dallek, *FDR and American Foreign Policy*, 199.
32. Cf. Edelgard E. Mahant and Graeme S. Mount, *An Introduction to Canadian-American Relations*, 2d ed. (Scarborough, Ont., 1989), 157.
33. Poll in Robert D. Schulzinger, *American Diplomacy in the Twentieth Century* (New York, 1990), 168.
34. Friedel, *Rendezvous with Destiny*, 350; "The Canada-United States Permanent Joint Board on Defense, 1940–1945," Dean Acheson Papers, Box 47, HSTL; Robert Dallek, *Franklin D. Roosevelt and American Foreign Policy, 1932–1945* (New York, 1979), 245.
35. Hugh L. Keenleyside, *On the Bridge of Time*, vol. 2 of *Memoirs* (Toronto, 1982), 49–51; Moffatt to Acting Secretary of State, Sumner Welles, 14 August 1940, *FRUS*, vol. 3 (1940), 144–45; poll in Stanley Dziuban, *Military*

Relations Between the United States and Canada (Washington, D.C., 1959), 25; "Defense Plans with Canada," *Chicago Daily Tribune*, 20 August 1940, 10; Welles to Jefferson Caffrey (Brazil), 22 August 1940, *FRUS*, vol. 3 (1940), 146.

36. *CHCD*, 12 November 1940, 55–58; Churchill cited in Eayrs, *In Defence of Canada*, vol. 2, *Appeasement and Rearmament* 209–10, and in John W. Dafoe, *Canada Fights: An American Democracy at War* (New York, 1941), 1; on the Royal Navy, C. P. Stacey, *Arms, Men and Governments: The War Policies of Canada* (Ottawa, 1970), 328–32, and *DCER*, vol. 8, 1939–41, 65–97; Reynolds, *Anglo-American Alliance*, 2–3.
37. R. D. Cuff and J. L. Granatstein, "The Hyde Park Declaration: Origins and Significance," *Canadian-American Relations in Wartime* (Toronto, 1975), 69–92; *CHCD*, 28 April 1941, 2286–89.
38. Donald Creighton, *Canada, 1939–1957: The Forked Road* (Toronto, 1976), 42–44; J. L. Granatstein, *How Britain's Weakness Forced Canada into the Arms of the United States* (Toronto, 1989).

6. World War to Cold War, 1941–1947

1. King in *CHCD*, 12 November 1940, 55–58; "U.S. Holiday Celebrated Here by Legionnaires; Fellowship Is Stressed," *Globe*, 5 July 1941, 1; Richard W. Van Alstyne, "New Viewpoints in the Relations of Canada and the U.S.," *CHR* 25, no. 2 (1944): 130.
2. Roosevelt in Thomas G. Paterson, ed., *Since 1914*, vol. 2 of *Major Problems in American Foreign Policy*, 2d ed. (Lexington, Mass., 1984), 209; Robert Divine, *Second Chance: The Triumph of Internationalism in America During World War II* (New York, 1967).
3. Stacey, *Arms, Men and Governments*, 137–80; King to Lord Moran, 9 June 1950, in *Churchill: Taken from the Diaries of Lord Moran* (Boston, 1966), 117 n. 3.
4. Keenleyside, *On the Bridge of Time*, 61–62; "The Canada–United States Permanent Joint Board on Defense, 1940–1945," Dean Acheson Papers, Box 47, HSTL; C. P. Stacey, "The Canadian-American Permanent Joint Board on Defence, 1940–1945," *International Journal* 9 (1954): 105–24.
5. Knox to Hull, 21 July 1941; John D. Hickerson, Assistant Chief, Division of European Affairs, DS, Memorandum of conversation with Hume Wrong, Minister Counsellor, Canadian Legation, 25 July 1941; Moffat to

Hull, 18 August 1941; Hull to Moffat, 16 October 1941, *FRUS*, vol. 3 (1941), 130–36; Stanley R. Dziuban, *Military Relations Between the United States and Canada, 1939–1945* (Washington, D.C., 1959), 72–76.

6. *FRUS*, vol. 3 (1941), 79–83; David Mackenzie, *Inside the Atlantic Triangle: Canada and the Entry of Newfoundland into Confederation, 1939–1949* (Toronto, 1986).
7. Waldo Heinrichs, *Threshold of War* (New York, 1988), 88; Stetson Conn and Byron Fairchild, *The Framework of Hemispheric Defense* (Washington, D.C., 1960), 46, 378; David G. Haglund, "'Plain Grand Imperialism on a Miniature Scale': Canadian-American Rivalry over Greenland in 1940," *ARCS* 11, no. 1 (1981): 15–36; Michael F. Scheuer, "On the Possibility That There May Be More to It Than That: Professor Haglund, The Documents on American [sic] External Relations Series and the Canadian-American Controversy over Greenland in 1940," *ARCS* 12, no. 3 (1982): 72–83.
8. Hull, *Memoirs*, 2:1128–31; Douglas Anglin, *The St. Pierre and Miquelon Affair of 1941: A Study in Diplomacy in the North Atlantic Quadrangle* (Toronto, 1966).
9. Hull, *Memoirs*, 2:1131; Granatstein and Hillmer, *For Better or for Worse*, 150.
10. Hull memorandum of conversation with British ambassador, 25 April 1942; Ambassador William Leahy (Vichy) to secretary of state, 27 April 1942, *FRUS*, vol. 2 (1942), 179–81. Hull, *Memoirs*, 2:1157–58; Paul M. Couture, "The Politics of Diplomacy: The Crisis of Canada-France Relations" (Ph.D. thesis, York University, 1981).
11. Conn and Fairchild, *The Framework of Hemispheric Defense*, 377.
12. *The Papers of George Catlett Marshall*, vol. 3, 7 December 1941 to 31 May 1943, 690–91; Hull, *Memoirs*, 2:1182; Dziuban, *Military Relations*, 252–59.
13. Stacey, *Canada and the Age of Conflict*, 2:339–41; Pearson quoted in John English, *Shadow of Heaven: The Life of Lester Pearson*, vol. 1, *1897–1948* (Toronto, 1989), 257.
14. Donald Creighton, *Canada's First Century* (Toronto, 1970), 242–43; Morton in *CHR* 45, no. 3 (1964): 320–21; King cited in James Eayrs, "The Road Past Ogdensburg," *Canadian Forum*, February 1971, 366.
15. S. McKee Rosen, *The Combined Boards of the Second World War* (New York, 1951), 232–33.
16. Winston Churchill, *The Hinge of Fate* (Boston, 1950), 374–77; Dean Acheson, *Present at the Creation* (New York, 1969), 165; Robert Bothwell and William Kilbourn, *C. D. Howe: A Biography* (Toronto, 1979), 168–69, 205.
17. Donald Avery, "Secrets Between Different Kinds of Friends: Canada's

Wartime Exchange of Scientific Information with the United States and the USSR, 1940–1945," *CHA Historical Papers* (1986), 225–53.

18. The story of Canol is more fully told in Stephen J. Randall, *United States Foreign Oil Policy: For Profits and Security* (Montreal, 1985), 160–65.
19. Worker quoted in Barry Broadfoot, *Six War Years, 1939–1945* (Toronto, 1974), 222; Curtis R. Nordman, "The Army of Occupation: Malcolm MacDonald and U.S. Military Involvement in the Canadian Northwest," and Richard J. Diubaldo, "The Alaska Highway in Canada-United States Relations," both in Kenneth Coates, ed., *The Alaska Highway* (Vancouver, 1985), 83–115; Coates and William Morrison, *The Alaska Highway in World War II: The U.S. Army of Occupation in Canada's Northwest* (Norman, Okla., 1992).
20. George Britnell and V. C. Fowke, *Canadian Agriculture in War and Peace, 1935–1950* (Stanford, 1962), 135–38; Lawrence R. Aronsen, "From World War to Limited War: Canadian-American Industrial Mobilization for Defence," *Revue internationale d'histoire militaire* 51 (1982): 210–16; Robert Bothwell, *Canada and the United States: The Politics of Partnership,* (Toronto, 1992), 23; McCarthy quoted in *King Diary,* 22 Mar 1943, cited in Bothwell, ibid., 22.
21. Danford W. Middlemiss, "Economic Defence Co-operation with the United States, 1940–1963," in Kim Richard Nossal, ed., *An Acceptance of Paradox: Essays on Canadian Diplomacy in Honor of John W. Holmes* (Toronto, 1982), 109; "The Permanent Joint Board on Defense," Box 47, Dean Acheson Papers, HSTL; Bothwell and Kilbourn, *C. D. Howe,* 171–2.
22. R. D. Cuff and J. L. Granatstein, "The Hyde Park Declaration: Origins and Significance," *Canadian-American Relations in Wartime,* 69–92; R. Warren James, *Wartime Economic Cooperation: A Study of Relations Between Canada and the United States* (Toronto, 1949), 394; "49th State?," *Time,* 23 February 1948, 46; William R. Willoughby, "The Canada-U.S. Joint Economic Agencies of the Second World War," *Canadian Public Administration* 50, no. 1 (1972): 59–73; Alan S. Millward, *War, Economy and Society, 1939–1945* (Berkeley, 1977), 233.
23. Beatrice Bishop Berle and Travis Beal Jacobs, eds., *Navigating the Rapids, 1918–1971* (New York, 1973), diary entry for 18 March 1941, 365; Keenleyside, *On the Bridge of Time,* 91–92.
24. Gary Gerstle, *Working-Class Americanism: The Politics of Labor in a Textile City, 1914–1960* (Cambridge, Mass., 1989), 278–309; Jacques Ducharme, *The Shadows of the Trees: The Story of the French Canadians in New England* (New York, 1943), 217–19; FDR to King, 18 May 1942, in Jean-François

Lisée, *Dans l'oeil de l'aigle: Washington face au Québec* (Quebec, 1990), 20–23, 454–55.

25. Cf. for the metaphor Seymour Martin Lipset, *Continental Divide: The Values and Institutions of the United States and Canada* (New York, 1990), 172–88; Allan Smith, "Metaphor and Nationality in North America," *CHR* 51, no. 3 (1970): 273; "The Permanent Joint Board on Defense," Box 47, Dean Acheson Papers, HSTL.
26. Roger Daniels, "Japanese Relocation and Redress in North America: A Comparative View," *Pacific Historian* 26, no. 1 (1982): 2–13.
27. *Sporting News* in David Pietrusza, *Baseball's Canadian-American League, 1936–1951* (Jefferson, N.C., 1990), 152–54; Richard Collins, *Culture, Communication and National Identity: The Case of Canadian Television* (Toronto, 1990), 59; Hanson in John Herd Thompson, "Comic Relief," *Horizon Canada* 8 (1987): 2174–79.
28. Michael Hirsh and Patrick Loubert, *The Great Canadian Comic Books* (Toronto, 1971).
29. Broadfoot, *Six War Years*, 215–16, 221, 286, 290; J. L. Granatstein, *Canada's War* (Toronto, 1975), 421–24.
30. Brinton, *The United States and Britain* (Cambridge, Mass., 1945), 222–23; Pearson in English, *Shadow of Heaven*, 257.
31. Department of State, memorandum for the President, "Visit of Prime Minister of Canada," 28 September 1945, President's Secretary's File, Subject File, Foreign Affairs, Box 172, Truman Papers, HSTL; J. L. Granatstein, *A Man of Influence: Norman A. Robertson and Canadian Statecraft, 1929–68* (Ottawa, 1981); John T. P. Humphrey, *Human Rights and the United Nations* (Dobbs Ferry, N.Y., 1984).
32. Stacey, *Canada and the Age of Conflict*, 2:379, 385.
33. Canadian reaction in report of U.S. Ambassador Atherton, 30 October 1945, forwarded to Truman, President's Secretary's File, Subject File, File Affairs, Box 172, Truman Papers, HSTL; Pearson in *DCER*, 11 and 12 November 1946, 1670–72; Kennan in Thomas Paterson, ed., *Major Problems in American Foreign Policy*, 2:296–97; Acheson, *Present at the Creation*, 150.
34. FBI, "Soviet Espionage Activities," 19 October 1945, President's Secretary's File, Subject File, FBI-A-Communism, HSTL; U.S. Department of War, Intelligence Division, "Soviet Espionage in Canada," 3 October 1946, Naval Aide Files, Alphabetical File, Box 17, HSTL; Central Intelligence Agency, "Canada," 5 May 1950, President's Secretary's File, Intelligence

File, CIA Reports, Box 261, HSTL; on Pearson, J. L. Granatstein and David Stafford, *Spy Wars: Espionage and Canada from Gouzenko to Glasnost* (Toronto, 1990), 47–75, esp. 58–60; Truman's speech in *Public Papers of the Presidents, Truman* (Washington, D.C., 1963), 176–80.

35. Department of State, memorandum for the President, "Visit of Prime Minister of Canada," 28 September 1945, President's Secretary's File, Subject File, Foreign Affairs, Box 172, Truman Papers, HSTL; Theodore Ropp, "Politics, Strategy and Commitments of a Middle Power," in David R. Deener, ed., *Canada-United States Treaty Relations* (Durham, N.C., 1963), 82.
36. Stacey, *Canada and the Age of Conflict*, 2:391.

7. Canada in the New American Empire, 1947–1960

1. Lawrence Aronsen and Martin Kitchen, *The Origins of the Cold War in Comparative Perspective: American, British and Canadian Relations with the Soviet Union, 1941–1948* (London, 1988), 205; T. G. Paterson, *Soviet-American Confrontation: Postwar Reconstruction and the Origins of the Cold War* (Baltimore, 1973) and *Meeting the Communist Threat* (New York, 1988); Gar Alperovitz, *Atomic Diplomacy*, 2d ed. (New York, 1985); Truman, *Memoirs*, vol. 2, *Years of Trial and Hope, 1946–52* (Garden City, N.Y., 1956), 250.
2. Text of NSC-68 in Paterson, *Major Problems in American Foreign Policy*, 2:310–15.
3. King in Swanson, *Summit Diplomacy*, 124; counselor quoted in David J. Bercuson, *True Patriot: The Life of Brooke Claxton, 1898–1960* (Toronto, forthcoming), 264–65. We thank our colleague for a prepublication peek.
4. Claxton in James Eayrs, *In Defence of Canada*, vol. 4, *Growing Up Allied* (Toronto, 1980), 45; G. F. G. Stanley, *Canada's Soldiers: The Military History of an Unmilitary People* (Toronto, 1960), 414.
5. Denis Smith, *The Diplomacy of Fear: Canada and the Cold War 1941–1948* (Toronto, 1988), 226–36; Lester Pearson, *Words and Occasions* (Cambridge, Mass., 1970), 70, 170; external affairs documents cited in Don Page and Don Munton, "Canadian Images of the Cold War," *International Journal* 32, no. 3 (1977): 585, 587, 595.
6. "Hard and fast" cited in Page and Munton, "Images of the Cold War," 593 (the conclusion we draw is at odds with theirs, however); J. W. Pickersgill

and D. F. Forster, *The Mackenzie King Record,* vol. 4, *1947–1948* (Toronto, 1970), 192.

7. Claxton in Bercuson, *Claxton,* 288, and in Eayrs, *Growing Up Allied,* 246.
8. St. Laurent in *CHCD,* 29 April 1948, 3449; charter, among many places, in Escott Reid, *Time of Fear and Hope: The Making of the North Atlantic Treaty, 1947–1949* (Toronto, 1977), 264–66.
9. John A. Munro and Alex Inglis, eds., *Mike: The Memoirs of the Right Honourable Lester B. Pearson,* vol. 2, *1948–1957* (Toronto, 1973), 33; Escott Reid, *Radical Mandarin: The Memoirs of Escott Reid* (Toronto, 1989), 267; St. Laurent in *CHCD,* 29 April 1948, 3449.
10. Dwight D. Eisenhower, *The White House Years: Mandate for Change, 1953–1956* (Garden City, N.Y., 1963), 12; statistics in John W. Warnock, *Partner to Behemoth: The Military Policy of a Satellite Canada* (Chicago, 1970), 322.
11. Claxton in Eayrs, *Growing Up Allied,* 200; Acheson in Walter LaFeber, *America, Russia and the Cold War, 1945–1975* (New York, 1976), 100; Truman to King, 5 January 1948; King to Truman, 8 January 1948, White House Central Files, Confidential Files, Truman Papers, HSTL; Acheson, *Present at the Creation,* 404–5.
12. Reid, *Radical Mandarin,* 257–66; NAC, Pearson to External Affairs, 6 November 1950, DEA File 50069-A-40, No. 324, cited in Charles M. Dobbs, "U.S.-Canadian Relations During the Korean and Vietnam Conflicts," paper presented to the Association for Canadian Studies in the United States, Boston, 1991; "Diplomats Hope General Ousted," *Globe,* 3 April 1951, 1; Claxton in Denis Stairs, *The Diplomacy of Constraint: Canada, the Korean War, and the United States* (Toronto, 1974), 212 n. 84.
13. Reg Whitaker, "The Cold War and the Myth of Liberal-Internationalism: Canadian Foreign Policy Reconsidered, 1945–1953"; Peyton Lyon, "Quiet Diplomacy Revisited," in Stephen Clarkson, *An Independent Foreign Policy for Canada?* (Toronto, 1968), 34.
14. Quotations from Raymond B. Blake, "An Old Problem in a New Province: Canadian Sovereignty and the American Bases in Newfoundland, 1948–1952," forthcoming in *ARCS* (1994); David J. Bercuson, "SAC vs. Sovereignty: The Origins of the Goose Bay Lease, 1946–1952," *CHR* 70, no. 2 (1989): 221.
15. Memorandum from Defence Liaison Division to Undersecretary of State for External Affairs, Canada, 9 July 1952, *DCER,* vol. 18, 1952, 1112–18. Woodward to Acheson, 13 January 1953, Papers of Stanley Woodward,

HSTL; Briefing Papers for President's Visit to Ottawa, 13–14 November 1953, Box 6, Whitman File, International Series, DDE; James E. Webb, Acting Secretary of State memo for Truman, 2 March 1951, outlining PJBD discussions in 1951 and subsequent correspondence, White House Central Files, Confidential Files, Truman Papers, HSTL; White House Central Files, PJBD-Canada-U.S. Files, Truman Papers, HSTL; Joseph T. Jockel, *No Boundaries Upstairs: Canada, the United States, and the Origins of North American Air Defence, 1945–1958* (Vancouver, 1987), 127.

16. Robert Bothwell and John English, "Canadian Trade Policy in the Age of American Dominance and British Decline, 1943–47," *Canadian Review of American Studies* 8 (1977): 52–56.
17. Howe in *CHCD,* 25 June 1948, 5845; J. L. Granatstein and R. D. Cuff, "Canada and the Marshall Plan, June–December 1947," *CHA Historical Papers* (1977): 196–213, Truman quoted; Willard Thorp Oral History, 118, HSTL; Granatstein and Norman Hillmer, *For Better or for Worse,* 175.
18. Quotations from Robert Cuff and J. L. Granatstein, "The Rise and Fall of Canadian-American Free Trade, 1947–48," *CHR* 57, no. 4 (1977): 469, 473; memo and text of the agreement in *FRUS* (1948) IX, *The Western Hemisphere* (Washington, D.C., 1972), 406–9.
19. *Mackenzie King Record,* 4:268–69.
20. Bruce Muirhead, "Trials and Tribulations: The Decline of Anglo-Canadian Trade, 1945–50," *Journal of Canadian Studies* 24, no. 1 (1989): 50.
21. Report cited in Lawrence Aronsen, "From World War to Limited War: Canadian-American Industrial Mobilization for Defence," *Revue Internationale d'histoire militaire* 51 (1982): 220. Eisenhower to Diefenbaker, 21 September 1958; Diefenbaker to Eisenhower, 28 October 1958; Eisenhower to Diefenbaker, 7 November 1958, Whitman File, International Series, Canada (5), Box 6, DDE. On Canadian concerns over lead and zinc exports, see also Canadian ambassador to Secretary of State, 29 June 1960, Official File 134-E-7, Lead and Zinc (2), Box 679, Eisenhower Papers, DDE.
22. Paul M. Litt, "The Massey Commission, Americanization, and Canadian Cultural Nationalism," *Queen's Quarterly* 98, no. 2 (1991): 375–87; Paul Rutherford, *When Television Was Young: Primetime Canada, 1952–1967,* (Toronto, 1990), 131.
23. Pierre Berton, *Hollywood's Canada: The Americanization of Our National Image* (Toronto, 1975), 167–200.
24. Department of State Press Release, 8 October 1957, Whitman file, "Dulles-October 1957," Box 7, DDE.

25. Department of State Press Release, 8 October 1957, Whitman file, "Dulles-October 1957," Box 7, DDE; Commission on Foreign Economic Policy, *Report to the President and the Congress* (Washington, D.C., January 1954); Eisenhower, *Mandate for Change,* 292–94.
26. Stephen Scheinberg, "Invitation to Empire: Tariffs and American Economic Expansion in Canada," in Glenn Porter and Robert Cuff, eds., *Enterprise and National Development* (Toronto, 1973), 95; Ralph Strauss, special consultant to Undersecretary of State for Economic Affairs, *Expanding Private Investment for Free World Economic Growth* (Washington, D.C., 1959); William Draper, Chairman, President's Committee to Study the U.S. Military Assistance Program, Third Interim Report, July 1959, Staff Series, Council on Foreign Economic Policy, Draper Committee (1), Box 5, DDE; Canadian figures from F. H. Leacy, ed., *Historical Statistics of Canada,* 2d ed. (Ottawa, 1983), series G191–96.
27. Woodward to Acheson, 13 January 1953, Papers of Stanley Woodward, HSTL; U.S. Chamber of Commerce Resolution, 1953, White House Central Files, Official File, Box 868, DDE; Middlemiss, "Economic Defense Cooperation," 86–109.
28. Peter Karl Kresl, "Before the Deluge: Canadians on Foreign Ownership, 1920–1955," *ARCS* 6, no. 1 (1976): 102–16.
29. Randall to Herter, 16 April 1957, Chronological File, Council on Foreign Economic Policy, Box 4, DDE; Randall Memorandum, 15 July 1957, and Department of State, "United States-Canadian Economic Integration," 27 June 1957, Eisenhower Papers, Office Series, Council of Foreign Economic Policy, Box 2, DDE; Dulles to Randall, 25 July 1957, Council on Foreign Economic Policy, Randall Series, Box 2, DDE; Briefing Papers for Eisenhower Visit to Canada, July 1958, International Meeting Series, Whitman File, Box 3, DDE.
30. Dulles Memorandum of conversation with Clarence Randall, 8 August 1957, General Correspondence and Memo Series, Box 1, Dulles Papers, DDE; "Specific topics for Discussion by the President at Ottawa," Whitman File, International Series, Eisenhower Papers, DDE.
31. Basil Robinson, *Diefenbaker's World: A Populist in Foreign Affairs* (Toronto, 1989), 85–87.
32. Robinson, *Diefenbaker.* Diefenbaker to Eisenhower, 2 July 1960, Whitman File, International Series, Box 6, DDE.
33. Diefenbaker to Eisenhower, 7 June 1960; Herter to Eisenhower, 27 May 1960, Whitman File, International Series, Box 6, DDE; Christian Herter

memorandum of conversation with Eisenhower, 8 April 1960, Miscellaneous Memoranda, Box 10, Herter Papers, DDE; St. Laurent in Swanson, *Summit Diplomacy*, 138.

34. *Montreal Star*, 26 and 29 June 1959.

8. The Moose That Roared, 1960–1968

1. Kennedy quoted in *NYT*, 25 August 1960, and in William E. Leuchtenburg et al., *Britain and the United States* (London, 1979), 11; Richard Walton, *Cold War and Counterrevolution: The Foreign Policy of John F. Kennedy* (Baltimore, 1973), 9.
2. Knowlton Nash, *Kennedy and Diefenbaker: Fear and Loathing Across the Undefended Border* (Toronto, 1990), 60; John Diefenbaker, *One Canada*, vol. 2, *1956–1962* (Toronto, 1977), 165–66, 172; Thomas Reeves, *A Question of Character: A Life of John F. Kennedy* (New York, 1991).
3. CIA, National Intelligence Estimates, "Trends in Canadian Foreign Policy," JFK trip to Ottawa, 5/61 (D), Folder 11, Canada, Security, Box 113, POF, JFK.
4. Basil Robinson, *Diefenbaker's World: A Populist in Foreign Policy* (Toronto, 1989), 168; *Public Papers of the Presidents, Kennedy, 1961*, 305–306.
5. Robinson, *Diefenbaker*, 193–94, 200–201. On Cuba, see Briefing Papers for Kennedy Visit to Ottawa, May 1961, Folder 8, Canada, Security, POF, Box 113, JFK; Randall confidential interview with former DEA official.
6. Kennedy in Swanson, *Summit Diplomacy*, 200–206; David MacKenzie, "'The World's Greatest Joiner': Canada and the OAS," *British Journal of Canadian Studies* 6, no. 1 (1991): 206–8.
7. Victor Levant, *Quiet Complicity: Canadian Involvement in the Vietnam War* (Toronto, 1986), 107–70; U.S. Department of Defense, *United States–Vietnam Relations, 1945–1967* (Washington, D.C., 1971), book 2, part B, pp. 53–57.
8. James M. Minifie, *Peacemaker or Powdermonkey: Canada's Role in a Revolutionary World* (Toronto, 1960), 126.
9. Diefenbaker, *One Canada*, 2:182–83; Rostow memorandum, 10 May 1963, Canada Security, 1963, Box 113, POF, JFK.
10. President's Trip to Ottawa, Briefing Papers, 12 May 1961, Canada, Security, Box 113, POF, JFK; *Public Papers of the Presidents, Kennedy*, 1961, 534–36; Robinson, *Diefenbaker*, 204, 228–30.
11. Soviet officials claim that there were nuclear warheads in storage in Cuba

during the crisis: Randall interviews with Georgy Shahknazarov, advisor to Mikhail Gorbachev, Moscow, March 1992, Calgary, June 1992. The most useful insider's account is Robert Kennedy's *Thirteen Days: A Memoir of the Cuban Missile Crisis* (New York, 1969).

12. Kennedy to Diefenbaker, 22 and 19 October 1962, Canada-Security, POF, Box 113, JFK; Diefenbaker, *One Canada,* 2:171.
13. Jocelyn Maynard Ghent, "Canada, the United States, and the Cuban Missile Crisis," *Pacific Historical Review* 48, no. 2 (1979): 169–70. Significantly, Robert Kennedy's account does not mention NORAD, and his only reference to Diefenbaker is to suggest that the Canadian prime minister was concerned about how to convince the rest of the world of the circumstances in Cuba: *Thirteen Days,* 52; George Ball, *The Past Has Another Pattern: Memoirs* (New York, 1982), 299–300; External Affairs Documents, 1962, 336–38.
14. The most authoritative account is J. L. Granatstein, "When Push Came to Shove: Canada and the United States," in Thomas Paterson, ed., *Kennedy's Quest for Victory* (New York, 1989), 86–104; Paul Martin, *A Very Public Life,* vol. 2, *So Many Worlds* (Toronto, 1983), 364; Diefenbaker in *One Canada,* 3:80, 82.
15. Nash, *Kennedy and Diefenbaker,* 238–57, press release, 243–44; Granatstein, "When Push Came to Shove," 98–99. Ball does not even mention these events in his memoirs, nor does Rusk's biographer; see Thomas J. Schoenbaum, *Waging Peace and War: Dean Rusk in the Truman, Kennedy and Johnson Years* (New York, 1988).
16. American Embassy to Department of State, 2 February 1963, Canada General, 1963, POF, Box 113, JFK.
17. Butterworth to Department of State, 12 February 1963, Canada General, 1963, POF, Box 113; William Brubeck, Executive Secretary to Bundy, the White House, 5 April 1963, Canada Security, 1963, Box 113, JFK; campaign quotations in J. Murray Beck, *Pendulum of Power: Canada's Federal Elections* (Scarborough, Ont., 1968), 356–57.
18. Berton cited in John English and Norman Hillmer, "Canada's Alliances," *Revue Internationale d'histoire militaire* 51, no. 18 (1982): 45; Martin, *Public Life,* 2:385–87. Martin also expressed these views to the authors during his terms as a visiting scholar at McGill University in the mid-1980s.
19. Denis Smith, *Gentle Patriot: A Political Biography of Walter Gordon* (Edmonton, 1973).
20. "Ice" from Douglas LePan quoted in James Eayrs, "The Road from Ogdensburg," *Canadian Forum* (February 1971): 364; David McClellan and

Dean Acheson, eds., *Among Friends: Personal Letters of Dean Acheson* (New York, 1980), 250.

21. *Public Papers of the Presidents, Kennedy,* 1963, 673.
22. Diary Backup, Box 3, LBJ; National Security File, Country File, Canada, Pearson Visit, LBJ; National Security File, Country File, Canada, Pearson Visit, 1964, LBJ. See also William Brubeck memorandum for the President, 24 January 1964, National Security File, Country File, Canada, Pearson Visit, LBJ.
23. Appointments File, 16 September 1964, Diary Backup, Box 9, LBJ; Robert Bothwell, *Canada and the United States: The Politics of Partnership* (Toronto, 1992), 93; James Keeley, "Cast in Concrete for All Time?: Negotiation of the Auto Pact," *Canadian Journal of Political Science* 16 (June 1983): 281–97; Hartke in Levant, *Quiet Complicity,* 35–36.
24. Rusk/Sullivan to Lodge, 1 May 1964, in Swanson, *Summit Diplomacy,* 239–40; Martin, *Public Life,* vol. 2, 428–29. The U.S. position on the Seaborn missions is in *Administrative History of the Department of State,* vol. 1, chap. 8, "Vietnam," 242–45, LBJ.
25. Editorial comments in *Globe,* 4 November 1964, 6, and *Winnipeg Free Press,* 4 November 1964, 57; Pearson in Swanson, *Summit Diplomacy,* 251–54. National Security Adviser McGeorge Bundy congratulated Pearson on his award, Bundy to Pearson, 30 March 1965, CO 43, LBJ.
26. Lawrence Martin, *The Presidents and the Prime Ministers* (Garden City, N.Y., 1982), 226–27; Gwyn, *The 49th Paradox,* 115; Pearson, *Memoirs,* 3:140–43; Appointments File, Diary Backup, Box 15, LBJ, 26.
27. Pearson, *Memoirs,* 3:143–44; Ronning mission in Martin, *Public Life,* 2:437–43, George C. Herring, ed., *The Secret Diplomacy of the Vietnam War: The Negotiating Volumes of the Pentagon Papers* (Austin, 1983), 159–207, and *Administrative History of the Department of State,* 1:249–50. The major Canadian study, Douglas Ross's *In the Interests of Peace: Canada and Vietnam, 1954–1973* (Toronto, 1984) argues that Hanoi was in fact unwilling to negotiate without a guarantee of the recognition of the NLF as a legitimate political force in South Vietnam.
28. Ross, *Interests of Peace,* 288–95, 308–9; Martin, *Public Life,* 2:444–45; statistics in John J. Kirton, "The Consequences of Integration: The Case of the Defense Production Sharing Agreements," in Andrew Axline et al., eds., *Continental Community: Independence and Integration in North America* (Toronto, 1974), 136; Levant, *Quiet Complicity,* 54–56.

29. Brewster Kneen to Moyers, 7 December 1965, CO 43 Canada, LBJ; *Montreal Gazette*, 26 May 1967, 14; *CHCD*, 30 May 1967, 771.
30. U.S. memorandum on Martin's proposal, Appointments File, Box 66, LBJ; *NYT*, 26 May 1967, 1; *Washington Post*, 26 May 1967, A1, A3; *Globe*, 26 May 1967, 1, 6.
31. Pearson, *Memoirs*, 3:146–47.
32. They also dated their movement's birth from the American student revolt of 1968: Peter Warrian, "From Colonized to Colonizer," in John H. Redekop, ed., *The Star-Spangled Beaver* (Toronto, 1971), 70–79.
33. William H. Chafe, *The Unfinished Journey: America Since World War II* (New York, 1991), 303; Robert Bothwell, Ian Drummond, and John English, *Canada Since 1945: Power, Politics, and Provincialism* (Toronto, 1981), 311–19 (we differ from these authors, however, on how much the NDP presence and example moved the Liberals to enact these programs); J. L. Granatstein, *Canada, 1957–1967: The Years of Uncertainty and Innovation* (Toronto, 1986), 169–97.
34. Lipset, *Continental Divide*, 39, 50, 136–51; Robert Bothwell, "More Than Kin, and Less Than Kind: The Political Cultures of Canada and the U.S.," in Stephen J. Randall, ed., *North America Without Borders?* (Calgary, 1992), 287, and *Politics of Partnership*, 166 n. 52, 174 n. 39.
35. Stephen J. Whitfield, *The Culture of the Cold War* (Baltimore, 1991).
36. Lawrence Aronsen, "Canada's Postwar Re-armament: Another Look at American Theories of the Military-Industrial Complex," *CHA Historical Papers* (1981), 175–96; Norbert MacDonald, *Distant Neighbors: A Comparative History of Seattle and Vancouver* (Lincoln, Neb., 1987), 138–63; "social security state" is borrowed from Bothwell, "Political Cultures," 291, and "national security state" from Daniel Yergin, *Shattered Peace: The Origins of the Cold War and the National Security State* (New York, 1990).

9. The Ambivalent Ally, 1968–1984

1. English and Hillmer, "Canada's Alliances," 40–48.
2. "Coming apart at home" is William H. Chafe's description in *The Unfinished Journey: America Since World War II* (New York, 1991); "U.S. Society Disintegrating, UAW Official Declares," *Globe*, 12 February 1968, 4; "Jubilant Negroes Take the Death of Dr. King as a Sign to Rampage," *Globe*,

6 April 1968, 9; *Le Devoir,* 9 April 1968, 4; *Winnipeg Free Press,* 6 April 1968, 3, 8 April 1968, 21; *Globe,* 6 April 1968, 6; Ryan, "Tragédie de Los Angeles," *Le Devoir,* 6 June 1968, 4.

3. Helen F. Eckerson, "United States and Canada Magnets for Immigration," *Annals of the American Academy of Political and Social Science* 316 (1958): 34, 38; Michael Bliss, "Cultural Tariffs and Canadian Universities," in Redekop, *Star-Spangled Beaver,* 88.
4. Clippings, Press Reaction to U.S. Exhibit at Expo '67, 25 May 1967, President's Appointment File, Box 66, LBJ; *NYT,* 28 April 1967; Edgar Z. Friedenberg, *Deference to Authority* (White Plains, N.Y., 1980).
5. James Eayrs, "The Road from Ogdensburg," *Canadian Forum,* February 1971, 365–66; coverage described in *Globe,* 18 November 1970, 1–2.
6. Charles Ritchie, *Storm Signals: More Undiplomatic Diaries* (Toronto, 1983), 114, 129; Kim Richard Nossal, *The Politics of Canadian Foreign Policy* (Scarborough, Ont., 1985), 133–43; J. L. Granatstein and Robert Bothwell, *Pirouette: Pierre Trudeau and Canadian Foreign Policy* (Toronto, 1990), 39; Trudeau in Dale C. Thomson, *Canadian Foreign Policy* (Toronto, 1971), 126.
7. Lawrence Martin, *The Presidents and Prime Ministers* (Garden City, N.Y., 1982), 12; Trudeau in Swanson, *Summit Diplomacy,* 275.
8. "Canada Tied to U.S. Plan for Asian Empire: Nixon," *Globe,* 25 May 1967, 4; "Trudeau Welcomes Draft Evaders," *Christian Century,* 8 April 1970, 414.
9. Douglas Ross, *In the Interests of Peace: Canada and Vietnam, 1954–1973* (Toronto, 1984), 339–68; Granatstein and Bothwell, *Pirouette,* 52–60.
10. Scowcroft in Granatstein and Bothwell, *Pirouette,* 93.
11. John Bullen, "The Ontario Waffle and the Struggle for an Independent Socialist Canada: Conflict Within the NDP," *CHR* 64, no. 2 (1983): 188–215; "Nixon Drinks Canada Dry" signified opposition to the plan of the North American Water and Power Alliance (NAWPA), which proposed to divert Canadian water to the American Southwest—see Lynton K. Caldwell, "Binational Responsibilities for a Shared Environment," in Charles F. Doran and John H. Sigler, eds., *Canada and the United States: Enduring Friendship, Persistent Stress* (Englewood Cliffs, N.J., 1985), 215–16.
12. Michael Bliss, *Northern Enterprise: Five Centuries of Canadian Business* (Toronto, 1987), 482–83, 508–13; Kari Levitt, *Silent Surrender: The Multinational Corporation in Canada* (Toronto, 1970); Kim Richard Nossal, "Economic Nationalism and Continental Integration," in Denis Stairs and Gilbert R. Winham, *The Politics of Canada's Economic Relationship with the United States* (Toronto, 1985), 55–94.

13. Canada, House of Commons, *Eleventh Report of the Standing Committee on External Affairs and National Defence Respecting Canada-U.S. Relations*, 28th Parliament, 2d session (Ottawa, 1970); Canada, Privy Council Office, *Foreign Direct Investment in Canada* (Ottawa, 1970).
14. Granatstein and Bothwell, *Pirouette*, 64–66; Nixon quoted in John Lewis Gaddis, *Strategies of Containment* (New York, 1982), 280. Paul Kennedy analyzes America's downward direction in the early 1970s in *The Rise and Fall of the Great Powers: Economic Change and Military Conflict, 1500–2000* (New York, 1987), 515–35.
15. Granatstein and Bothwell, *Pirouette*, 67–70. On Kissinger, see Nixon's *The White House Years* (New York, 1979). Significantly, Nixon makes no reference to Canadian problems in his own memoirs.
16. Wallace C. Koehler, Jr., "Foreign Ownership Policies in Canada: 'From Colony to Nation' Again," *ARCS* 11, no. 1 (1981): 80–97.
17. Edward Shaffer, *The United States and the Control of World Oil* (London, 1983), passim; Daniel Yergin, *The Prize* (New York, 1990), passim; S. J. Randall, "United States Strategic Petroleum Policy in the Twentieth Century: The Canadian Dimension," in A. W. Rasporich, ed., *Oil in Canada*, forthcoming; Department of Defense, *The Oil Import Program* (Washington, D.C., 1970), 37–70, 81, 132; Department of State, *Bulletin*, 7 May 1973; U.S. Senate, Committee on Interior and Insular Affairs, *The Geopolitics of Energy*, Energy Publication No. 95–1 (Washington, D.C., 1977), 9–10. The main author was Melvin Conant, a former member of the U.S. War College.
18. U.S. Congress, Senate, Foreign Relations Committee, Subcommittee on Multinational Corporations, *Direct Investment Abroad and the Multinationals: Effects on the United States Economy* (Washington, D.C., 1975), 27–29; *Multinational Oil Corporations and United States Foreign Policy, Report* (Washington, D.C., 1975), 4, 7–8.
19. Paul Audley, "Book Publishing in Canada," in Abraham Rotstein and Gary Lax, *Getting It Back: A Program for Canadian Independence* (Toronto, 1974), 204, 206; *Time* executive quoted in *Business Week*, 20 October 1975, 52.
20. John Herd Thompson, "Canada's Quest for Cultural Sovereignty: Promotion, Protection and Popular Culture," in Helen Holmes and David Taras, *Seeing Ourselves: Media Power and Policy in Canada* (Toronto, 1992), 188–201.
21. Isaiah A. Litvak and Christopher J. Maule, *Cultural Sovereignty: The "Time" and "Reader's Digest" Case in Canada* (New York, 1974), and "Bill C-58 and

the Regulation of Periodicals in Canada," *International Journal* 36 (1980): 70–90; Roger Frank Swanson, "Canadian Cultural Nationalism and the U.S. Public Interest," in Janice L. Murray, ed., *Canadian Cultural Nationalism* (New York, 1977), 54–79.

22. Martin Knelman, *Home Movies* (Toronto, 1987), 4; Dave Chenowith, "Does the Quantity Equal the Quality?," *Montreal Gazette*, 21 March 1980.
23. Paul Audley, *Canada's Cultural Industries: Broadcasting, Publishing, Records and Film* (Toronto, 1983), 257, statistics 259; Charles Pullen, "Culture, Free Trade, and Two Nations," *Queen's Quarterly* 95, no. 4 (1988): 888; Swanson, "Canadian Cultural Nationalism," 63.
24. Martin, *Presidents and Prime Ministers*, 262–76, Carter quoted 266.
25. Jean-François Lisée, *Dans l'oeil de l'aigle: Washington face au Québec* (Montreal, 1990); Jurgen Schmandt and Hilliard Roderick, *Acid Rain and Friendly Neighbors* (Durham, N.C., 1985), 63.
26. Granatstein and Bothwell, *Pirouette*, 219–20; Warren Christopher et al., *American Hostages in Iran* (New Haven, 1982).
27. Canada, Department of Energy, Mines and Resources, *The National Energy Program, 1980* (Ottawa, 1980); *The National Energy Program Update, 1982* (Ottawa, 1982); Robert N. McRae, "A Major Shift in Canada's Energy Policy: The Policies and Impact of the National Energy Program," *Journal of Energy and Development* 7, no. 2 (1982): 173–98.
28. Stephen Clarkson, *Canada and the Reagan Challenge: Crisis and Adjustment, 1981–1985* (Toronto, 1985), 23–41, 55–82; Edward Wonder, "The US Government Response to the Canadian National Energy Program," *Canadian Public Policy* 8 (1982): 480–93; U.S. House of Representatives, Committee on Government Operations, *The Adequacy of the Federal Response to Foreign Investment in the United States* (Washington, D.C., 1980).
29. U.S. Department of State, "Note on National Energy Program to the Government of Canada," 5 March 1981; Reagan press conference, 6 March 1981, *American Foreign Policy, Current Documents, 1981* (Washington, D.C., 1982), 639; Myer Rashish, "Approach to Foreign Economic Issues," *Department of State Bulletin* (October 1981): 40–46. An example of the oil industry response may be seen in the *Oil and Gas Journal* 79 (26 January 1981). The *Oil and Gas Journal* noted that Canadian ownership had been on the increase in the 1970s without such interventionist policies, from 22.4 percent in 1971 to 38.5 percent in 1979.
30. *Globe*, 23 September 1981, 1; Eagleburger, *Department of State Bulletin*,

December 1981, 34–37; on Trudeau-Reagan differences over the USSR and NATO, see Canadian ambassador Allan Gotlieb's memoir, *"I'll Be with You in a Minute, Mr. Ambassador": The Education of a Canadian Diplomat in Washington* (Toronto, 1991). Stephen Randall is grateful to Mr. Gotlieb for sharing, in the fall of 1991, his personal reflections on the Trudeau-Reagan relationship.

31. Granatstein and Bothwell, *Pirouette*, 324–25; Clarkson, *Canada and the Reagan Challenge*, 36–50, 51–114.
32. Randall confidential interview, Toronto, July 1973; *Canadian Annual Review of Public Affairs* (Toronto, 1973), 270–71.
33. Liisa North, *Bitter Grounds: Roots of Revolt in El Salvador* (Toronto, 1981); Clarkson, *Canada and the Reagan Challenge*, 350.
34. Canada, Department of External Affairs, 2 November 1983.
35. Peter C. Newman, *True North Not Strong and Free: Defending the Peaceable Kingdom in the Nuclear Age* (Toronto, 1983), passim, NATO statistic 143.
36. Thomas J. McCormick, *America's Half-Century: United States Foreign Policy in the Cold War* (Baltimore and London, 1989), 229. Not only the Reagan administration ignored Trudeau—there is not a word in McCormick about the "peace initiative."
37. Eagleburger in Granatstein and Bothwell, *Pirouette*, 371–72; Gotleib, *Education of a Canadian Diplomat*, 97; Adam Bromke and Kim Richard Nossal, "Trudeau Rides the 'Third Rail,'" *International Perspectives* (1984): 3–10.
38. John English review of Granatstein and Bothwell's *Pirouette*, *Globe*, 25 August 1990, C8.

10. Republicans and Tories, 1984–1993

1. *Weekly Compilation of Presidential Documents* 21 (11 February 1985): 146; George Ball, *The Past Has Another Pattern: Memoirs* (New York, 1982), 486.
2. Carter in *NYT*, 16 July 1979, 1.
3. "Principled realism," in Department of State, *Bulletin* (June 1988): 33.
4. Mulroney in Michael K. Hawes, "Canada and the United States in a Changing Global Context," *ACS Newsletter* 13, no. 1 (1991): 9.
5. J. L. Granatstein, *Yankee Go Home?: Canadians and Anti-Americanism* (Toronto, 1996), 251.
6. Department of State, *Bulletin* (May 1986): 57; John C. Polanyi, "Time for

More 'No' in NORAD?," *Globe,* 2 December 1985; for the case against SDI, see Jerome B. Wiesner, former scientific adviser to the White House, quoted in *NYT,* 27 March 1983; David Leyton-Brown, in Maureen Molot and Brian Tomlin, eds., *Canada Among Nations, 1985: The Conservative Agenda* (Toronto, 1986), 180, 187–88.

7. Department of State, *Bulletin* (January 1986), 42–45, for Clark-Schultz meeting in Ottawa; Gotlieb provides an insightful and often witty account of these years in *"I'll Be With You in a Minute Mr. Ambassador": The Education of a Canadian Diplomat in Washington* (Toronto, 1991); Reagan radio address, 4 January 1986, Department of State, *Bulletin* (March 1986): 10.
8. Lynton K. Caldwell, "Binational Responsibilities for a Shared Environment," in Charles F. Doran and John H. Sigler, eds., *Canada and the United States: Enduring Friendship, Persistent Stress* (Englewood Cliffs, N.J., 1985), 207; Gotlieb, *Education of a Canadian Diplomat,* 61–62.
9. Michael Weisskopf, "Canada Is Still Waiting for the Administration to Do Something," *Washington Post,* 14 December 1987, 31; Gotlieb, *Education of a Canadian Diplomat,* 66–74.
10. Mulroney in *Globe,* 29 March 1988, A10; John Maggs, "Acid Rain Pact 'Codifies' Clean Air Act," *Journal of Commerce,* 10 July 1990, 3A; Hugh Winsor, "Canadian Quits Joint Commission," *Globe,* 10 September 1996, A1.
11. Justine Kaplan, "The Not-So-Great Lakes," *Omni,* February 1989, 32; lip service in *Vancouver Sun,* 13 January 1990; Co-chairs quoted in *Winnipeg Free Press,* 13 October 1989, 14; radioactive lamprey in *Globe,* 14 October 1989, D6.
12. Donald Barry, "The U.S. Senate and the Collapse of the East Coast Fisheries Agreement," *Dalhousie Review* 62, no. 3 (1982): 495–503; "Sub a Surprise to Scallop Poachers," *Globe,* 24 March 1993, 1.
13. Bruce Doern and Brian Tomlin, *Faith and Fear: The Free Trade Story* (Toronto, 1991), 2; poll in *Globe,* 24 February 1988, A1, A4.
14. Canada, Department of External Affairs, *Canadian Trade Policies for the 1980's: A Discussion Paper* (Ottawa, 1983); *Globe* and *Maclean's* editorials, both 6 August 1985; Doern and Tomlin, *Faith and Fear,* 24–25, 106, 310 n2.
15. Mulroney in Graham Fraser, "Popularity Is Long Gone," *Globe,* 28 February 1993, A9; *NYT, Durham Morning Herald,* both 5 October 1987, 1.
16. There is a full but negative overview of the agreement in Duncan Cameron, ed., *The Free Trade Deal* (Toronto, 1988), and in Doern and Tomlin, *Faith and Fear,* 70–99.
17. *Statement of Administrative Action* (Washington, 1988), 72, 88.

18. *Statement of Administrative Action,* 62–63.
19. Black, "Our Own Meech Shoot-Out," *Saturday Night* (September 1990): 76.
20. There are many examples of this perspective, but one of the most broadly representative is Ed Finn, Duncan Cameron, John Calvert, eds., *The Facts on Free Trade* (Toronto, 1988), which contains short essays by, among others, Eric Kierans (former cabinet minister); prominent Canadian author Margaret Atwood; president of the Canadian Labour Congress Shirley Carr; political scientist Stephen Clarkson; economist and women's rights activist Marjorie Cohen; Bob White, president of the Canadian Auto Workers; Scott Sinclair, coordinator of the Coalition Against Free Trade.
21. Reagan speech in Department of State, *Bulletin* (December 1988): 23.
22. Colin Mackenzie, "Old Allies Are Nice; Votes Are Essential," *Globe,* 13 October 1993, A10; "Sand in the Wheels of Trade," *The Economist,* 10 April 1993, 25–26.
23. *NYT,* 25 February 1993, A10; Sherbrooke *Record,* 25 February 1993; cartoon from the *Victoria Times-Colonist,* reprinted in *Globe,* 26 February 1993; Trillin in *Triangle Comic Review,* September 1992; Storer H. Rowley, "Well-Being of Northern Neighbor Significantly Affects U.S.," *Durham (NC) Morning Herald,* 25 October 1992; Robert Karl Manoff and Michael Schudson, *Reading the News* (New York, 1986), 60, 74.
24. Frank Hyland, "Message to Toronto: This Is *Our* Game," *Atlanta Constitution,* 17 October 1992; Stephen Brunt, "Canadian Fans Forgiving about Their Inverted Flag," *Globe,* 21 October 1992, 1.
25. Robert Pastor, "The Salinas Opening," *Journal of Interamerican Studies and World Affairs* 32, no. 3 (Fall 1990): 1–24.
26. Department of External Affairs and International Trade, *Highlights of the North American Free Trade Agreement* (Ottawa, August 1992).
27. Department of State, *Bulletin* (April 1989): 28.
28. See Stephen J. Randall, Herman Konrad, Sheldon Silverman, eds., *North America Without Borders? Integrating Canada, the United States and Mexico* (Calgary, 1992); Gary Clyde Hufbauer and Jeffrey Schott, *North American Free Trade: Issues and Recommendations* (Washington, D.C., 1992); Michael Hart, *A North American Free Trade Agreement: The Strategic Implications for Canada* (Ottawa, 1990).
29. Henry J. Jacek, "Public Policy and NAFTA: The Role of Organized Business Interests and the Labor Movement," *Canadian-American Public Policy,* 19 (1994); Matilde Luna, "Entrepreneurial Interests and Political Action in Mexico: Facing the Demands of Economic Modernization," in Riordan

Roett, ed., *The Challenge of Institutional Reform in Mexico* (Boulder, 1995), 77–94; Fen Osler Hampson and Christopher Maule, eds., *After the Cold War: Canada Among Nations, 1990* (Ottawa, 1991), 69.

30. Testimony to the House Committee on External Affairs and International Trade, Fall 1990.

Epilogue: "Plus ça change . . ."

1. "Thinking About Tomorrow," *Maclean's*, 1 February 1993, 36.
2. The U.S. balance of trade with both Canada and Mexico fell severely between 1993 and 1995, with Canada from a negative balance of trade of $10.8 billion U.S. to –$18.2; with Mexico from a trade surplus in 1993 of $1.7 billion to a trade deficit of $15.4 billion in 1995. U.S. Department of Commerce, Census Basis.
3. Landers in *Durham (NC) Herald-Sun*, 26 February 1993, B7; Marty York in *Globe*, 20 November 1992, A15.
4. Robin Winks, "Imagining Canada," in Karen Gould, Joseph T. Jockel, and William Metcalfe, eds., *Northern Exposures: Scholarship on Canada in the United States* (Washington D.C., 1993), 15.
5. Charles F. Doran, "Will Canada Unravel?," *Foreign Affairs* 75, no. 5 (1996), 108–9.
6. John H. Redekop, "A Reinterpretation of Canadian-American Relations," *Canadian Journal of Political Science* 9, no. 2 (1976): 227–243.
7. United States Information Service, "Background on the Helms-Burton Bill," 5 September 1996, www.usis-canada.usia.gov/helms.htm.
8. "Cautious Policy to Continue on Bosnia, Clinton Indicates," *Washington Post*, 6 February 1993, 1; "PM, Clinton Agree Generally But Not Entirely," *Globe*, 6 February 1993, A1.
9. Ronald Inglehart, Miguel Basañez, and Neil Nevitte, *American Convergence: Trade, Politics and Values* (Mexico City, 1993), and see the suggestions by the same authors in "Directions of Value Change in North America," in Stephen J. Randall, Herman Konrad, Sheldon Silverman, eds., *North America Without Borders? Integrating Canada, the United States and Mexico* (Calgary, 1992), 245–60.

Bibliographical Essay

The endnotes to *Ambivalent Allies* provide the reader with the sources for specific references in the text, in particular to those archival and government sources that have been used in preparing this study. This bibliographical essay will guide those students and general readers who wish to read more widely on a particular aspect of U.S.-Canadian relations. It is not all-encompassing, and includes neither master's and doctoral theses nor all relevant academic periodical literature.

There is a wide range of general studies of U.S.-Canadian relations, as well as of U.S. and Canadian foreign policy and the various topics of a social, political, and economic nature that have been alluded to in this volume. On the United States side, there is no substitute for Thomas G. Paterson, J. Garry Clifford, Kenneth T. Hagan, *American Foreign Policy, A History* (third edition, 1988). The Paterson volume is balanced but inclined toward revisionist scholarship. Those wishing a different perspective might consult Norman Graebner's realist interpretation of American diplomacy or Alexander DeConde's *History of American Foreign Relations* (1971). Some of the more theoretical underpinnings of this volume, in particular the world systems model, may be explored in Michael J. Hogan and Thomas G. Paterson, eds., *Explaining the History of American Foreign Relations* (1991). On world systems analysis, we have relied on Immanuel Wallerstein, *The Modern World System* (1974), *The Capitalist World Economy* (1979), and Terence Hopkins, *World-Systems Analysis: Theory and Methodology* (1982). More specialized are the volumes in the *American Secretaries of State and their Diplomacy* series, which began in 1928 under the editorship of Samuel Flagg Bemis and continued under Robert H. Ferrell. Frank Merli and Theodore Wilson, eds., provide a briefer and more interpretive approach to the same subject in *Makers of American Diplomacy* (1974). All students of U.S. foreign policy rely on the documents contained in the Department of

State, *Foreign Relations of the United States,* published in annual volumes since the late nineteenth century and now complete into the 1960s. This can be supplemented with the considerably less useful Department of State *Bulletin,* and by the Council on Foreign Relations, *Documents on American Foreign Relations, 1938–1970* (1939–73).

The most useful general study of Canadian foreign policy is C. P. Stacey's two-volume *Canada and the Age of Conflict: A History of Canadian External Policies,* (vol. 1, *1867–1921* [1979]; vol. 2, *The Mackenzie King Era, 1921–1948* [1981]), which is impeccably researched, written, and argued. G. P. deT. Glazebrook's *A History of Canadian External Relations* (2 volumes, 1950, repr. 1966) is a dated exegesis of modern Canadian foreign policy. James Eayrs's thoughtful series *In Defence of Canada* (1964–) begins in the 1920s and is now, in its sixth volume, in the 1960s. For the period since World War II, general studies include Dale Thomson and Roger Swanson's *Canadian Foreign Policy: Options and Perspectives* (1971), and Peyton Lyon's *Canada in World Affairs* (vol. 12, *1961–1963* [1968]), which is part of the valuable series on Canada in world affairs. For the very recent period, Carleton University has published the *Canada Among Nations* series of incisive annual volumes, which will remain the most important source until archival materials open for these years. The Canadian equivalent to the *Foreign Relations of the United States* volumes is the Department of External Affairs, *Documents on Canadian External Relations.* Unfortunately, these do not begin until 1909, and at present they encompass only the years until 1952. Those wishing more documentary material on recent Canadian foreign policy should consult the Department of External Affairs, *Annual Review,* the title of which has varied but which nonetheless carries into the 1980s. The *International Journal,* published under the auspices of the Canadian Institute for International Affairs, is valuable for specialist and generalist alike.

The study of Canadian-American relations is a distinct subdiscipline of Canadian foreign policy, although few historians of U.S. foreign policy specialize in the field. An important exception in this regard is provided in the insightful analysis by Gordon Stewart, "A Special Contiguous Country Economic Regime: An Overview of America's

Canada Policy," *Diplomatic History*, 6, no. 4 (Fall 1982), and in his book *The American Response to Canada Since 1776* (1992). Given the importance of Britain as a factor in Canadian-American relations, it is understandable that a number of studies adopt a trilateral approach. Valuable general studies include: J. L. Finlay, *Canada in the North Atlantic Triangle* (1975), and John Bartlett Brebner, *The North Atlantic Triangle* (1945), which is still the classic account. Kenneth Curtis and John Carroll focus on more contemporary issues in *Canadian-American Relations: The Promise and the Challenge* (1983), as does author/diplomat John Holmes in *Life with Uncle: The Canadian-American Relationship* (1981). More general is the collection of primary and secondary sources edited by Richard Bowles, James Hanley, Bruce Hodgins, and George Rawlyk, *Canada and the U.S.: Continental Partners or Wary Neighbours?* (1973), and by Norman Hillmer, *Partners Nevertheless: Canadian-American Relations in the Twentieth Century* (1989). The best general interpretive study is J. L. Granatstein and Norman Hillmer's engaging *For Better or For Worse: Canada and the United States to the 1990s* (1991), which unfortunately for those who wish to read further eschews notes and an extensive bibliography. More extensive documentation is available in Edelgard Mahant and Graeme Mount's workmanlike synthesis *An Introduction to Canadian-American Relations* (second edition, 1989). Robert Bothwell's recent study of the post-1945 years, *Canada and the United States: The Politics of Partnership* (1991) is an outstanding work of interpretation with strongly expressed opinions on most controversial issues. John Sigler and Charles Doran, eds., *Canada and the United States: Enduring Friendship, Persistent Stress* (1985), and Doran's *Forgotten Partnership: US-Canada Relations Today* (1984) provide insights into the more recent relationship.

The literature on Canadian-American relations between the American Revolution and the Treaty of Washington in 1871 appropriately concentrates on critical turning points in the relationship. An outstanding book that brackets the period is Reginald Stuart's *United States Expansionism and British North America, 1775–1871* (1988). Gerald M. Craig's 1968 study of the eighteenth and nineteenth centuries in *The United States and Canada* remains valuable, as is the first edition of H. L.

Keenleyside's *Canada and the United States* (1929). Especially useful because of its focus on the history of ideas is Sidney F. Wise and Robert Craig Brown's *Canada Views the United States: Nineteenth-Century Political Attitudes* (1967). More specialized is Jane Errington's, *The Lion, the Eagle, and Upper Canada: A Developing Colonial Ideology* (1987).

The years from the American Revolution through the War of 1812 have attracted considerable scholarly interest. George Rawlyk's collection of contemporary documents and later historical accounts in *Revolution Rejected, 1775–1776* (1968) is invaluable, as is his *Nova Scotia's Massachusetts: A Study of Massachusetts–Nova Scotia Relations, 1680–1784* (1973). William H. Nelson provides the analysis of the Tory experience in the revolutionary era on which this study relies in *The American Tory* (1960). Among the many important analyses of the loyalist/Tory migration and adaptation to what remained of British North America are Wallace Brown, *The Good Americans: The Loyalists in the American Revolution* (1969); Leslie Upton, *The United Empire Loyalists: Men and Myths* (1967); Robert Calhoon, *The Loyalists in Revolutionary America 1760–1781* (1965); Neil MacKinnon, *This Unfriendly Soil: The Loyalist Experience in Nova Scotia* (1986). Studies of the War of 1812 focus either on causation, for example, Patrick White's *A Nation on Trial: America and the War of 1812* (1965), and Harry Coles's, *The War of 1812* (1965), or on the details of combat. Pierre Berton's two volumes on the war, *The Invasion of Canada* (1980) and *Flames Across the Border* (1981), as well as George Stanley's *The War of 1812: Land Operations* (1983), and William Dudley, ed., *The Naval War of 1812: A Documentary History* (1985), all fall into the latter category. Kenneth Bourne, *Britain and the Balance of Power in North America, 1815–1908* (Berkeley, 1967) examines the century in meticulous detail; C. P. Stacey's brief Canadian Historical Association booklet, *The Undefended Border: The Myth and the Reality* (1962), will be beloved by students seeking a shorter overview.

The years of manifest destiny, westward expansion, and continentalism have evoked passionate interest among historians. Stuart's study mentioned above is excellent on the Canadian-American relationship, but readers should also be aware of important studies of American expansionism in which Canada receives little direct attention. These include William H. Goetzmann's, *Exploration and Empire: The Explorer and the Scientist in the Winning of the American West* (1966), and Michael Hunt's study of American ideology in these years, *Ideology and U.S. Foreign Policy* (1987). West Coast Anglo-American rivalry receives its due in Frederick Merk's *The Oregon Question: Essays in Anglo-American Diplomacy and Politics* (1967), as well as in his *Manifest Destiny and Mission in American History.* The continentalist theme is explored by Donald F. Warner, *The Idea of Continental Union: Agitation for the Annexation of Canada to the United States, 1849–1893* (1960). More general but thorough is Lester B. Shippee, *Canadian-American Relations, 1849–1874* (1939).

Cross-border intellectual, political, and economic issues during the late Jacksonian era and the rebellions in Upper and Lower Canada are treated in a wide range of sources. Wilson Shortridge provides an early account in "The Canadian-American Frontier During the Rebellion of 1837–1838," *Canadian Historical Review,* 7 (1926); more recent are Gerald M. Craig's "The American Impact on the Upper Canadian Reform Movement Before 1837," *Canadian Historical Review,* 29, no. 4 (1948); more narrowly focused is Colin Read's study *The Rising in Western Upper Canada, 1837–38: The Duncombe Revolt and After* (1982). Alastair Watt provides a now badly dated account of the Alexander McLeod affair, which almost provoked war, in the *Canadian Historical Review,* 12, no. 2 (June 1931). Important work on the debate over American cultural influences include: Susan Houston, "Politics, Schools, and Social Change in Upper Canada," *Canadian Historical Review,* 53, no. 2 (1972); and Bruce Curtis, "Schoolbooks and the Myth of Curricular Republicanism: The State and the Curriculum in Canada West, 1820–1850," *Histoire Sociale/Social History* 16 (1983). The economic dimension is explored by Arthur M. Lower, et al., *The North American Assault on the Canadian Forest: A History of the Lumber Trade Between Canada and the United States* (1938). On reciprocity one must still consult D. C. Masters, *The Reciprocity Treaty of 1854* (1937); Lawrence Officer and Lawrence Smith, "The Canadian-American Reciprocity Treaty of 1855 to 1866," *Journal of Economic History* 30, no. 2 (June 1970); Graeme S. Mount, "Maine and the End of Reciprocity in 1866," *Maine Historical Society Quarterly* 26, no. 1 (Summer 1986). Western contacts are thoroughly treated by George F. G. Stanley's *Birth of Western Canada* (1936) and *Louis Riel* (1963).

The standard accounts of the impact of the American Civil War on the trilateral relationship remain Robin Winks, *Canada and the United States: The Civil War Years* (1960), and the two volumes by Brian Jenkins, *Britain and the War for the Union* (1974, 1980); Winks's study *The Blacks in Canada* (1971, 1997) is also important for the Civil War years and before, as is the collection *The Black Abolitionist Papers,* vol. 2, *Canada 1830–1865* (1986). More general work on the diplomacy and politics of the period includes David P. Crook, *Diplomacy During the American Civil War* (1975) and *The North, the South and the Powers, 1861–1865* (1974). Recognition of the importance of the war to Canada is evident in John A. Williams's, "Canada and the Civil War," in Harold Hyman, ed., *Heard Round the World: The Impact Abroad of the Civil War* (1969). Two works on the Trent Affair warrant attention: Norman B. Ferris, *The Trent Affair* (1977), and Gordon Warren, *Fountain of Discontent: The Trent Affair and Freedom of the Seas* (1981). The Fenian issue during and in the aftermath of the Civil War receives its due in Hereward Senior, *The Fenians and Canada* (1978), and Charles Stacey's "Fenianism and the Rise of National Feeling in Canada at the Time of Confederation," *Canadian Historical Review* 12, no. 3 (September 1931). They and others underline the importance of the American threat to confederation. See in this connection Donald Creighton's classic *The Road to Confederation* (1964) and C. P. Stacey's "Britain's Withdrawal from North America, 1864–1871," *Canadian Historical Review* 36, no. 3 (September 1955), which emphasizes Canadian vulnerability during and after the Civil War. The Treaty of Washington in the aftermath of the Civil War is the focus of an analysis by late nineteenth-century continentalist Goldwin Smith [Jr.], *The Treaty of Washington, 1871: A Study in Imperial History* (1941). Also useful for this topic and period are Donald Creighton's biography of John A. Macdonald, *The Old Chieftain* (1955), and Allen Nevins's biography of Grant's secretary of state, *Hamilton Fish* (1957). Lawrence Martin's useful *The Presidents and the Prime Ministers: The Myth of Bilateral Bliss, 1867–1982* (1982) is well written and provides many exciting leads, but is unfortunately scantily documented.

The major development of the period from the Treaty of Washington to the Alaska boundary dispute of 1903 was the emergence of the United States as a major world player. The rise of the United States touched Canada very directly in these years, as Great Britain turned its attention away from the Western Hemisphere. Walter LaFeber's *New Empire: An Interpretation of American Expansion, 1860–1898* (1963) has the best discussion of Canada's exceptional place in American policy during the period when the U.S. changed (in James G. Blaine's words) from "annexation of territory" to "annexation of trade." A. K. Weinberg, *Manifest Destiny: A Study of Nationalist Expansionism in American History* (1935), stretches from the eighteenth to the twentieth century, and has much discussion of Canada. Several other authors provide the important context in which American policy toward Canada was formulated, among them are William A. Williams, *The Roots of the Modern American Empire* (1969); Milton Plesur, *America's Outward Thrust* (1971); Mira Wilkins, *The Emergence of Multinational Enterprise: American Business Abroad from the Colonial Era to 1914* (1970). Very useful for trade policy is Tom Terill, *The Tariff, Politics, and American Foreign Policy, 1874–1901* (1973). The transformation of Anglo-American relations, which so affected Canada, is skillfully traced in Kenneth Bourne, *Britain and the Balance of Power in North America, 1815–1908* (1967), and Charles S. Campbell, *From Revolution to Rapprochement: The United States and Great Britain, 1783–1900* (1974).

Continued cross-border contacts are discussed in Alvin C. Gluek, Jr., *Minnesota and the Manifest Destiny of the Canadian Northwest* (1965), and in Douglas Owram, *The Promise of Eden: The Canadian Expansionist Movement and the Idea of the West, 1856–1900* (1980). The flight of Sitting Bull and the Sioux into Canada is the subject of several works, which treat both the specific incidents and the larger question of Indian policy in both countries. Among the more useful are Joseph Manzione, *"I Am Looking to the North for My Life": Sitting Bull, 1876–1881* (1991), and articles by Gary Pennanen, "Sitting Bull: Indian Without a Country," *Canadian Historical Review* 51, no. 2 (1970); Christopher Joyner, "The Hegira of Sitting Bull to Canada: Diplomatic Realpolitik, 1876–1881," *Journal of the West* 16 (1974). Hana Samek, *The Blackfoot Confed-*

eracy, 1880–1929: A Comparative Study of Canadian and U.S. Indian Policy (1987) is an excellent monograph that merits emulation by scholars on other comparative U.S.-Canada topics. The Canadian National Policy in its broadest sense is ably analyzed in Robert Craig Brown's *Canada's National Policy, 1883–1900: A Study in Canadian-American Relations* (1964). Richard A. Preston provides a military dimension in *The Defense of the Undefended Border: Planning for War in North America, 1867–1939* (1977).

The debate over continentalism and imperialism on the Canadian side is considered in Carl Berger's *The Sense of Power: Studies in the Ideas of Canadian Imperialism, 1869–1914* (1970), and by Goldwin Smith, one of the protagonists, in *Canada and the Canadian Question* (repr. 1971 edition). The literature on the American side of the debate over imperialist expansion is very rich, although there is a striking lack of attention to turn-of-the-century views toward Canada. The best starting place for an understanding of anti-imperialist ideas in the era is Robert Beisner, *Twelve Against Empire* (1968).

Migration and immigration receive their due in several works, although there is still no recent examination of the topic. Marcus Lee Hanson and John B. Brebner, *The Mingling of the Canadian and American Peoples* (1940), remains useful but badly dated; more recent is Yolande Lavoie, *L'Emigration des Canadiens aux Etats-Unis avant 1930* (1972), and Bruno Ramirez's work *On the Move: French Canadian and Italian Migrants in the North Atlantic Economy* (1991). On the experience of one sector of the immigrant experience see Gerard Brault, *The French-Canadian Heritage in New England* (1986); Yves Roby, *Les Franco-Américaines de la Nouvelle Angleterre, 1776–1930* (1990), and Tamara Hareven, *Amoskeag*, which discusses French-Canadians in Manchester textile mills.

The beginnings of the Canadian branch-plant economy with the migration of United States capital are traced in Hugh G. J. Aitken, *American Capital and Canadian Resources* (1961); Michael Bliss, *Northern Enterprise: Five Centuries of Canadian Business* (1987); Bliss, "Canadianizing American Business: The Roots of the Branch Plant," in Ian Lumsden, ed., *Close the 49th Parallel* (1970); Mira Wilkins, *The Emergence of Multinational Enterprise*, noted earlier; and Scott Nearing and Joseph Freeman's Marxist analysis, *Dollar Diplomacy* (1925). H. V. Nelles, *The Politics of Development: Forests, Mines & Hydro-electric Power in Ontario, 1849–1941* (1974), is a splendid study of one province's development strategy *vis à vis* American capital.

Norman Penlington provides a broader treatment of Canadian external policy in the period of American expansionism in *Canada and Imperialism, 1896–1899* (1965). Bradford Perkins provides the larger context of Anglo-American relations during the Alaska boundary dispute in *The Great Rapprochment: England and the United States, 1895–1914* (1968). The best single volume on the dispute is Norman Penlington, *The Alaska Boundary Dispute: A Critical Reappraisal* (1972); J. A. Monroe (ed.) provides contemporary documents in *The Alaska Boundary Dispute* (1970). See as well the still valuable study by Charles Tansill, *Canadian-American Relations, 1875–1911.* The most useful studies of the foreign policies of Theodore Roosevelt include: Howard K. Beale, *Theodore Roosevelt and the Rise of America to World Power* (1956); David H. Burton, *Theodore Roosevelt: Confident Imperialist* (1968); William Harbaugh, *The Life and Times of Theodore Roosevelt* (1975), which is the best biography and political analysis, while Henry Pringle's *Theodore Roosevelt* (1956) is vigorously hostile. More comprehensive on Roosevelt's foreign policy are: Frederick Marks, *Velvet on Iron: The Diplomacy of Theodore Roosevelt* (1979); Raymond Esthus, *Theodore Roosevelt and the International Rivalries* (1970).

Volume 1 of Charles Stacey's *Canada and the Age of Conflict* mentioned above is the best survey of Canadian foreign policy in the early decades of the twentieth century. Volume 2, *The Mackenzie King Era, 1921–1948,* is essential for the years after World War I. The best sources for the study of United States foreign policy, with relevance to Canadian-American relations, in the period between the Alaska boundary dispute and the 1920s include: works by Pringle, Harbaugh, Beale, and Burton noted above for chapter two; the eight volumes of Elting R. Morison, ed., *The Letters of Theodore Roosevelt* (1951–54); Walter and Marie Scholes, *The Foreign Policies of the Taft Administration* (1970); Ralph Minger, *William Howard Taft and United States Foreign Policy* (1975). On Woodrow Wilson, the multivolume edition of his letters and papers by Arthur Link is indispensable, as are several volumes by Link, which focus on various aspects of Wilson's career and diplomacy. See for instance, *Wilson the Diplomatist* (1960); *Woodrow Wilson: Revolution, War, and Peace* (1979); Edward Buehrig, ed., *Woodrow Wilson's Foreign Policy in Perspective* (1957). The papers and memoirs of several of Wilson's ambassadors and cabinet members are also worth consulting. See Burton Hendrick's three-volume *Life and Letters of Walter Hines Page* (1922–1925); William Jennings Bryan and Mary Bryan, *Memoirs* (1925). The best overview of Canadian-American relations in two world wars is Robert D. Cuff and J. L. Granatstein, *Canadian-American Relations in Wartime* (1975), and the essays in their *War and Society in North America* (1971) repay attention. For important specific topics in Canadian-American relations in these years, see Robert Spencer, John Kirton, Kim Richard Nossal, eds., *The International Joint Commission Seventy Years On* (1981); Alvin C. Gluek, "The Invisible Revision of the Rush-Bagot Agreement, 1898–1914," *Canadian Historical Review* 60 (December 1979). Broader treatment of the environmental issue and the International Joint Commission is provided by John E. Carroll, *Environmental Diplomacy: An Examination and a Prospective of Canadian-U.S. Transboundary Environmental Relations* (1983).

Post-1900 migration between the two countries is discussed by Harold Troper in *Only Farmers Need Apply* (1972). Mormon and the agricultural migration to the Canadian west are the subjects of Rennie Warburton, "Mormonism on Vancouver Island," *B. C. Studies,* no. 43 (Autumn 1979); R. W. Sloan, "The Canadian West: Americanization or Canadianization?" *Alberta Historical Review* 16, no. 1 (Winter 1968), and is covered in the fine history of Alberta by Howard and Tamara Palmer. Migration is only a sideshow for Pierre Berton in his study of the Klondike Gold Rush, *Klondike: The Life and Death of the Last Great Gold Rush* (1963).

The ubiquitous question of Canadian-American commercial relations is the subject of a number of studies, including those that focus on the contentious election of 1911, including: Peter Neary, "Grey, Bryce, and the Settlement of Canadian-American Differences, 1905–1911," *Canadian Historical Review* 49, no. 4 (December 1968); L. Ethan Ellis, *Reciprocity 1911* (1939); Paul Stevens, ed., *The 1911 General Election* (1970);

W. M. Baker, "A Case Study of Anti-Americanism in English-Speaking Canada: The Election Campaign of 1911," *Canadian Historical Review* 51, no. 4 (December 1970); R. E. Hannigan, "Reciprocity 1911: Continentalism and American *Weltpolitik*," *Diplomatic History* 4, no. 1 (Winter 1980). Paul Wolman, *Most Favored Nation: The Republican Revisionists and U.S. Tariff Policy, 1897–1912* (1992), provides a reinterpretation of the U.S. decision to seek reciprocity with Canada.

Binational labor and working-class history has been graced with suggestive studies by Robert H. Babcock, *Gompers in Canada: A Study in American Continentalism Before the First World War* (1974), and Carlos Schwantes, *Radical Heritage: Labor, Socialism and Reform in Washington and British Columbia, 1885–1917* (1979), but the field cries out for more such comparative work.

Aspects of Canadian-American relations in the aftermath of World War I and Versailles and the course of the 1920s are covered by a variety of authors, although there remains no thorough overview of the period except Stacey's general history of Canadian external relations. James Eayrs's *In Defence of Canada*, volume 1, *From the Great War to the Great Depression* (1964) was written before much of the archival record was available. On American statesmen in the 1920s, a good starting point is Norman Graebner's essays on secretaries of state Charles Evans Hughes, Frank Kellogg, and Henry Stimson in *An Uncertain Tradition* (1961). Dexter Perkins is most helpful on the most important secretary of state in the period, Charles Evans Hughes, in *Charles Evans Hughes and American Democratic Statesmanship* (1956). Robert Bothwell discusses early diplomatic relations in "Canadian-Representation at Washington: A Study in Colonial Responsibility," *Canadian Historical Review* 53, no. 2 (June 1972), as does Richard Kottman, in "Hoover and Canada: Diplomatic Appointments," *Canadian Historical Review* 51, no. 3 (September 1970), and a half-dozen other articles cited in our notes to chapters 4 and 5. John S. Galbraith treats the Canadian role in the breakdown of the Anglo-Japanese naval alliance in "The Imperial Conference of 1921 and the Washington Conference," *Canadian Historical Review* 29, no. 2 (June 1948). Ian Drummond, *Imperial Economic Policy, 1917–1939* (1975) is useful for the international economic history of the 1920s. U.S. accounts of the 1920s, even of major issues such as international trade and investment, tend to ignore relations with Canada. The tariff does receive attention from Richard N. Kottman in *Reciprocity and the North Atlantic Triangle, 1932–1938* (1968), and in the same author's "Herbert Hoover and the Smoot-Hawley Tariff: Canada, A Case Study," *Journal of American History* 50, no. 3 (December 1975). For a firsthand account of early diplomatic relations, see the memoir of William Phillips, *Ventures in Diplomacy* (1952), and that by Canada's first minister in Washington, Vincent Massey, *What's Past Is Prologue* (1963). There is brief reference to Canada and oil resources in Stephen J. Randall, *United States Foreign Oil Policy* (1985); Mira Wilkins treats Canadian developments in *The Maturing of Multinational Enterprise: American Business Abroad from 1914 to 1970* (1974). Important for understanding American foreign economic policy in the 1920s, although it does not address relations with Canada, is Joan Hoff Wilson's *American Business and Foreign Policy* (1971). Especially important for its interpretation is Ellis Hawley, ed., *Herbert Hoover, Secretary of Commerce, 1921–1928* (1981). The development of the automobile industry in Canada is the concern of Tom Traves, *The State and Enterprise: Canadian Manufacturers and the Federal Government, 1917–1931* (1979).

The 1920s was a decade of at least official prohibition, a source of considerable traffic between Canada and the United States. That dimension is the subject of C. W. Hunt, *Booze, Boats and Billions* (1988), and Richard Kottman, "Volstead Violated: Prohibition as a Factor in Canadian-American Relations," *Canadian Historical Review* 43, no. 2 (June 1962).

Mary Vipond documents Canadian concern about U.S. popular culture in "Canadian Nationalism and the Plight of Canadian Magazines in the 1920s," *Canadian Historical Review* 58, no. 1 (March 1977), a theme she pursues more fully in *The Mass Media in Canada* (1989) and for radio in *Listening In: The First Decade of Canadian Broadcasting, 1922–1932* (1992). Peter Morris, *Embattled Shadows: A History of Canadian Cinema, 1895–1939* (1978), and Ian Jarvie, *Hollywood's Overseas Campaign: The North Atlantic Movie Trade, 1920–1950* (1992), offer very different explanations of U.S. dominance of Canadian movie screens. All of these things are considered in a wonderful Ph.D. dissertation that should have been published: John Weaver, "Imperilled Dreams: Canadian Opposition to American Empire, 1918–1930," (Duke University, 1973). For a broader understanding of U.S. foreign policy and cultural expansion, see Emily Rosenberg, *Spreading the American Dream: American Economic and Cultural Expansion, 1890–1945* (1982); Rosenberg's near-exclusion of Canada is remarkable, given its primary importance as a consumer of "American dreams."

The abrupt transition from prosperity to depression and then world war in U.S. foreign policy and Canadian-American relations is discussed in several of the studies noted above, including Kottman, Bothwell, Wilkins, and Stacey. Works on the Hoover presidency and foreign policy, Kottman excepted, pay less attention to Canada than Hoover did: Robert H. Ferrell, *American Diplomacy in the Great Depression* (1957), and McGeorge Bundy and Henry Stimson, *On Active Service in Peace and War* (1948). An important biography of Hoover is Joan Hoff Wilson, *Herbert Hoover, Forgotten Progressive* (1975), as is Martin Fausfold's more recent *The Presidency of Herbert C. Hoover* (1985).

The Franklin Roosevelt era continues to hold fascination. The standard account of Roosevelt's foreign policy is Robert Dallek's *Franklin D. Roosevelt and American Foreign Policy, 1933–1945* (1979), although its strength lies in narrative rather than analysis. The older account by James McGregor Burns, *The Lion and the Fox* (1956), is still valuable, as are the multivolume biographies by Frank Friedel, *Franklin D. Roosevelt* (1953–73), and Arthur Schlesinger, Jr., *The Age of Roosevelt* (1957–60). Neglectful of Canadian relations but important for an understanding of economic policy are the essays in William Becker and Samuel Wells, eds., *Economics and World Power* (1984).

There is no standard account of Canadian-American relations in the 1930s. The most perceptive of the one-volume studies of Canadian policy, with particular attention toward Britain and the United States, is C. P. Stacey's *Mackenzie King and the Atlantic Triangle* (1976), which should be read in conjunction with Stacey's larger study of Canadian foreign policy noted earlier. Robert Bothwell and Norman Hillmer, eds., have provided an excellent introduction to various facets of Canadian foreign policy prior to the onset of world war in *The In-between Time: Canadian External Policy in the 1930s* (1975). Canadian historians have given excellent attention to the trade and economic relationship with the United States in the 1930s, notably Ian Drummond and Norman Hillmer, *Negotiating Freer Trade: The United Kingdom, the United States, Canada and the Trade Agreements of 1938* (1989), and Marc Boucher's extremely useful article "The Politics of Economic Depression: Canadian-American Relations in the Mid-1930s," *International Journal* 41 (Winter 1985–86). Stacey provides a sound account of Canadian wartime policies, including relations prior to Pearl Harbor, in *Arms, Men, and Governments: The War Policies of Canada, 1939–1945* (1970), and Stanley Dziuban focuses on the military aspects of Canadian-American cooperation in *Military Relations Between the United States and Canada, 1939–1945* (1959).

Dziuban's study noted above, combined with Stacey's study of the Mackenzie King era, and Robert Dallek's work on Roosevelt foreign policy provide a good understanding of the wartime relationship between the two North American countries. The more valuable studies of the Roosevelt administration and World War II include Robert Divine, *Roosevelt and World War II* (1969); Gaddis Smith, *American Diplomacy and the Second World War* (1985); Stephen Ambrose, *The Supreme Commander* (1970); James McGregor Burns, *The Soldier of Freedom* (1970). As in the case of the depression years, Cordell Hull's *Memoirs* (1948) has little insight for Canadian affairs. More useful personal accounts of the war and early cold war years by Americans are Adolph Berle's memoirs, *Navigating the Rapids* (1973), edited by Beatrice Bishop Berle and Travis Beale Jacobs, and Dean Acheson's *Present at the Creation* (1969). Given the importance of lend-lease in the Anglo-Canadian/United States economic relationship, see Warren F. Kimball, *The Most Unsordid Act: Lend-Lease, 1939–41* (1969). David Reynolds's *The Creation of the Anglo-American Alliance, 1937–41* (1969) provides the major context in which Canada had to develop its relations with the United States.

Robert D. Cuff and J. L. Granatstein, *Canadian-American Relations in Wartime* (1975) is the only solid analysis of the economic impact of the war, and their sequel volume follows the discussion into the early cold war years, *American Dollars, Canadian Prosperity: Canadian-American Economic Relations, 1945–1950* (1978). S. J. Randall, *United States Foreign Oil Policy* provides a brief discussion of the Canol oil project. Kenneth Coates, ed., *The Alaska Highway* (1985), and Coates and William Morrison, *The Alaska Highway in World War II: The U.S. Army of Occupation in Canada's Northwest* (1992), discuss the American wartime presence in the Canadian north. *The Mackenzie King Record,* in four volumes (1960–68), is drawn from King's Diary and covers the years from 1939 through 1948. John Holmes effectively links war and postwar Canadian policy in *The Shaping of Peace: Canada and the Search for World Order, 1943–1957,* 2 vols. (1979, 1982). Robert Bothwell (with William Kilbourn), J. L. Granatstein, and David J. Bercuson provide biographical studies of three figures important to the development of Canadian defense, economic development, and statecraft in, respectively: *C. D. Howe: A Biography* (1979); *A Man of Influence: Norman A. Robertson and Canadian Statecraft* (1981); and Bercuson's *True Patriot: The Life of Brooke Claxton, 1898–1960* (1993). Danford Middlemiss, "Economic Defense Cooperation with the United States, 1940–1963," in Kim Richard Nossal, ed., *An Acceptance of Paradox: Essays in Honour of John Holmes* (1982), links the war and cold war years.

General Canadian accounts of the transition from war to cold war and into the 1950s include the several volumes in the *Canada in World Affairs Series.* The pertinent volumes for these years are: Frederic Soward, *From Normandy to Paris, 1944–1946* (1950); Robert Spencer, *From UN to NATO, 1946–1949* (1967); Donald Masters, *Canada in World Affairs, 1953–1955* (1959). James Eayrs has contributed *Growing Up Allied* (1980), volume 4 of *In Defence of Canada;* Denis Smith, *The Diplomacy of Fear: Canada and the Cold War, 1941–1948* (1988); and Lawrence Aronsen and Martin Kitchen, *The Origins of the Cold War in Comparative Perspective: American, British and Canadian Relations with the Soviet Union, 1941–48* (1988).

John L. Gaddis provides the best postrevisionist overview of U.S. cold war policies in *The United States and the Origins of the Cold War, 1941–1947* (1972). Canadian official perspective on the cold war and after is provided by John A. Munro and Alex Inglis, eds., *Mike: The*

Memoirs of the Right Honourable Lester B. Pearson (1973), which covers the 1948–1957 years, and by the Mackenzie King diaries noted above, whereas Harry Truman's insights are advanced in *Years of Trial and Hope, 1946–1952* (1956), volume 2 of his *Memoirs.* For the subsequent presidency, see Dwight Eisenhower, *The White House Years: Mandate for Change* (1963). On Eisenhower and Dulles, the better studies are Stephen Ambrose, *Eisenhower the President* (1984); Ronald Pruessen, *John Foster Dulles* (1982), which deals with the pre–secretary of state period; and Townsend Hoopes, *The Devil and John Foster Dulles* (1973).

More specialized work on Canada and the cold war includes Lawrence Aronsen, "Canada's Postwar Re-Armament: Another Look at American Theories of the Military-Industrial Complex," Canadian Historical Association, *Historical Papers* (1981); Aronsen, "Imperialism and Dependency: Some Reflections on Canadian-American Economic Relations, 1945–1957," *Bulletin of Canadian Studies* 4, no. 1 (April 1990). Two other important unpublished papers by Aronsen are "A Leading Arsenal of Democracy: American Re-Armament and the Continental Integration of the Canadian Aircraft Industry, 1948–1953" (1991), and "An Open Door to the North: The Liberal Government and the Expansion of American Foreign Investment, 1945–1953" (1991). Robert Cuff and J. L. Granatstein address similar issues of bilateral free trade possibilities in "The Rise and Fall of Canadian-American Free Trade," *Canadian Historical Review* 58 (December 1977). A major development in Canadian-American economic relations, the St. Lawrence Seaway, is discussed by William Willoughby, *The St. Lawrence Waterway: A Study in Politics and Diplomacy* (1961). The ongoing saga of the Columbia River treaty in the 1950s is treated fully and fairly by Neal Swainson, *Conflict over Columbia: The Canadian Background to an Historic Treaty* (1979). Joseph Jockel explains the origins of NORAD in *No Boundaries Upstairs: Canada, the United States and the Origins of North American Air Defence, 1945–1958* (1987), but also worth consulting is William Willoughby, *Joint Organizations of Canada and the United States* (1979).

The sensitive issues of espionage, Communist subversion, and anticommunism are discussed in several sources. See Robert Bothwell and J. L. Granatstein, eds., *The Gouzenko Transcripts: The Evidence Presented to the Kellogg-Taschereau Royal Commission of 1946* (1982). Richard Freeland, *The Truman Doctrine and the Origins of McCarthyism* (1971), analyzes the important relationship between domestic anticommunism and cold war foreign policies, which contributed to the significance of the Gouzenko affair in Canadian-American relations.

For the Marshall Plan and NATO, see Timothy P. Ireland, *Creating the Entangling Alliance* (1981); Lawrence Kaplan, *The United States and NATO* (1984); and Escott Reid, *Time of Fear and Hope: The Making of the North Atlantic Treaty, 1947–1949* (1977) and *Radical Mandarin: The Memoirs of Escott Reid* (1989); Michael Hogan, *The Marshall Plan* (1987); Immanuel Wexler, *The Marshall Plan Revisited* (1983).

On Korea, the standard Canadian account is Denis Stairs, *The Diplomacy of Constraint: Canada, the Korean War and the United States* (1974), which states its thesis in its title. Robert S. Prince casts serious doubt on the sincerity and effectiveness of Canada's attempts at "constraint" in "The Limits of Constraint: Canadian-American Relations and the Korean War, 1950–51," *Journal of Canadian Studies* 27, no. 4 (1992–3), 129–52.

On John Diefenbaker's foreign policy, see Basil Robinson, *Diefenbaker's World: A Populist in Politics* (1989); Diefenbaker's somewhat unreliable memoirs, *One Canada: The Memoirs of the Right Honourable John G. Diefenbaker* (1976); and Knowlton Nash, *Kennedy and Diefenbaker: Fear and Loathing Across the Undefended Border* (1990). J. L. Granatstein provides the best account of the implications for Canada of the Cuban Missile crisis in "When Push Came to Shove," in Thomas Paterson, ed., *Kennedy's Quest for Victory* (1989). The best insider's account from an American perspective is Robert Kennedy's *Thirteen Days* (1969), although Canada again is absent from the crisis.

John English has written a fine two-volume *Life of Lester Pearson* (1989, 1992) which has importance for the U.S.-Canada relationship from the 1920s until his prime ministership in the 1960s. Pearson himself provides a useful account of his views on Vietnam in volume 3 of his memoirs, as does Paul Martin in volume 2 of *A Very Public Life* (1983). The best secondary account of the Vietnam War and Canada is Douglas Ross, *In the Interests of Peace: Canada and Vietnam, 1954–1973*

(1984), but one should also consult Peter Stursberg, *Lester Pearson and the American Dilemma* (1980); James Eayrs, *Indochina: Roots of Complicity* (1983); and Charles Taylor's less balanced *Snowjob: Canada, the United States, and Vietnam* (1974). See also George C. Herring, ed., *The Secret Diplomacy of the Vietnam War: The Negotiating Volumes of the Pentagon Papers* (1983). Another major development of the 1960s, the Autopact, is assessed by James Keeley, "Cast In Concrete for All Time? Negotiation of the Auto Pact," *Canadian Journal of Political Science* 16 (June 1983).

Robert Bothwell and J. L. Granatstein's *Pirouette: Pierre Trudeau and Canadian Foreign Policy* (1990) is a brilliant scholarly synthesis, well written and based on original research. Charles Doran's *Forgotten Partnership: U.S.-Canada Relations Today* (1984) remains useful. Stephen Clarkson provides a vigorous critique of U.S. policy toward the National Energy Policy and foreign investment controls in the final Trudeau government in *Canada and the Reagan Challenge: Crisis and Adjustment* (1982, rev. 1985). See also Edward Wonder, "The U.S. Government Response to the Canadian National Energy Program," *Canadian Public Policy* 8 (1982), and a collection of essays edited by E. Erickson and Leonard Waverman, *The Energy Question: An International Failure of Policy* (1974). A more comprehensive study is Denis Stairs and Gil Winham, eds., *The Politics of Canada's Economic Relationship with the United States* (1985). A useful study of one of the early advocates of Canadian economic nationalism is Denis Smith's *Gentle Patriot: A Political Biography of Walter Gordon* (1973). Richard Nixon provides no insights into his views of Canada during his troubled presidency, although Henry Kissinger, perhaps because of his own relationship with Pierre Trudeau, is more forthcoming in his memoirs. See *Years of Upheaval* (1982), and *The White House Years* (1979). On the early Reagan presidency, see Robert Dallek, *Ronald Reagan: The Politics of Symbolism* (1984), and David Schwartz, *NATO's Nuclear Dilemmas* (1983).

Unfairly overlooked in Canadian-American relations and indeed in world affairs is the Jimmy Carter presidency. These years are given their due in Bothwell and Granatstein, *Pirouette,* noted above. One should also consult Zbigniew Brzezinski, *Power and Principle* (1985), which demonstrates in its neglect of Canadian affairs that the former secretary of state had transcended his Polish-Canadian background and education.

Stephen Clarkson's study noted earlier provides insights into the Trudeau–Brian Mulroney transition, and one should consult the work cited above on Reagan's presidency. Canadian ambassador Allan Gotlieb's memoirs of the 1981–89 years, *"I'll Be with You in a Minute, Mr. Ambassador": The Education of a Canadian Diplomat in Washington* (1991), is truly indispensable, given the recent nature of these events and the lack of solid historical evidence. The *Canada Among Nations* series must suffice for the moment on the Canadian side for general accounts of the period. Among the best of those volumes are Maureen Molot and Brian Tomlin's compilation on 1985 (1986), and Fen Osler Hampson and Christopher Maule, eds., *After the Cold War: Canada Among Nations 1990* (1991). The emergence of trilateralism with Mexico is evident in Michael Hart, *A North American Free Trade Agreement: The Strategic Implications for Canada* (1990) and in the essays in Stephen J. Randall, Herman Konrad, and Sheldon Silverman, eds., *North America Without Borders?* (1992). For the negotiation of the Free Trade Agreement between Canada and the United States, see Bruce Doern and Brian Tomlin, *Faith and Fear* (1991), and Michael Hart, et al., *Decision at Midnight: Inside the Canada-U.S. Free-Trade Negotiations* (1994). Marci McDonald's *Yankee Doodle Dandy: Brian Mulroney and the American Agenda* (1995) captures Canadian nationalist resentment of Mulroney's rapprochement with the United States.

On Canadian cultural nationalism, see Isaiah A. Litvak and Christopher J. Maule, *Cultural Sovereignty: The "Time" and "Reader's Digest" Case in Canada* (1974); Janice L. Murray, ed., *Canadian Cultural Nationalism* (New York, 1977); Paul Audley, *Canada's Cultural Industries: Broadcasting, Publishing, Records and Film,* (1983); and David Flaherty and Frank E. Manning, eds., *The Beaver Bites Back?: American Popular Culture in Canada* (1993). Richard Collins, *Culture, Communication and National Identity: The Case of Canadian Television* (Toronto, 1990) takes a skeptical look at the history of Canadian television policy, while Manjunath Pendakur does the same for Canadian feature film policy, albeit from a very different perspective, in *Canadian Dreams and American Control:*

The Political Economy of the Canadian Film Industry (Detroit, 1990). The notes to John Herd Thompson, "Canada's Quest for Cultural Sovereignty: Promotion, Protection and Popular Culture," in Helen Holmes and David Taras, *Seeing Ourselves: Media Power and Policy in Canada* (1992), will provide references to other scholarly articles.

For the United States in these years, Ronald Reagan provides a rare presidential perspective on Canadian relations, brief as it may be, in *An American Life* (1990). On the contentious issue of the Strategic Defense Initiative (SDI) see Sidney Drell, ed., *The Reagan Strategic Defense Initiative* (1985). The almost consuming Reagan administration involvement in the Central American crisis and the Canadian position is outlined in Walter LaFeber, *Inevitable Revolutions: The United States in Central America* (1983). Liisa North, *Bitter Grounds: Roots of Revolt in El Salvador* (1981), contains an article by Tim Draimin that provides Canadian perspective: "Canadian Foreign Policy and El Salvador." For a more general analysis of the emergence of Canada as a factor in the inter-American system, see James Rochlin, *Canada as a Hemispheric Actor* (1992).

Literature on NAFTA and the developing trilateral U.S.-Canada-Mexico relationship is beginning to appear. Gustavo del Castillo and Gustavo Vega Cánovas, *The Politics of Free Trade in North America* (1995), consider the agreement in detail, while the essays in Stephen J. Randall and Herman W. Konrad, *NAFTA in Transition* (1995), look at social and cultural as well as economic implications. The contributors to Robert L. Earle and John D. Wirth, eds., *Identities in North America: The Search for Community* (1995), speculate about the effects of regional integration on national and subnational "identities." In *After the Fifth Sun: Class and Race in North America* (1994), James W. Russell attempts an ambitious synthesis of the historical experiences of the three North American nation-states. *The North American Trajectory* (1996), by Ronald F. Inglehart, Neil Nevitte, and Miguel Basañez, explores *Cultural, Economic, and Political Ties among the United States, Canada, and Mexico*.

Index